INVESTMENTS: Analysis and Management

INVESTMENTS:
Analysis

SECOND EDITION

and Management

Douglas A. Hayes, Ph.D.

PROFESSOR OF FINANCE
THE UNIVERSITY OF MICHIGAN

The Macmillan Company, New York

Collier-Macmillan Limited, London

CANISIUS COLLEGE LIBRARY
BUFFALO, N. Y.

HG
4521
.H38

© Copyright, Douglas A. Hayes, 1966

All rights reserved. No part of this book
may be reproduced or transmitted in any form
or by any means, electronic or mechanical,
including photocopying, recording or by
any information storage and retrieval
system, without permission in writing from
the Publisher

Second Printing, 1967

Earlier edition © Copyright 1961
by Douglas A. Hayes.

Library of Congress catalog card number:
66–19096

THE MACMILLAN COMPANY, NEW YORK
COLLIER-MACMILLAN CANADA, LTD.,
TORONTO, ONTARIO

Printed in the United States of America

Preface

A number of major changes and additions have been incorporated into this revised edition as a consequence of emerging developments both in the economy and in analytical concepts. First, as to the economy, it has become increasingly clear that national economic policy is firmly committed to stimulate economic growth and promote a high degree of stability. Moreover, there is considerable evidence that the implementation of this policy has been quite successful. From the end of World War II through 1965, a period of about twenty years, the economy has been able to avoid serious and prolonged economic downturns, although minor recessions have occurred. Over the entire period long-term growth has been achieved on a broad front and at a generally salutary rate.

However, it is also true that the growth rate has not been consistent on a year-to-year basis, particularly with respect to corporate earnings, which are of paramount importance to investment results. In addition, as might be expected in a dynamic competitive economy, the growth rates of different industries and companies have been quite different. Some have achieved above-average growth for several years but then for one reason or another have suffered a serious retardation in their rate of growth. Others have enjoyed a fairly consistent growth pattern, and still others have vacillated between periods of relative stagnation and highly satisfactory growth.

Taken together, these characteristics suggest that the analytical format for the appraisal of securities, and particularly common stocks, should include a heavy emphasis on (1) the appropriate means for measuring corporate growth rates and (2) the interpretation of the alternative causes of past growth, with a view to deriving some useful indications of the probable dimensions of future growth rates. Therefore, in this edition a completely new and extended analysis of these crucial elements has been developed which uses several analytical tools evolved in recent years.

The development of such new appraisal concepts has made it possible to integrate the conclusions on potential growth rates into the comparative evaluation and decision process in specific and tangible ways. Because they involve the treatment of dynamic variables, some of the concepts may require intensive study if we are to understand their application and interpretation. However, because these techniques sharpen considerably the ability to distinguish between the investment potentials of different stocks, they should enable the discerning student to understand more clearly the probable implications of alternative investment decisions. Although much recent literature in the field has relied primarily on abstract mathematical and statistical concepts, the author has not considered it desirable, because unrealistic assumptions have clearly been inherent in the purely mathematical approaches to portfolio decisions.

The material on the several broad alternative strategies of portfolio management is also entirely new in this edition. It is hoped that the comparative critical evaluations of the potential advantages and drawbacks of the major alternative strategies will encourage clear thinking with respect to the various options that are available and will eliminate much of the confusion about what can be reasonably expected from commitments in the securities markets.

As in the previous edition, extensive use has been made of illustrative material taken from actual companies and industries. My experience has indicated that a discussion of analytical concepts without specific illustrations of their applicability tends to be vague. Only through interpretative illustrations taken from the real world can the student be made aware of the essential issues involved in the selection and management of a security portfolio. Criticism of the interpretations offered in the case material is encouraged; only in this way can the analytical and reasoning powers of the student and practitioner alike achieve their maximum development.

From experience the author has also found that the scope of this book extends beyond what can be adequately covered in a one-semester or a one-quarter course in investment principles. Therefore, it might be helpful to indicate some personal views about the relative priorities for such a course, but of course, the preferences of individual instructors might well justify some modifications.

In Part I, Chapters 1 through 5 are essential, but Chapter 6 might be assigned a lower priority. The author prefers to cover Parts II and III in their entirety, although the chapters on corporate fixed-income securities have sometimes been omitted because these are usually of limited appeal to most individual investors.

In Parts IV and V the priority should be given to the chapters on public utilities and investment companies, with commercial banks added if time is available. Because of their limited investment appeal, the lowest priority might be assigned to railroads and insurance companies.

Part VI could be entirely left out of a one-semester course, although some knowledge of government securities and yield curves is often considered desirable. The author is inclined to assign all of Part VII at the end of the course, because these chapters serve to integrate the selection decisions on individual securities with the overall portfolio requirements of different types of investors.

In the preparation of the revised edition, the author is indebted to a number of past students and colleagues for their helpful suggestions concerning the desirability of new material and possible improvements of the previous edition. Mr. John B. Watkins, Vice President of the Detroit Bank and Trust Company, provided materials and assistance in connection with the chapters on municipal obligations. Messrs. Herbert Hunter and Charles Willings, partners in Watling, Lerchen & Co., were most cooperative in supplying illustrative material on the handling of security transactions and brokerage accounts. Finally, a special note of gratitude is due Professor C. James Pilcher, the author's colleague at the Graduate School of Business Administration, for reviewing the entire manuscript in detail and providing many helpful suggestions to improve both accuracy and clarity.

D. A. H.

Ann Arbor, Michigan

Contents

PART I

INVESTMENT MEDIA
AND STRATEGIES

CHAPTER 1

Financial Investments: Media and Approach

Financial Assets: Consumer Holdings

One of the ironies of our time is that both the flow of liquid savings and the consumer debt assumption rate have steadily increased during the great majority of the postwar years. In 1964, for example, household units acquired about $49 billion of financial assets and incurred about $25 billion of liabilities; these amounts were both at record historical highs, and it seems likely that in an affluent society their trend will continue to be upward. These data and their trend clearly suggest that decisions on the allocation of financial assets are becoming an increasingly important problem for many household units.

The change between 1950 and 1962 of the aggregate values of the several types of financial assets held in the consumer sector of the economy is shown in Table 1-1. Although the data, particularly on corporate stock, reflected market appreciation of existing holdings as well as net acquisitions, the totals and the implied rate of growth in discretionary financial assets of most kinds have been quite impressive. The discretionary assets would include savings accounts, securities, and credit instruments, as contrasted to equities in life insurance and pension fund reserves, which for the most part are not obtained as a consequence of voluntary investment decisions.

TABLE 1-1
HOLDINGS OF FINANCIAL ASSETS *(in billions of dollars)*
(Consumers and Nonprofit Organizations)

	1950	1962
Savings accounts	$ 68.7	$209.5
Life insurance reserves	57.9	98.9
Pension fund reserves	23.4	104.3
Securities and credit instruments:		
U.S. governments	69.9	70.3
Municipal obligations	15.1	31.2
Corporate and foreign bonds	4.9	6.3
Corporate stock	133.5	436.6
Mortgages	17.3	38.2

Source: Federal Reserve Board, *Flow of Funds Accounts 1954–62, 1963 Supplement,* p. 4.

The breadth of portfolio holdings as well as their total quantity has also increased substantially since 1950. For example, it has been estimated that the number of individuals holding common stocks advanced from about 7 million in 1950 to more than 17 million in 1965.[1] Moreover, it would seem significant to note that as the level of family income improves, the proportion of families holding investment assets greatly increases. Data on consumer financial characteristics showed that only 20% of families with incomes below $5,000 hold investment assets and only 10% common stocks. But the proportion of families holding such assets advanced to more than 70%, including 52% that held common stocks, when the income levels increased to between $15,000 and $25,000.[2] Therefore, as it is expected that the average level of incomes will continue to improve substantially in subsequent years, the growth trend in the breadth of asset holdings probably will continue, and perhaps at an increasing rate. As a result, improving the ability to make intelligent investment decisions would seem to be a highly desirable educational objective. Moreover, college graduates, in particular, might well be required to make such decisions recurrently throughout their productive careers, as their income expectations are notably higher than the population as a whole.

[1] *Business Week,* "Are Stockholder Ranks Thinning?" February 1, 1964, p. 72.
[2] "Survey of Financial Characteristics of Consumers," *Federal Reserve Bulletin,* March, 1964, p. 292. For income levels between $25,000 and $50,000, investment assets were held by 89% of the group and stocks by 78%.

The Financial Investor. The financial investor can usually be found only in an advanced free-enterprise economic society. As exemplified in the United States it is marked by (1) great accumulations of capital by large-scale corporate enterprise, (2) negotiable evidences of pro-rata claims against and equities in these accumulations (bonds and stock certificates), (3) a relatively large flow of liquid savings to individuals and institutions not directly involved in the acquisition of real capital goods, (4) the need for these funds by governmental units and corporate enterprise, (5) organized markets for the negotiable instruments issued to acquire the use of these savings.

Under these conditions the financial investor emerges as an important element in the economic process. Either as a private individual or as an employee of a financial intermediary, he is primarily concerned with deciding which evidences of debt or equity offer the optimum combination of safety and prospective returns for the funds entrusted to his use. Decisions must be made for both new funds and those already invested; one must decide whether probable optimum results can be obtained by retaining present holdings or by selling some and using the proceeds to acquire others. In brief, the financial investment process is a continuing affair that involves both the investment of new savings and the continuous management of existing negotiable instruments representing claims against or equities in accumulated real wealth.

Financial Investor: Role in Economy. The role of the financial investor in promoting economic welfare is a controversial issue. For the most part the role does not include deciding on the nature of the capital assets which may result from the investment. There are, however, certain exceptions—notably, when the investor is an institution and direct negotiations are undertaken with the business firms requiring funds. Even in this case the decision is usually negative; a request for funds may be vetoed for purposes considered questionable, but the original development of capital needs is left to the entrepreneur or business firm. Therefore, in the economic-theory sense, the acquisition of financial assets does not include direct participation in investment decisions.

But through the capital markets, financial investors supply a significant quantity of new funds to corporations and governmental units each year. Table 1-2 shows the amounts of securities purchased in the years 1959–64, inclusive. Although some of the proceeds were devoted to the refunding of outstanding issues, the majority was used to expand the productive resources of corporations, to extend local governmental services, or to finance the chronic deficits of the federal government. Moreover, these figures do not include investments in real estate mortgages—individual investors increased their holdings of such mortgages by $5 billion in 1964.[3]

TABLE 1-2

MAJOR TYPES OF NEW SECURITY ISSUES: 1959–64 *(in millions of dollars)*

	Noncorporate		Corporate		
Year	U.S. Government Bonds	State and Municipal Bonds	Bonds	Preferred Stock	Common Stock	Total
1959	$13,029	$ 7,681	$ 7,190	$531	$2,027	$30,458
1960	9,578	7,230	8,081	409	1,664	26,962
1961	13,701	8,360	9,420	450	3,294	35,205
1962	9,778	8,558	8,969	422	1,314	29,041
1963	8,381	10,107	10,872	342	1,022	30,725
1964	11,861	10,544	10,372	412	2,679	35,868

Source: *Federal Reserve Bulletin*, March, 1965, p. 465.

Second, the acquisitions of financial assets in the secondary markets provide an indirect incentive to economic progress. Individuals and institutions acting in this capacity do not, to be sure, provide much capital to new enterprises. For the most part the original capital of new business firms comes from an "inside" group of individuals who are either closely connected to management or are synonymous with it. This, combined with the fact that corporate expansion is largely financed by retained earnings, has led one economist to suggest that economic progress is not likely to be inhibited by steeply progressive income taxes on individuals who would otherwise save the funds and engage in financial investments.[4]

But this implicit disparagement of the financial investor ignores his role in providing a major means whereby a successful innovator can realize the fruits of his success. Although its importance cannot be measured statistically, a major incentive for "insiders" to risk funds on a new business project is likely to be the knowledge that "outside" financial investors will purchase the equity at a handsome profit to the original owners if and when the firm becomes reasonably well established and

[3] *Federal Reserve Bulletin*, March, 1965, p. 469.
[4] Hansen, *Fiscal Policy and Business Cycles*, New York: Norton, 1941, Chapters XVIII and XIX.

profitable.[5] In addition, by providing liquidity to the equity in established business enterprises, capital is thereby made more mobile and can be released for diversion to new projects.

Media of Financial Investors: Securities.   The media most commonly used in a financial investment are securities of one sort or another. These take various forms, and the implications of the major types will be considered in the next chapter. The direct approach to an investment of this kind is the outright purchase of a bond, preferred stock, or common stock. The indirect approach is the purchase of some kind of contract with a financial institution which in turn typically invests the proceeds to a very considerable extent in securities or their equivalent.

Perhaps the most common instances of the latter are (1) time deposits with banks, (2) shares in savings and loan associations, and (3) life insurance contracts. However, in the case of time deposits and savings and loan shares, the contracts are simple and a minimum of analysis of the institutions is required. The reason is that government insurance programs cover the liabilities of these institutions, so the investor need not rely on the soundness of the individual company for the ultimate safety of his commitments.[6]

Media: Life Insurance Contracts.   Life insurance contracts, however, offer a wide variety of choice to the purchaser, but the purpose of acquiring these contracts is usually quite different from that associated with security acquisitions. The motivation for acquiring life insurance is to obtain protection for dependents against the untimely decease of the major earning member of the family. When used in this way, it provides no return on the commitment; it is in essence an expense payment designed to eliminate the impact of a special risk by "pooling" individual risks into an actuarial universe. Security commitments, on the other hand, usually involve the conscious assumption of risk in order to obtain a positive return. Some life insurance contracts, however, do have quasi-investment attributes. The most notable is the annuity. In this case, the investor makes payments through a series of years or possibly turns over

[5] For example, in 1965 three officials of the Wolverine Shoe and Tanning Corporation were able to realize more than $5 million from the sale of 150,000 shares of the common stock after making the company a significant factor in the shoe industry from modest beginnings a decade earlier. *Wall Street Journal*, April 21, 1965, p. 24.

[6] Government insurance on these liabilities is limited to $10,000 per person per institution. It is doubtful if more than this sum would be allocated to this form; if so, then diversification among different institutions will cover the matter.

to the insurance company a single lump sum. The company then invests the proceeds and agrees to return a specified annual amount starting at a specific age and ending at the death of the annuitant (or specified beneficiaries if the contract so stipulates). The annual annuity per dollar of premium payment depends both on the investment returns guaranteed by the company and the actuarial life expectancy of the beneficiary at the time the payments are initiated. Upon the death of the specified beneficiaries, all rights to any remaining accumulation revert to the insurance company, but the company in turn must continue the annual contractual benefits regardless of whether a specific individual's accumulation is extinguished.

The annuity contract, therefore, represents a combination of investment returns with an actuarial "pooling" of risk. Its advantage is that it guarantees a dollar life income at a certain age; its disadvantages are that it assumes stability in the purchasing power of the dollar and that nothing remains for heirs not specifically stipulated in the terms of the contract. The first of these disadvantages may possibly be removed in future years by the variable-annuity concept, which relates the annuity payments to the current market value of and income on a common-stock portfolio, but these were not generally available as of 1965. By and large, the conventional annuity contract covers a rather special need. As presently constituted, it resembles a "pooled" bond portfolio from which income and principal are mixed to meet the payments to the participants. Since it is not transferable, continuing management is not necessary once a decision has been made, nor does the investor make any decision as to the form of investment taken by his premium payments.

There are, therefore, a minimum of discretionary problems involved in an annuity decision. Once their nature is understood, it is merely a matter of deciding whether such a contract fits the specific need of the investor. Benefits do not vary much between companies, nor is it really possible to appraise the soundness of insurance companies from the published data, so these elements of the investment problem are also removed.[7] For these reasons, this type of investment does not require detailed analysis.

Media: Real Estate. Apart from some type of a security portfolio, the media of financial investment are most commonly found in the real

---

[7] On this point it may be generally recommended that a large insurance company with many years of operating history be chosen. This recommendation is based on the theory that large companies are most likely to have greatest diversification of risk exposure and also to have the ability to afford the employment of skilled management.

estate field. Here the commitment may take the form of a bond or stock, but there is also a great amount of investment in direct mortgages against or fee ownership of the properties concerned. The source of returns on a real estate investment is sometimes a business operation, such as rent derived from apartments and commercial or industrial buildings, but the source may be the personal income of individuals. This would ordinarily be true of the returns on residential mortgages. When the properties are unimproved, the source of returns depend upon land development in the particular geographic area.

Real estate investments in all their varied forms are particularly suitable for wealthy individuals, for those closely related by business interests to this field, and for institutional investors. Their rather singular characteristics justify this observation. These may be summarized as follows. First, the unit of investment tends to be relatively large. A mortgage on a given property is usually held by a single investor or a closely related syndicate of investors. Similarly, fee ownership of improved or unimproved property is typically restricted to one or a few individuals. Second, the direct purchase of real estate usually includes some aspects of business management, such as decisions on maintenance or improvements. Third, detailed knowledge about the character and availability of properties is restricted; it seems often to be concentrated in the hands of local business interests. Fourth, the results derived from most real estate investments depend upon purely local matters. Therefore, it is highly desirable to be aware of new and impending developments in the community as soon as possible. Such information may not be easy to obtain, and businessmen in the vicinity tend to have an inherent advantage in this respect. Finally, successful operations in real estate investments involve knowledge and techniques which are both highly complex and unique to this field.[8]

The fact that the real estate departments of financial institutions are

[8] In the 1960–62 period, small participations in real estate syndicates owning or leasing commercial properties became quite fashionable for a time. On the whole, the subsequent record of such syndicates was not favorable. In their special study of the securities markets, the Securities and Exchange Commission felt obliged to make the following revealing comments: "The recent spectacular expansion of public participation in real estate securities has created new problems and intensified existing ones. . . . Further study is necessary to determine whether the Commission's power to compel disclosure is adequate to deal with the problems presented by speculative offerings, promoters' benefits, insider transactions, and cash flow distributions. The complexity of the problems as well as the specialized use of familiar terms and the high degree of risk of some of the offerings, all make disclosure especially important. . . ." Securities and Exchange Commission, *Report of the Special Study of Securities Markets, Part 5,* Washington, D.C.: U.S. Govt. Printing Office, 1963, p. 76.

typically entirely separate from the investment departments is evidence of the singular approach to this type of investment. Therefore, although investments in real estate operations are indeed widespread, these activities will not be discussed in any detail. For those desiring competence in this area, a specialized course of study is recommended.

Approach to Investment in Securities

Basic Premises. As already suggested, the subsequent analysis will concentrate on the corporate and governmental securities available in the public markets. The first premise is, therefore, that discretionary financial investments arise from purchases of securities in the open market. It will further be postulated that there is no direct connection with the firm or governmental unit in which an investment is contemplated. To express this relationship, the term *outside investor* may be applied.

This postulate, which seems to fit the majority of individuals today, orients the approach of the outside investor in the following ways. First, because security acquisitions do not result in control of managerial policies, the evaluation must be made on the basis of how the company will fare at the hands of the existing management rather than how it might fare if drastic managerial changes could be effected. Second, it implies that portfolio decisions must be made largely upon the basis of published information. Very large institutional investors find it expedient to supplement this information with personal interviews of management, but the practice is regarded as exceptional. Therefore, the discussion of analytical techniques will be confined to those predicated upon the type of information readily available to the public.

The next, related premise is that there must be a reasonable amount of specific validated information before any situation is considered for investment purposes. This means that market tips or a vague impression that the products of a company have a favorable outlook cannot be the sole framework for sound investment decisions. In all candor, however, it must be admitted that spectacular results have sometimes been enjoyed from casual operations on this basis, although it is quite possible that a distorted view is obtained from the daily press.[9]

[9] For example, Texas Gulf Sulphur reported the discovery of a "significant" body of ore in Timmins, Ontario in 1964. Purely on the basis of this information, the common stock of the company advanced from about $21 per share to more than $60 per share within several months. Wide publicity concerning these events was given in the press, so to many it may have appeared that it is only necessary to obtain "tips" in the news to achieve spectacular market results. The S.E.C. study, however, detailed a number of instances where such operations were disastrous. *Ibid.*, Part 3, pp. 70–78.

Two corollary precepts for outside investors follow from this premise. First, such investors are advised to devote their attention to reasonably seasoned companies with a demonstrated record of earnings and financial integrity. This means there will be little if any participation in new companies in their formative years, because the data necessary for an intelligent appraisal are simply not available. On the other hand, it does not mean exclusive concentration on companies of dominant size and prestige. These may of course be considered, but there are also a number of moderate-sized companies with an adequate history of demonstrated performance. Just when reasonable seasoning is obtained cannot be indicated precisely; as a rough rule of thumb, it might be suggested that profitable operations of from five to ten years would be required. Second, if commitments are to be based on an analysis in depth of validated information, then considerable effort will be required to select and manage a discretionary investment portfolio. Competence in making selection decisions might logically come about in several steps. First, an academic education in the techniques of investment analysis and portfolio management may be the original step. Here there should be heavy emphasis on understanding the significance of analytical techniques rather than on their arithmetical computation. Second, the prospective investor might endeavor to make a thorough application of these techniques to specific companies and to hypothetical or actual portfolios. Third, it should then be ascertained through subsequent observation whether the conclusions derived from the appraisals were reasonable. The major purpose would be to establish the merits and shortcomings of specific analytical tools and to suggest the need for others. This experience, if critically and intelligently evaluated, should provide the educational background for most financial investment operations. The sequence of steps in a "training program," in summary, involves both academic education and practical experience in the selection and management of security portfolios.

The selection recommendations of brokerage houses and investment advisory firms may often be quite useful in reaching portfolio decisions, but the trouble is that the quality of this information varies widely.[10] Therefore, a thorough understanding of investment theory and principles seems essential to weigh judiciously the reliability of the advice that is so freely offered. Although it is possible to establish trusts in reliable institutions or obtain competent investment counsel, these means are generally oriented to relatively large investors. In any case, it would still

---

[10] The S.E.C. special study of securities markets was quite critical of much investment "research" sent to prospective customers and in some instances found serious conflicts of interest. *Ibid.*, Part 1, pp. 237–323.

seem desirable to understand the major implications of the decisions recommended by the professionals managing the account.

To summarize, for the most part the outside investor is limited to investments which can be made in the security markets. Additional premises are that (1) all commitments will be based on a thorough and intelligent appraisal of adequate data and (2) the investor will be willing to devote considerable effort to the selection and management of his investment portfolio. Finally, the basic objective is not to suggest specific securities, but to develop the capacity to reach prudent selection decisions.

Approach to Subject: Scope and Sequence. The scope will include the major areas in which securities are available, and the sequence will offer a logical development of the subject material. There seem to be three major dimensions of an academic education in investment analysis and management. First, there is the need to analyze the major investment characteristics of security types and their related return opportunities and risk problems. This dimension should also include a discussion of the alternative strategies which may be used in the selection and management of security portfolios. These matters must be settled at the outset, as the conclusions reached will control the entire frame of reference of the other dimensions. For example, a decision to employ an investment strategy designed to profit by the short-term swings in the stock market will lead to analytical procedures quite different from those designed to estimate the desirability of securities for long-term investment. Therefore, the first section will be concerned with the nature of the various types of securities and the alternative strategies guiding their use in investment operations. In addition, the technical means of implementing investment decisions in the secondary markets will receive some attention.

The second dimension is that of obtaining a critical and thorough understanding of the theories, principles, and analytical techniques which are relevant to making specific selection decisions from the wide array of companies and securities that are available in the market. In this connection it has become increasingly evident that common stocks probably deserve an important role in most investment programs. Therefore, considerable emphasis will be placed on the concepts and techniques pertinent to the selection of common stocks.

Corporate fixed-income securities (bonds and preferred stocks) have, for reasons which will be discussed later, become increasingly concentrated in the hands of financial institutions. Individuals are quite likely to concentrate their fixed-income commitments in either government obligations or municipal bonds; the latter, because of their tax-exempt feature, are particularly appropriate for large investors. In the case of government securities, the problems concerned with their selection are minimal because their credit quality cannot be questioned. Municipal obligations, however, have many analytical features which are entirely unique and are rather complex. However, because some students may be actual or potential institutional investment analysts, the appraisal of corporate bonds and preferred stocks is separately considered. It should be noted that many of the factors pertinent to a decision on a company's common stock are also relevant to the fixed-income securities.

The third dimension involved in the selection of financial investments is that of structuring the portfolio as a whole. The problem is to consider (1) the unique needs and limitations of the investor and (2) the potential risks and returns, and then select a portfolio in keeping with these considerations. This section of the book is confined to discussing alternative programs for individual investors, based on the supposition that primary interest is in establishing or recommending portfolios for individuals. However, in the section devoted to an analysis of the common stocks of certain financial institutions, their portfolio-management policies are necessarily considered in the appraisal of their investment attractiveness. Therefore, in an indirect way the major investment management problems of financial institutions receive consideration.

The fact that investment-management considerations are treated as the last stage in the investment process should not be interpreted to mean that they are less important than the others. Indeed, it may be suggested that the sequence indicates just the reverse is true. A thorough appreciation of the problems involved in the selection of individual securities should allow a more penetrating insight into the possible implications of alternative decisions as to the portfolio structures. Put another way, some of the major factors requiring consideration in portfolio management decisions are related to the merits and shortcomings inherent in the analysis of specific securities. Finally, it is hoped that the section on investment management will provide an integration of investment-decision problems through relating conclusions on individual securities to the portfolio structures of specific investors.

Investment Characteristics:
Bonds and Preferred Stocks

Introduction

The purpose of the following two chapters is to examine and evaluate the essential investment characteristics of the various types of securities commonly available in the market. It should be emphasized that
these characteristics are considered solely from the standpoint of their
potential advantages and disadvantages to the investor. Although this
viewpoint might seem to be the obvious one for a book on investment
analysis, this is not always the case. The reason seems to rest in the fact
that, both in education and business, there is a tendency to identify with
the corporate point of view. The study of business finance, for example,
considers at some length the relative desirability of certain types of securities to the financial management of the corporation, considering only
incidentally the specific interests of the investor. The investor, of course,
is concerned with the success of the company, and in this respect the interests of the investor and the operating management unquestionably
coincide. At the same time, it is possible for the corporation to seek certain privileges or options on their security issues which reduce their investment attractiveness. Therefore, it should be clear at the outset that
the objective is to appraise the various features of securities solely on
their desirability for investment purposes.

By and large, the investor must choose between two major types of investment contracts. First, there is the fixed-income class. This type can be further subdivided into bonds and preferred stocks because the legal obligation of the corporation is substantially different on bonds than on preferreds. Nevertheless, the investor logically approaches both with the same objective in mind—a fixed income. Second, there is the equity or common-stock security which does not provide for any specific income in the investment contract. In addition sometimes it is possible to find combinations of the two basic types in a single issue. For purposes of classification, such securities may be designated "hybrids," and the major investment characteristics of several such combinations are considered in a separate section.

In the case of bonds and preferred stocks, the specific terms of the contract result from an arm's-length bargaining process. The company attempts to secure capital funds at the least cost and on the most flexible terms, whereas the investor seeks to maximize the returns and solidify his claim on the company, so far as it can be done via the contract. To consummate the bargain, many special contractual terms are added which set forth in detail the specific rights and obligations of the company and the investor. A complete discussion of all the possible ramifications of these contractual provisions would require a book by itself.[1] Therefore, it will only be possible to discuss the investment significance of the most important and typical contractual features found in these securities.

The specific terms of common stocks are much less complex, but at the same time, the relationship between the management of the corporation and the investor is more ambiguous for two reasons. In the first place, a strictly legal view of common stocks results in a relationship concept which differs a great deal from what actually exists in the world of finance. And in the second place, there is a much greater commonality of interest between the common stock and the corporation than between fixed-income securities and the corporation.

Fixed-Income Securities: Bonds

Essential Contractual Provisions. The essential features of a bond contract are relatively simple. First, the borrower promises to pay a specific amount of dollars per bond unit (par value) on specified dates

---

[1] One excellent book more or less confined to the various provisions of security contracts is Dewing, *Corporation Securities,* New York: Ronald Press, 1934

each year. Because it is an unconditional promise, a failure to meet the required income payments means insolvency and resultant legal proceedings for nonpayment of debt. Second, the contract promises to return principal amount of the debt at a specified future date; this date is known as the maturity of the bond.[2]

These two provisions are the heart of the bond contract, and taken alone they have a great deal of significance for the investor. There are two major advantages of this investment contract to some investors. There is (1) a known amount of income in dollar terms and (2) considerable pressure on the corporation to pay. It may be assumed that the debtor will meet these obligations if at all possible, because the penalties for default are drastic. Under ordinary circumstances, therefore, default will occur only if the flow of corporate income and other sources of cash are insufficient to meet the required payments. As a result, *relative* to the other types of investment contracts, the bond provides a greater certainty of a given income. But the contract alone does not and cannot guarantee payment of the return. Actual payment will still depend upon the continued financial ability of the borrower to fulfill the promise. In brief, the mere fact that a contract is a bond does not insure safety; it is still necessary to appraise the quality and prospects of the company.

The main disadvantage of the bond is the fact that the income return is restricted. The bondholder continues to receive only the indicated contractual income even if the profits of the company grow a hundredfold. This may be a considerable sacrifice in a dynamic economy where many corporations either show substantial growth or ultimately fall by the wayside. Moreover, although the rewards of growth cannot be realized, the penalties of failure may still be suffered to a large extent. As already indicated, the mere fact that bonds have an unconditional promise and relative preference over other investors in a given company does not guarantee payment of either income or principal. If the assets are practically valueless in relation to the obligations—and in the case of a bankrupt corporation this might well be the case—then all investors are likely to incur substantial losses regardless of the relative priority of claims. In other words, it is small comfort to know that other investors in the company are wiped out while you receive 5 or 10 cents on the dollar of principal invested.

Typical Discretionary Contractual Clauses. Although a specified amount of income and a fixed maturity are the essential components of

---

[2] In a very few cases, e.g., British Consols, there is no maturity. Also some bonds have been issued with such exceedingly long maturities, e.g., 2300 A.D., that they may be considered perpetual for practical purposes. They are, however, quite rare.

a bond contract, there are other typical provisions which may be of considerable significance to the investor. First, a bond issue is often granted a specific lien on a part of the corporate assets, generally in the form of a mortgage on the land, plant, and possibly the equipment. In the past the importance of such liens has often been overestimated. Although it is true that they give the bond issue exclusive claim to the mortgaged property, on all other assets they are merely on an equal footing with all the general creditors of the company. Therefore, the practical protection afforded by a lien depends for the most part on the independent value of the property covered. For example, if the assets pledged are highly specialized and would have little independent use outside the business, then the position of a first-mortgage bondholder may not be substantially better than a general creditor. On the other hand, if the pledged assets have substantial *alternative* value, then the lien position may actually add a great deal to the prospects of payment independent of the fortunes of the company as a whole.[3] But as modern technology has tended to make fixed assets more specialized, alternative uses of such property are more often than not quite limited.

In addition to the familiar lien clause, the redemption, or call, provision deserves special mention. Although it is not always found in the bond contract, it is typical of the great majority of cases. It gives the corporation the right to redeem the outstanding bonds at any time after proper notice at a specified price, which is usually a few dollars more than the par or stated principal of the debt.[4]

It can be categorically stated that the call provision is always disadvantageous to the investor. A company will exercise its option to redeem its bonds at the call price only if it is to their advantage to do so. In most cases, the company advantage arises from a decline in interest rates or an improvement in the credit position of the company (or both). As a result of such developments, it becomes possible for the company to redeem a high-cost issue with the proceeds from the sale of a new issue at a lower interest cost. The investor has no choice in the matter. The bonds, which were originally purchased with the expectation of receiving a favorable return until maturity, must be surrendered at the call price specified in the indenture. On the other hand, if interest rates

---

[3] Those bonds of railroads known as "Equipment Trust Obligations" are good examples of a special type where the lien position is regarded as highly significant. These are secured by liens on railway cars or locomotives; here the collateral can literally be "run off" the tracks of a defaulting road and onto the tracks of a solvent road needing equipment.

[4] Often the call premium will decline through time. For example, a bond may be callable at 105 for the first five years after issuance, then at 104 for the next few years, and so on at lesser premiums until maturity.

rise or the financial position deteriorates, the company will not exercise its option to call the issue and the full brunt of any market or credit losses will be borne by the investor holding the issue.

The unusual contractual features of Government Savings Bonds deserve special mention in this respect. These obligations in effect offer the investor the redemption clause in reverse, which is a highly desirable feature. The government cannot redeem these bonds prior to maturity, but the investor, after holding them for six months or so, has the option of redeeming, although at a yield sacrifice. Therefore, if interest rates rise materially above those paid on savings bonds, the investor can redeem and obtain the higher yields offered elsewhere. But in the event prevailing interest rates fall below the yields offered on outstanding savings bonds, the Treasury cannot redeem them and offer in exchange a lower-yielding obligation. The option also means these bonds can be used as a source of immediate cash at any time. Because of the favorable redemption terms on savings bonds, it is often recommended that callable corporate or municipal bonds should offer a greater net yield after taxes of at least 0.5% as compensation for the less favorable terms.

When the call provision is included in the bond contract, it is usually advisable to avoid new bond issues carrying high-coupon rates during periods of high interest rates unless the call price is substantially above par—say, 10 or 15%.[5] The alternative during such periods is to buy low-coupon bonds, issued during an earlier era of lower interest rates, at a discount from par values. On these issues, part of the return will take the form of a capital gain (amortization of the discount) between the time of purchase and maturity. It is true that the result is a somewhat lower current income, which may be a drawback to certain types of investors. On the other hand, these "discount" issues are not likely to be called if and when interest rates decline in the future, because it is the coupon rate which determines whether the company will find it advantageous to redeem the bonds. Further, if interest rates decline, the bond bought at a discount will immediately appreciate in the market and a moderate capital gain will be obtained.

One might expect that a high-coupon bond would also appreciate

---

[5] In relatively "tight" bond markets, where the bargaining position of the investor is strong, the delayed redemption clause has been increasingly inserted into the contract at the insistence of important bond investors. This clause prevents the refunding of the new bonds for a specified number of years, usually five or ten. The delayed-call feature of course improves the attractiveness of a bond to a considerable extent, because the investor is assured of being able to hold his high yield obligation for at least the period of the delay.

if interest rates were to fall subsequent to its issue. If it were merely a matter of mathematical yield, such would be the case, but here we have another aspect of disadvantage associated with the redemption provision. Regardless of the extent of a decline in interest rates, the price will not advance much above the redemption price because of the capital loss that would be incurred if the company suddenly decided to refund its obligations.

Factors Affecting Bond Prices. To illustrate, Table 2-1 shows the *theoretical* price pattern of two bond issues, one with a 5% coupon and one with a 3% coupon, should interest rates decline from a 6% level to a 3% level. In the absence of the redemption clause, the 5%, thirty-year bond would appreciate to slightly more than 139 from 86, or by 61.6%. But in actual practice the market price of this bond would probably not advance much above the call price of 105, because the market undoubtedly would reflect the good possibility of redemption. The 3% coupon bond, on the other hand, will advance in price the full amount from 58 to 100, or by 70.9%, under the same conditions, as it would still sell under call price in a market where prevailing interest rates were 3%. In the absence of a considerable market yield differential, therefore, it is clear that the investor should prefer a low-coupon bond selling at a discount when interest rates are at a relatively high level.

TABLE 2-1

Coupon Rate	Maturity	Call Price	Theoretical Price at Interest Rate Levels of:			Per Cent Theoretical Appreciation on Cost from 6% to 3% Market
			6%	5%	3%	
5%	30 years	105	86+	100	139+	61.6
3%	30 years	105	58+	69+	100	70.9

This example shows the several practical limits of price appreciation resulting from the terms of the bond contract. First, the call provision tends to put a practical ceiling on the price in response to a decline in interest rates. But secondly, a near-term maturity will also tend to restrict the appreciation prospects of a bond. However, a short maturity also limits price depreciation during periods of rising interest rates, because as a bond approaches maturity, its price reflects the fact that the principal is going to be returned in the near future. For example, a bond with a 3% coupon and a one-year maturity will sell for about 98 in a market where prevailing yields are 5%. In nontechnical terms, the price can be explained by noting the course of events until maturity. The purchase at 98 is followed one year later by repayment at 100; it is evident, therefore, that a $2 gain is obtained on the transaction. And in addition the investor receives $3 during the year as an interest payment. The net annual return is thus $5, or roughly 5% of the purchase price of 98. The same analysis also shows that a very substantial decline in interest rates can take place with only a small rise in the price of near-maturity obligations. Thus investors desiring stable prices (banks, for example) tend to stress the acquisition of short-maturity bonds.

If maturity is in the distant future, price variations in response to a given change in interest rate levels are greatly magnified. The thirty-year, 3% coupon bond, shown in Table 2-1, would sell at only about 69 when interest rates in the market were at a 5% level, as compared to the 98 price indicated for a one-year obligation. If the same bond matured in 50 years, it would sell for about 63 under similar conditions.[6] The market record of the Atchison, Topeka and Santa Fe Railroad non-callable General Mortgage 4s of 1995 illustrates the actual effects of removing both the redemption price and near-term maturity as an effective limitation on price. This high-quality issue sold as high as 140 after World War II, and as low as 89 in 1959. Then as interest rates declined again in 1961–62, the price advanced to 98.

A substantial long-term growth in the sales and earnings of a company will probably produce an appreciation in the price of its bonds only if there had been some appreciable credit risk with respect to the issue at the time of purchase. It is, of course, possible for a low-quality bond to return a 5 or 6% yield on market price at a time when high-quality bonds of a similar maturity are only paying a return of 3%. A subsequent improvement in the financial stature of such a company can remove all question of credit risk. As a result, with no change in the general level of interest rates, the bonds move upward in price to equalize their market yield with other top-credit issues. However, even then the participation in the success of the company may be moderate. If the bonds are callable, they will not advance much above call price; the very success of the company will make possible a refunding at a much lower interest cost to the company.

----

[6] However, it should be recognized that both the absolute and relative variations in yields through time are less pronounced in the long-term than in the short-term area. For example, from 1959 through 1964, ninety-day Treasury obligations showed yield variations of from 2% to about 4%, or more than a 100% range, whereas during the same period long-term Treasury obligations varied in yield from about 3.5 to 4.8%, which is a range of about 37%. Even so, the price variations were much more extensive in the long-term market because of the importance of maturity as a limiting factor on price.

Implications to Bond Analysis Procedures. In general, therefore, the bond investor does not share in the growth of a company to any appreciable extent. The practical significance of this conclusion is that although serious losses can accrue to bond holders if a company suffers financial reverses, they cannot profit to any significant degree by a spectacular improvement in the company's position. It is a case of heads they lose and tails they cannot win. Therefore, their primary role in an investment portfolio is to provide continuity of income under all reasonably conceivable economic conditions. This fact in turn means that in the bond area security analysis is concerned primarily with estimating performance under conditions of possible adversity. It is not concerned to any great extent with appraising growth prospects, because the nature of the investment contract limits the rewards for successful corporate performance.[7]

Bonds: Yield Computations. In the course of the preceding analysis it was necessary to refer to certain measures of the yields on bonds. Because inexperienced investors are sometimes confused by the different concepts, a brief review of the various yield computations and their significance is considered desirable at this point. There are three possible measures of yields on bonds (1) the coupon rate, (2) current income yield, and (3) yield to maturity.

The first of these, the coupon rate, represents the amount of annual income promised in the contract per $100 of par value. It is customarily specified in the title of a bond. For example, in Table 2-2 the coupon rates are shown as part of the description of the unsecured (debenture) obligations of the Columbia Gas System. The prominence given the coupon rate in bond descriptions is somewhat unfortunate, as it may lead to a superficial impression that it corresponds to the actual yield obtainable on the issue. This would be true only if the bond happened to sell in the market precisely at par, which is unlikely. Therefore, the coupon rate is only one factor in the determination of the prevailing yield at any given time, the other factors are the actual price in the market and the number of years remaining until maturity.

---

[7] A minor exception is the case of bonds in bankruptcy or nearly so. Such bonds may be selling at a very small fraction of the principal of the debt and rejuvenation of earnings and/or reorganization may result in very substantial speculative returns. The favorable workout of many real estate and railroad obligations in recent years that were in or near default in the late thirties are examples of this special case. In these instances, while the investment contract is technically the bond form, they are essentially equities because their position is essentially a residual claimant to assets and earnings along with the other creditors.

TABLE 2–2
BOND-YIELD COMPUTATIONS
Selected Columbia Gas System Debentures

Description	Price October, 1964	Current Income Yield	Yield to Maturity
Debenture 3%, Series B, of 1975	86	3.49%	4.70%
Debenture 3½%, Series D, of 1979	88½	3.97%	4.52%
Debenture 5%, Series I, of 1982	104	4.81%	4.67%

The second measure, current income yield, is computed by dividing the coupon rate by the prevailing price. It represents, therefore, the percentage of market price that will be obtained in the form of cash interest payments from the issuer each year. When there is no maturity, this represents the "true" yield; also in the occasional case wherein maturity is very far in the future—say, a hundred years or more—the current income yield may be constructively the most realistic measure of the returns offered over the life of the investor. In addition, investors primarily interested in cash income from the portfolio find the current income yield of some significance.

But when a bond matures within the foreseeable future, the current-income yield computation is defective as a true measure of the total return on a bond. It fails to recognize that the difference between the actual price paid for a bond and amount that will be received at maturity must be considered in determining the "true" yield obtainable over its remaining life. This element in the determination of yield is incorporated into the yield-to-maturity computation. It is, therefore, the most realistic measure of the percentage return offered on a bond over its remaining life.

If a bond is purchased at a premium above par, the Columbia Gas 5% debenture at 104 as per Table 2-2, for example, then the yield-to-maturity computation assumes that a proportionate amount of the premium is written off against the interest payments each year for the number of years remaining until maturity. To be specific, the yield-to-maturity concept considers that the $4 premium should be proportionately deducted from the $5.00 annual income during its remaining life, which was about eighteen years as of 1964. On the other hand, when a bond is available in the market at a price below par, then the yield-to-maturity concept considers that a regular portion of the discount should be added to the indicated coupon income each year, although it is not actually received as a cash "gain" until maturity. Thus on the Columbia

Gas debenture 3s, the annual yield to maturity of 4.70% represents the sum of the $3 interest income per year plus an appropriate annual accrual of the $14 discount related to the market price of 86. It will be noted that when a bond sells at a premium, the yield to maturity is below the current yield; whereas when one sells at a discount, the yield to maturity is above the current yield. The reason of course is that premiums are deducted from cash income in computing yield to maturity, whereas discounts are added to such income.

The mathematical theory involved in the computation of yield to maturity is quite complex, but there is no need to understand the mathematics to grasp the investment significance of the computation. If these general concepts are understood, then intelligent investment decisions can be made. The main point is that the yield-to-maturity computation is based on combining the current interest income with an accrual or amortization of the difference between the price in the market and the maturity value. These yields can be easily computed from standard bond tables after a few minutes of clerical instruction in their use.

In case a bond table is not readily available, a rough approximation of the yield to maturity can be easily computed by using the following procedure. First, estimate the average accrued or amortized value of the bond over its remaining life; splitting the difference between price and par is reasonably accurate. This would result in an average amortized value of 102 on the Columbia Gas 5s. Second, divide the total premium or discount by the number of years remaining to maturity on the bond. This would be $4 divided by 18 in our example, or $.22. Third, subtract the average annual premium from (or add the average annual discount to) the coupon rate and divide by the average accrued value. In the example, it would be $5.00 minus $.22, or a net annual return of $4.78 divided by 102, which equals about 4.69%. This compares with the true yield to maturity taken from a bond table as shown in Table 2-2 of 4.67%.

Fixed-Income Securities: Preferred Stocks

Nature of Contract. The investment implications of the preferred-stock contract are for the most part analogous to those of a bond. In the typical case there are two important provisions which are found in both bonds and preferred stock. First, both provide a limited fixed income. Second, both typically include the redemption provision. Because

of the resemblance, the techniques for analyzing the two types of securities are almost identical. The grouping of preferred stocks with bonds
for analysis purposes is in distinct contrast to legal and accounting concepts which view the preferred shareholder as a part of the equity along
with the common stock and establish the creditors in a separate category. In one major respect only the preferred contract resembles common
stock more closely than bonds: like common stock, there is no maturity.[8] But this is of much less significance than the fact that both bonds
and preferreds are fixed-income securities.

Major Weakness of Preferred-Stock Contracts.   From the standpoint
of the investor, however, preferred stock is less desirable than bonds.
The corporation is under much less compulsion to pay preferred
dividends than it is to pay bond interest because preferred stock is
merely given the right to receive its specified dividend before any dividends are paid on the common. When a corporation fails to meet interest charges on bonds, the result is receivership, which may result in
liquidation or (more probably) a reorganization with a complete turnover of management. Therefore, it may be presumed that a company
will pay bond interest so long as it is at all possible to do so. But the
penalty resulting from a failure to declare preferred dividends is not
particularly onerous. Such a default merely means that the company
cannot pay dividends on the common stock until the preferred dividends
have been paid in full.[9]

And if the cumulative provision is assumed, any dividends not paid in
any series of years must be settled before common stock dividends can
be resumed. On noncumulative preferreds there is not even the pressure

---

[8] In recent years there has been a tendency to include an annual sinking fund
requirement in the preferred stock indenture and to require that the fund be used
to retire stock either through purchase in the market or at a special sinking-fund
call price. When the stock is selling at or above this call price, the provision in
effect makes a part of the issue "mature" each year. The particular shares redeemed
in this manner are determined by lot; thus the shareholder does not know in advance
whether his shares will "mature." If such a stock is purchased at a price above the
sinking-fund call price, the investor does assume some risk of partial loss of his
principal, although the mathematical probability of his shares being drawn by lot
may be quite small. When the market price is less than call price, the operation of
the sinking fund may be advantageous to the investor in the sense that an artificial
demand for the stock is introduced into the market and prices are thereby kept
higher than otherwise would be the case.

[9] Once in a while the preferred stock, when in default, is given the sole right
to elect a portion of the board of directors. This provision may increase the incentive
to maintain regular preferred dividends, but its practical significance is open (
doubt. For a further discussion of this point, see Chapter 16.

of this claim. However, noncumulative preferreds ar rare; furthermore, they are so unattractive that the investor may be categorically advised to avoid them except under the most unusual circumstances.

Because preferred dividends can be omitted with relative impunity, the holder of such stocks can expect to obtain dividends only so long as it is expedient for the corporation to pay them, and it must be realized that the board of directors is elected by and thus represents the interests of the common shareholders. Moreover, in practice the board is often controlled by operating management. Suppose, then, that there is a setback in general business conditions and the directors decide to suspend common dividends in order to conserve working capital against the unknown vicissitudes of the future. Assuming such a decision has been reached, what incentive remains to continue payments on the preferred? The answer is, in fact, very little.

It is even quite possible that the suspension of preferred dividends for a period of years may involve less in *total* distributions on the stock than if continuity of payments had been maintained. The practical realities of finance are that dividend arrearages may sometimes be settled for something less than their arithmetic total. The reason rests in the weak bargaining position of preferred stock. Sole power over dividend distributions is vested in the board of directors, and it is quite rare for the preferred stock as a class to have any real voice in the selection of the board.

Preferred-Stock Weakness: Illustrations. During the extended depression years of 1931–40, a number of companies found it prudent to suspend preferred dividends. As a result, substantial arrearages of dividends were built up. It is in such circumstances that compromise settlements are most likely, because cash availability will probably be far short of the total accumulated dividend requirements. For example, in 1941 Jones and Laughlin Steel Corporation was faced with an arrearage of $46 per preferred share. And while their cash position appeared adequate at the time, the wartime requirements for expansion and modernization of their plant capacities were great. As a consequence, the preferred was offered common stock with a market value of about $34 as a complete settlement of the $46 arrearage, and as part of the package, the old preferred had to be exchanged for a new preferred with a lower dividend requirement. The offer, it is interesting to note, was accepted within a few months despite the fact that the preferred stock appeared to be in a strong bargaining position because of the large earnings then in prospect for the duration of World War II.

Because of the generally favorable economic conditions that have prevailed in the postwar period, large arrearages of this sort have been rare. Even so, some companies have suffered wide fluctuations in their earnings, and several instances can be found to demonstrate the inferior contractual position of preferred stocks. First, the case of A. S. Beck Shoe Corporation illustrates the point that when common dividends are suspended, there is little compulsion to continue preferred dividends. During the decade, 1951–60, the company showed average net earnings of about $800,000 per year and the $141,000 annual requirement on the 4¾ % preferred was paid regularly along with common dividends. In 1961, however, earnings declined to about $100,000 but the preferred dividend was paid as usual. Moreover, despite the fact that earnings after deducting the preferred requirement were negative, regular dividend payments amounting to about $260,000 were continued on the common stock. In 1962, operating results declined further and the company incurred a deficit of $700,000, yet it continued to pay regular dividends to both the preferred and common until the last quarter of that year. At that time payments were suspended on both completely and simultaneously.[10]

It is true that the adverse operating conditions undoubtedly were a cause for concern, but a legitimate question can be raised as to why the $35,000 preferred dividend requirement could not be paid in the last quarter of 1962 when during the same year the directors felt able to pay common dividends of about $190,000. Apparently the policy was to suspend all preferred dividends as soon as a decision was reached that common dividends were no longer expedient. Earnings continued to be unfavorable through 1964, and as of mid-1965, the accumulated arreage was about $12 per share. The preferred, listed on the New York Stock Exchange, then sold for about $65 per share, which suggested that investors had at least fair expectations for an ultimate resumption in dividends. However, the experience of the A. S. Beck preferred indicates clearly the lack of incentive to continue preferred dividends once common dividends have been suspended.

The postwar record of the Cudahy Packing Company, one of the largest meat-packing firms in the United States, can also be cited to indicate the problems that may be encountered on preferred stocks. As

---

[10] A similar case: "For the first nine months of 1964, (Wheeling Steel Corp.) earned $3,554,900, or $1.09 a share. Third quarter net, however, nosedived to 14 cents a common share. . . . The company promptly omitted its dividend on common and deferred dividends on preferred to conserve capital for a major equipment improvement program." *Wall Street Journal,* January 18, 1965, p. 4.

shown on Table 2-3 the company obtained excellent earnings immediately following World War II, but then suffered a large deficit in 1949. At that time common dividends were eliminated, but the company, to its credit, continued payments on the preferred. As earnings recovered somewhat, preferred dividends were paid in full through 1952, but the large deficit of that year led to a suspension of preferred payments in the following year. Then when earnings recovered in 1955–56, the arrearage was completely discharged and the regular annual preferred requirements were paid through 1961.

TABLE 2–3
CUDAHY PACKING COMPANY
Earnings and Dividend Data: 1946–64

Year	Net Income before Dividends	Preferred Dividends	Common Dividends
1946	$6,721,000	$ 450,000	$1,028,000
1947	7,121,000	450,000	1,259,000
1948	152,000	450,000	925,000
1949	(4,650,000)	450,000	463,000
1950	3,019,000	450,000	—
1951	1,350,000	450,000	—
1952	(6,904,000)	450,000	—
1953	543,000	—	—
1954	(7,162,000)	—	—
1955	2,703,000	1,125,000	—
1956	5,268,000	1,125,000	—
1957	2,006,000	450,000	—
1958	2,670,000	450,000	—
1959	2,640,000	450,000	—
1960	811,000	450,000	—
1961	(374,000)	450,000	—
1962	(1,849,000)	112,500	—
1963	(1,985,000)	—	—
1964	1,753,659	—	—

But unfavorable earnings levels were again encountered in 1961–63 with the result that preferred dividends were suspended for the second time within a decade. Some recovery in earnings was obtained in 1964, and in view of the earlier policy to meet arrearages as soon as earnings levels permit, it may be conjectured that a continued earnings recovery in 1965–66 would result in attempts to meet both current and past requirements on the preferred.

In this case, management has clearly made considerable efforts to meet its obligation to the preferred stock, especially in view of the fact that the common stock has received no dividends since 1949. At the same time, the lack of a legal compulsion to meet preferred dividends led to suspensions whenever temporary earnings setbacks were encountered. During these same intervals, interest and sinking fund payments on funded debt continued without interruption. In fact, in 1962 the company found it necessary to retire $1.5 million of long-term debt, which may have been one reason for suspending preferred dividends. Therefore, the conclusion seems warranted that because of a weak contractual position, the continuity of income payments on preferred stocks depends heavily upon the ability of the company to maintain earnings levels consistently above the preferred dividend requirements.

High-Quality Preferreds.   There are indeed a number of preferred stocks where earnings in relation to their dividend requirements have been consistently very large or alternatively have been favored by a highly stable earnings performance. In the large earnings category, the 5% preferred of General Motors might be cited. In the stable category, the preferred stocks of a number of the electric utilities can be noted; for example, Consumers Power Company alone has three different preferred stocks outstanding. In these instances, the stocks may be desirable for fixed-income security investment, not because the contract per se is attractive but because analysis suggests there is little possibility that the company will find it expedient to take advantage of the contractual weakness and suspend payments.

However, an institutional factor has tended to make high-quality preferred stocks less attractive to the individual investor. Taxable corporate investors are allowed to exclude 85% of dividends received from other corporations from their taxable income.[11] Such institutional investors, the fire and casualty insurance companies for example, are naturally greatly attracted to preferred stocks as compared to corporate bonds because of the substantial tax exemption feature of the former. As a consequence, the yields prevailing on high-quality preferred stocks are often lower in relation to long-term corporate and government bond yields than would appear justified so far as the individual investor is concerned. Therefore, while occasional exceptions may be noted, preferred stocks under ordinary conditions are likely to occupy a very minor role in the portfolios of individual investors.

---

[11] The reason for this provision of the corporate tax law is to prevent double taxation of corporate income. As a corporation cannot deduct preferred dividends in determining its own taxable income, it is reasoned that another corporation receiving such dividends on stocks held as investments should be allowed to exclude them (for the most part) in their determination of taxable income.

CHAPTER 3

Investment Characteristics:

Common Stocks

and Related Securities

Common Stocks and Management. In a great many small corporate enterprises there is a close relationship between the holders of the common stock and the operating management, and sometimes they are identical. In a few instances such identity exists for very large corporations; the DuPont family, for example, own a substantial proportion of the common stock of DuPont Chemical Company and also represent a substantial proportion of the top management. With respect to these situations, it would be somewhat fanciful to discuss the common stock "investment contract," which implies certain rights and duties between separate and independent parties.

But the development of the large corporation during the last fifty years or so has typically resulted in a widespread diffusion of stock ownership among many relatively small holders. It is commonplace today to find that no single stockholder or his immediate family owns as much as 1 or 2% of the total outstanding common stock. For example, at the end of 1964, National Dairy Products Corporation had 14.5 million shares outstanding distributed among 70,000 stockholders of which 3,000 were institutional investors.[1]

Under the typical conditions of widely dispersed stock ownership it seems realistic to view corporate management policies, including the

---

[1] National Dairy Products Corp., *Annual Report for 1964*, p. 4.

policy with respect to the treatment of the common stockholders, as determined more or less independently of the legal owners of the corporation.[2] In considering the investment characteristics of common stocks, therefore, it is assumed that the so-called control rights are negligible, except perhaps as a latent factor that might arise if the corporation attempted to treat the holders of the common stock with gross injustice. Now and again there has been a successful revolt of a shareholder group against an entrenched management, but these occasions have been mostly notable for their rarity. The de facto divorce of corporate ownership and control suggests that the common stockholder must generally rely on tradition and the ethical standards of directors for a representation of their interests in the corporation; there are, however, certain basic rights which fundamentally control the relationship between the directors and the common stock.

Rights of Common Stock. Perhaps the most fundamental right of common stockholders is to have the net earnings of the corporation (after all prior charges for expenses, taxes, and senior capital claims) devoted to their *immediate* or *ultimate* benefit. The principal *immediate* benefit derived from earnings is, of course, dividend distributions. Their rights, however, do not extend to either a specific dollar amount of dividends or to a proportion of the total applicable earnings. Decisions on dividend policy rest entirely with the board of directors, who, as already indicated, may be almost entirely independent of the rank-and-file stockholders. Many factors may be considered in establishing dividend policy. The current level of earnings, the availability of cash relative to the capital requirements of the business, the general economic outlook, and a desire to maintain some degree of consistency are usually among the important considerations which govern the deliberations of the directors.

But the directors are obliged to devote all earnings not paid out in dividends to the acquisition of additional corporate assets, to the reduction of senior capital claims, or in rare cases to the purchase of the company's common stock in the market. In brief, the ostensible purpose of all retained earnings is to add to the asset facilities or financial strength of the company, or both. Therefore, the retention of a part of the earn-

[2] Recognition of this fact seems to be implicit in many of the provisions of the Securities Act of 1933 and the Securities and Exchange Act of 1934 and in the administrative regulations promulgated by the Securities and Exchange Commission. The classic study which considered the implications of this development to economic society and may have influenced the subsequent legislation considerably was A. Berle and G. Means, *The Modern Corporation and Private Property*, New York: Macmillan, 1932.

ings is supposed to increase the value of each share of common either through reducing risk or increasing the earnings potential. In some cases, the probable increases in value may appear to justify a substantial retention of earnings; in other cases, retained earnings may appear to have little value. An evaluation of the probabilities in this regard clearly is one of the most important aspects of an analysis of a company in which a common stock investment is contemplated.

The pre-emptive right of common stock might also be mentioned. This is the legal right under common law to subscribe for any new sales of common on a pro-rata basis. It is, however, not a general right; the statutes of many states specifically allow the corporate charter to include a provision waiving the pre-emptive right. The reasons for the pre-emptive right are to allow the existing shareholders to maintain their proportionate voting power and claim on the earnings and assets, but as the right to vote for directors has been shown to be of academic interest only, this reason is of nominal significance. Moreover, its importance to protect against dilution of the equity in earnings and assets depends on the probability of new stock offerings from time to time. In some instances (public utilities, for example) in which there are large capital needs, new issues of stock are more probable. In others, retained earnings and senior security offerings have provided all the required capital for a great many years; as a consequence, the existence of the pre-emptive right is usually of small importance to a decision on the attractiveness of these common stocks.

Absence of Restrictions.   Although the positive rights are limited and to some extent ambiguous, it is also true that the common stock contract does *not* include certain restrictive provisions that are typically found in fixed-income securities. The absence of a contractual amount of income means there is no limit to the ultimate dividends that might be received if the company turns out to be exceptionally profitable. Furthermore, the common stock contract does not give the corporation the option to redeem the shares at a given price. In brief, there are no inherent limits imposed on the potential value by restrictive features of the investment contract. These same elements, however, provide the investor with less assurance as to current income and make for substantially wider price variations. Therefore, common stocks are generally less attractive for investors who require price stability and certain income.

In spite of these drawbacks, a strong case can be made that of the types of securities available common stock is the most attractive from the investor's standpoint. It is true that the common equity must bear first impact of any adversity, but it is also true that the common stock is the only class of securities privileged to enjoy the maximum participation in any extensive growth of the company. The risk of the one may be regarded as commensurate with the opportunity of the other.

Theory of Common Stocks as Long-Term Investments. The fact is that the common-stock contract appears to be superior in theory to any type of fixed-income arrangement, although special objectives of certain investors may lead to an emphasis on the latter in a specific portfolio. It is paradoxical to note, therefore, that common stocks did not achieve any real investment respectability until after World War I. Prior to that time, it was customary to regard these securities as suitable only for short-term traders, implying that the sole objective in their purchase was quick profits through the recurrent fluctuations in market prices.

Then an empirical study was published showing the long-term results obtained from sample portfolios of common stocks.[3] All the data assembled in the book indicated that a diversified portfolio of common stocks was by far superior to fixed-income securities if the stocks were *purchased* and *held* for a number of years. The superiority was manifested in two ways. First, the average long-term dividend yield on cost prices was markedly greater than the yield on high-grade fixed-income securities. Second, it was found that common stocks enjoyed a long-term appreciation which was not available to the holder of bonds or preferreds. The source of the appreciation was found to be the growing earnings capacity that most companies were obtaining from the profitable reinvestment of that portion of earnings not distributed in dividends.

This empirical study revolutionized the thinking of the financial community and the public on the subject of common stocks; unfortunately the pendulum moved to the opposite extreme. Common stocks, it was concluded, had been shown to be the most attractive investment medium; therefore, investment policy was simple and obvious; buy a diversified group of such stocks, and they would yield a substantial appreciation ultimately, in addition to a good average current income. Individuals and institutions who had never before even thought of common stock commitments bought them with increasing fervor. As might be expected, the stock market surged upward to almost unbelievable levels and then collapsed in the debacle of 1929. Since then most common stocks have appreciated to levels in excess of their 1929 peaks, but in the vast majority of such cases it required many years and the inflation

[3] Smith, *Common Stocks as Long-Term Investments*, New York: Macmillan, 1924.

subsequent to World War II to accomplish this result. And in spite of the postwar inflation other stocks have never exceeded the price they reached in the early fall of 1929.

Qualifications of Theory. The short review of historical developments suggests that something was seriously wrong with the unqualified theory that common stocks of well-established companies will *always* yield both appreciation and dividend returns substantially greater than fixed-income securities throughout a decade or so. It is possible, however, that a more realistic theory of common stocks as long-term investments can be suggested by introducing appropriate qualifications of the original theory developed by Smith.

First, it may be observed that the results of statistical studies of economic phenomena are largely dependent upon the major characteristics of the particular periods included. Therefore, to extrapolate these results into the future implicitly assumes that the economy will continue to follow the same patterns as during the years covered by the investigation. Smith's data on the performance of common stocks were drawn from the years 1866–1922. This period, in turn, was broken down into eras of declining prices for goods and services in general (1866–99) and rising price levels (1901–22). However, its tremendous economic growth was the crucial characteristic of the entire period. Developments in the industrial scene were almost revolutionary. The introduction and assimilation of the automobile alone provided a tremendous impetus to industry as a whole. The electrification of homes and industry was also a major development, and many others could be mentioned. Therefore, it was possible for corporations to commit capital on a very profitable basis to new methods of production and to new products. As already mentioned, one of the cornerstones of the theory of common stocks as long-term investments is that appreciation in the value of common stocks is obtained from continuous opportunities to reinvest retained earnings profitably.

It is entirely possible, of course, that economic growth will continue to be as rapid in the future as in the years studied by Smith. There is, in fact, considerable evidence that the rate of economic progress since 1922 has not been greatly different than in the forty years preceding that date. In spite of the reassuring evidence, however, it is still not absolutely certain that future decades will enjoy an equivalent growth rate. And if the same rate of economic growth is not maintained, then it may be presumed that the general performance of common stocks, especially with respect to appreciation, will not measure up to the results indicated by empirical studies of the past. Particular companies quite probably will show favorable long-term growth even if the rate of general economic progress is not maintained, but then favorable long-term investment results would depend upon superior selectivity; it would no longer be possible to depend upon the continued appreciation of common stocks as a whole.

Perhaps an even more important qualification of the original theory is a factor which was not mentioned specifically by Smith, although it might be inferred from his statistical presentations. This is the matter of acquisition price. Unlike bonds and preferred stocks, there are no contractual features of common stocks to limit market prices. Therefore, market prices can vary over an exceptionally wide range as expectations of investors and speculators move from unbounded optimism to extreme gloom.

As a consequence, it is significant to note the character of the stock markets which prevailed at the time Smith's hypothetical commitments to common stocks were made. As indicated, the study covered several different periods, and numerous tests using various methods of mechanical selection were employed within each period in order to avoid the charge of hindsight. Table 3-1 summarizes the results of the major tests for the particular years in which the stocks were purchased with respect to dividend income as a percentage of cost price.

TABLE 3-1
PORTFOLIO YIELDS ON ACQUISITION COSTS

Years	Cost of Portfolio	Dividend Income First Year	First-Year Percentage Dividend Yield
Test 1 1901–22	$10,002	$ 818	8.2
Test 2 1901–22	9,877	607	8.2
Test 3 1901–22	10,012	616	6.1
Test 4 1880–99	10,163	739	7.2
Test 5 1866–85	10,013	1,093	10.9

Source: E. L. Smith, *Common Stocks as Long-Term Investments*, New York: Macmillan, 1924, pp. 21–43.

Note that the data in Table 3-1 show that *in every instance it was possible for the common investor to buy these securities at prices on which the current dividend yields were in excess of high-grade bond yields.* At the same time it was found that these companies were also reinvesting additional earnings which were believed to be the essential cause of the subsequent appreciation in long-term market values. In short, total earnings (consisting of dividend distributions plus the amounts re-invested) as a percentage of original cost prices were consistently and significantly higher than bond yields.

Importance of Price: Earnings Yield. To illustrate, assume common stocks in general are returning a 6% dividend yield on existing market prices and retained earnings amount to another 4% of such market prices; then the total average earnings yield is 10% at the prevailing level of the market. The quantitative advantage of common stocks over bonds may be measured by the difference between the total earnings yield on market price and the rate of return on bonds, because it is total earnings which are managed for the benefit of the common stock-holder. In a reasonably stable and growing economy, there would be reason to expect that the acquisition of common stocks at prices where earnings yields are 10% would produce better investment results than would bonds yielding 4% or so.

Suppose, however, that the market prices of common stocks advance to levels where their earning yields actually fall below bond yields. Under these conditions a highly favorable growth rate in corporate earn-ings would be required for a continued superior performance of common stocks. For example, if most common stocks sold at prices where the earn-ings yield was only 4% at a time when bond yields were 5%, then a very profitable use of retained earnings would be required to make the total current income and appreciation returns on stocks compare favorably with bonds. In other words, it would then be necessary for future earn-ings to be materially higher than current levels. A very favorable growth rate in the economy and corporate earnings might produce the desired result, but the point is that the probabilities in favor of common stocks would be reduced under these conditions.

Qualifications Related to Empirical Performance: 1926–64. Table 3-2 shows the record of common stock prices, earnings, dividends, and the related yield computations as indicated by the Standard and Poor's Composite Index for the years 1926–64. (The years of World War II were omitted because of the temporary institutional factors introduced into the economy at that time, particularly price controls and excess profits taxes.) The pronounced upward trend in stock prices, earnings, and dividends over these years clearly confirms the view that common stocks generally have been superior for long-term investment, but the record also suggests that the results for periods up to a decade or so were heavily dependent upon (1) the rate of growth of corporate earnings

TABLE 3-2

STANDARD AND POOR'S COMPOSITE INDEX 1926–41 AND 1947–64
(Earnings and Dividends Adjusted to Index)

Year	Price High	Low	Average	Earn-ings	Divi-dends	Earnings Yield°	Dividend Yield°	High-Grade Corporate Bond Yields†
1926	13.7	10.9	12.6	$1.24	$ .69	9.05%	5.04%	4.77%
1927	17.7	13.2	15.3	1.11	.77	6.27	4.35	4.65
1928	24.3	16.9	19.9	1.38	.85	5.68	3.50	4.63
1929	31.9	17.7	26.0	1.61	.97	5.05	3.04	4.90
1930	25.9	14.4	21.0	.97	.98	3.74	3.78	4.71
1931	18.2	7.7	13.7	.61	.82	3.35	4.51	4.55
1932	9.3	4.4	6.9	.41	.50	4.41	5.38	5.28
1933	12.2	5.5	9.0	.44	.44	3.61	3.61	4.69
1934	11.8	8.4	9.8	.49	.45	4.15	3.81	4.14
1935	13.5	8.1	10.6	.76	.47	5.63	3.48	3.61
1936	18.0	13.4	15.5	1.02	.72	5.67	4.00	3.34
1937	18.7	10.2	15.4	1.13	.80	6.04	4.28	3.30
1938	13.8	8.5	11.5	.64	.51	4.64	3.70	3.20
1939	13.2	10.2	12.1	.90	.62	6.82	4.70	3.02
1940	12.8	9.0	11.0	1.05	.67	8.20	5.23	2.92
1941	10.9	8.4	9.8	1.16	.71	10.64	6.51	2.82
1947	16.2	13.7	15.2	$1.61	$ .84	9.93%	5.19%	2.58%
1948	17.1	13.8	15.5	2.29	.93	13.39	5.44	2.80
1949	16.8	13.6	15.2	2.32	1.14	13.81	6.79	2.65
1950	20.4	16.6	18.4	2.84	1.47	13.92	7.21	2.59
1951	23.8	20.7	22.3	2.44	1.41	10.25	5.92	2.84
1952	26.6	23.1	24.5	2.40	1.41	9.02	4.30	2.95
1953	26.7	22.7	24.7	2.51	1.45	9.40	5.43	3.18
1954	36.0	24.8	29.7	2.77	1.54	7.69	4.28	2.87
1955	46.4	34.6	40.5	3.62	1.64	7.80	3.53	3.04
1956	49.7	43.1	46.6	3.41	1.74	6.86	3.50	3.38
1957	49.1	39.0	44.4	3.37	1.79	6.86	3.65	3.91
1958	55.2	40.3	46.2	2.89	1.75	5.24	3.17	3.80
1959	60.7	53.6	57.4	3.39	1.83	5.58	3.01	4.38
1960	60.4	52.3	55.8	3.29	1.95	5.45	4.23	4.41
1961	72.6	57.6	66.3	3.21	2.02	4.42	2.78	4.36
1962	71.1	52.3	62.3	3.67	2.13	5.16	2.99	4.29
1963	75.0	62.6	69.8	4.02	2.28	5.36	2.95	4.24
1964	86.8	74.8	80.8	4.56	2.50	5.24	2.87	4.35

° Based on high for average of each year; price divided into earnings and dividends.

† Average for year.

and (2) the spread between earnings yields on common stocks and bond yields.

Because these propositions are crucial to the selection and management of a security portfolio, it might be useful to review briefly the empirical evidence on which they are based. First, it may be noted that the late 1920's witnessed a favorable growth rate in corporate earnings and dividends. However, stock prices advanced at a much more rapid rate. As a consequence, earnings yields declined from 9% at the market highs of 1926 to about 5% at the highs of 1929. With bonds yielding 4.90%, the differential between earnings yields and bond yields had by then largely disappeared. Therefore, to justify 1929 stock prices, corporate earnings would have had to continue their favorable trend. Unfortunately, the impact of the Great Depression caused a large decline in earnings. As a result, in 1932 common stocks sold for less than a third of 1929 levels.

As a matter of fact, the earnings on common stocks declined even more than prices, with the result that earnings yields in 1931–34 were even lower than in 1929. But the low earnings yields which prevailed during the depression clearly did not reflect overvaluations of stocks, but merely a temporary and abnormal disappearance of corporate earning power. Parenthetically, if corporate earnings should encounter a similar disaster in the future, the same reasoning would be applicable. However, such an event is considered to be highly improbable in view of structural changes in the economy, particularly the unquestioned commitment today to vigorous governmental action to combat business recessions. But the fact remains that the combination of high prices in mid-1929 (low earnings yields under reasonably prosperous economic conditions) and the interruption of the earnings growth trend produced results in the following two decades which were clearly at odds with the unqualified version of the common stock theory presented by Smith and others.

However, the empirical data on the stock market (shown in Table 3-2) since about 1950 have certainly vindicated the following qualified version of the theory: long-term holdings of diversified common stocks, although subject to cyclical fluctuations, are a superior investment medium if (1) the economy maintains a favorable growth rate, (2) the economy avoids serious downturns in business activity, and (3) if stocks are not acquired at earnings yields below bond yields. In fact, from 1950 through 1964 the total returns on long-term investments in common stocks have probably exceeded those obtained for any equal period in this century. But note that these results were obtained by the acquisition of stocks at prices where earnings yields were at the unprecedented level of more than three times prevailing bond yields. In short, the highly favorable returns that have been enjoyed on common stocks acquired in the early postwar years were due both to favorable economic growth and to a correction of the low valuations placed on corporate earning power at the beginning of the period.

By 1959, however, earnings yields on stocks had declined to about 5.6%, whereas bond yields had advanced to 4.38%. At this point prices of common stocks in relation to earnings were clearly above the norms of the past, and historically oriented analysts were inclined to suggest a possible overvaluation of stocks and consequent limited opportunities for adequate future long-term results.[4] But despite a downward drift in corporate earnings through 1961, common stock prices continued to advance with the result that the spread between earnings yields and bond yields actually became less than in 1929. The dangers of this situation were then reiterated by a substantial decline in stock prices in mid-1962, but the decline proved to be merely a temporary interruption in the upward trend. The fortunate result can only be ascribed to the fact that it became clear late in 1962 that corporate earnings were again increasing at a favorable rate after a disappointing performance in the previous several years. Indeed as corporate profits achieved new highs in 1964, the prices of common stocks responded accordingly, although earnings yields remained modestly above their postwar lows registered in 1961.

Therefore, one element which has historically contributed to the long-term superiority of common stocks was absent in the 1959–64 period; namely, earnings yields on stocks were not well above bond yields. On the other hand, the growth factor continued to favor common stocks. As of 1965, therefore, superior future returns on common stocks seemed to depend upon the continuance of a favorable growth rate in corporate earnings. If corporate earnings reach a plateau, as in 1955–61, or decline, as after 1929, then subsequent returns may be less favorable than suggested by empirical studies of the past long-term results.

Conclusions. To generalize from the above discussion, common stocks have proved to be a favorable long-term investment medium in a progressive economy when they are purchased at prices which are reasonable relative to the demonstrated earning power of the companies

[4] See, for example, Graham, *The Intelligent Investor*, New York: Harper & Row, 1959, pp. 44–59.

concerned. Because it is difficult in many cases to ascertain probable earning power, investment in common stocks requires competence in investment analysis and usually some diversification in order to protect the investor against the errors in judgment which are almost inevitable. Further, the investor must be reconciled to rather wide movements in the prices of his holdings. This fact has two practical implications. First, recoverability of principal is highly uncertain; second, the long-term investor must be emotionally equipped to experience substantial declines in market prices without becoming unduly disturbed.

It is less clear whether long-term returns on common stocks will be relatively favorable if they are acquired at earnings yields, computed on the basis of earning power during reasonably prosperous periods, close to or below bond yields. Under such conditions, dividend yields will be less than bond yields for a considerable period of time, and sustained growth in earnings plus consistently generous valuations of such earnings will be required to offset the lower income with adequate appreciation. The uncertainties surrounding the realization of these contingencies would seem to reduce the probability of favorable results. However, if in fact they are realized, the total returns on common stocks may even then compare favorably to alternative forms of investment over a decade or so.

Hybrid Security Contracts

Corporations have developed many special contractual devices to make security issues more palatable to investors. One of the more significant additions to fixed-income security contracts is the conversion privilege, which confers on bonds or preferred stock some of the aspects of common stock. The nature of the provision is relatively simple: it gives the investor in the senior issue the option to turn in all or part of his holdings to the company in exchange for a specified number of common shares.

Convertible Securities: Theoretical Advantages. In theory the convertible option is a very attractive addition to the security contract. Without disturbing the prior claim on income and the resultant greater *relative* safety and consistency of the current income return, the offsetting disadvantage of being unable to participate in the growth of the company is partially removed. The potential call on a given number of common shares provides this participation. When and if a growth in earning power is reflected in the price and the income paid to the common shares, the holder of the convertible security has three options. First, he can convert to the common and enjoy the increased income and all subsequent appreciation on such shares. Second, he can participate in the appreciation of the common without converting as the market price of the convertible will always reflect the total market price of common stock represented by one bond or preferred share. (For example, if an issue with a par value of 100 is convertible into two shares of common stock and the market price of the common appreciates to say 75, then the senior security will sell for at least 150.[5]) Third, he can of course sell the convertible issue (or the common after conversion) if a review of the company's prospects in relation to the prices of the securities suggests such an action is desirable.

On the other hand, if the growth in earnings and dividends on the common stock does not materialize, the convertible issue may still be a satisfactory investment based on its inherent merits as a fixed-income security. But, of course, if the company suffers a significant economic decline, there may be a corresponding reduction in the value of the senior issue because of the greater risk which may then be involved in the situation.

Convertible Securities: Disadvantages.   Although a strong case can be made for the theoretical advantages to the investor of the conversion privilege, in practice there are certain drawbacks connected with their use. In the first place, the conversion privilege is not a "free" addition to the contract. This merely means that the fixed-income security would probably sell at a lower price and at higher yield if it did not possess the conversion right. In other words, the purchase of a convertible bond or preferred results in a lower yield than could be obtained on an ordinary bond or preferred of comparable quality. The amount of yield sacrifice will depend upon the apparent attractiveness of the common stock and the terms of the conversion clause as set forth in the contract.

In the second place, continued retention of a convertible bond or preferred may not be warranted when and if appreciation on the common forces a substantial increase in the price of the convertible, because

---

[5] The possibility of arbitrage will assure at least this price for the convertible issue. If the convertible sold for 145 (say), the arbitrager could simultaneously buy it and sell short two shares of common for 150. He could then deliver the common sold short by converting the senior security. For this reason, convertible securities cannot sell for less than the price of the common multiplied by the number of shares into which they are convertible.

the yield may become negligible on the basis of market price. A practical illustration from the security markets may indicate the dilemma that arises in such circumstances. In early 1965, the price of the Dow Chemical Convertible 3s of 1982 was 165. At this price the current income yield was about 1.8%. The extraordinary price resulted from the fact that the bond was convertible into 2.26 shares of common which sold at about 78. Under these conditions there was no real justification for a true investor to continue to hold the debenture. As an ordinary bond, the issue was worth perhaps 82; at that price it would yield 4.5% to maturity, which was approximately the return on nonconvertible high-grade bonds at that time. Therefore, in essence the price of 165 really represented the market value of the common shares into which it was convertible. As a result, if the common appeared attractive for investment purposes, conversion would have been indicated as the yield on the common was about 2.4%, or well above the current income yield on the bond. On the other hand, if the common did not appear attractive for investment purposes, then sale of the convertible issue would be indicated.

Although the case is an excellent demonstration of the appreciation possibilities on a convertible security due to the growth in the value of the common stock, prudent investment considerations would have dictated conversion or disposal of the issue long before it reached the price prevailing in 1965. On the basis of market price, the Dow Chemical convertible bond was essentially nothing more than the common stock without the income return of the common. As a rule of thumb, it may be suggested that sale or conversion would be indicated when and if the current income yield on the senior security becomes less than one half the yield on comparable quality senior issues without the convertible feature.[6]

The investment attractiveness of convertibles is also reduced to some extent by the call feature. Because of this provision, the participation of the investor in the growth of the common can be held to within relatively narrow limits by the issuing corporation. In effect, conversion can be "forced" when the market price of the common pushes the price of the senior security to a level above the call price. To illustrate, assume that an issue is redeemable at 105 and is convertible into two shares of

[6] It is more appropriate to use the current income yield than the yield to maturity as a measure of the indicated return on a convertible bond when its price has been "forced" up by the appreciation in the common stock. In this special instance, the investor does not intend to accept par at maturity, because the value of the common stock incorporated into the bond is by definition greater than the par value of the bond.

common stock. Assume further that the common stock appreciates to 55; as indicated above, the price of the senior security will then be at least 110. A notice of redemption of the issue will require the investor to sell or convert it before the effective call date (usually thirty days after notice of call), or ultimately to surrender it for payment at 105. Under the assumed conditions it would be unwise, of course, for anyone to surrender it at the call price; therefore, sale or conversion would be indicated. In any event, the investor would have forfeited an advantageous position as a senior-security holder with an option on the common, and the company would have retired a senior claim by only increasing the number of common shares.

But it is by no means certain or even probable that companies will exercise their option to call convertible issues under such conditions. Forcing conversion results in an increase in the number of common shares outstanding, and the earnings to the common stock are increased only by the amount of the senior security requirements.[7] Therefore, earnings per share of common may be significantly diluted as a result of conversion. Consequently, no categorical statement about the probability of a given company exercising its option to force conversion can be made. However, when the cost to the company of the senior security (as indicated by the coupon rate) is low in comparison with prevailing interest rates and the payment of the interest or dividend requirement on the senior security appears to offer no problem, then action to redeem the issue would seem less probable. On the other hand, if the company seems likely to need new money and thereby to market a new senior issue, then eliminating an outstanding convertible security via forcing conversion may be a reasonable probability.

Another possible shortcoming to the use of convertibles as a practical avenue of investment is that one reason for attaching the privilege to the contract may be to assist in the distribution of a senior security which is intrinsically weak.[8] It is possible, therefore, that some issues which appear attractive from the standpoint of the convertible feature may not measure up to the standards of financial performance expected on senior securities. Therefore, if an analysis of the company indicates con-

[7] When the convertible is a bond, only about one-half the bond interest is added to common stock earnings as a result of conversion, because interest is deductible for tax purposes and the corporate tax rate is about 50%.

[8] The statement should not be interpreted to imply that the majority of convertibles are issued for this reason. There are other reasons for a corporation to employ these securities, such as the ability to obtain a more favorable yield or because of an expectation that ultimately a convertible issue will end up as equity capital when and if the common appreciates. The "forcing" of conversion, when the total value of the common stock controlled by the senior security is above the call price, is applicable to this latter point.

siderable risk on the senior issue, then a major segment of its attractiveness is lost.

However, under unusual technical circumstances an investor may find it more desirable to acquire the convertible security of a given company than the common stock, even though his main objective is to obtain the common stock for long-term investment. There are, therefore, two possible reasons for considering convertibles: (1) when the investment objective is principally a senior-security investment but some participation in the potential growth of the company is desired, (2) when the objective is really a common stock investment, but certain temporary aspects favor the convertible as a short-term alternative.

Convertibles: Appraisal Factors.   The preceding analysis of the nature of convertible securities suggests there are three distinct tasks involved in appraising their investment merits. First, it is necessary to evaluate their position as a senior security per se. The task here requires an investigation of the company with a view to ascertaining its ability to meet senior charges under all reasonably conceivable economic circumstances. Such an investigation requires, of course, an extensive treatment which would be inappropriate at this point.

Second, it is necessary to analyze the attractiveness of the convertible provision as a special feature. This phase of the analysis first requires an investigation of the investment value of the common stock. The conclusions derived from the investigation of the quality of the senior security are pertinent in this connection, but additional techniques and standards are also required.

Third, the attractiveness of a convertible issue also depends on certain technical features and yield relationships derived in large part from the investment contract. It is these features which are pertinent to the present discussion.

Convertibles: Illustrative Analyses.   The following analysis of technical terms assumes that the fixed-income securities are of satisfactory investment quality and that the common stocks at prevailing prices have been appraised as reasonably attractive long-term investments. Once these basic conclusions have been reached, then the following more or less technical measurements are pertinent to a final decision on the convertible security:

1. The indicated cost of the common stock which would result from the purchase of the convertible at its existing price and then converting it.

2. Comparison of this cost with the price of the common stock (the "closeness ratio").
3. The yield of the convertible compared to yields on nonconvertible senior securities of similar quality.
4. The amount of loss (if any) which would result if the convertible was called for redemption.
5. The duration of the convertible privilege.
6. The relative yields of the convertible and the common stock.

To demonstrate the computation and interpretation of these techniques, Table 3-3 shows the pertinent data and computations for two convertible issues, a bond and preferred stock, as of November, 1964. Measurement (1) above on the Phillips Petroleum bond is obtained from two separate computations. First, the number of common shares into which the senior security is convertible is obtained by dividing the *conversion price* into the par value of the bond. The conversion price is set forth in the bond indenture and represents the amount of par value of bond exchangeable for one share of common. Second, it is then necessary to divide the prevailing price of the convertible security by the number of common shares into which it is convertible. Table 3-3, for example, shows that the conversion price of the Phillips Petroleum debenture 4¼ s was 50; dividing into the par of 100 gives two shares into which it was convertible. As the price of the bond was 117 and it was convertible into two shares, the market conversion price became 58½, determined by dividing the bond price by the number of shares that could have been obtained in exchange for the convertible issue.

Measurement (2) related the "market conversion price" to the prevailing price of the common stock in order to find the percentage amount that the common stock must appreciate before any additional appreciation will mathematically be reflected in the price of the bond. The percentage relationship in this respect is known as the *closeness ratio*. Table 3-3 shows that Phillips Petroleum common stock sold at 53. Therefore, to reach the "market conversion price" of 58½ it would have to appreciate by 5½, or by about 10.4% (5½ ÷ 53). In brief, if the bond was purchased in preference to the common, the first 10% appreciation might have been foregone. Therefore, the closeness ratio is one major indication of a convertible's attractiveness; 30% or less would perhaps justify placing at least moderate value on the conversion option, but the value of the conversion privilege would seem dubious if the closeness percentage was greater than 30%.

Measurement (3) above gives two significant indications to the in-

TABLE 3-3
CONVERTIBLE SECURITIES: ANALYSIS DATA
(as of November, 1964)

Contract and Price Data	Phillips Petroleum 4¼s of 1987	Standard Oil of California $3.30 Preferred
Conversion price	$50.00	1.45 sh. of common
Market price—common	53	$67.00
Market price—convertible	117	99
Call price—convertible	103½	80 at 10/1/66
Date of change in conversion price	2/15/67	None
Common-stock dividends—1964 rate	$2.00	$2.20
Approximate yields of similar nonconvertible issues	4.40%	4.2%
Computed Data		
Number of common shares convertible into	2	1.45
Market conversion price	$58.5	$68.3
Closeness ratio	10.4%	1.8%
Dividend yield—stock	3.9%	3.2%
Current-income yield—bond	3.6%	3.3%

vestor. First, it shows the sacrifice in income incurred by buying the convertible instead of an ordinary bond or preferred. For example, Table 3-3 indicated that the investor obtained a current-income yield of 3.6% on the Phillips Pete bond, whereas nonconvertible bonds of similar quality gave yields of about 4.4%.[9] In percentage terms, the bond offered 84% as much yield as ordinary issues, which was well within the 50% level suggested earlier. Therefore, if other factors seemed attractive, the investor would not have felt compelled to reject it on the grounds that the yield sacrifice was too great.

Secondly, this comparison also indicated the estimated "price floor" on the convertible bond which would become operative in case the stock market suffered an extensive decline in the future. The price floor may be defined as the independent value of the senior security without the conversion feature at prevailing levels of interest rates. It may be estimated by determining the price which would give a yield to maturity equal to nonconvertible issues of similar quality or, as of November,

---

[9] The yield to maturity would be used only if the convertible bond had not been "forced" to a premium price above maturity value by the value of the common stock into which it was convertible.

1964, a yield of 4.4%. A bond table shows that a twenty-three-year bond (1987 maturity) with a coupon of 4.25% would sell at about 97.80 to give this yield. As the actual bond price was 117, the price floor was 19.20, or about 16%, below its existing price, In an adverse stock market, many common stocks show declines of more than 16%. The price floor was, therefore, one advantage of acquiring an interest in the common stock through the bond.[10]

Measurement (4), the amount of loss in case of redemption, is only applicable when the convertible security is selling above call price. However, it is not necessarily determined by the difference between market price of the convertible and call price. Instead, in a convertible issue the amount of the call risk is the lesser of the difference between (1) the market price and the call price or (2) the market price and the value of the common stock obtained through conversion. In the case of the Phillips Pete bond, although the call price was 103½, the value of common stock embodied in the bond was 106 (two shares times the prevailing price of 53). The loss in case of redemption would be 117 less 106, or 11 per bond; in percentage terms the loss would be about 10%.

This situation was an obviously undesirable feature of the convertible security, but the prospects of call should also have been considered. As factors deterring redemption, it can be noted that the 4.25% coupon rate was relatively low in comparison with prevailing money rates of about 4.4%. Moreover, the company may desire to avoid diluting the common stock. On the other hand, Phillips may ultimately decide to engage in new bond financing, which would probably be expedited if this issue was converted to common stock by a redemption notice and forced conversion. But the difference between call price (103½) and the common stock value of the bond (106) appeared too small to assure conversion, because the price of the common stock would probably react unfavorably to a redemption notice on the bond. This fact may inhibit a redemption notice unless the company was prepared to redeem in cash, which was unlikely.

Therefore, the probability of a future redemption notice was rather dubious, but even so it detracted from the desirability of this bond at a price of 117. On the other hand, the closeness ratio of about 10% was fairly attractive and the yield sacrifice was only 0.8% (3.6% as related to 4.4% on ordinary bonds), so if redemption was considered unlikely

[10] If the stock market decline was precipitated by a deterioration in business activity, then Federal Reserve authorities would probably follow a policy of monetary ease and as a consequence interest rates would decline. This could have the effect of raising the "price floor" on the bond to an upper limit of the call price.

on balance, the bond might have been considered technically desirable as a convertible security.

However, except for the slightly lower yield and the related factor of the price floor, the technical position of the Standard Oil of California $3.30 preferred appeared clearly superior to that of the Phillips Petroleum convertible bond. The closeness ratio of 1.8% was especially favorable; its significance was that all appreciation beyond 1.8% on the common would be certain to be enjoyed by the preferred. The call problem was also less on the Standard Oil preferred. It was not callable until late 1966, although at that time at 80, or well below the prevailing price of 99. More importantly, however, if the common stock maintains or increases its price in the meantime, any redemption of the preferred in 1966 would not result in any significant loss, as conversion would result in a holding of common stock worth almost 99. To be precise, if the common stock remained at its late 1964 price, the indicated loss on call would be equal to the closeness ratio, or 1.8%. Moreover, forcing conversion would not be particularly advantageous to the company as the dividend rate of $2.20 in effect on the common stock in 1965 would cost the company about $3.20 on 1.45 shares, as compared with the $3.30 paid on the preferred.

Although reasonably attractive as a fixed-income security with the convertible option, a case could also have been made for the preferred as a temporary substitute for an outright investment in the common stock. Its yield was slightly greater than the common (3.3% as compared to 3.2%) and its price floor, or investment value, as a straight preferred was approximately 80, or 20% below the price of 99. Therefore, at prevailing levels of interest rates, even if the common declined substantially, the decline in the preferred would be limited to about 20%. The only disadvantage to the purchase of the preferred as a substitute for the common would be a possible sacrifice of the first 1.8% of any subsequent appreciation. The decision, therefore, came down to whether the slightly higher yield and the defensive "floor protection" was worth a sacrifice of 1.8% in potential appreciation. On balance, assuming the common stock appeared attractive, the acquisition of the common stock through a temporary position in the convertible preferred seemed entirely reasonable.

Participating Securities.   The special feature of participating securities which distinguishes them from ordinary senior securities is the right to participate in dividend distributions on the common stock in addition to their fixed income. In theory at least, it can be argued that this right has an even greater investment attractiveness than does the conversion privilege, because a substantial improvement in the profitability of the issuing company can increase the total returns on these securities in two ways. First, the current income return can increase and this share in the increased profits can be enjoyed year after year. Second, there may be some appreciation return as the market takes recognition of the larger income payments. However, these securities have usually been issued in order to achieve acceptance of a poor-quality issue. As a consequence, they are quite rarely offered by the type of companies attractive to the outside investor.

Moreover, the other contractual terms can reduce the theoretical advantages to a very considerable extent. First, the inclusion of the redemption provision means that the appreciation return might be strictly limited. Investors are naturally reluctant to pay much more than call price for any security, except a convertible security under certain circumstances, and such reluctance might be considered especially advisable for a participating issue. It might be presumed that the directors would have a strong incentive to redeem a participating senior security when and if total earnings increase and greater dividends on the common can be paid only if distributions are increased on the participating security.

Second, the extent of the participation may be strictly limited. For example, the Arden Farms Company $3 participating preferred stock is entitled to receive one-quarter of the total common dividends in any year in addition to the $3 contractual dividend. During 1964 common dividends amounted to $1; thus the preferred received $3.25. However, the contract limits the extra participation to a maximum of $1 per share. As a result, this stock has a maximum potential income of $4 per share, which would be paid when the common stock also received $4 per share. All further distributions would go solely to the common stock.

Common-Stock Warrants. As long-term options to buy common stock at a specified price, warrants are not, in a strict sense, securities at all. Their origin is usually in the form of an attachment to a fixed-income security either to obtain a lower cost of capital or more probably to make possible the sale of a marginal-quality issue. But as warrants can be detached from the related senior security and sold in the market (some are listed on the organized exchanges), they have an independent technical status of their own as possible substitutes for the outright purchase of the common stock. However, as they are very seldom used by quality companies, their practical significance as an investment medium is not great. But it is true that during the extremely tight money market conditions of 1957 and 1959-60, several companies of reasonable investment stature, such as Sperry Rand and Kerr McGee Oil, did issue senior securities with warrants attached.

There is sometimes a tendency to confuse stock rights with stock warrants, but aside from the fact that they are both options to buy common stock, they are quite different.[11] Rights arise from new issues of common stock where holders of the existing common are given the right to subscribe to the new shares on a pro rata basis at a price modestly *below* the prevailing market price. Stock rights are good for perhaps thirty days and have a mathematical value whose precise amount depends upon the number of rights required to obtain a new share and the difference between the market price and the subscription price. American Telephone and Telegraph is perhaps an outstanding example of a company which from time to time has sold new stock through rights offerings.

In contrast, when they are first issued, warrants invariably give the holder the option to buy common stork at a price well *above* the prevailing market, but the option extends for a considerable period of time, usually ten years or more. Therefore, only a qualitative value, which may be defined as the value placed on the probabilities that the future price of the common stock will exceed the option price, can be determined. Of course if the common stock subsequently appreciates to a point above the option price, then the warrant will have a mathematical value equal to the price differences plus a probable qualitative value related to expectations for further appreciation.

As warrants are merely options to buy stock, their price is usually modest in comparison with the prevailing prices of the related common stock. The result is that a given percentage increase in a common stock's price may well have a magnified percentage effect on the warrant's price. For example, the Martin Marietta Corporation, a large aerospace and construction materials company, had warrants outstanding in 1964 which allowed each warrant to buy, for $45, 2.73 shares of common stock until November 1, 1968, or at a price of about $16.50 per share. The price of the common in late 1964 was 20, or $3.50 more than the price per share prescribed in the warrant. Therefore, each warrant had an arithmetic value of 2.73 times $3.50, or $9.55, but the actual market price of the warrants was about $21. To make the subsequent exercise

[11] The term *warrants* is in fact often used in connection with offerings of new stock issues under the pre-emptive right of the stockholder; for example, it might be stated that several warrants are required to buy one new share.

of the warrant profitable at that price, the common stock would have to appreciate to slightly above $24 ($21 plus $45 divided by 2.73), or by approximately 20%. The latter percentage may be defined as the "closeness ratio" of the warrant as of that date, or alternatively, as the "expectation value" of the warrant.

But note the effects should the common stock double in price to $40 before the end of 1968. Then each warrant would have an arithmetic value of 2.73 times $23.50 ($40 − $16.50), or about $64.15, more than three times the warrant price as of late 1964. In short, any dramatic price appreciation of the common would have a magnified effect on the warrant, but the effect tends to operate both ways. A substantial decline in the common stock's price would probably result in an even larger percentage decline in the price of the warrant as the possibility of profitable exercise became more remote.

Because warrants are essentially a means of obtaining a leverage position in a common stock, similar to the purchase of a stock on margin, they are usually considered to be a vehicle for traders rather than for long-term investors. But in exceptional circumstances, if current income can be completely sacrificed, warrants may be considered as a substitute for an investment in the common stock if the technical closeness and duration factors are reasonable and the prospects for the company appear to be good.

CHAPTER 4

Investment Strategies:
Fixed-Income Securities

Introduction

The selection and management of security portfolios generally include the following areas of analysis and decisions. First, as background perspective, it is important to examine the dynamic behavior of security markets over a considerable period of time and to investigate the possible causes and consequences of these behavioral characteristics. Second, on the basis of this evaluation, a decision is required as to which basic investment strategy or combination thereof appears to offer the best prospects for both returns and risk protection. Third, there is the area of security analysis per se, which covers the development of specific analytical techniques to appraise the desirability of individual issues. Fourth, in the context of the accepted strategy and from the conclusions derived from the security analysis procedures, specific securities would be purchased for, or perhaps eliminated from, the portfolio. Certain principles of portfolio management, such as reasonable diversification, would of course also be applicable to the continuing decisions about the appropriate composition of the portfolio.

The discussion in the following two chapters will be devoted to the first two of these areas: (1) an analytical examination of the dynamic behavior of the several securities markets and, (2) a consequent critical

CANISIUS COLLEGE LIBRARY
BUFFALO, N. Y.

appraisal of the alternative strategies which may be used to guide selections for and management of a security portfolio. At the outset it should be indicated that there are wide differences in views on these matters; considerable controversy continues to exist among even professional portfolio managers as to which strategies offer the best possibilities for favorable investment results. It will, however, be necessary to reach positive decisions as to which strategies are most promising because the orientation of the subsequent material dealing with appraisal and selection will heavily depend upon the fundamental strategies considered appropriate for operations in the securities markets. For example, the selection procedures pertinent to an operational strategy of trading in the market for short-term swings are entirely different from the techniques required when securities are to be bought and held for the long pull.

Bond Market Characteristics: 1926–64

Short-Term Price Movements.   Figure 4-1 indicates the major price characteristics of the bond market for the past forty years. These data, it might be noted, would also be relevant to the market for high-quality preferred stocks, which are essentially similar in their investment characteristics to bonds. Observation and analysis of the data shown on Figure 4-1 suggest the following comments. First, the intrayear or short-term price movements have usually been of minor proportions, except in those years when major cyclical changes took place in general business activity. In other words, violent swings in interest rates, which cause the movements in high-grade bond prices, do not take place except over a considerable span of time unless unusual developments occur in the economy. Prices moved fairly widely during the depression years of 1931–34 because the entire world was then marked by convulsive panics and uncertainty. Again in 1956, for example, the intra-year price range was relatively wide, but on this occasion the apparent inflationary developments within that year led the monetary authorities to create a tight money environment at a rapid rate. These events, however, were clearly atypical. Therefore, because short-term variations in bond prices have been quite limited, strategies directed at profiting by such fluctuations do not seem particularly relevant for most investors. Indeed in practice they are limited almost entirely to professional bond-trading houses.

FIGURE 4-1. HIGH-GRADE CORPORATE BOND INDEX

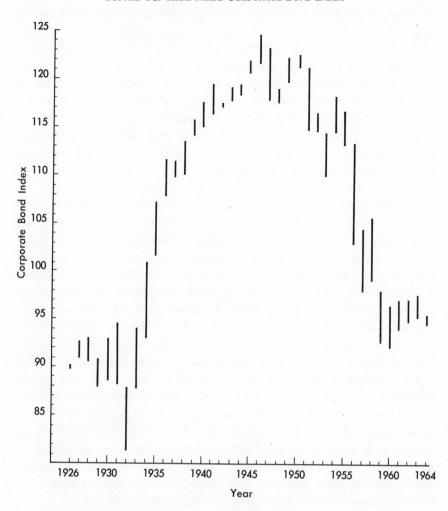

Source: Standard and Poor's, *Security Price Index Record.*

Cyclical Movements. Cyclical swings in bond prices, however, are quite another story. From the high of 1931, for example, to the low of 1932, prices declined by about 12%, and between 1954 and 1957 the decline was about 16%. And in the other direction, prices rose by about 30% between 1932 and 1936. However, the relation of these movements in bond prices to the course of business activity has been somewhat different in the postwar years than during the prewar years. Perhaps because the concepts of contracyclical monetary and fiscal policy were less well understood in the prewar years, bond prices in the late 1920's and early 1930's were often high during prosperous years and low during depression years. In the postwar period, on the other hand, monetary policy has been directed at bringing about "tight" money during booms and "easy" money during recessions. As a consequence, bond prices have typically declined cyclically during recoveries and booms in business activity (1958–60 and 1962–65) and have increased during recession periods (1953–54 and 1957–58). Therefore, there is some grounds for arguing that operations in the bond market may include a strategy to increase returns via appropriate adjustments of the portfolio in accord with cyclical expectations for bond prices.

Long-Term Trends. The data in Figure 4-1 further suggest that in-addition to the price swings resulting from fluctuations in business activity and contracyclical monetary policy, there have also been long-term trends in bond prices, in the sense that a general movement in one direction or another has extended over several business cycles.[1] Two such long-term trends seem apparent since 1926. The first, in an upward direction, can by hindsight be dated from 1932 through 1946. During these years, interrupted only by minor cyclical variations, bond prices moved upward substantially from the low in 1932 of 81.7 to the high in 1946 of 124.6. In total the advance of some forty points in the index represented an increase in bond prices of about 50%. The second long-term trend, in a downward direction, can be dated from perhaps 1947, clearly extended until 1959, and may yet be in progress as of 1965. In this case, prices declined about 27% from their highs in 1947. As these trends have been substantial, an investment strategy aimed at their exploitation could have been profitable, but the fact that about fifteen or more years were required for their consummation reduced the return opportunities measured on an average annual basis.

Strategy to Improve Returns: Medium-Quality Obligations

Yield Differentials. As brought out earlier, the inherent nature of the bond contract suggests that its primary function in an investment portfolio is to supply a high degree of certainty of dollar income. A sec-

---

[1] For a highly detailed and complete discussion of the several types of fluctuations in bond prices in the United States since 1900, see Homer, *A History of Interest Rates*, New Brunswick, N.J.: Rutgers University Press, 1963, Chapter XVII.

ondary function may be to obtain recoverability of principal which is, however, associated only with short maturities. But maximization of income and perhaps obtaining some moderate capital gains may also be legitimate objectives. One strategy aimed at increasing returns is to purchase medium- or low-quality fixed income securities, which of course carry an income premium for the increased risk. Between 1955 and 1964, for example, top-quality industrial bond yields showed average annual yields between 2.97% to 4.26%, whereas the range of yields on similar type medium-grade bonds was between 3.34% and 4.93%.[2] In short, about a ½ % income premium was typically obtainable on medium-grade bonds.

Empirical evidence in favor of this strategy was indicated in a detailed study of a large universe of bonds over the period 1900 to 1944 (note the inclusion of the Great Depression years). This study found that whereas bonds rated in the fourth class for quality showed a default rate of 19.1% as compared to a 6% default rate for top-quality obligations, the total realized net yields, including liquidation returns, were 5.7% on the fourth-quality class as compared to 5.1% on those of top quality.[3]

Use by Life Insurance Companies.   Therefore, at first glance, the results suggest that investors might be well advised to improve returns by the deliberate purchase of low-quality bonds. Indeed the bond portfolio policies of the very large life insurance companies indicate that this strategy is actually used in practice. These companies often emphasize the acquisition of private placements from moderate-sized companies of less than prime quality and the portfolios tend to be dominated by several hundred of such issues. But life insurance companies, it should be noted, can afford to operate for the *average* long-term yield, rather than a *steady annual* yield. Moreover, because of the very extensive diversification, there is a strong probability that their loss experience will approximate that of the entire universe. Thus if defaults average, say 15%, and recoveries on defaults average 50% of the original principal values for the entire universe of many thousands of such bonds, it can be anticipated that insurance company portfolios of a thousand or so such

[2] Standard and Poor's, *Security Price Index Record*, 1964 edition, pp. 190 and 193.
[3] Fraine, *Valuation of Securities Holdings of Life Insurance Companies*, Richard D. Irwin, Inc., Homewood, Ill., 1962, pp. 29–40, reporting on data taken from Hickman, *Corporate Bond Quality and Investor Experience*, Princeton, N.J.: Princeton University Press, 1960.

issues should have a similar experience. In addition, it would seem likely that the use of comprehensive screening techniques may improve the portfolio experience in relation to the unscreened universe.

Drawbacks. It may be seriously questioned, however, whether the individual investor can successfully emulate the large life insurance companies. In the first place, these investors are usually interested in continuous stability of income from their fixed-income security portfolio rather than in the average returns. If fluctuating dollar income can be tolerated, then common stocks have usually been a more desirable investment medium. The life companies, however, for legal reasons cannot hold common stocks to any significant extent.

In the second place, it would be very difficult if not impossible to acquire a sufficient number of issues to achieve a reasonable probability that the experience would be similar to the entire universe of such bonds. For example, the choice of one unsatisfactory issue could seriously impair the results on the entire portfolio of a few bonds. This, of course, is not the case for the large life companies. Therefore, it is concluded that most individual investors should not adopt a strategy of improving yields on their fixed-income security portfolios through the acquisition of medium- or low-quality bonds or preferred stocks.

Strategy to Improve Returns: Cyclical Timing

Maturity Switching. A second strategy to improve returns might be to switch the portfolio in accordance with the cyclical outlook for interest rates. The typical technique adopted to implement such a strategy is to concentrate on short maturities when interest rates are low and are expected to rise, and to acquire long maturities when rates are high and are expected to decline. Some commercial banks are known to operate along these lines to some degree, but again there are real problems in achieving successful results.

First, the current income yields would probably tend to vary widely as short maturities historically have given very modest yields during periods of low interest rates. Among other possible reasons, the very tendency of important investors to concentrate on these issues during low rate periods produces this result. When and if the short maturities were liquidated and invested in longer-term issues consequent to a general advance in interest rates, current income would increase, but then it would subsequently decrease again as the process was reversed.

Second and perhaps more important, interest rate movements are quite difficult to forecast accurately. Although it is clearly possible to establish whether rates are currently high, low, or average in relation to the past several years, it is still a highly uncertain business to predict the duration and extent of any movement then in progress. During early 1958, for example, predictions were widespread that interest rates would decline for the entire year because of the prevailing recessionary conditions, yet by the end of the year a reversal in business conditions and monetary policy brought bond prices down to about their lows of 1957. Again during 1963 and 1964, a number of bond analysts freely predicted the probability of "tight" money policies ahead (falling bond prices), yet prices remained remarkably stable during these years.

But some modest action to lengthen average maturities when rates appear relatively high may be a tempting strategy for two reasons. First, it ties down the higher rates then available for a longer period ahead. Second, it increases the capital gain potentials when and if rates turn downward. The same reasons in reverse are applicable to a strategy to shorten average maturities when rates seem low. Capital losses will be reduced and the low level of income derived on new commitments can be improved if and when rates rise. As brought out earlier, however, during periods of generally low interest rates, the difference between yields at the short end and the long end of the maturity schedule is usually relatively substantial. Therefore, if interest rates generally stubbornly remain low for a long period (1941–51, for example), then a considerable sacrifice in income may be involved.

Strategy to Obtain Average Yields: Staggered Maturities

A third strategy of bond portfolio management can be used to guard against the possibility that the yield obtained on a large commitment in the market at any one time will be less than the average level of yields subsequently available. It consists of structuring the original portfolio with staggered maturities, say at regular intervals between one and twenty years. Then as a given maturity comes due, the proceeds are reinvested at the long end, say twenty years or so. As a result, there is a reasonably constant flow of reinvestment at various levels of interest rates. Therefore, the portfolio through time should obtain about the average level of long-term rates that are obtainable in the bond market.

The strategy, it may be observed, is somewhat defensive in the sense that its purpose is to avoid the consequences of a serious miscalculation of future interest rate levels. For this reason, conservative investors may be attracted to it. There is, however, the drawback that the income returns on the original staggered maturity account may be less than if the account was invested entirely in long-term obligations because short maturities typically carry lower returns than long maturity items.[4] For example, Table 4-1 shows the approximate yields available during much of the 1962–64 period on a government bond account of $100,000 invested in equal maturities of one through eleven years. For purposes of comparison the returns obtainable on such an account invested entirely in ten-year maturity bonds are also shown. On the staggered account, it will be noted that the average yield was about 3.8%, whereas 4.1% was available on ten-year obligations. If interest rates rise in subsequent years, the yield on the staggered account will gradually increase as maturing issues are reinvested at the higher eleven-year rate, and there will also be less price depreciation on the account as a whole than on the long-term account. In brief, the staggered-maturity strategy produces greater stability of market values but usually less income for a number of years than the long-term account unless the latter was invested at rates which in retrospect turn out to be abnormally low.

Combination Strategy: Adjusted Staggered Maturities

Finally, there is the possibility of combining a general strategy of staggered maturities with a policy to institute moderate actions to lengthen or shorten maturities in accord with the cyclical outlook for rates. The large commercial banks are perhaps the most common advocates of such a combined strategy. In this case, as maturities come due they may not be completely reinvested at the long end of the maturity schedule, instead they are placed partially or entirely in short- or intermediate-term obligations if expectations seem to favor an increase in rates. For example, if such an expectation seemed reasonable at the end of one year when $10,000 of the obligations shown in Table 4-1 came due, the proceeds may be put into maturities of one and two years. The decision will increase the one- and two-year maturities at that time to $15,000 each and eliminate the eleven-year maturity. Then when and if rates do in fact rise, some of the near-term maturities may be sold and perhaps committed to twelve- or fifteen-year maturities. Such obliga-

---

[4] During periods of tight money, short maturities offer yields about equal to longs, but these occasions have been relatively infrequent in the past twenty years.

TABLE 4–1
STAGGERED MATURITY VS. LONG-TERM BOND ACCOUNTS
(Comparison of Alternative Yields: Government Obligations)

	Staggered Maturity Account		
Amount	Maturity	Yield to Maturity*	Total Return
$10,000	1 year	2.5%	$ 250
10,000	2 years	2.7	270
10,000	3 years	2.9	290
10,000	4 years	3.1	310
10,000	5 years	3.2	320
10,000	7 years	3.8	380
10,000	8 years	3.9	390
10,000	9 years	4.0	400
10,000	10 years	4.1	410
10,000	11 years	4.1	410
		Total	$3,800

	Long-Term Account		
Amount	Maturity	Yield to Maturity*	Total Return
$100,000	10 years	4.1%	$4,100

* Based on average yield approximations during 1962–64.

tions of course have a greater appreciation potential consequent to a later cyclical decline in rates. Therefore, if the forecasts are reasonably accurate, some capital gains can be generated. In addition, yields may be improved over a considerable span of years. Finally, because the implementation tends to proceed gradually as reinvestment of maturing obligations is required, the consequences of an erroneous forecast at any given time are less serious than if large structural changes in the maturity distribution were made on the basis of a given forecast.

CHAPTER 5

Investment Strategies:

Common Stocks

Stock-Market Characteristics: 1926–64

Types of Price Movements. Because market phenomena were an integral factor in appraising the nature of common stocks as an investment medium, Table 3-2 in Chapter 3 showed many of the essential behavioral characteristics of the stock market for the years 1926–64. The data in that table are relevant to the present discussion, and in addition, Figure 5-1 is offered to give a graphical view of the stock market for those years.

It is clear from these data that several types of price movements have been characteristic of the stock market. First, intrayear fluctuations have often been wide, and although not specifically indicated in the yearly data, minor price movements in one direction or another over a few weeks or months can also be identified. Second, a cyclical pattern of market prices is apparent in Figure 5-1; these may be defined as movements which are precipitated by expectations of or developments in the course of business activity. Third, the long-term trend of stock prices has certainly been in an upward direction over the entire period.

But a fact which may be of great importance to a decision on an appropriate investment strategy is that the magnitude of cyclical fluctuations in relation to the long-term trend was quite different between the years 1926–50 than between 1950–64. Cyclical variations without question

FIGURE 5-1. Dow-Jones Industrial Average: 1926–64

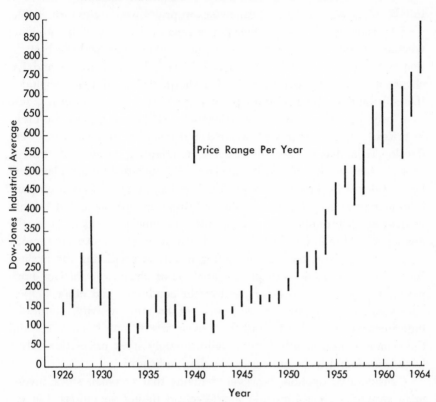

dominated the 1926–50 period. In fact, based on the data for those years alone, serious doubts could be raised about the actual existence of any upward long-term trend. After all the market was no higher in 1950 than it had been in 1928 and it was well below the highs of 1929. But since about 1950 the long-term trend of prices has been rapidly upward, so that stocks in 1965 were more than four times their level fifteen years earlier. Downward movements during these years were of short duration and generally could be characterized as merely interruptions for a year or so in the upward course of stock prices. In brief, although cyclical movements dominated the stock market between 1926 and 1950, a rapid upward long-term trend has dominated the market since that time.

Characteristics and Strategy Decisions. It is perhaps entirely natural to expect that the major empirical characteristics of a given market for the preceding decade or so will heavily influence decisions about the appropriate strategy for action in that market. Thus it is not surprising to note that after 1929 and up until about 1954, various techniques designed to take advantage of the cyclical swings in prices were quite fashionable.

For example, the Dow Theory, a mechanical means of determining whether the market was in a "bull" or "bear" phase, received much attention in those years. It was so widely followed that a Securities and Exchange Commission investigation of a sharp decline in 1946 concluded that substantial selling on the part of Dow Theory followers in response to a "bear signal" may well have triggered a significant part of the break in prices.[1] Again, rather sophisticated and complex formula plans were developed in that era for the purpose of adapting investment strategy to a predominantly cyclical stock market.[2] Although formula plans will be considered in somewhat more detail in a subsequent section on portfolio management principles, suffice it to note at this point that the objectives of all formula plans are to entice buying of stocks at cyclically low levels and selling at high levels. Finally, as might be expected, much time and effort was devoted to finding means of predicting the cyclical swings in stock prices through the analysis of changes in various business indices, such as monetary and credit conditions and other supposedly sensitive indicators of the course of business activity. Naturally, indicators which tended to lead the movements of both stock prices and the economy were avidly sought; unfortunately stock prices themselves have been found to be among the leading indicators.[3]

Considerable opinion, however, remains that common stock investment strategies should include some cyclical timing operations. For example, many investment advisory services continue to comment on the outlook for stock prices for the next year or so and to orient their recommendations accordingly.[4] And indeed it is not altogether clear that some attention on this score may not be advisable. Even though the long-term trend has been upward at a remarkable rate since about 1950, on several occasions the market has experienced sharp declines. The dates and extent of the more serious setbacks are shown on Table 5-1. The time span of these declines, measured by hindsight from a preceding high to a subsequent low, has varied between three and eight months, although it should be recognized that in most cases it required a year or so for the market to surpass its prior high point. But in comparison with the two

[1] *Commercial and Financial Chronicle*, Volume 166, August 28, 1947, p. 17.

[2] Perhaps the most comprehensive treatise on formula plans is Cottle and Whitman, *Investment Timing—The Formula Plan Approach*, New York: McGraw-Hill, 1953. (Note the date of publication.)

[3] Moore, *Business Cycle Indicators*, Volume I, National Bureau of Economic Research, Princeton, N.J.: Princeton University Press, 1961, pp. 27–29.

[4] See, for example, *Moody's Stock Survey*, New York: Moody's Investors Service, and Standard and Poor's, *The Outlook*, New York: Standard and Poor's Corporation.

TABLE 5-1
STOCK MARKET DECLINES: 1950–65
(Dow-Jones Industrial Average)

Date	High	Date	Low	Amount of Decline	Percentage of Decline
January, 1953	293.8	September, 1953	255.5	38.3	13
July, 1957	520.8	October, 1957	419.8	101.0	19
January, 1960	685.5	October, 1960	566.1	119.4	17
December, 1961	734.9	June, 1962	535.8	199.1	23
May, 1965	942.1	June, 1965	835.4	106.7	11

decades of 1929 through 1949, where downturns of 50% or more were witnessed and several years were generally required for a complete recovery, these more recent downward movements have been very limited in extent and duration.

Market Declines: Causation. By and large, over the years the major declines in stock prices have been associated with downturns in general business activity, although the stock market has rather consistently anticipated the course of business activity rather than moving concurrently with it. It is for this reason that such setbacks are usually characterized as cyclical in origin. But in several postwar instances, substantial declines have taken place which cannot realistically be related to the subsequent direction of business activity. The first of these was witnessed during 1946–48. By hindsight this decline was almost incredible, because during these years corporate earnings more than doubled (see Table 3-2), yet stock prices at the end of 1948 were about 16% lower than at their highs in 1946. One can only conjecture about the reason for the unprecedented action of the market; the most reasonable explanation may be that a severe business recession has usually followed a major war and that the market rather stubbornly continued to anticipate a recession which never took place.

The second occasion was in 1962. In this instance, the 23% decline in the Dow-Jones Industrial Average represented the most severe setback since 1940–42, yet the direction of business activity moved slowly but steadily upward for several years thereafter. It is clear, therefore, that the decline was not cyclically oriented in the usual sense, although it may again be argued that, as in 1946–48 and in 1965, the market was anticipating a recession which did not take place.

Another reason, however, may be advanced to explain the adverse market performance of 1962. It can be noted that at the end of 1961, the Standard and Poor's Composite Stock Index was selling at 22.5 times the realized earnings of that year on the constituent stocks. This level of prices in relation to earnings of a moderately prosperous year (neither boom nor clearly recessionary conditions) was well above previous experience, in fact matched only by the levels of 1929, which had proved nonsustainable. It is true, as Table 3-2 showed, that prices had exceeded twenty times earnings in several years during the 1930's. But in those years the cause was clearly the effects of the Great Depression on corporate earnings and not consequent to a major advance in stock prices.

In view of past experience, therefore, there is some reason to believe that stock prices may be vulnerable to a major decline under two conditions. First, setbacks may be associated with cyclical influences in the economy generally. Second, they may occur when average stock prices advance generally to levels of perhaps twenty-two to twenty-five times earnings realized under reasonably favorable economic conditions.[5] If the rate of growth in corporate earnings can be accelerated in some way (and such growth, it may be added, may be different than that achieved for such general economic indexes as Gross National Product), then levels of general stock prices of twenty-two to twenty-five times earnings may be sustainable. The reason is that the rapid growth in earnings will rapidly reduce the earnings multiple associated with any given price level of common stocks. Although conjectures that the future long-term growth rate in corporate earnings will be highly favorable have been widely advanced, such predictions remain to be proved. Therefore, there is reason to suggest that the probability of a major market decline increases as stocks advance at a more rapid rate than corporate earnings. Past experience suggests that when prices exceed perhaps twenty-two times earnings, the exposure to an unfavorable subsequent performance becomes more probable, but experience also suggests that the exposure is reduced during periods of rapid growth in corporate earnings.

Common-Stock Strategy: Trading

Types of Trading.   A trading operation may be defined as one where the objective is to obtain market profits through forecasting the short-term

[5] It should be emphasized that the reference in this statement is to prices of common stocks generally as reflected in a comprehensive stock average and *not* to prices of individual stocks whose unusual growth prospects may justify higher prices than average.

swings in prices and buying and selling accordingly.[6] Although any precise definition of a short-term transaction must necessarily be arbitrary, a rough bench-mark might be those completed within a year. At one extreme in this regard, it is possible to trade stocks hourly on the basis of the immediate indications for supply and demand as revealed by successive transactions. Individuals conducting such operations are known as "tape readers." By a study of technical market factors, they try to predict whether a stock will move up or down a fraction of a point in the next transaction or so; securities are turned over hourly, and, while unit profits are necessarily low, the volume of trades is correspondingly high. As commissions and odd-lot premiums amount to more than a fraction of a point per share, this type of operation is customarily identified with members of the stock exchange actually on the floor who do not pay commissions.

Second, there are the "general market" traders, who attempt by a variety of means to predict the course of the market over the succeeding few weeks or months. To illustrate the irregular timing and extent of this type of market action, Table 5-2 shows the significant intrayear fluctuations in the Standard and Poor's 425 Industrial Index for 1964.

A great deal of effort apparently goes into making such forecasts. Some members of this family are known as "chartists." The term means that the past price record of the market or of a particular security is depicted in detail on various kinds of graphs; from these records it is felt that certain price patterns emerge which can be used to predict the

TABLE 5-2
STANDARD AND POOR'S 425 INDUSTRIALS
(Intrayear Fluctuations 1964)

Period	Level of Average	Amount of Change
January 2 to April 16	79.1–85.7	+6.6
April 16 to April 28	85.7–83.8	−1.9
April 28 to May 12	83.8–87.0	+3.2
May 12 to June 9	87.0–82.8	−4.2
June 9 to July 20	82.8–89.4	+6.6
July 20 to August 5	89.4–85.4	−4.0
August 5 to November 20	85.4–91.9	+6.5
November 20 to December 15	91.9–87.2	−4.7

[6] These operations are usually visualized as the purchase of certain stocks which, it is hoped, will move upward in the next several months. However, through the short-sale technique, described in Chapter 6, the sale can precede the purchase and the profit be derived from a decline in price.

probability of future movements. The great difficulty here is that the past record does not provide conclusive evidence and in some cases the several indicators may be contradictory. In brief, it is possible to know a great deal about the pattern of the market and its historical record, and still not know enough to formulate reliable predictions of the future.

Others in this group may prefer to rely on economic and political indications. Elections, developments in the international arena, reports on new developments within companies, etc., are the source materials to provide the clues for buying and selling securities. But, like the "chartists," the "news traders" have a problem of interpretation which prevents the realization of consistently dependable forecasts on which a net return can be assured.

Problem of Trading Strategies. The great difficulty of forecasting the short swings of the market has been clearly indicated in several correlation analyses of the behavior of stock prices using modern mathematical techniques. For example, two such independent studies both concluded that stock prices perform a "random walk," or in other words, there is no significant and consistent correlation between any past market data and subsequent price behavior.[7] As a result, it is concluded that a strategy designed to obtain profits from the short-term swings of the market should be left to professional traders and avoided by the average individual investor.

Common-Stock Strategy: Cyclical Timing

As mentioned earlier, until evidence became available in the mid-1950's that the long-term trend in stock prices was again upward, strategies designed to profit from alternatively buying at major cyclical lows and selling at highs probably dominated investment operations aimed at producing appreciation rather than current income. This orientation, it might be repeated, appeared entirely justified in view of the market characteristics of the twenty years preceding 1950: a flat trend marked by wide fluctuations upward and downward over periods of several years. In such a market, to achieve any significant appreciation returns the only alternative was to attempt to single out the minority of companies with upward growth trends, despite the absence of such a trend for corporations in general.

[7] Molodovsky, "Lessons from the Recent Past," *Financial Analysts' Journal,* January–February, 1964, p. 50.

Forecasting Problems. In theory at least, the strategy was and remains an incontestable one: buy stocks when they are low and sell them when they are high. It would be difficult indeed to argue with this advice. The real controversial issue in connection with this strategy is a practical one: the question of whether there are reliable devices to indicate when the market is high and a decline is imminent and when it is low and a rise is likely to follow. Unfortunately, it must be concluded that reliable, known techniques for forecasting the major price fluctuations of the stock market do not exist. It was indicated above that the market itself has rather consistently anticipated the course of business activity. Therefore, the changes in various indexes which allegedly portend cyclical fluctuations in economic conditions have not been consistently useful to predict the stock market, although many financial publications continue to comment on the "market outlook" as presumably revealed by business or political developments.[8]

Market-Norm Approach. A second approach to a cyclical timing strategy has been to establish market "norms" and to recommend selling or buying when the market is respectively well above or below the indicated "norms."[9] The main hypothesis of this strategy is that the stock market tends to be influenced by recurrent waves of excessive optimism and pessimism. Therefore, it is argued that prices tend to move to levels well above and below those justified by objective and intelligent valuation procedures based on the long-term probabilities. In short, it is held that the market is likely to exaggerate the importance of phenomena which are likely to have only a short-term effect, such as the outlook for business conditions and perhaps domestic or international political events. As the present discussion is oriented to a brief outline of the alternative strategies, it is not appropriate to consider at this point the various detailed techniques used to determine the "norms" of the market; suffice it to note that they are generally based on an assumption that the empirical past average relationships of the market are likely to continue into the future. For example, a smoothed long-term trend line might be used; alternatively, attempts have been made to formulate the appropriate relationship of prices to earnings and dividends. To illustrate, one view is that the long-term historical record indicates that the market is

[8] See, for example, the weekly column in *Barron's* entitled "The Trader Gives His Views of the Market."

[9] Perhaps the most widely known proponent of this hypothesis and approach is Benjamin Graham. For his reasoning and detailed techniques for implementation see Graham, Dodd, and Cottle, *Security Analysis*, 4th ed., New York: McGraw-Hill, 1962, pp. 405–433 and pp. 507–538.

probably in an overvalued position when it sells much above fifteen times earnings of reasonably prosperous years.[10]

Appraisal: Cyclical Timing Strategies. There are both theoretical and empirical grounds to favor a common-stock strategy along these lines. On the theory side, it is argued that common stocks should have definable long-term values based upon the probabilities for earnings and dividends in the future. But it is also argued that the market may become heavily influenced by emotional buying based on mass behavioral reactions to favorable economic and market activity. As a result, it can be carried to levels which are unreasonably high based on any realistic appraisal of the probabilities for future earnings and dividends. Finally, the theory concludes, excessive movements in one direction are ultimately likely to produce excessive reactions in the other direction. The prudent investor, therefore, would be well advised to sell common stocks in overvalued markets and buy them in undervalued markets.

On the empirical side, Table 5-3 shows the position of the market in relation to the approximate earnings data then available at several cyclical highs and at the lows registered within one year thereafter.[11] (It may be noted that the fluctuations associated with the Great Depression and World War II have been omitted on the grounds they are abnormal in character.) The data for the prewar years suggest that the market was vulnerable to decline when it sold significantly above fifteen times earnings. In the postwar years the record is less clear because the decline of 1957 took place when the market was not demonstrably high on the basis of the fifteen times earnings benchmark. However, the market performance of 1961–62 strongly supports the case for a strategy of selling stocks when the market proceeds to levels well above twenty times earnings. In this case even though earnings continued to move upward in 1962, the market index declined by about 28%. Therefore, for the most part the empirical evidence tends to support the view that the market may become overvalued at times, and as a consequence be exposed to a sharp and extensive subsequent decline of a temporary nature.

But despite the evidence, the record does not prove that a strategy to sell stocks at such times and then buy them back at lower levels would

[10] *Ibid,* pp. 511–512 and pp. 745–748.

[11] Apparent trends in earnings at the time undoubtedly influenced the levels of the market at the respective dates. Unfortunately, in a historical analysis where hindsight information is available, the dynamic expectations as to the earnings outlook which influenced the course of prices at a given time cannot be introduced because such expectations contain subjective elements which may or may not have been realized in subsequent earnings results.

TABLE 5–3
STANDARD AND POOR'S 425 STOCK INDUSTRIAL AVERAGE
(Data at Selected Market Highs and Lows)

Year	Index High	Index Low	Earnings*	Price-Earnings Ratio
1929	25.4		1.25	20.3
1930		11.3	1.03	11.2
1937	18.1		1.00	18.1
1938		8.4	.82	10.2
1957	53.3		3.51	15.5
1958		42.0	3.22	13.0
1961	76.7		3.39	22.5
1962		54.8	3.62	15.2

* Average for year indicated and preceding year.

have been or will be successful. The principal problem has been the fact that the stock market even at the lows of 1957 and 1962 sold at price-earnings ratios appreciably above those witnessed at the lows of the pre-war years. Moreover, because of the highly favorable trend pattern in effect since about 1950, these lows in an absolute sense were well above the highs of a few years earlier. Thus the low registered in 1957 on the Standard and Poor's 425 Industrial Index of 42.0 was well above any high point in the market reached prior to 1955. Similarly, the low in 1962 of 54.8 was above the preceding market high of 53.3 reached in 1957. As a result, although the "norm" approach to common stocks could have logically suggested sales in 1960–61, it is doubtful if replacements would have been recommended at the 1962 lows, because the market did not then indicate a level significantly below the historical normal pattern. In short, as of 1965 the investor committed to a strategy of purchasing common stocks only when below norm levels and selling them when above might well have held no stocks since 1961 or perhaps even since 1959.

The major controversial issue surrounding the strategy is whether a structural change in the relation of stock prices to earnings and dividends may not have emerged in the latter part of the 1950's. The advocates of the norm approach argue that historical precedents back to the turn of the century indicate that common stocks are ultimately likely to sell at levels below about fifteen times earnings. On the other side, it is held that structural changes in national economic policy have materially improved the growth and stability characteristics of corporate earnings, and perhaps in addition have introduced a distinct long-term inflationary bias into the economy. As a result, it is claimed that the probabilities favor normal levels of stock prices in relation to earnings well above those usually prevailing up to about 1955.[12] On the whole, there seems to be plausible evidence to suggest that such a structural change may have occurred. Therefore, efforts to conduct a cyclical timing strategy may be quite difficult to consummate successfully until and unless new normal patterns emerge in subsequent years.

Common-Stock Strategy: Buy and Hold

Concepts. The buy-and-hold strategy may be defined as the purchase of stocks for the long-term results obtainable from the earnings and dividends of the related corporations over a period of a decade or more. Under this approach analytical techniques are applied to industries and companies to estimate their probable long-term value potentials on the one hand, and the risks of achieving them on the other. Sales of particular issues may be contemplated if analysis suggests quality has deteriorated or perhaps if it appears that prices have moved well above value potentials. But it is usually expected that the proceeds from such sales will be directed to other common stocks and not converted into cash or bonds, as might result from the various timing strategies outlined previously. It is hoped that the returns obtained, both in the form of current income and appreciation, will be somewhat greater as a consequence of the selection techniques than would be obtained from a diversified random sample of common stocks. In addition, the selection procedures should assist in obtaining the type of stocks which appear most relevant to the particular needs of each investor.

Empirical Justification. Over a period of a decade or more when the economy and the stock market have enjoyed a remarkable upward trend and fluctuations around the trend line have been modest in degree, this strategy would by definition have produced quite favorable results. And indeed as shown in Figure 5-1 such characteristics have dominated the stock market through the period 1949–64. To illustrate the record in more detail, Table 5-4 shows the prices, earnings, and dividends

---

[12] The growing institutional demand for quality stocks has also been cited as a reason for a change in the normal relationship of prices to earnings and dividends. The argument also notes that the supply of such stocks has been growing at a less rapid rate than the demand on the part of pension funds and other institutional investors.

TABLE 5-4
DATA ON STANDARD & POOR'S INDUSTRIAL AVERAGE
(425 Stocks)

Year	Yearly Price Range (1941–43 = 10)			Earnings	Ratio Mean Price to Earnings	Dividends	Yield on Mean Price
	High	Low	Mean				
1964	91.86	79.08	85.47	$4.83	17.8	$2.60	3.0%
1963	79.25	65.48	73.39	4.22	17.4	2.38	3.2
1962	75.22	54.80	65.01	3.87	16.8	2.20	3.4
1961	76.69	60.87	68.78	3.37	20.4	2.08	3.0
1960	65.02	55.34	60.18	3.41	17.6	2.00	3.3
1959	65.32	57.02	61.17	3.53	17.3	1.90	3.1
1958	58.97	43.20	51.09	2.95	17.3	1.79	3.5
1957	53.25	41.98	47.62	3.50	13.6	1.84	3.9
1956	53.28	45.71	49.50	3.53	14.0	1.78	3.6
1955	49.54	35.66	42.60	3.78	11.3	1.68	3.9
1954	37.24	24.84	31.04	2.89	10.7	1.57	5.1
1953	26.99	22.70	24.85	2.59	9.6	1.47	5.9
1952	26.92	29.30	25.11	2.46	10.2	1.44	5.7
1951	24.33	20.85	22.59	2.55	8.9	1.45	6.4
1950	20.60	16.34	18.47	2.93	6.3	1.53	8.3
1949	16.52	13.23	14.88	2.42	6.1	1.14	7.7

on the Standard and Poor's Average of 425 Industrial Stocks for these years. In retrospect, these data suggest that a program of constant accumulation of representative stocks would have produced highly adequate returns both in the form of dividends and appreciation.

For example, a portfolio (representative of the index) might be assumed to have been acquired under such a program at an average cost of about the mean price of the median years (1956–57), or at about a price of 50 on the index.[13] Based on the mean price for 1964, the portfolio would have appreciated by about 60%. In addition, the dividend yield on cost prices would have been in excess of 4% per annum. As a conservative estimate, the average annual total rate of return, including both dividends and appreciation, would have approximated 8%. Although undoubtedly less than would have been obtained by shrewd

---

[13] If it is assumed that a constant number of dollars was committed to stocks in each of these years (dollar cost averaging) the average cost would be lower as a larger number of shares would have been acquired at low prices than at high prices, and as a consequence, average cost would be weighted more heavily with low-priced shares. But as the purpose here is merely to show the results on a buy-and-hold program acquired in any way, the assumption of the median price for the entire period gives results less affected by the low prices prevailing from 1949–53, when common stocks clearly lacked popular appeal.

timing operations, the results at least confirm the view that over a period of years the purchase of common stocks for long-term investment will produce returns in excess of those obtained on fixed-income securities.

Moreover, it should be emphasized again that the highly favorable long-term trend would not necessarily have increased the probability of favorable returns through a timing strategy. In fact, as suggested previously, the rapid upward trend in itself created serious problems for a timing program because although temporary setbacks in stock prices occurred, they were not sufficient to bring stocks to levels which might have been expected from previous experience. Therefore, although by hindsight timing profits were possible, it seems only reasonable to conclude that they would have been very difficult to obtain in actual practice during the 1949–64 period.

Qualifications. It has been argued, however, that investors can hardly expect the record of 1949–65 to be duplicated in the future. During this period the upward trend in prices greatly exceeded the trend of the value fundamentals (earnings and dividends). The ratio of prices to earnings increased from about 6 in 1949 to about 18 in 1965. A similar increase in the price-earnings ratio, it is held, would not seem probable for the future. Therefore, unless some unusual structural changes occur in the economy, such as an acceleration in inflationary propensities, the results of 1949–65 may be difficult to duplicate in succeeding decades.

But the basic hypothesis of the buy-and-hold strategy does not include the presumption that price-earnings ratios will continually increase. It is rather that the economy, corporate earnings, and dividends will continue to increase over periods of a decade or so and common-stock returns in the form of both dividends and appreciation will be commensurate with this growth. Moreover, it is conceded that setbacks to the earnings growth pattern are likely to occur, such as occurred between 1955 and 1961, but this fact merely means that recoverability of funds committed to common stocks should not be expected. Even though the long-term trend is favorable, corporate earnings and stock prices may well decline for a number of months and perhaps up to several years. To suggest otherwise would be entirely contrary to the market record of even the highly favorable postwar years.

It must be further conceded that it may be possible for prices to be bid up to levels which anticipate a more rapid rate of increase in earnings and dividends than is subsequently realized. Under such circumstances even though earnings and dividends continue to advance at a moderate rate, returns on stocks may be unfavorable for a considerable period of time. Therefore, an investment program in common stocks based on the buy-and-hold strategy carries no guarantee of highly satisfactory results. However, the long-term characteristics of both the economy and the stock market indicate that it offers a greater probability of at least adequate returns than do alternative strategies.

Buy and Hold: Growth-Stock Strategy

Concepts. The above discussion related the buy-and-hold approach to the average probabilities on a representative sample of listed common stocks where selection procedures are minimal. It is possible of course to seek greater than average returns through refined appraisal techniques applied to the selection of the individual issues. In fact, some efforts along these lines would seem axiomatic in any common-stock program. The general objectives are to find stocks where the risk exposure seems acceptable in relation to the prospective returns that might be realized. And the analytical and valuation procedures developed in subsequent chapters are to a considerable extent aimed at assisting investors in this connection.

But it has also been advocated that the selection process should concentrate on certain types of stocks to obtain greater than average results. One of the most widely recommended strategies is that of seeking out growth stocks. These are typically defined as the equities of companies whose per share earnings demonstrate the probability of future growth at a more rapid rate than corporations in general. Although the future period to be covered by superior growth expectations is not always made clear by advocates of the growth-stock approach, it usually seems to encompass five years or more.

Controversial Issues. In principle, the concept of growth stocks appears quite appealing, as it suggests that investors should concentrate their commitments in the highly dynamic companies and profit by their rapid expansion in subsequent years. Moreover, empirical evidence can be introduced to show how certain stocks showed astronomical results during a rapid growth period.[14] It is very difficult to disagree with

---

[14] For example, on one page of a book devoted to advocating the growth-stock theory, the following results are mentioned to tempt the investor: (1) the quadrupling of Sprague Electric during 1947–57; (2) an increase of two-and-one-half times in the price of Friden Calculating between 1954–57; (3) a twenty-four-fold increase in Foote Minerals between 1947–57. Fisher, *Common Stocks and Uncommon Profits,* New York: Harper & Row, 1960, p. 124.

the proposition that, other things equal, companies with superior growth prospects should be preferred. The essential controversial issue arises from the fact that in connection with these companies other things are not equal. Their prices in relation to prevailing levels of earnings and dividends are almost invariably well above those of the leading, good-quality, nongrowth companies because their superior records and outlook attract a great deal of investor interest. For example, in early 1965 Xerox, a widely acclaimed growth company at the time, sold at 130, or at sixty-eight times its 1964 earnings of $1.88 per share. This compared to about nineteen times 1964 earnings for the Standard and Poor's 425 Industrial Index.

To justify the wide price differentials, proponents of the growth-stock strategy advance one or both of the following two arguments. First, it is held that the prevailing market expectations for a favorable growth trend produce the existing price "premiums." Therefore, if these expectations continue to be justified, there is no reason to believe the "premium" (in the form of a high price-earnings ratio) will decline.[15] If this is so, the argument continues, then so long as the growth outlook continues to be favorable, it is logical to expect at least a continuation of the existing price-earnings ratio, in which case the percentage appreciation return will be equal to the percentage growth in per share earnings. The second argument is that although the price in relation to the existing earnings performance may be high, a rapid growth in earnings will correct this situation within a reasonable time. Thus in the case of Xerox the proposition may be advanced that earnings within five years are likely to be $8.00 per share, which was only a moderate sixteen times the current price in 1965.

Opponents of the growth-stock strategy are inclined to emphasize the substantial risks involved in these propositions. First, it is held that the "premium" may include a considerable element of transitory popularity. Considerable attention may be attached to certain stocks as a consequence of some promised but as yet unproved development which seems to offer a strong growth potential. Earnings progress may be quite attractive for a time, but more importantly the stock prices may rise very rapidly as investors and traders are attracted to both the growth in earnings and the market price performance. It is then noted that the price action of these stocks often becomes cumulative in the sense that the upward surge in prices itself attracts buying which in turn engenders a further price rise. During such a period, the equities receive wide attention in the financial press and it becomes quite fashionable to include

[15] *Ibid.*, p. 112.

them in a portfolio. As put by one analyst, they are then in "vogue."[16]

But, it is observed, such vogues by their very nature often tend to burn out as traders are induced to take profits and prices stabilize or even retreat somewhat. Then more cautionary notices receive attention and even if subsequent earnings performances are reasonably favorable, prices may suffer a decline on balance as more objective appraisals of the actual earnings outlook are made. The rise and fall of the electronic, vending-machine, book-publishing, and the so-called leisure-time companies in the late 1950's and early 1960's can be cited as examples of this sequence of developments.

The second risk noted in connection with the popular growth stocks is the difficulty of maintaining a given percentage rate of growth in per share earnings. Growth areas attract widespread competition, product markets become saturated, and the relative influence on earnings of additional new products tends to be reduced as companies become larger. In brief, the economic principle of diminishing returns comes into operation. Therefore, although many companies may show a fantastic growth rate for several years, only very exceptional companies are able to maintain high growth rates for long periods of time. As a result, it is concluded that substantial risks are connected with the purchase of common stocks at substantial premiums where the justification is that a rapid growth trend has been enjoyed for the past several years and as a consequence, it is likely to continue for the indefinite future.

Examples. Table 5-5 illustrates both the opportunities and risks that are related to the growth-stock strategy. The opportunities for substantial returns are indicated most dramatically by the instances of Xerox and to a lesser extent by International Business Machines. In both of these cases, even though price-earnings ratios based on the earning power of each year have been consistently high in relation to the general market, subsequent appreciation returns have been most satisfactory. The possible exception would have been the purchase of IBM at a price close to its 1961 high. In these cases, the trend in earnings has been upward at both a rapid and continuous rate over the 1957–64 period, with the consequence that premium prices in relation to demonstrated earnings have been rather consistently maintained. The result has been that the rate of appreciation has approximated the rate of growth in earnings.

Xerox, for example, trebled its per share earnings between 1957 and 1961. As a result, its high price of 34 in 1961 was more than 100 times

[16] L. O. Hooper, "Market Comment," *Forbes,* March 1, 1962, p. 38.

TABLE 5–5

SELECTED DATA ON GROWTH COMPANIES: SELECTED YEARS 1957–64

	1957	*1958*	*1959*	*1960*	*1961*	*1964*
Texas Instruments						
Earnings per share	$ .89	$1.47	$2.87	$3.13	$1.89	$3.59
Price range—common	25–13	69–21	155–49	205–118	165–76	94–60
Polaroid						
Earnings per share	$1.44	$1.86	$2.78	$2.26	$2.07	$4.64
Price range—common	53–25	110–43	188–96	261–163	238–175	186–129
Helene Curtis Ind.						
Earnings per share	$ .27	$ .90	$1.24	$1.58	$1.53	(d) $.23
Price range—common	12–6	10–6	13–8	29–10	74–27	42–13
Holt, Rinehart & Winston, Inc.						
Earnings per share	$ .44	$ .54	$ .82	$ .97	$ .95	$1.24
Price range—common	9–4	13–6	22–12	37–25	45–34	30–23
Xerox						
Earnings per share	$ .09	$ .10	$ .12	$ .13	$ .29	$1.88
Price range—common	3–2	5–2	7–4	15–5	34–13	132–70
International Business Machines						
Earnings per share	$2.62	$3.70	$4.25	$4.90	$6.02	$12.30
Price range—common	127–84	191–104	260–175	320–217	486–309	494–407
Standard & Poor's 425 Industrial Index						
Earnings per share	$3.50	$2.95	$3.53	$3.41	$3.37	$4.83
Price range—common	53–42	59–43	65–57	65–55	77–61	92–79

earnings of that year. If earnings had failed to increase much beyond the $.29 per share registered in 1961, the stock probably would have subsequently declined substantially. But earnings in fact increased six-fold between 1961 and 1964; consequently, a very high price-earnings ratio continued to persist. Measured by its 1964 high price, an investor would have enjoyed about a fourfold appreciation even if it had been purchased at its 1961 high. But as the stock then sold for about sixty-five times 1964 earnings, the risk again existed that subsequent results would be unfavorable if earnings failed to grow substantially in the future. On the other hand, if the same rate of growth continued to be maintained, results similar to 1961–64 might well be obtained in future years.

The cases of Polaroid and Helene Curtis are in sharp contrast. After remarkable earnings growth between 1957 and 1959, both were widely acclaimed as growth stocks. But between 1959 and 1962, earnings not only failed to grow but actually declined. The inevitable consequences followed: prices of these stocks at the end of 1964 were well below those prevailing at the time when they were in vogue as growth situations. Although Texas Instruments and Holt, Rinehart have not suffered absolute declines in earnings since the peak of their popularity (1960 for Texas Instruments and 1961 for Holt) the growth rate has diminished. Consequently, the prices of both stocks in 1964 were disappointing relative to those prevailing in 1960–61, especially in view of the fact that the general market had advanced in levels well above the 1961 peak. In short, unless a highly favorable growth rate is maintained on stocks of this type, long-term results may be unfavorable. Therefore, outstanding long-term returns are certainly possible by following the growth-stock strategy, but it is by no means clear that the average returns on a portfolio of growth stocks will be superior to those derived from a general list of high-quality issues.[17]

Common-Stock Strategy: Undervalued Issues

Concepts. In a sense, the basic objective of all analysis of common stocks is to seek out those equities whose probable value in relation to price appears to be most attractive. Therefore, it can be argued that any strategy of investment wherein selection of individual issues involves a price-value comparison is implicitly using the concept that some stocks are selling at undervalued prices in relation to others. From this point of view, it would appear that any stock selections based on a thorough and intensive valuation process have been made through the application of this approach.

But as a special strategy designed to obtain greater than average returns available on common stocks generally, it has come to be identified with a particular type of company emerging from a behavioral theory of the market. The behavioral theory is that the market tends to exaggerate the importance of unfavorable developments or perhaps the mere absence of a highly dynamic potential.[18] By the same token it is held that the market also tends to overemphasize favorable factors. In

[17] Because of the "premium" prices typically associated with such stocks, dividend yields relative to nongrowth issues are quite low. Thus appreciation returns must be greater than average merely to compensate for the sacrifice in current income yield. Tax considerations, however, make the sacrifice of varying importance to investors in different tax brackets.

[18] The following argument is typical of this theory: "The market is always making mountains out of molehills and exaggerating ordinary vicissitudes into major setbacks." Graham, *The Intelligent Investor*, New York: Harper & Row, 1959, p. 110.

short, the theory is the logical extension of the vogue theory, noted in connection with growth stocks, to an anti-vogue theory. The view is that prices of certain stocks may be unreasonably depressed because of an undue emphasis on the immediate past earnings performance or on some unfavorable information of a general sort.

Substantial returns may well be obtained, it is argued, when and if it becomes clear that the adverse performance was indeed temporary or that the potential problems were not as catastrophic as was generally believed. Recognition of the improved situation may take time, but ultimately, it is held, the market price will reflect the improvement. Note that it is not growth that is anticipated, but only a reasonable recovery to former levels of earnings performance. Such a recovery should, it is argued, ultimately produce investment returns well in excess of the secular performance of the market as a whole. Moreover, because prices are depressed at the time of acquisition, dividend yields on cost are usually quite satisfactory if further reductions in the dividend rate do not subsequently take place.

Evaluation of Strategy. However, the risks surrounding the under-valued-issue strategy should not be minimized. In essence, they are that the problems may prove to be permanent rather than temporary. Then instead of recovery, further declines in earnings and dividends may well be experienced. And under these conditions, the inherent investment qualities of the companies become open to serious question. Thus it is possible that a portfolio constructed under this approach may ultimately end up with a substantial number of mediocre and low-quality issues which continue to suffer declines.[19]

Moreover, these stocks are, by definition, unpopular in the market, and prejudices are often slow to change even after there are clear signs of recovery. As a result, market performances may be quite disappoint-

[19] The case of Brunswick Corporation might be cited as a most unfortunate example. For the five years ending with 1961, this company enjoyed a remarkable growth in earnings, largely due to sales of automatic pin spotters. In 1962, some problems of market saturation appeared and during the sharp market decline of that year the stock declined to about 25 from a high in 1960–61 of about 70. At 25 it was selling at only about ten times 1961 earnings, and on the basis of a conclusion that bowling and leisure-time goods still enjoyed a favorable demand outlook, it appeared undervalued. However, instead of alleviating, the market problems became increasingly serious and earnings steadily declined to merely nominal amounts in 1964. As a result, in early 1965 at a price of about 8, it sold for about one-third of its apparent bargain price in 1962, yet during the interim the market as a whole had advanced substantially.

ing for periods up to several years even if the analyses appear to be vindicated by earnings recoveries. Therefore, with some possible exceptions from time to time, the undervalued-issue strategy is usually not appropriate for portfolios where a high-quality list is essential (trust accounts, for example) or for investors without considerable patience and skill.

Examples. The records of Socony-Mobil Oil Company and Penn-Dixie Cement, shown in Table 5-6, are illustrative both of the opportunities and risks of the undervalued-issue strategy. First, as to Socony-Mobil, after a strong postwar performance ending in 1956, earnings declined substantially, until in the relatively prosperous year of 1959 they were less than 60% of 1956 levels. In addition, overcapacity problems and a weak price structure in the oil industry received widespread attention in the financial press, although the total sales of oil products continued to increase. It was not surprising, therefore, that although the general market advanced considerably between 1956 and 1960, the average price of Socony declined from about 57 in 1956 to about 39 in 1960. At a price of 39, however, it was selling at about twelve times its depressed earnings levels of 1958–59 and offered a dividend yield of more than 5%. At the same time the Standard and Poor's 425 Industrial Index sold at about eighteen times 1958–59 average earnings with a dividend yield, based on the 1960 rate, of 3.3%. It was clear, therefore, that Socony was definitely "out of vogue" as a consequence both of its earnings and market price performance of the preceding three years.

At the average price prevailing in 1960, the opportunity in Socony might have been considered twofold: (1) a favorable dividend yield even at the lower dividend rate then in effect after the slide in earnings and (2) ultimate appreciation on a long-term basis if and when earnings showed evidence of some permanent recovery. The dimensions of the price appreciation might reflect: (1) the percentage recovery in earnings and (2) possibly some increase in the price-earnings ratio as the "anti-vogue" status of the stock was overcome by the improved earnings performance. The risk, of course, was that the problems of the industry would intensify and earnings and dividends would decline further.[20]

---

[20] A complete analysis of all the pertinent economic and financial factors would then have been required to indicate whether on balance the probabilities seemed to favor some recovery or continued decline. A discussion of these analytical techniques will be the subject of Part II of this book.

TABLE 5-6
SELECTED FINANCIAL AND PRICE DATA

	1955	1956	1957	1958	1959	1960	1961	1962	1963	1964
Socony-Mobil Oil Co.										
Earnings per share	$4.76	$5.70	$4.56	$3.24	$3.37	$3.76	$4.35	$4.97	$5.44	$5.79
Dividends per share	$2.30	$2.50	$2.00	$2.00	$2.00	$2.00	$2.25	$2.60	$2.60	$2.60
Price range, common	54–40	66–49	65–45	52–45	52–39	43–35	52–39	60–44	75–58	93–68
Penn-Dixie Cement										
Earnings per share	$2.72	$3.12	$2.14	$3.07	$2.84	$2.26	$1.90	$1.71	$1.27	$1.39
Dividends per share	$1.00	$1.00	$1.20	$1.40	$1.55	$1.40	$1.40	$1.40	$1.00	$1.00
Price range, common	38–25	44–30	40–21	39–23	39–30	32–24	33–26	28–15	19–14	19–15
Std. & Poor's—425 Industrial Index										
Earnings per share	$3.78	$3.53	$3.50	$2.95	$3.53	$3.39	$3.37	$3.87	$4.22	$4.83
Dividends per share	$1.68	$1.78	$1.84	$1.79	$1.90	$2.00	$2.08	$2.20	$2.38	$2.60
Range of index	50–36	53–46	53–42	59–43	65–57	65–55	77–61	75–55	79–65	92–79

As matters turned out, the industry in general and this company in particular managed to adjust successfully to their problems. By 1964 the earnings of Socony had fully recovered to 1956 levels. As a consequence, the price of the stock in 1965 was more than double the average price of 1960. But, it should be emphasized, considerable patience and fortitude would have been required in the interim. In 1961 when the market advanced substantially, Socony moved upward only modestly to an average price of about 45. Thus for a considerable period, it appeared that Socony was destined to remain "out of vogue" indefinitely, despite convincing evidence that its earnings decline had been halted and recovery was under way. Actually it was not until late in 1962 that the stock responded with a significant advance in price. An important maxim for investors is suggested by this sequence of events—*after an investment decision has been reached, subsequent review should focus primarily on the corporate performance rather than on the market action of the stock*. If the anticipated earnings progress does take place, then an unfavorable market action should be disregarded by the long-term investor. For periods up to several years, market inertia due to prior prejudices may give disappointing results, but ultimately a favorable earnings performance almost always obtains recognition in the market price.

In contrast to Socony, the case of Penn-Dixie Cement illustrates the substantial risks associated with the undervalued-issue strategy. Here a creditable earnings performance between 1955–59 was followed by a moderate decline, despite the fact that the volume of cement sales continued to advance. Intensive price competition, generated by an overcapacity in the industry which was caused by an excessive rate of expansion in plant capacities, was the apparent cause of the problems. But again, like the oil situation, further increases in demand appeared likely. Therefore, there was considerable justification, on the grounds that the overcapacity problems were likely to be temporary, for the conclusion that at a price of perhaps 20 in 1962 the stock was undervalued. Recovery of earnings to even the average levels enjoyed between 1955 and 1959 might have produced a substantial appreciation. In the meantime the dividend rate of $1.40 per share produced the highly satisfactory current yield of 7%.

However, adverse operating results continued to plague this company. Earnings declined further through 1963, and results were not much improved in 1964, especially in the light of the record performance of corporate earnings in general. As a consequence, the stock not only failed to participate in the general market advance since the middle of 1962, but its investment quality appeared to have deteriorated. However, despite a reduction in the dividend rate, the current yield has been quite satisfactory and ultimately some recovery in earning power may bring some appreciation in the market price. But as of 1965, it could only be concluded that although a good case could have been made for an investment in Penn-Dixie as an undervalued issue in 1962, its subsequent earnings record has not vindicated such a conclusion. As a consequence, in relation to alternatives, the returns on this stock had been highly unfavorable as of 1965 and there was little reason to expect substantial improvement for possibly several years.

In summary, although the undervalued-issue strategy can be made to appear quite attractive in principle, its implementation in practice is very difficult. The investor following this approach as an aggressive means of obtaining greater than average long-term returns on common stocks may in some instances fare quite well, but substantial risks also must be assumed. Although the market may exaggerate temporary adadversity, there is the real problem of distinguishing temporary from permanent adversity. Moreover, because "problem" companies are involved, there may be a temptation to compromise basic standards of investment quality, particularly when the market as a whole is at advanced levels in relation to earnings.

The Buy-and-Hold Strategy and Market Fluctuations

Reaction to Market Fluctuations. One major concept implied in the undervalued-issue approach is considered to represent a sound maxim for the long-term investor. It is that a decline in price, either of an individual stock or the general market, should ordinarily be regarded as a possible opportunity to acquire common stocks at a favorable price-value relationship. This recommended reaction is in sharp contrast to the observed behavior of many investors who are inclined to interpret a sharp market setback as evidence that stocks should be sold and then avoided until a substantial recovery has taken place.

Vice versa the maxim is that stocks become less attractive long-term commitments as they advance in price over periods of from one to several years. These maxims are based on the observed characteristics of the postwar stock market which were analyzed previously—an upward long-term trend which is also subject to setbacks from time to time. During this period at least, it is clear that in retrospect market setbacks should have been regarded as buying opportunities rather than as the occasion to dispose of stocks on the grounds that a long period of decline might take place.

Continuous Purchases. The buy-and-hold strategy, however, is based on the propositions that: (1) the timing of a market decline cannot be determined in advance, and (2) while a decline is in progress, its extent and duration similarly defy prediction. Therefore, it is not suggested that buy-and-hold investors should wait until the market reaches a certain prescribed level to institute purchases; this approach would in all probability turn into a version of the cyclical-timing strategy. On the contrary, to the extent that a portfolio is in an acquisition phase, purchases would presumably be made continuously so long as prospective long-term returns on stocks considered eligible for the portfolio appear reasonable.

A strategy of continuous purchases implies that future average corporate earnings over the following decade or so, which largely determine total returns, are not affected per se by stock market fluctuations. As a result, it is quite possible that investors following the buy-and-hold strategy may not be able to increase their acquisitions should a market setback take place. On the other hand, *such purchases would continue to be made all during such a period* rather than stopped, with a view to reinstituting them at considerably lower prices.

Problem of High Prices. The appropriate reaction of buy-and-hold investors to a substantial advance in the market is a more controversial issue. There are of course three possible reactions: (1) dispose of some or all common stocks, (2) continue regular acquisitions on a selective basis, (3) continue to hold past acquisitions but delay new purchases. The argument for portfolio sales is that the market has in the past advanced to excessively high levels; the term *excessive* in this context is used to describe a condition in which the market seems to reflect the exuberant optimism of traders rather than the considered judgment of investors. Then for one reason or another, if behavioral attitudes change for the worse, it may require a decade or more for a combination of corporate growth and a revival of investor confidence to bring the market back to the levels prevailing before the collapse.

Proponents of this view further argue that corporate growth has proceeded at an irregular rate and if the collapse of the stock market is followed by a declining or stagnant corporate performance, two decades or more might be required for stocks to reach a break-even level.[21] This sequence of events, it has been noted, occurred after 1929, and also after 1906. Therefore, it is concluded that unless stocks are sold at some point during extended bull markets, subsequent results for a decade or more might be highly unfavorable.

On the other side, it can be argued that most buy-and-hold investors are best advised to emphasize continuous accumulation of an appropriate amount of common stocks and not attempt to decide whether the market in general is vulnerable to a decline. The following observations are cited in support of this position. First, it is probable that only a portion of any portfolio will turn out to have been acquired at unreasonably high prices if regular purchases have been made through time. As a consequence, *average* portfolio results are not likely to be as unfavorable as would be indicated by the assumption that an *entire* portfolio is acquired at a market peak. For example, the assumption of complete acquisition at a market peak is implicit in the typical illustration which shows that the results on common stocks were unfavorable for twenty-five years after 1929.[22]

Second, it is held that structural changes in the economy, mainly a heavy orientation of national economic policy to avoid a major deflation, make long periods of corporate earnings stagnation unlikely in the future. Therefore, the probabilities are clearly against a long-term decline in corporate earnings such as followed 1929; instead the probabilities, it is maintained, favor corporate growth which even if not regular and continuous will produce adequate returns over a decade or so. Although returns might be even larger if acquisitions were delayed until the market declines, there is no assurance that substantially lower prices will in fact prevail at any time in the future.

In addition, there may well be a psychological barrier to reinstituting purchases in a declining market, where it always appears that further declines are in prospect to justify continued procrastination. For example, in 1962 when the market declined sharply, many investors might well have anticipated even further declines on the basis of widespread predictions that the great bull market of 1949–61 was now over, yet within less than a year the market had recovered the greater part of the decline. As a result, such investors might still have been waiting for the "time to buy" as of 1965.

[21] F. Salz, "Is the Long-Term Investor Facing Bleak Years Ahead?" *Financial Analysts Journal*, September–October, 1964, p. 34.
[22] *Ibid*, p. 34.

Finally, there is considerable evidence that generalizations concerning the attractiveness of all common stocks on the basis of the level of a market index is unsound. The market does not move as a unit; even though average prices may increase substantially, some may remain stagnant or even decline. Therefore, although general buying opportunities may diminish during an advancing market, some reasonably priced stocks are likely to be found even when the market indexes are at a high level.[23] The stagnant, and in retrospect attractive, prices of the leading oil stocks during the substantial 1959–61 advance in the general market may be cited as an example.

On balance, although it is conceivable that all common stocks of acceptable quality may advance to price levels well above objective estimates of long-term values, there is no convincing evidence that such a condition has existed at any time during the postwar era through 1965. Therefore, the buy-and-hold strategy would ordinarily seem best implemented by a continuous search for individual values, despite the possibility of some sharp temporary declines of the general market from time to time.

This conclusion does not mean that such investors should neglect to review the value-price relationship both for stocks already in the portfolio and for contemplated purchases. Indeed some individual issues may be sold because their prices advance well above their estimated values or because of some clear evidence of a possible deterioration in quality. In such a case, other suitable issues should be found to replace those sold. What it does mean is that the proportion of common stocks in a portfolio will not be reduced because of an advance in the market.

In addition, it means that as funds become available for additional investment in securities the investor's positive objectives and needs for risk protection should govern his selection of securities. The alternative prospective returns offered on various types of securities at a given time may affect the allocation to some extent, but this fact would not mean complete cessation of common-stock purchases, as is suggested by those who emphasize the dangers of high market levels to the long-term investor.

---

[23] The following comment of a professional portfolio manager is illustrative of this view: "Mr. Moore said the trust looks for undervalued situations and, despite the high level of the market, they can be found 'if you dig hard enough.'" *Wall Street Journal*, October 21, 1964, p. 2.

CHAPTER 6

Mechanics of
Security-Market Operations

A number of different options for executing transactions in the securities markets are available to investors. Entire books in fact have been largely devoted to the mechanics of stock market operations.[1] But many technical market procedures are useful chiefly to short-term traders executing frequent transactions. These would include, for example, short-term "put" and "call" options and most "stop-loss" orders. In addition, the frame of reference is assumed to be the moderate-sized individual investor and not the large institutional investor, the sheer size of whose transactions may require special precautions in market techniques.

Therefore, the objectives of the following discussion may be summarized as follows: (1) to describe and compare the characteristics of the several securities markets, (2) to show the major techniques used by long-term investors to acquire and dispose of securities in these markets, (3) to suggest the conditions under which each seems reasonably appropriate, and (4) to inform investors of their obligations and rights in connection with the holding and transfer of securities.

[1] Two of the best-known are Eiteman, Dice, and Eiteman, *The Stock Market*, New York: McGraw-Hill, 1965; and Leffler, *The Stock Market*, New York: Ronald Press, 1957.

Types of Security Markets

The Security Exchanges.   There are two national security exchanges, the New York and the American Exchanges, one located on and the other near Wall Street. There are in addition regional exchanges located in other major cities that more or less concentrate on companies located in their geographic area. The New York Stock Exchange is the largest and best known, and most of the largest publicly owned companies have their securities listed thereon. The American Exchange has some major companies, but by and large it concentrates on smaller and less seasoned companies in addition to numerous foreign listings. Because of the predominant role of the New York Stock Exchange, the specific illustrations will be taken from it, although most of the other exchanges operate generally in the same way.

A security exchange is a formal association of members organized to trade securities for their own account or as an agent for others. Procedures are controlled by exchange rules, and they are also subject to federal regulation under the Securities and Exchange Act, 1934. This statute was designed to protect the interests of the public against certain abuses which had been detected through an investigation of practices during the speculative spree of the 1920's. For the most part, trading is limited to "listed" securities, although unlisted trading is conducted in some securities on the American Exchange.

A company must make a formal application to list its securities, and acceptance is dependent on its showing sufficient size and public holdings of the securities to justify a need for a secondary market. All listed companies must conform to the reporting requirements of the exchange and the Securities and Exchange Commission acting under the authority of the statute. Therefore, one advantage of listed securities to investors is the knowledge that reasonably complete audited financial information will be forthcoming.

The public investor almost always acquires listed securities through a commission brokerage house which owns a seat on the exchange and acts as his agent in the transaction. The general legal rules of agency apply and the customer is further protected by exchange rules and the S.E.C. For example, under such rules the commission brokers must give precedence to a customer's order over any order which they would like to execute for their own account as investors or traders.

Transactions in listed securities are expedited by an instantaneous nationwide communications system. Ticker services to the commission brokerage offices throughout the country report the prices of each round-lot transaction in a matter of minutes after the actual trade. Moreover, most offices can obtain firm quotations on any of these securities within a few minutes. Metropolitan newspapers generally carry a detailed summary of New York Stock Exchange transactions, and numerous market averages or indexes are computed from these prices. For these reasons, the general public typically associates the securities market with the organized exchanges.

The Over-the-Counter Market. However, although the dollar volume of daily transactions is probably greater on the exchanges, the so-called over-the-counter market serves a larger number of companies. In general, these are securities of smaller firms or those of local interest only, but there are certain important exceptions. First, all municipal bonds are traded in this market. Second, most financial institutions' common stocks, such as those of insurance companies and commercial banks, are not listed on the exchanges. Third, most Government bond transactions take place in this market. And, finally, there are some large industrial companies that for one reason or another have not found it expedient to list their securities on an exchange.

In this market, securities are bought from or sold to dealer inventories for the most part. In practice the over-the-counter dealers are established investment banking or brokerage houses that undertake to "make markets" in certain securities. This means that they maintain continuous bids and offers for the securities concerned, and their normal profit is presumably the "mark-up" of the offering price above the bid price. For example, a dealer may give a bid price on a stock at $5 and offer it at $6. In effect, the dealer hopes to buy from some investors at $5, mark it up 20%, or $1, and sell it to others at $6. The risk is, of course, that a large number of investors will decide to sell, thereby increasing the dealer inventory to unwieldy proportions, so that price concessions will be necessary to move the inventory to other investors.

The National Association of Securities Dealers has greatly improved the status of the over-the-counter market in the past twenty years or so. Through the association, quotations are obtained and published in the financial journals, although these are merely rough guides and not necessarily firm bids and offers. The source of the market on each security is not indicated, but member firms can obtain this information (about which dealers make markets in specific securities) from the association.

However, transactions are not reported via ticker service in this market and the task of obtaining firm quotations might be more difficult on these securities. Particularly during periods of severe market declines, such as the one that took place in the middle of 1962, price quotations on less active over-the-counter stocks may be difficult to obtain. For a few days during the 1962 decline, some stocks reported a complete absence of bids or very large declines compared to the previous sale.

Comparison of Markets: Listed vs. Over-the-Counter. There seems to be a general impression that securities traded in the over-the-counter market are of lower investment quality than listed securities. But, as stated earlier, some highly regarded issues, such as municipal bonds and bank common stocks, are available only here. Perhaps the publicity given to the rise and fall of a number of so-called "hot" issues in the market between 1960 and 1962 is responsible for this unfavorable impression. It is true that most of the leading industrial, utility, and rail stocks are listed on the exchange. Therefore, differences in company size and quality are probably wider in the over-the-counter market than on the New York Exchange.

There is also less investor interest in unlisted stocks simply because only the transactions in listed stocks are reported in most daily newspapers. In general, therefore, the broadest market is obtained in listed securities, although again there are notable exceptions such as the stocks of certain large banks. Thus the intrinsic value of a security is more likely to be recognized if it is listed on a stock exchange.

If the securities are obtained from a reputable dealer or broker, the acquisition costs in the form of commissions and transfer taxes are roughly identical in both markets. However, the percentage spread between the bid and ask prices often seems greater in the over-the-counter market, possibly because dealer inventories on many securities may move slowly and the mark-up on each transaction must, therefore, be greater. As a result, the effective costs on a "round trip" buy and sell are probably greater in this market.

Finally, as stated previously, the published price information on securities traded in the over-the-counter market is tentative, and firm quotations can sometimes be obtained only with difficulty. This situation contrasts with the immediate reporting of all transactions on listed securities and with the availability of direct wires in member firms' offices to obtain firm data on prices in a matter of minutes. This feature expedites acquisition (or disposal) of listed issues, but it is only of minor significance to long-term investors for whom day-to-day price fluctuations are relatively unimportant.

Exchange Regulation. All listed securities are subject to the regulatory safeguards of the Securities and Exchange Act of 1934 and the rules of the several exchanges. The statute and the rules govern in important respects both the conduct of listed companies and members of the exchange. There are two objectives of these regulations: (1) to assure that adequate financial information on the companies is forthcoming so that investors may regularly appraise the status of their investments, and (2) to guard against procedures by members or companies which might mislead or injure the interests of the public stockholder.

The specifics of these regulations are highly detailed; therefore, only a few illustrative highlights can be mentioned. First, listed companies must publish certified annual statements and provide the Securities and Exchange Commission with prescribed financial details. In addition, a 1964 regulation requires annual reports to show "in substance" the same breakdown of financial information as provided in the reports filed with the S.E.C. Second, some limits are imposed on the ability of company "insiders" to profit at stockholder expense. Salaries of officers and directors must be given in proxy statements and reported to the S.E.C. Short-term profits (less than six months holding) by "insiders" derived from speculating in their own stocks are recoverable by the company. Third, the S.E.C. is given the power to prevent manipulation of stock prices, and the exchanges also constantly review the actions of their members in their dealings with the public. In brief, although a questionable transaction may occur from time to time, the S.E.C. and the exchanges have succeeded in imposing high standards of conduct on members in their dealings with the public.

Securities of companies traded in the over-the-counter market with assets in excess of $1 million and with 500 stockholders or more are subject to the same reporting requirements under a law passed in August of 1964. Smaller companies, however, may furnish only limited information to their stockholders. And although the conduct standards of dealers in this market are regulated to a considerable extent by the National Association of Securities Dealers, subject to the review of the S.E.C., there have been many more instances of unethical and fraudulent activities in the over-the-counter markets than on the organized stock exchanges.

Analysis of Stock-Exchange Orders

Round-Lot versus Odd-Lot Orders. In order to limit the number of transactions on the floor of the exchange, a specified unit of trading is established for each stock. With the exception of a few inactive (mostly preferreds) and very high-priced stocks, the unit of trading is 100 shares. For the most part, therefore, round-lot orders are for quantities of 100 shares or any multiple thereof. It is these transactions that are reported on the ticker service throughout the country. Further, the published statistics on the volume of trading are solely in terms of round lots.

Odd-lot orders are those for less than the unit of trading. Although any commission broker may receive such an order, it is turned over to a brokerage firm specializing in odd lots for actual execution. On the New York Exchange, two brokerage houses make odd-lot markets in all the listed issues, and they deal only with regular members of the exchange who in turn act as agents for the public. In a sense, each firm is a complete exchange by itself, although the prices charged are controlled by round-lot transactions. As far as the ordinary investor is concerned, the only difference is that a small premium is charged for odd-lot transactions. For stocks selling at $40 per share or more, the investor must pay one-fourth of a point more per share than the price of the related round lot with which it is associated. For stocks selling at less than $40 the premium is one-eighth of a point per share. The premium is of course in addition to the regular commission of the broker.

Market Orders. A market order is the least complex and perhaps the most widely used of all types of orders. In the case of a round lot it directs the floor broker to proceed immediately to the post where the stock is traded and buy at the lowest price or sell at the highest price obtainable at that time. Although the floor broker, as agent for the customer, may try through auction to obtain a slightly better price, the customer in giving such an order should be willing to pay the ask price or accept the bid price prevailing at the time. The current bid and ask quotations can be obtained by brokers anywhere in the country in a matter of minutes.

However, reasonably active stocks under orderly market conditions can be purchased or sold at prices very close to the last transaction price reported on the tape. Therefore, when investors have predicated their investment analysis on the prevailing price, market orders to implement the decision will naturally follow. Moreover, because the value of common stocks cannot be determined precisely, it is usually "hair-splitting" for a long-term investor to decide, for example, that a stock is desirable when it reaches $40 per share but should not be bought at the prevailing market price of $42.

Market orders also expedite the operational aspects of investment management by keeping the portfolio clear of contingent commitments. If a number of buy orders, for example, are outstanding at specified prices below the prevailing market prices, it may result in the need to keep an undue amount of idle cash to take up the possible future purchases. Although these contingent orders can always be canceled, there is a natural tendency toward inertia and even stubbornness which makes it difficult to reverse these decisions. For these reasons, long-term investors are usually well advised to conduct most of their transactions via market orders.

Market Orders: Odd Lots. An odd-lot market order is executed at the price of the next round-lot transaction after the order reaches the odd-lot broker plus or minus the appropriate odd-lot premium. All odd-lot orders are time-stamped when they reach the proper post on the floor and are then related to the time of the next round-lot transaction. On occasion a dispute will arise about the proper round-lot order that should be related to a given odd-lot order. These disputes, however, are rare and are decided by comparing the time of the odd-lot order with the time that the round-lot transaction appeared on the ticker less a minute or so for the interval between the execution of a transaction on the floor and its appearance on the tape.

Because an odd-lot market order is consummated only when and if there is a subsequent round-lot transaction, there is no absolute assurance that it will be executed within a given time. Hypothetically, weeks could pass before such an order was filled for a very inactive stock. Although this circumstance is rather rare, it can be avoided altogether by specifying that the order be executed "without waiting." Such orders are fulfilled from the bid or ask quotation on the stock. For example, if an investor wished to buy ten shares of a stock quoted at 45 bid and 46 asked, he could do so immediately at the ask price of 46 plus the odd-lot premium of one-fourth point.

Limit Orders: Round Lots. As the name suggests, limit orders prescribe the maximum price that will be paid for a purchase or the minimum price that will be accepted for a sale. A more favorable price than that established by the limits is of course acceptable. When a limit order is placed it may specify a restricted time period for which it is in effect (a day, week, or month). If no instructions are given, it is presumed to be an "open" order, which will remain in force indefinitely. Many brokers, however, follow the practice of asking monthly confirmation of GTC (Good Til Canceled), or open, orders, and in any case they must be confirmed every six months by rule of the New York Exchange.

When a limit order cannot be executed immediately—the usual reason being that it represents an attempt to buy stock at less than the prevailing market or to sell above it—it is left with the specialist in the stock for entry on his book. The specialist is a combined broker-dealer who stays at one post and "makes" a market in a specified stock or stocks. The limit order is executed by the specialist when and if orders to sell or buy stock are subsequently received in sufficient quantities to cause the price to move to the level established by the price limits. The specialist is also allowed to act in the capacity of a dealer by maintaining an inventory and making purchases and sales for his own account.[2]

Limit orders at a given price placed on a specialist's book are filled in chronological order. For example, if an order is given to buy 100 shares of a stock at 40 and 500 shares are already on the book to buy at this price, then this particular order will not be filled until 600 shares are offered at this price. The specialist can reveal to other brokers only the number of shares covered by the high bid and low ask, so unless the customer establishes his limits at those prices, it is impossible for him to ascertain how many orders have priority at the specified price. Therefore, even though a stock reaches the limit price, there is no assurance that a particular order will be executed.

Although most long-term investors are well advised to use market orders for most transactions, there are certain possible exceptions. First, if a large investor desires to obtain a substantial bloc of a rather inactive stock, limit orders may be preferable, because the specialist may have wide gaps between the successive asked prices on the book. As a result, the cost of such a bloc may be substantially higher than the indicated asked quotation on 100 shares or so. Second, if a stock seems to be advancing to a level well above its appraised value range, a limit order to

[2] Specialists are supposed to use dealings for their own account to keep the market "orderly," i.e., to prevent wide changes in price between successive transactions. Because they know the demand-and-supply conditions more intimately than anyone else, they conceivably could take advantage of this knowledge; the exchange therefore follows their activities closely. In fact, because of alleged abuses on the part of some specialists, recommendations have been made that the specialist system be abandoned.

sell might be placed at a point where the price has definite speculative implications. In this instance the price factor is the sole reason for selling, and the investor presumably would be entirely content to retain the stock at reasonable price levels. Third, under very unsettled market conditions (which have been experienced only infrequently), prices may be changing so rapidly that market orders may be executed at levels materially different from those that were indicated by the last sale price or the apparent quotation. However, here the investor may well decide to delay all orders until more settled market conditions prevail.

In operations where the avowed objective is to profit by the short-term swings in the market, the occasions to consider limit orders relative to market orders are described differently.[3] Here the long-standing advice has been to recommend limit orders to buy in declining markets and to sell in rising markets. Conversely, market orders are considered desirable when selling in declining markets or buying in rising markets. The reasoning is that there is no hurry to buy when the market is going down (therefore use limit orders), but if sales are contemplated under such circumstances, the speed of market orders will obtain execution before the market falls further. In a rising market rapid execution seems necessary to the trader on the buy side (market orders) but not on the sale side (limit orders).

Limit Orders: Odd Lots. All limit orders for odd lots are placed with one of the two odd-lot brokerage houses on the New York Stock Exchange; on other exchanges the specialists may handle these transactions. Because of the odd-lot premiums, a limit order to buy or sell is consummated only when a round lot trades at a price equal to the limit price minus or plus the premium. For example, if the investor places a limit order to buy twenty shares of a stock at 30, it will only be executed when a round lot trades at 29⅞; on a sell order at 30 the stock must trade at 30⅛ before execution.[4] Unlike a round-lot limit order, however, once the stock reaches the required price, all orders at that price are filled. There is no chronological priority needed on these orders, as the odd-lot broker agrees to take up all limit orders then on the books once the related round-lot price is registered through an actual sale.

---

[3] In Chapter 5 these activities were found to be mostly the concern of the speculator rather than the investor. As this book is directed primarily at the long-term investor, only brief mention of the technical market rules used by traders will be made.

[4] When the price is 40 or more, the respective prices must be one-quarter point below or above the limit price.

Bond Quotations: Special Features. The prices of corporate and Treasury bonds are quoted in terms of an assumed $100 par, although most have denominations of $1,000 or more. Therefore, a single point represents $1 in terms of the standard $100 bond, which, of course, would be $10 on a $1,000 bond. Then for some mysterious reason municipal bonds are usually quoted on the basis of their yield, which must then be converted from a bond table into a price.[5] For example, a ten-year municipal with a 2% coupon might be quoted on a 1.50% basis. This means the price is that required to yield 1.5% to maturity, and inspection of a bond table shows this to be 104.63. In considering bond prices, reference is often made to a certain number of "basis points." A basis point is defined as .01% of yield. Thus, if the yield on a given bond is described as having increased by ten basis points, this means the price has decreased sufficiently to raise the yield to maturity by .10 of 1%.

In addition to the quoted price, the investor must also pay the seller of a bond the amount of accrued interest from the last interest payment date to the date of purchase. If this is not so, for example on a bond in default, then the price is specifically described as being on a "flat" basis.

Short Sales. By and large short sales belong in the arsenal of the speculator rather than of the long-term investor, but to understand why this is so it is necessary to describe the mechanics of their execution and the consequent position of the several parties involved. A short sale reverses the ordinary sequence of security trading. Instead of buying the stock and then selling it, the stock is first sold and then "covered" or bought back. The general purpose should be evident—the trader forecasts a downward market movement, and it is expected that a sale now can be covered by an acquisition at a lower price later on.

At first glance it would appear that selling a security (or anything else) which is not owned would be illegal. However, a well-defined procedure has been established in the securities markets to make these transactions routine. Essentially, a short sale is made possible through having the short-seller's broker borrow the stock from established channels. The borrowed stock is then delivered to the purchaser in the ordinary manner, and the cash received from the sale is turned over to the lender of the stock or his broker. In effect, therefore, the short-seller lends money in return for the borrowed stock. The loans are on a demand basis and can be terminated by either party on twenty-four-hour notice.

---

[5] There has been some welcome agitation to change this practice, and it is notable that many municipal revenue bonds are now quoted on a standard-price basis.

There are other aspects of the relationship which deserve brief mention. First, the amount of cash held by the lender of the stock is regularly adjusted to the prevailing market price. If the stock goes down, a notice called a "mark to the market" is given the lender of the stock by the short-seller's broker, and cash must be returned. If the stock goes up, however, additional cash must be deposited by the short-seller with the stock lender. For example, if 100 shares were sold short at 50, the original cash loan would be $5,000. Suppose the stock declined to 45, then $500 would be returned to the short-seller; but if the stock went to 55, then $500 more cash would have to be turned over to the lender of the stock.

Second, under Federal Reserve regulations a short-seller must have cash in his account equal to the margin requirements then in effect. Under 70% margin requirements, for example, cash of about $3,500 would have to be in the account on the above hypothetical transaction to assure a source of funds in case the stock increased in price. The New York Stock Exchange requires a minimum cash balance of $1,000 before a short sale can be made and margins of at least 30% of the value of the stock at all times. The Federal Reserve regulation is concerned only with the initial margin and not with what happens subsequently. To illustrate, the original margin of 70% would change on an assumed stock-price increase following a 100-share short sale at 50 as follows:

Stock Price	Stock Value	Cash in Account	% Margin
$50	$5,000	$3,500	70
60	6,000	2,500	41
65	6,500	2,000	30.7

Therefore, if the price increased to slightly above 65, the cash margin would fall to less than 30% of the prevailing market value, and the short-seller would be required to deposit more cash under the rules of the Stock Exchange.

Third, all dividends declared on a stock must be paid by the short-seller. The requirement results from the fact that the lender of stock is no longer the registered owner per company records, but under the loan relationship he is still entitled to dividends. For a few weeks or so, this should theoretically occasion no loss to the short-position trader, because stocks presumably decline ex-dividend by the amount of the dividend. But if the short position is maintained for any length of time, the payment of dividends may represent a constant attrition of the short-sellers' anticipated profit.

Another factor giving a probability bias against profits from a long-extended short position is that the upward secular trend of the economy and market has operated against short positions. Of course, there have been periods of several years when the general market declined, but on the average these have been far outweighed by advancing markets. On individual stocks, however, long-term declining trends have often taken place, so that in particular instances profits from long-term short positions may be realized.[6]

Some short sales may be undertaken for certain technical reasons aside from purely trading operations. First, there are those known as sales "against the box." Here the stock is already owned (in the safe deposit box), and a decision to sell might seem appropriate for investment reasons. However, by selling short first in one year and then delivering the stock already owned to cover in the next year, the profit or loss can be carried to the second year for tax purposes. Second, hedging against a possible loss in market value of an existing portfolio from a general market decline may sometimes seem desirable to some investors. Short sales of market leaders will presumably hedge this contingency, but the risk is that the stocks selected for short sale may be selectively strong relative to the shares then in the portfolio. Therefore, this type of transaction is not a hedge in the strict sense of eliminating all of a given risk. Third, short sales are sometimes the consequence of arbitrage transactions on (1) the same security selling at slightly different prices in two markets, (2) convertible securities wherein common stock is sold short and the sale is later covered by conversion of the senior security bought at the same time.

Short-sale orders may either be at the market or at a limit price above the market. However, an S.E.C. rule requires that stocks cannot be sold short at successively lower prices. If the most recent sale price on a stock represented a decline from the preceding transaction, then a short sale is possible only at a price one-eighth of a point higher. But if the last sale price was above the preceding transaction price, then short sales are possible at this last sale price but no lower. The purpose of the

---

[6] In the days before S.E.C. regulation short-sellers sometimes were drastically hurt by "corners" on the floating supply of the stock that made it almost impossible to acquire stock to cover their transactions. This danger may still exist in the case of relatively small companies, as witnessed by the Artloom Carpet Co. case in September of 1958. According to the *Wall Street Journal* of Sept. 3, 1958 (p. 16), a short position of almost 36,000 shares existed on August 15, 1958, compared to total outstanding shares of 505,000 of which at least 50,000 shares were held by the chairman of the company. Between August 26 and September 2 the stock rose from 17⅞ to 27⅝ before the Exchange suspended certain types of orders and the SEC announced that it was opening an investigation of trading in the issue. Brokers reported that the rise may have been due to a squeeze on short-sellers who were having difficulty finding stock to cover their transactions.

regulation is to prevent "bear raids" on a stock by driving the market price down with repeated large short-sale orders.

Stop-Loss Orders.   Orders to buy or sell a stock at the market when and if it sells at or below a certain price are known as "stop-loss orders." Perhaps the most common example is the stop-loss order to sell at a price below the prevailing market. Such an order is often based on a major precept of traders: let profits run but cut losses short. For instance, a stock may be purchased at 40 with the expectation that it will rise, but the trader may desire to limit his loss in case the expectation proves wrong. A stop-loss sell order may be placed at, say, 35; this means that when and if the stock sells at or below 35, the broker is to sell the stock at the market. There is no assurance that a price of 35 will be realized, but only the hope that it can be disposed of close to that price when and if another round lot sells at that figure. Similarly, stop-loss orders to buy at a price above the prevailing market are used to limit losses on short sales.

As stop-loss orders are not usually executed immediately, the customer's broker places them with the specialist or the odd-lot broker and it becomes his responsibility for execution at the proper time. On odd-lots all stop-loss orders on the books are executed when the specified price is reached less the usual premium. On round lots, however, chronological preference operates on stop orders as on limit orders, except that all of them must be executed even at lower prices.

By and large, stop-loss orders are of use to short-term traders rather than investors. However, a long-term investor might conceivably use a stop order to protect a profit on a stock which has moved to a level considered speculative but which, because of market conditions, may move even higher. Investors may be perfectly willing to accept speculative profits if their basic investment objectives are being achieved; a stop-loss order is a possible technique to accomplish this aim.

A possible danger in these orders is known as the "whip saw." Stocks seldom move in a straight line. Even during a rising trend the price will move upward in a zigzag fashion. For example, the following weekly price pattern was shown by General Motors common for the five weeks ended January 1, 1965.

Week Ended	High	Low	Close
December 4	96¼	93	94¼
December 11	94⅞	91⅝	93½
December 18	96½	93½	96½
December 25	97¾	95½	95¾
January 1	98	95⅛	98

For the entire period a modest advance was indicated from 94 to 98, but any stop-loss order down to a price of 91⅝ would have been executed in the week ended December 11th. Any stop order near this price would have been subject to an unfortunate "whip saw" during this particular period.

The danger of being whip-sawed on stop orders is a constant one, as the market is notoriously subject to quick sell-offs following some sudden dramatic development in the news. The possibility of sudden short-term market movements suggests that stop-loss orders should not be placed too close to the prevailing market quotation, but, on the other hand, the greater the difference between the stop order and the market price, the less the protection that is afforded.

Acquisition Costs and Custodial Services

Commissions. Besides the price of the security itself, the major costs of acquisition are brokers' commissions. Under current practice the percentage acquisition cost decreases as the money value of the transaction increases. This practice appears entirely reasonable, as the effort of executing a small order is not materially different from that for a large one. In fact, it might be suspected that on very small orders the brokerage house does not cover its costs, despite the higher-percentage commission. Table 6-1 shows the specific rates prevailing as of 1965.

TABLE 6–1
SCHEDULE OF BROKERS' COMMISSION RATES: 1965

Transaction Money Value	Commissions	
	Round Lots	Odd Lots*
Under $100	As mutually agreed	As mutually agreed
$100 to $399	$3 plus 2%†	$1 plus 2%†
$400 to $2,199	$7 plus 1%	$5 plus 1%
$2,200 to $4,999	$19 plus ½%	$17 plus ½%
$5,000 and up	$39 plus 1/10%	$37 plus 1/10%

* The odd-lot premium of $.125 or $.25 per share is added to get the total applicable brokerage costs. It is understood that these commissions apply to both exchanges in New York and to over-the-counter transactions as well. This standardization of commission rates is relatively recent, having been adopted when the increases of 1958 were put in effect.

† A $6 minimum commission applies to all orders so rates shown apply only when total exceeds $6.

The only major question of analytical interest applies mostly to small investors operating by necessity in odd lots. The commission rates apply, after all, on a standard basis to all securities, and there is no reason to prefer one security to another because of acquisition costs. However, it is true that transactions in round lots of modestly priced securities are usually slightly preferable to odd lots of higher-priced situations, because the odd-lot premium of $.25 or $.125 per share typically exceeds the $2 lower-base commission (see Table 6-1) applicable to odd-lot orders. A more important consideration is the sliding scale, which reduces the percentage commission as the money value of an order increases. This method of computing commissions means that small investors should decide upon the minimum amount of funds to accumulate before placing an order.

To resolve the problem, one possible approach would be to consider the effective percentage acquisition costs on orders of successively higher money value and then note the point where the percentage costs do not seem unduly high. Table 6-2 gives some illustrative commission costs. These computations show that the percentage acquisition costs decline quite rapidly as the size of the order increases up to about $300 and then at a much reduced rate. Therefore, as a very rough rule of thumb, it might be suggested that small investors might be advised to consider accumulating about $300 before placing orders for common stocks.

TABLE 6-2

COMMISSION EXPENSE ON ODD-LOT TRANSACTIONS

Size of Order	Commission	Odd-Lot Premium* (ten-share lots)	Total Cost: Percentage of Order
$ 50	$ 6	$1.25	14.5
100	6	1.25	7.25
200	6	1.25	3.62
300	7	1.25	2.75
400	9	2.50	2.81
500	10	2.50	2.50

* Interpreted as a commission to the odd-lot broker.

Monthly Investment Plan. In 1954 the member firms of the New York Stock Exchange introduced MIP for small investors desiring to acquire stocks on a regular basis from current savings. Under the plan periodic payments are sent to the broker in amounts of not less than $40 nor more than $1,000. Additional payments may also be made at any time within the prescribed limits. Upon the receipt of cash, stock is then purchased in a predetermined company. Because the plans are set up on the basis of constant dollar contributions, fractional shares are purchased and usually dividends are reinvested as paid. Custodial services for the shares are provided without charge. On MIP purchases of less than $100 the commission charge is 6%, but on orders above $100 the regular odd-lot commissions apply. Therefore, even investors using this plan can keep percentage acquisition costs down by buying in units of about $300 every three months or so rather than in smaller monthly amounts.

Broker's Services: Custodial. Most brokerage firms offer investors custodial services on their securities upon request and after determination of responsibility. These are known as brokerage accounts and are relatively simple to open, although a bank reference and perhaps one other reference are usually required. As might be expected, these can be opened in a single name or jointly with other parties. It has been customary to impose no fees for services rendered on brokerage accounts, but formal proposals to establish mandatory service charges on such accounts were made in 1965, and moderate charges on such accounts may ultimately be made.

The securities held in these accounts are registered in the name of the firm, "street name" in the popular jargon. The brokerage firm thereupon receives all dividends or interest from the companies and credits these receipts to the account of the customer. Monthly statements are rendered on most accounts; Figure 6-1 shows a hypothetical statement with certain typical illustrative transactions indicated. The monthly statement shows the net cost or proceeds from each transaction, and the customer is also sent a regular confirmation of each executed order as per Figure 6-2. The confirmations and statements are the basic records for the investor in making out tax returns and reviewing the status of the portfolio. It should be mentioned, of course, that confirmation of individual transactions are sent to all investors after each transaction, and not merely to those having custodial brokerage accounts.

The services are purely custodial on the so-called cash accounts wherein the investor pays cash in full upon receiving a confirmation of each purchase transaction. Dividends and net proceeds from any sales of securities held in the account may be left on deposit and of course represent an automatic source of funds for additional purchases. The advantages to investors in keeping their securities in this way are the

FIGURE 6-1

DATE		SHARES OR PAR VALUE OF BONDS		DESCRIPTION
MO.	DAY	BOUGHT OR REC'D	SOLD OR DEL'D	

MO. DAY YR.
1 1 2 5 6 4   PETER KENNEDY
8868 CAVELL
PERIOD ENDING   GARDEN CITY MICHIGAN

MEMBERS
NEW YORK STOCK EXCHANGE
DETROIT STOCK EXCHANGE
MIDWEST STOCK EXCHANGE
AMERICAN STOCK EXCHANGE

DATE		SHARES OR PAR VALUE OF BONDS		DESCRIPTION
MO.	DAY	BOUGHT OR REC'D	SOLD OR DEL'D	
10	28			BALANCE FWD
11	2			SO CAL EDISON CO COM
11	2			NORTHERN PACIFIC RY
11	4	100		CATERPILLAR TRACTOR
11	4	50		DELTA AIRLINES INC
11	4		50	CLUETT PEABODY & CO
11	4		100	SO CAL EDISON CO COM
		100		CATERPILLAR TRACTOR
		100		CORN PRODUCTS CO
		50		DELTA AIRLINES INC
		100		DETROIT EDISON CO
		100		GENL DYNAMICS CORP
		50		GENERAL ELECTRIC CO
		100		GENERAL MOTORS CORP
		100		NIAGARA MOHAWK POWER
		50		NORTHERN PACIFIC RY
		200		PAC NOWST BELL TEL
		100		REPUBLIC STEEL CORP
		50		SEARS ROEBUCK & CO

If this is a general account and we maintain a special miscellaneous account for you under Section 4 (f) (6) of Regulation T of the Board of Governors of the Federal Reserve System, this is a combined statement of your general account and special miscellaneous account. The permanent record of the special miscellaneous account as required by Regulation T is available for your inspection at your request.

Any free credit balance represents funds payable upon demand which, although properly accounted for on our books of record, are not segregated and may be used in the conduct of this firm's business.

YOU MAY INSPECT A FINANCIAL STATEMENT OF THIS PARTNERSHIP AT ITS OFFICES.

convenience and facilitation of regular investment of dividend income. By using custodial brokerage accounts, transactions can be executed without any physical handling of stock certificates, and permanent records of income and costs are forthcoming. Moreover, holding the cash dividends in the account and not commingling them with any other sources of cash income serves as a device to discipline many investors to regular investment of these funds. Needless to say, however, the cash credit balance can be withdrawn on demand should the investor so desire.

STATEMENT OF ACCOUNT WITH

WATLING, LERCHEN & CO.

FORD BUILDING

DETROIT, MICHIGAN, 48226

TELEPHONE 962 - 5525

ANN ARBOR - JACKSON - PONTIAC
BIRMINGHAM - DEARBORN - NEW YORK
LANSING - PORT HURON - WARREN

ACCT. NUMBER		
1	5 0 4 2 0	6 2

OFF.	ACCT.	T	REP

TYPE OF ACCT.
1 - CASH
2 - MARGIN
3 - SHORT

PRICE OR SYMBOL	DEBIT	CREDIT	ACCT. NUMBER OFF.	ACCT.	T	REP
D I V		3 3 5 7 9	1	5 0 4 2 0		
D I V		3 0 0 0	1	5 0 4 2 0		
		3 0 0 0	1	5 0 4 2 0		
37½	3 7 8 7 7 5		1	5 0 4 2 0	2	6 2
61¾	3 1 1 9 9 4		1	5 0 4 2 0	2	6 2
56¾		2 8 0 3 1 3	1	5 0 4 2 0	2	6 2
36⅞		3 6 4 4 5 0	1	5 0 4 2 0	2	6 2
B A L			1	5 0 4 2 0	2	
B A L			1	5 0 4 2 0	2	
B A L			1	5 0 4 2 0	2	
B A L			1	5 0 4 2 0	2	
B A L			1	5 0 4 2 0	2	
B A L			1	5 0 4 2 0	2	
B A L			1	5 0 4 2 0	2	
B A L			1	5 0 4 2 0	2	
B A L			1	5 0 4 2 0	1	
B A L			1	5 0 4 2 0		
B A L			1	5 0 4 2 0	2	

YOUR BALANCE IS	6 4 2 7	Keep this statement for income tax purposes. If it is not correct please advise us at once. When writing please mention your account number.

DEBIT UNLESS MARKED CR

OR A COPY WILL BE MAILED UPON YOUR WRITTEN REQUEST.

E. & O. E.
FORM IBM 900 REV. 5/64

There are, however, certain drawbacks to holding securities in brokerage accounts. First, the customer is merely a general creditor of the firm, and its insolvency could conceivably result in a loss. For many years, there were no failures of stock exchange firms, so that the credit risk on brokerage accounts appeared academic. But between 1962 and 1964, two firms of significant size failed; one of these, Ira Haupt & Co., received wide publicity, as it was associated with alleged fraud on large inventories of vegetable oils and fraudulent warehouse receipts of many

FIGURE 6-2

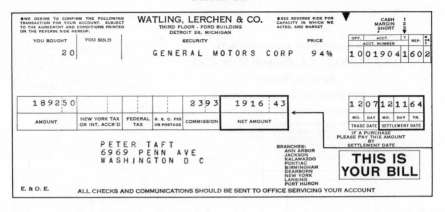

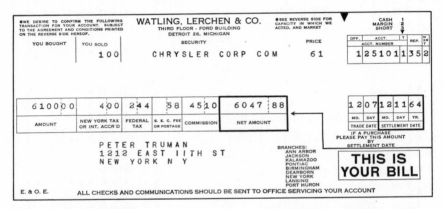

millions of dollars. In both instances, however, the New York Stock Exchange through assessments on members and by other means made up all losses to holders of brokerage accounts, although no guarantee was given that the same policy would be followed in the future. But the Exchange indicated that means of protecting investors against loss due to failure of member firms were under consideration.

Second, annual reports and interim information on the company are not sent to the investor by the companies, because the securities are not registered in his name; but it is possible to arrange to be placed on the mailing list for these data upon request to the companies concerned. Third, although there is no minimum size of accounts required, brokers do not encourage this arrangement for small accounts where transactions are likely to be few. Finally, the broker has the right to close the account at any time and may sell the securities outright in case of death of the principal. This latter right is not, however, used in actual practice by most brokers.

Margin Accounts. When part of the cost of a stock is borrowed, the purchase is called a *margin* transaction. When the broker advances the funds, it is necessary to leave the securities in a brokerage account, because they provide security for the loan. Moreover, in order to obtain the funds to lend customers, the broker typically borrows from banks using the same securities as collateral.[7]

The New York Stock Exchange requires that an initial balance of $1,000 in cash or market value of securities must be deposited in an account before a margin transaction can be executed. In addition, the percentage of original cost that can be borrowed is subject to Federal Reserve regulations. As of 1965, the margin requirements were 70%, which means that only 30% of the dollar value of a transaction could be borrowed. However, once the stock is purchased, it can decline in value until the customer's equity is much less before additional margin is required. The New York Exchange requires a minimum equity of 25% of the market value of the account, but some brokers require a somewhat higher percentage. Suppose, however, that the 25% minimum margin applies. Then if stock worth $1,000 were purchased and $300 of this amount borrowed (maximum under existing Federal Reserve regulations), the stock could decline to a total market value of $400 before the customer's equity would only be 25% of the value. If the value became less than $400, the broker would require part of the loan be paid off. An amount sufficient to restore the customer's equity to about 33% would typically be required.

The major purpose of margin accounts is usually to obtain capital-gains leverage. For example, suppose half of a $1,000 stock purchase was borrowed (assuming the Federal Reserve allows a 50% margin); then if the market price of the securities advanced 10% ($100), the percentage gain on the owner's equity would be 20% ($100 as a percentage of $500). Because the objective of market gains predominates in margin accounts, they are typically associated with traders rather than long-term investors.

However, enterprising long-term investors could conceivably make moderate use of margin accounts for perhaps two reasons. First, the expected annual rate of return in the form of both income and appreciation may exceed the rate of interest charged on the borrowed funds. If this is so, then profitable leverage results, and it may be used indefinitely. Second, some investors find that borrowing in anticipation of dividend

---

[7] The customer could conceivably borrow directly from a bank to finance a margin purchase, but this is not customary. Such direct borrowings are also subject to the Federal Reserve margin requirements.

income is a good way to keep fully invested. In this instance funds are borrowed against an existing portfolio to buy more securities, and the loan is then repaid from the regular credit of dividend income to the account. Nevertheless, it is probable that most investors following a long-term philosophy of investment operations do not use margin accounts.

Sources of Investment Information

Basic Data on Corporations. Information on a company's activities and finances is usually obtained in the first instance from either the annual reports of the company or from one of the several statistical investment services. For the most part this material is purely factual; it provides the raw material for analyzing the company's merits for investment purposes.[8]

There are two major statistical services: Moody's and Standard and Poor's Corporation. Their annual volumes give a summary description of each company's products and its securities, plus the financial statistics for a considerable period of time. In addition, current interim information is sent out weekly for inclusion in loose-leaf volumes. Standard and Poor's also publishes the *Industry Surveys,* which includes extensive analytical reviews of each major industry in a "basic report," revised once a year, plus a "current analysis," sent out quarterly. This service, in addition, gives statistical summaries of the leading companies in each industry. Although these services provide valuable information, many individual investors would not find it expedient to have personal copies of these services, as the annual charge for subscriptions is approximately $200. However, they are available in many city libraries as well as in banks and brokerage offices.

Annual reports are generally available free of charge upon a written request to the corporation. Some will also place interested persons on a permanent mailing list to receive all future reports and other information published by the company. The average quality of these reports has greatly improved through the years, so that a wealth of data is customary today. Naturally, however, most annual reports tend to emphasize the favorable aspects of the company's record and outlook. Therefore,

---

[8] Quality ratings of publicly owned bond issues are incorporated into the statistical services' report on each company, and these seem to be constructed on a reasonably conservative basis, although no reasons for the determination of the rating is given in the course of the discussion of the company.

the investor must exercise considerable care to analyze the material objectively before an investment conclusion is reached.

Investment Advisory Services. To complement the purely factual material given in the manuals, the statistical services also publish weekly reports giving specific advice to investors. Standard and Poor's *Outlook* and Moody's *Stock Survey* and *Bond Survey* are typical of these reports. These publications are entirely separate from the statistical manuals. They usually devote considerable space to a forecast of economic activity and the stock market, with consequent conclusions for investment policy at the moment. In addition, specific stocks and bonds are recommended for various portfolio purposes on the basis of summary analyses of individual companies.

Although these services are valuable to obtain candidates for potential commitments and also as a source of supplementary information, it would seem unwise for long-term investors to base their decisions solely on these recommendations for two reasons. First, many of the recommendations are oriented to the near-term price outlook for both the stock market as a whole and the individual stocks. This is natural, because many people are highly disturbed by an unsatisfactory short-term price performance after the purchase of a security. However, it has been strongly emphasized that a long-term investment philosophy would regard short-term price movements of minor significance. Second, the analyses are quite cursory in nature and give heavy emphasis to the current performance of the company rather than to the long-term appraised value of the security.

Brokerage Houses. There is a wide variety of material published by brokerage firms. Its classification into topical areas is difficult, but most fall into one of several categories. First and perhaps most voluminous are the market letters. These generally review the status of the market and the economy and then reach some conclusion about the prospects for the near term. These are by nature primarily of interest to traders rather than long-term investors. But even traders may find it difficult to predicate their operations on this material. Often the recommendations are hedged to a considerable extent, and there is usually considerable diversity of opinion among the market analysts.

Second, many brokerage houses prepare analytical brochures on various industries and companies. These vary in length and quality, but in general the investor can obtain much helpful information from these analyses. The large nationwide firms, which can support considerable research activity, are in general the best source of this material. Such research work of course is primarily intended for customer use, although most firms are very cooperative in making specific items available to others upon request.

Third, a number of firms publish special reports on various aspects of investment management, such as taxation and determination of portfolio objectives. In addition, some houses offer personalized analyses of portfolios to their actual and prospective customers with reviews from time to time of their status. These services may be very useful even to experienced investors who wish to obtain as many clues as possible to guide their decisions. A possible drawback is that brokerage firms are naturally interested in transactions and may have a natural tendency to suggest switches in the accounts. This is not to say that such recommendations are capricious and are designed solely to generate transactions, but an inclination in this direction could conceivably result because of the dependence of brokerage firms on commissions from the turnover of securities.

Financial and Market News. The financial pages of most metropolitan newspapers publish the daily price summary of the stocks on the New York Stock Exchange and perhaps the same information for any local exchange. In addition, some current business and financial news can be found, but, except in the very largest city newspapers, this news is usually locally oriented. The *New York Times* has perhaps the most complete financial news coverage of any regular daily newspaper.

The *Wall Street Journal* is devoted almost entirely to business and financial news. It is published every weekday and offers very complete market price data on securities traded both on the organized exchanges and in the over-the-counter market. All current developments and summarized financial data on a great many companies are reported in the *Journal*. In addition, interpretive articles on general business conditions and on specific industries are relatively frequent. The *Wall Street Journal*, therefore, is probably the best over-all source of financial news, and a great many informed investors make a regular practice of daily perusal of this paper. The *Journal of Commerce* is another weekday paper which may be useful to investors. While it gives considerable data on the financial markets, this paper tends to emphasize commercial and commodity news more than financial news on corporations. But it provides a good source of qualitative information on trade and industry developments.

Financial Magazines. In this context a magazine is defined as a publication which is not published every day. Some resemble newspapers in physical appearance; for example, *Barron's* and the *Commercial and Financial Chronicle.* The former is a weekly, and its material includes a regular column on the stock-market outlook, articles on industries and companies, plus a statistical summary of stock prices accompanied by earnings and dividend data. The *Chronicle* is published twice a week. The Monday issue gives a summary of the news on a great many corporations, plus information on new security offerings and a detailed record of prices in security markets both in this country and in Canada. The Thursday issue is mostly devoted to articles on investment policies, industries, and the business outlook. Spot financial news is also included. Besides furnishing a background of information, the investor can often obtain clues to specific candidates for acquisition from these publications.

Other magazines of possible interest include *Forbes, Business Week, U.S. News and World Report, The Weekly Bond Buyer,* and *Fortune.* All of these review business conditions and offer analytical articles on various industries and companies. *Forbes* also gives specific buy-and-sell recommendations on individual securities. In a sense, therefore, this publication almost provides an investment counsel service, except that it does not review the personal investment policies of the investor.

Government Publications. The *Federal Reserve Bulletin,* published by the Board of Governors, and the *Survey of Current Business,* published by the U.S. Department of Commerce, are good sources of background information on economic developments, statistical data on the economy as a whole, and some industry statistics. These are available to individual subscribers at modest cost and probably are available in the great majority of public libraries throughout the country. The data offered in these publications are quite useful for the purpose of measuring the performance of a given company or industry against that of the entire economy. These volumes do not, however, give any specific data on individual companies which are the direct tools of security analysis.

Summary: Sources of Information. The above review of possible sources of information on companies, industries, security markets, and general economic developments is by no means exhaustive, and the investor may well find other publications which serve these purposes equally well. Even so, the problem is often to limit rather than to expand the amount of data reviewed in the course of investment decisions. While professional analysts may use all the above publications and more, the average individual investor cannot be expected to have the time available for such extensive investigations.

Therefore, as a reasonable compromise, the investor might consider the following procedures: (1) regular scanning of a daily financial page or, preferably, a financial newspaper; (2) requesting, as a customer of a brokerage house, its reports on industries, companies, and investment policies for clues to possible commitments; (3) using annual reports or the statistical services to investigate more thoroughly those companies which seem interesting from the above reading; (4) possibly reading a financial magazine to obtain additional clues for prospective security purchases or an independent confirmation of the analytical work. Finally, it should be reiterated that there are no reliable short-cuts to a thorough appraisal of a security.

ANALYSIS OF CORPORATE PERFORMANCES

Qualitative Factors

CHAPTER 7

Product Demand

Introduction

For the most part, returns to long-term investors in corporate securities are derived from the future earnings stream of the related corporations. Fixed-income securities obtain their specified income payments from the first claim on the earnings. The balance, if any, is then available for either dividend payments on the common stock or reinvestment in the corporation, presumably to the benefit of the common. Therefore, the logical first step in appraising a corporation and its securities for investment purposes consists of an orderly analysis of the economic information and financial data pertinent to an estimate of the probable earnings characteristics of the corporation. This section of the book will be concerned with this phase of the investment decision-making process.

The second step is to evaluate the prevailing price of the security in the market. Therefore, the subsequent section will consider the techniques appropriate to estimating a value for the specified claim on potential earnings (in the case of fixed-income securities) or for their possible amount (in the case of common stocks). The quality and estimated pattern of the earnings are of course relevant to the decision on an appropriate price, but in addition, prospective returns offered on alternative commitments must also be considered at this point.

In a dynamic free-enterprise economy, earnings of most corporations are derived from the competitive sale of goods and services. There-

fore, an investigation of a company's ability to achieve market acceptance of its products in a competitive environment is one major element
to consider in an investment analysis.

But a favorable outlook for product sales is not sufficient by itself to
achieve an adequate level of earnings. It is also necessary to keep the
costs incurred in production and distribution reasonable in relation to
the selling prices of the products. As a result, the prospective behavior
of costs and a company's ability to control them effectively is also an
important element in appraising the earnings potential.

Role of Qualitative Analysis. The raw material for appraising the
prospective earnings performance of a company can be roughly classified into two areas: (1) general economic information, and (2) the
specific financial or physical data covering operations of prior years. The
first type of information is conventionally termed *qualitative* and it includes such matters as the economic characteristics of the products, new
product potentials, competitive conditions, and the nature of the cost
structure.

Taken as a whole, the analysis of qualitative information serves two
purposes. First, it serves to provide a general impression of the desirability of the company and the related industry for investment purposes.
Second, it may provide considerable assistance in interpreting the significance of the quantitative data covering past performance. For example,
because replacements and new acquisitions can be postponed during
recessionary periods, the heavy durable-goods companies would appear to be exposed to wide cyclical swings in their sales and earnings.
This qualitative conclusion would suggest that it would be questionable
to project earnings trends for such companies on the basis of quantitative data which covered only a period of rising levels of general business
activity.

However, although a grasp of the essential qualitative factors bearing on a company's future prospects for sales and earnings is clearly
desirable, there is a real problem of assessing their significance in the
determination of investment values. In most instances, some appear
favorable and others appear unfavorable. Because of their inherent intangible nature, the actual impact of the qualitative conclusions on earnings is quite difficult to evaluate on a rational basis. For this reason, most
investment analyses depend heavily upon an analysis of the important
quantitative data, and the qualitative factors become modifying elements rather than the basic determinants of investment values and decisions.

A penetrating qualitative analysis is very useful in reaching a decision as to the desirability of a company, but it should be brief and pertinent. A major problem is often that of distinguishing the important from the trivial. The modern large corporation is a very complex institution with widely diversified activities. Under these conditions, it may be difficult to avoid becoming immersed in the innumerable details of the operation. Only a general rule can be suggested on this point: unless the information is likely to have a significant bearing on the long-term sales and earnings, discard it.

Qualitative Analysis: Scope of Coverage. It would be exceedingly difficult, if not impossible, to discuss a complete list of the qualitative economic and perhaps political factors that might be pertinent to all the various companies in which an investment might be contemplated. Unique problems and opportunities are the rule rather than the exception in a highly developed and complex economy. For example, in the oil industry there is the unique problem of import quotas on crude oil and the differential impact of such quotas on the international and domestic companies. On the other hand, it would hardly be useful to conclude (as sometimes is done) that because of the complexities, specific guidelines for analysis cannot be established, yet admonish that somehow the essential economic features should be considered. Therefore, recognizing that special features are likely to emerge in many individual situations, the following qualitative inquiries are pertinent in most instances:

1. The growth potential for product demand.
   a. Record and prospects for development of new products.
   b. Trends in consumer preferences and needs.
   c. Outlook for sales in foreign markets.
   d. Indicated trends of major industries using products (derived demand).
2. The stability of product demand.
   a. Durability and prices of products.
   b. Stability of companies using products (derived demand).
   c. Diversification of products and customers.
3. The competitive forces bearing on the company.
   a. Intra-industry competition: price behavior.
   b. Inter-industry competition: loss of product demand.
4. The cost and production characteristics.
   a. Productivity improvement prospects.
   b. Degree of integration of productive process.
   c. Adequacy of raw materials.
   d. Status of labor relations.

Qualitative Analysis: Growth of Product Demand

New Product Prospects. This source of growth is largely identified with industries and companies where technological advances through research programs have been rapid and continued developments along these lines seem probable. The chemical, drug, electrical equipment, and business-machine industries are good examples of where growth in sales has been achieved largely through new product developments. However, when considering specific companies, it is usually quite difficult to assess the impact that new product developments might have on future sales revenues. First, there is often considerable reluctance, for competitive reasons, to divulge specific information on new products in the embryonic stage. Second, most investor analysts are not technically trained to evaluate the probable results from research activities even to the extent they are disclosed. Third, although companies often list or comment on new product developments in their annual reports, they do not usually give any indication of the additional sales that might be obtained from these developments.

For example, Merck & Company, the ethical drug manufacturer, offered the following statement in its annual report for 1963:

> We introduced four new products for human health in the U.S. in 1963: Aldomet and Aldonil, both for the treatment of hypertension; Rubeovax, an attenuated live-virus measles vaccine; and Cuprimine, for treatment of Wilson's disease, a rare hereditary ailment.
>
> Aldomet and Aldonil represent 13 years of research and an investment of more than $12,000,000, not including the large investment and the 15 years of research which led to Hydrodiuril, a component of Aldvoil.
>
> Aldomet has been well received by the medical profession here as well as abroad. It meets the need for an agent that is relatively free from distressing side effects to treat sustained moderate to severe hypertension.[1]

Accompanied with the knowledge that hypertension and measles are common human ailments, it might be concluded that the prospects for these new products are favorable. But whether they were technically superior to drugs offered by other companies and what their sales potentials were in relation to the $264.6 millions of total sales generated in 1963 could not be determined. In brief, the impression might be favorable, but translating the impression into some more tangible indica-

[1] Merck & Company, Inc., *Annual Report for 1963*, p. 14.

tion of the sales growth that might be incident to these developments would be highly conjectural.

Consumer Preferences and Needs. Unlike many areas of the world, consumers in the United States are offered the choice of a wide variety of goods and services to which their incomes might be allocated. In addition, the proportion of income required for the basic living essentials (food, clothing, and shelter) has been decreasing. Moreover, as productivity has consistently improved, the time available for discretionary consumption has greatly increased as work weeks have been reduced and vacations extended to a larger proportion of the labor force.

It is generally agreed that these trends are likely to continue in the future. Therefore, the qualitative analysis might inquire into whether the products or services of a given industry or company are likely to absorb a larger proportion of future increases in discretionary incomes or less. Certain industry areas (such as recreation, airlines, broadcasting, and household conveniences) have been favored by these developments, but others (such as flour milling and shoes) have taken a reduced proportion of consumer disposable incomes.

Demographic projections or other data on long-term social and economic trends may assist in appraising the qualitative growth outlook for some products. For example, Table 7-1 shows the projected increases in total households in the United States and in the population by various age groups. These data show that in succeeding decades new household formation should be favored by a large percentage increase in the 20–29 age groups, but that small increases will be registered in the 30–49 group until after 1975. The percentage of population over 64 is also expected to grow at a relatively rapid rate. As these projections are based on the known distribution of the population as of 1963, the growth in each segment, with the possible exception of those under 9 years of age, can be predicted with confidence. Markets for products used primarily by teen-agers, young married people, and old people would appear to be favored by consumer needs of the succeeding decade, but those used principally by the 30–64 age group may well have a reduced growth rate.

Foreign Markets. Extensive foreign markets may be both an opportunity and a risk. They may be an opportunity in the sense that percentage growth in discretionary incomes may be larger in some areas than in the United States, because of the low base from which the growth is measured. In Western Europe, for example, the growth rate in

TABLE 7-1

POPULATION AND HOUSEHOLD PROJECTIONS (BASED ON 1963 DATA)

Actual (in millions)	Total Households	Population Distribution by Age					
		to 9	10–19	20–29	30–49	50–64	64 and Over
1963	55.2	40.7	33.5	23.6	47.2	26.6	17.6
Projected (in millions)							
1970	63.0*	—	—	—	—	—	—
1975	68.8*	45.3	41.2	36.3	48.1	31.7	21.2
1980	75.1*	—	—	—	—	—	—
1985	—	55.5	45.5	41.6	61.5	31.8	25.0
Percentage Increase from 1963:							
1970	14.2%	—	—	—	—	—	—
1975	24.7%	11.3%	23.3%	53.0%	1.9%	18.8%	20.5%
1980	36.3%	—	—	—	—	—	—
1985	—	36.1%	36.3%	75.0%	30.4%	19.2%	41.1%

* Average of high and low projections.
Source: Department of Commerce.

auto sales has exceeded that in the U.S. and is expected to continue higher for a number of years, as the percentage of the population owning cars is still well below that of this country. This fact in turn suggests a more favorable sales growth for oil, auto parts, and rubber companies operating in foreign markets as compared to those operating entirely in domestic markets. Therefore, if pertinent, the qualitative appraisal might note apparent trends in the demand for the products abroad and whether the company in question has facilities to take advantage of any favorable prognosis on this score.

However, many areas of the world continue to have difficulties in maintaining reasonably stable economic and political conditions. Restrictions on currency exchanges, devaluations, expropriations, and import quotas are among the risks assumed by companies with extensive operations in foreign markets. In the fiscal year ended October 31, 1964, for example, Firestone Tire and Rubber Company reported losses due to devaluations of foreign currencies of $11.65 million, or more than half total foreign income of $21.8 million.[2] Therefore, although Firestone

[2] Firestone Tire and Rubber Company, *Annual Report for 1964*, p. 9.

reported that foreign markets are expected to show favorable growth, earnings resulting therefrom may be exposed to greater risks than those derived domestically. This conclusion would be particularly applicable to Latin American and African markets as of 1965, but unfortunately in most cases the companies do not break down foreign sales and earnings by geographic areas.

Growth Analysis: Derived Demand. Companies producing capital equipment, raw materials, or component parts for other companies are characterized as derived-demand situations. Some products in this area, particularly basic raw-material items such as steel, are incorporated into such a wide variety of end products that sales growth may be largely correlated with that of general industrial production. In these instances other factors may affect growth, such as location of plants or competition from alternative materials, and some qualitative impression of these factors may be desirable. Otherwise it would seem sufficient to conclude that the trend of general economic activity will largely control growth without a detailed analysis of the many industries using the products.

Some companies, however, particularly those of moderate size, may indicate heavy dependence upon one or two other industries, in which case the qualitative growth analysis would properly focus on the outlook for the customer industries. Finally, it may be noted that companies with a derived demand can through diversification, technology advances, or new products, achieve growth in excess of the related industries. For example, some farm-equipment manufacturers, particularly Deere and Company, have enjoyed a rate of growth through these means in excess of the growth rate of the agricultural sector of the economy.

Qualitative Analysis: Stability of Product Demand

Significance of Stability. Before considering the factors pertinent to appraising stability, the significance of stability to the investment merits of a company might be indicated. In the first place, the feature has sometimes been overemphasized. Instability should not be regarded as synonymous with unprofitability; a company can be highly variable but still show evidence of good average earnings. It is, however, appropriate to hold that instability makes a projection of the past earnings record a less reliable indication of future earning power. This follows because when a company's past earnings have been largely controlled by the particular cyclical pattern of the past, the record can be used to forecast only on the assumption that the same pattern will prevail in the future. Thus the 1959–65 record of a company subject to a highly cyclical demand for its products would be a less reliable indication of the future than would the same record for a highly stable company. As a consequence, a common stock of an unstable company is more difficult to appraise and has inherently more risk, for there are greater uncertainties surrounding its future performance.

In the second place, the interpretation of the risk associated with a given capital structure may largely depend upon an analysis of the company's vulnerability to cyclical disturbances. A very modest amount of fixed-income securities relative to the common stock equity may involve a considerable risk when sales and earnings are exposed to very wide fluctuations. In contrast, a large proportion of debt and preferred stock may mean only moderate financial risk in a highly stable situation. As a consequence, the standards established to appraise financial policies will vary according to the stability outlook. This point will be developed in more detail in a subsequent chapter.

Third, even though a volatile company may show a reasonably favorable average performance under a composite of both good and bad general economic conditions, the common stock might well experience wide fluctuations in both market price and dividend payments. This means, of course, that persons requiring a high degree of regularity of income from their stock portfolios should avoid such stocks. In addition, nervous investors (those greatly upset emotionally by price declines) might well give careful attention to the stability factor. In brief, an analysis of stability reveals some of the probable *characteristics* of a common stock but does not necessarily show whether long-term results are likely to be favorable on the average.

Stability: Nature of Products and Customers.   If the products are primarily nondurable expendable items with a low unit cost, the probabilities should favor a reasonably constant volume of sales regardless of cyclical developments. The dairy products companies are good illustrations of stability arising out of these product characteristics. The cost of milk, ice cream, and cheese is relatively nominal; in addition, they are clearly essential for a balanced diet. Therefore, because of these factors, the dairy companies have traditionally been classified as stable situations from an investment standpoint.

At the other extreme, the most volatile companies would be those producing high-cost durable items for industries which are themselves subject to wide cyclical variations. In this situation the customers are reluctant to purchase anything except necessary operating supplies during periods of declining business activity. Therefore, if the items in question are both durable and expensive, effective demand may almost disappear. A good example is railroad locomotives. Traffic on the railroads has been cyclically vulnerable for the past twenty-five years or so, and locomotives of course are both durable and relatively costly. This qualitative picture suggests an extreme degree of inherent instability, and it is not surprising to note that the sales of Alco Products, Inc., a leading locomotive builder, varied between $170 million and $86 million during the 1955–64 period.

In the consumer sector, automobiles and housing represent high-priced durable items for which demand is postponable, and as a consequence sales volumes have varied widely in these industries in response to cyclical variations in the economy. And of course auto parts and construction materials sales are derived from these industries and also show wide fluctuations, although replacement and repair sales for existing cars and houses may moderate the fluctuations in the sales of these companies.

As in the case of growth in product demand, there may be substantial differences in the stability characteristics of companies in the same general industry. The important chemical companies may be cited as an illustration of this point. By and large, their products enter into a cross-section of industrial output, so fluctuations in line with the general index of industrial production might be expected. But certain companies tend to specialize in certain types of chemical products for which the stability outlook is widely different, depending on the end products for which the chemicals are used. Du Pont, for example, supplies chemicals to a wide variety of industries, but sales to the nondurable industries, notably textiles, are by far the most important. Moreover, its growth, generated from new product development, has been outstanding. For these reasons its sales revenues have enjoyed both better stability and growth than the average industrial company. There are other chemical companies, however, where the growth factors have not been able to offset their dependence on heavy industry for sales, and as a result greater instability than average has been indicated.

Sales: Diversification. Finally, the evaluation of the reliability of product demand should consider the degree to which both products and customers are diversified. There are considerable advantages in not having the entire fortunes of a company committed to a single product or to one or two large customers. Although it may appear at the moment that a given product has a favorable demand outlook, unexpected developments can change the picture radically and quickly. The aircraft companies also provide an example of this risk. The government is in many cases the only significant customer, and the decision to substitute missiles for manned aircraft has proved significantly injurious to some companies unable to develop acceptable missiles or components for them. Concentration in single products with very few customers is usually an undesirable qualitative factor both from a growth and stability point of view.

However, the quest for diversified product lines by management has not always been advantageous. It is quite possible for a company to commit corporate resources to projects not suited to the productive and distributive facilities. As a specific instance, the experience of Olin Mathieson Chemical Corporation may be cited. This company diversified its operations into a number of fields unrelated to chemicals, including aluminum, brass, and firearm production. On the whole, it may be questioned if these acquisition projects were desirable, for through 1964 both the stability and growth record have been unfavorable in comparison to other major chemical companies, such as Monsanto and Union Carbide. It would seem unwise, therefore, to consider that product diversification always improves the stature of a company. If the new areas seem reasonably related to the existing product line, then a company's efforts in this respect may improve the quality of the revenue stream. But if it appears that a company has merely scattered its product lines, then diversification can result in the actual impairment of over-all growth and stability.

CHAPTER 8

Competition and Costs

Qualitative Analysis: Competition

Competitive forces bearing on industries and companies are highly important factors in appraising their general quality for investment purposes. Because of severe competitive pressures, a company can be favored with a growing demand for its product line and yet fail to obtain a satisfactory level of earnings. More often than not, the result is brought about by severe competitive conditions. Therefore, it is important to analyze the sources of very intense competition and then inquire if they are pertinent to the particular situation under investigation.

The inquiry might properly be directed along the following channels: (1) the possible intensity of competition from other companies with about the same product line, (2) the competitive position of the companies within the industry, and (3) the possibility of products from another industry encroaching on this industry. The first two of these inquiries are concerned with the potential intraindustry competition; the third is concerned with the possibility of interindustry competition. The latter is closely related to the long-term sales outlook for the products, but it is primarily concerned with a special, and in a sense a negative, aspect of this factor—can the economic services of the products be provided in a better or less costly way by other types of goods?

Intraindustry Competition. Except for the regulated, or "natural monopoly," industries, the free-enterprise system relies on competitive pressures to provide the incentive for companies to produce the best products at the lowest prices. That the system has worked remarkably well is evidenced by the tremendous productivity of the American economy. But although industry as a whole is competitive, in some instances it is relatively orderly and in others it appears to be destructive. Destructive competition is indicated when there is an inability of most firms in an industry to obtain adequate earnings despite a reasonably favorable trend in the demand for the products.

The major symptom of an unhealthy intraindustry competitive situation is a chronic excessive capacity relative to the demand for the products. Under these conditions, prices often decline to levels which greatly reduce profits for even the low-cost firms. But there remains the question of what circumstances are likely to bring about productive capacities in excess of demand. One possibility is that total demand has suffered a secular decline, but in this case the source of the difficulty is not a competitive problem. When the trend of total demand is favorable, but at the same time capacity seems to increase at an even more rapid rate, there is evidence of destructive competition.

One source of extreme competition is the ability of a large number of producers to get into the industry quickly and easily. In short, severe intraindustry competition is often associated with the ease of entry into a field. And this in turn is primarily a function of (1) the amount of capital required to produce on a relatively efficient basis, (2) the ability to capture sales strictly on a price basis, without large-scale promotional programs to obtain product recognition, and (3) the degree to which processes and products are free to be used by everyone.

Several illustrations of destructive competition because of ease of entry are available in the postwar record of certain industries. Some of the difficulties of the vending industry in recent years can be traced to ease of entry and consequent capacity problems. As capital requirements for the assembly or renting of vending machines were modest and product preferences difficult to achieve, a number of companies moved into the field. The result was that earnings of many companies in the industry have failed to increase, although total sales have grown rapidly. A similar experience can be noted for the producers of certain types of electronic components.

A second source of excess capacity and resultant severe price competition is forced expansion of productive facilities. This occurs when firms, in order to be technically efficient, must expand productive facilities in large increments, thereby obliging each company in the industry to expand in order to share in the growing market for the products. The consequence is that total additions to capacity may well exceed even a substantial growth in physical sales, thus prices weaken as the firms attempt to keep their facilities operating at a reasonable proportion of capacity. For example, the aluminum, cement, and paper industries have in the past been subject to severe competitive conditions because of chronic overcapacity problems.

In aluminum, for example, the operating rate declined from 108% of capacity in 1955 to 85% in 1962, despite a growth in physical consumption of about 33%. As a result, prices of aluminum ingots declined during this interval, although labor and other costs continued to increase. The effects of the severe price competition on the earnings of the aluminum companies were drastic. The largest domestic company, Aluminum Company of America (Alcoa), showed a growth in sales of over 30%, yet earnings declined by 25%. Because of the favorable demand outlook, the aluminum industry has continued to be regarded as a "growth" industry, but as of 1965, net earnings of Alcoa had yet to recover to 1955–56 levels.

Competitive Position: Qualitative Evaluation. Although it is important to evaluate the intensity of competition within an industry, this alone will not suffice in appraising the competitive risk faced by a company. The competitive position of a company in its industry is also highly significant to a conclusion on its general investment quality. A strategic competitive position can result from two general sources. First, the company can possess certain natural advantages that are not available to other firms in the industry. Second, a superior position can be achieved by sheer proficiency in all phases of management.

There are several origins of a natural competitive advantage. First, a company may have an especially favored location. Second, in the extractive and integrated industries, discoveries of unique supplies of natural resources may confer an inherent cost advantage. Third, patent rights can sometimes dictate the relative competitive positions of the firms within an industry. However, competitive advantages due to patent rights should be regarded skeptically; competitors are often exceedingly ingenious in developing products and processes which sidestep patent protections.

The location factor is particularly relevant in industries where high transportation costs tend to restrict the geographical scope of the markets and where, in addition, large capital costs are required to initiate production and, as a result, mobility of firms is restricted. Cement and steel are good examples of this type of situation. For example, the Inland Steel Company has enjoyed a favorable competitive position because its plants are entirely in the Chicago area, where demand for steel normally exceeds productive capacity. In contrast, the situation is reversed in the Pittsburgh area.

Control over low-cost sources of raw materials may be of major significance in the extractive industries. Kennecott Copper, for example, has owned for many years a large open-pit deposit of copper ore in Utah, which made it an inherently low-cost producer. As a consequence, the company has enjoyed a strong competitive position in its industry.

The second source of a strong competitive position is superior management proficiency. This is perhaps the most typical means of achieving dominance in an industry. The results show up in the existence of industry "leaders" of substantial size that enjoy a strong customer preference for their products. Many phases of management may be involved, such as more successful research and development operations, better distribution methods, and more efficient production techniques.

General Motors exemplifies an exceedingly strong competitive position which management has attained. It has become the leading firm in the automobile industry, both in terms of sales and earnings, without any natural advantages that were not available to others. Aggressive and successful engineering, styling, production, and merchandising have marked its activities, and these factors, essentially managerial in nature, are responsible for its eminent position.

However, whether due to location or management, the main evidence on the competitive position of a given company consists of the comparative sales and earnings record over the years. Therefore, although impressions as to the reputation of the firm and its products are of considerable value, the major tests of competitive position and management are to be found in certain quantitative techniques. These are considered of sufficient importance to warrant a subsequent chapter on their nature and interpretation.

Interindustry Competition.   Interindustry competition may be defined as the rivalry between products of two or more industries to satisfy the same economic purpose. It is of particular importance in a dynamic economy where new products are constantly appearing that may perform certain economic services better than existing goods.

It should be emphasized that this phase of the competitive process is both a risk and an opportunity. The risk is that products from other industries may successfully invade the subject's markets, forcing either a substantial decline in sales, a reduction in prices to unprofitable levels, or a combination of both. But to the aggressive company the prospects of capturing markets held by firms in other industries may represent a major source of growth. But this feature of interindustry competition should be included in the analysis of the prospective demand for the product line considered above.

Interindustry competition, on the whole, has probably constituted a more significant source of investment losses than intraindustry competition; an entire industry can literally be wiped out when remediable measures are unavailable. Perhaps an extreme case was the fate of the interurban rail transit companies. Today these companies have all but disappeared; automobile and bus have eliminated the demand for their services. Although less extreme, the same effects have been felt by the railroads, because of truck and airline competition.

These examples illustrate the nature of the analytical problems posed in this area. First, it is pertinent to inquire if products from other industries can satisfy some of the economic purposes provided by a company's products. Second, if so, the question becomes whether these other products can accomplish these purposes better, at lesser cost, or both. Finally, there is the question of whether the resources of the company have any degree of mobility. In some instances corporate facilities are irrevocably committed to one type of product—railroads, for instance—whereas in other cases interindustry competition might be met by shifting resources to the production of other items. Textron's disposal of their unprofitable northern textile properties and entry into the production of electronic components illustrates a successful adjustment to severe competitive problems arising from foreign textile mills and from synthetic fibers produced by chemical companies.

Qualitative Analysis: Cost and Production Characteristics

Productivity Improvement. Hourly wage rates and salaries have advanced substantially and constantly since World War II, and continued union pressures and shortages of managerial talent make a continuation of the trend highly probable. Therefore, a general impression of potential productivity improvement is of considerable significance in the qualitative appraisal of a company. Indications on this score are frequently found in the annual reports of leading companies. References to the installation of new automation devices, new processes, and plant modernization programs give evidence of efforts to improve productivity.

In many instances, the total number of employees is given for a period of years, and if so, a more tangible indication of productivity improvement is the relation of the percentage increase in sales to the number of employees. For example, a ten-year operation summary contained in the annual report of Standard Oil of California showed that between 1955 and 1964 inclusive, employees increased from 36,400 to 43,400, or by about 20%, whereas sales increased from $1.4 billion to $2.7 billion, or by almost 92%.[1] As there were no significant changes in product prices, the ability of this company to increase sales at a more rapid rate than the number of employees suggested good productivity improvement.[2]

Degree of Integration. In some important industries, oil and steel for example, companies may produce and market the same end products, but the degree of vertical integration in the structure of production may vary widely. Some enter the production process at a late stage through the purchase of raw or semi-finished materials, whereas others own and produce the basic natural resources. By and large, integrated companies have the advantages of control over their raw material sources and greater cost stability under inflationary conditions, when raw material prices may rise rapidly. Shares of vertically integrated companies are, therefore, preferable when one purpose of the commitment is to obtain some protection against inflation. On the other hand, nonintegrated companies may show better results under conditions of declining commodity prices as open-market prices of raw materials typically decline more than prices of end products sold at wholesale or retail.

Adequacy of Raw Materials. For nonintegrated companies, the analytical problem is whether any shortages in open-market offerings of raw materials have occurred in the past and may occur in the future. For integrated companies, the question is one of adequate raw material reserves. Some oil companies, for example, report the actual amounts of proven reserves; annual increases of course are favorable indications. Others, such as Standard of California, merely report without specific data whether discoveries have offset production for the year. Deterioration in raw material reserves is of course a negative factor, and a sub-

[1] Standard Oil of California, *Annual Report for 1964*, pp. 28–29.

[2] If possible, it might be useful to compare the performance with competitors, although differences in operating characteristics might make the comparisons not completely indicative of comparative productivity improvements.

stantial improvement, such as occurred for Marathon Oil with its Libyan discoveries in 1961–62, is a definite positive factor for a company.

Labor Relations. Favorable indications on this score would be (1) a record of amicable wage settlements without prolonged and repetitive strikes, and (2) evidence of enlightened policies of the unions with respect to the introduction of means to improve productivity. On balance, the second feature would seem more important as increases in wage rates appear inevitable, and even partially successful resistance to productivity improvements might well result in cost increases in excess of the ability to increase prices. The unsatisfactory cost trends of the railroads in the postwar years can be cited as an example of the problems that might arise in this connection.

The Qualitative Analysis: Summary

The purpose of the qualitative analysis is to obtain some general impressions of a company and its related industry. But at most only a rough insight into the investment opportunities on the one side and the risks on the other can be obtained. Investment values, therefore, cannot be estimated on the basis of a qualitative appraisal, because value determination implies measurements which inherently cannot be estimated from these factors alone.

However, brief qualitative impressions of the following areas are usually desirable. First, and perhaps of most significance, is an inquiry into the demand characteristics for the products. The major objectives are to appraise the potential growth and stability of the sales revenues.

Second, the qualitative appraisal should inquire into the prospective competitive conditions faced by the subject company. Intense competition, it was argued, is likely to be found on an intraindustry basis when there is a tendency for productive capacities to exceed normal demand for the products. Under these conditions, it is possible for sales to expand to a favorable rate, but earnings may not respond because of a weak product price structure. A qualitative review of the relative competitive positions of the companies in an industry is also desirable. A strong competitive position may arise from certain natural advantages, but more typically a strong management is likely to be the crucial factor. A second possible competitive problem is that of interindustry competition. Unfortunately, it is very difficult to appraise the factor satisfactorily. It really involves answering this question: are there any significant prospects for products from other industries being substituted on a large scale for the products of this industry?

Finally, there is the question of whether the prospects for future earnings are improved or reduced by the nature of and trends in the cost and production characteristics. The record of productivity improvements, control over raw material sources, and labor relations are among the elements which may be of some significance.

ANALYSIS OF CORPORATE PERFORMANCES

Quantitative Factors

CHAPTER 9

Analysis of Reported Earnings

Concepts and Scope

The major quantitative data on corporate performances are contained in the two conventional financial statements. These are, first, the income statements, showing the flow of sales and expenses during the past years and, second, the balance sheets which indicate the assets and liabilities at given times. As a series of financial statements represent the raw material for most of the quantitative analysis, a few comments on the approach to their use would seem appropriate.

First, because these statements reflect the application of accounting principles, it is necessary to be at least moderately familiar with conventional accounting practices. But although a working knowledge of basic accounting concepts is a prerequisite to intelligent analysis, it is not necessary to be fully trained in all the technical ramifications of this profession. The subsequent discussion will assume only a modest degree of proficiency in accounting.

Second, the financial statements portray the results of the past; these data are, in brief, water over the dam. Investment analysis is not greatly concerned with financial history as such. The primary objective is to appraise the probabilities for the *future* economic performance of an enterprise. Therefore, the use of the historical financial record presumes that this record is likely to reveal significant clues to the future potential. In other words, there is an implied assumption of some reasonable continuity in corporate affairs.

In certain cases it may appear that radical structural changes in a company have taken place recently. As a result, it may be concluded that the long-term patterns and trends revealed by the financial statements are not relevant indications of the investment opportunities afforded by the company's securities. However, there should be a heavy preponderance of evidence indicating that the new developments are actually revolutionary in scope before the past performance is rejected as a clue to the future, because experience indicates that only infrequently do seasoned companies incur revolutionary changes in their performances.[1]

Third, because the quantitative data are used only to obtain an estimate of future prospects, a high degree of arithmetical accuracy is not necessary. For instance, the appropriate ratios do not need to be accurate to several decimal places. And, again, if certain minor items appear to be improperly treated in the statements, there is no need for an elaborate reworking of the data to obtain absolute technical accuracy. A preoccupation with statistical refinements should not consume time and effort out of proportion to their significance in investment decisions. This observation does not, of course, condone cursory analysis or imply that company reports should always be accepted as presented if there are significant distortions of important data. Moreover, because many analysis techniques involve the comparison of results on two or more similar companies, care must be exercised to establish that significant differences do not arise solely because of variations in accounting practices.

Fourth, although the financial statements constitute most of the source material, additional data may be required in order to obtain some bench marks of performance. For example, comparisons with comparable data from one or more major competitors may be desirable. Alternatively (or in addition), statistics on the entire economy or on the particular industry may be useful for comparative purposes and may greatly en-

---

[1] Perhaps natural resource companies of moderate size which discover a large new source of reserves may be the most common exception. For example, in 1961, Marathon Oil Company reported the discovery of a large oil field in Libya with a large production potential relative to existing total output of crude. From zero production in 1961, the Libyan field output increased in 1964 to an amount almost equal to Marathon's total production elsewhere. Therefore, the data prior to 1964–65, when production from the new field reached its indicated optimum level, seemed to be of very little significance in evaluating the future potential of this company.

hance the value of the analysis. Therefore, reference should be made to such data when it is felt a substantially greater insight into a company can be obtained by their use.

Finally, the approach will be considerably different from the traditional organization of the subject. The typical technique has been to consider an analysis of the balance sheet, and then a completely independent section is devoted to the income statements. The traditional approach, it is felt, results in some confusion, because elements on both statements may be relevant to particular topics for which clues to future performance are desired.

The alternative to the conventional presentation may be termed the *functional approach*. A decision is first made about the pertinent elements in an investment appraisal. Then it is appropriate to develop the analytical techniques (which might be derived from either or both statements) that are relevant to a decision on each element. Special procedures are applicable to certain industries, but attention will be concentrated on those that pertain to the typical industrial company. Therefore many "special case" techniques, useful only in certain unusual situations (such as a company in the process of liquidation), will not be considered.

With this limitation in mind, the quantitative analysis of an industrial company would ordinarily include the following elements:

1. Elements pertaining to indications of general investment strength or weakness.
   a. Review of the reliability of reported earnings and the consistency of accounting practices.
   b. Appraisal of managerial capacities and the competitive position in the industry.
   c. Analysis of the stability characteristics of revenues and earnings.
   d. Analysis of the long-term growth potential (or alternatively, exposure to decline) of revenues and earnings.
   e. Appraisal of the financial policies, i.e., use of senior securities in capital structure.
2. Elements pertaining to a decision on the attractiveness of a common stock.
   a. Estimation of the probabilities for future earnings and dividends per share.
   b. Evaluation of the price in relation to probable earnings and dividends.

3. Elements pertaining to decisions on the senior securities.

    a. Review of the earnings protection afforded income payments on the securities.

    b. Analysis of the ability to manage debt obligations in future.

    c. Appraisal of the contractual terms and comparative yields.

Reported Earnings: Reasons for Review

The objectives of a critical review of the reported past earnings are as follows: (1) to ascertain that earnings have been stated on a basis which gives the best clue to the future operations, (2) to establish so far as possible the different sources of earnings, (3) to apportion, in preparation for the appraisal of the common stock, the total earnings on an appropriate per share basis. It should be added that these are theoretical objectives, and, unfortunately, it is not always possible to achieve them satisfactorily. Sometimes, to be sure, very precise quantitative adjustments are possible. However, in other instances the desired adjustments cannot be shown in specific amounts, and it is only possible to conclude that future earnings under circumstances similar to the past are likely to be somewhat greater or less than the reported figures.

In connection with objective (1), there has been considerable controversy within the accounting profession about the basic hypothesis which should guide the preparation of the income statement. One school of thought has supported what is termed the *all-inclusive* concept. In its view the responsibility of the accountant is to set forth on the income statement all the transactions of whatever nature which result in an increase or decrease in the ownership equity. The only possible exceptions to the rule are the changes produced by dividend payments and the sale or purchase of its own common stock by the corporate entity.[2] Although full disclosure of the pertinent facts is considered essential, the final net income figure will not differentiate between earnings derived from normal operations of the business and gains or losses arising from extraordinary events which may have transpired during the year. It is left for the analyst to decide if the reported net income should be considered indicative of future performance.

The second school of thought takes the position that the amount

[2] Committee on Accounting Procedure, *Restatement and Revision of Accounting Research Bulletins,* New York, American Institute of Accountants: Accounting Research Bulletin No. 43, p. 60.

reported as "net income" should exclude gains or losses foreign to the normal operating activities of the business. This view holds that the income statement should be prepared so that it will be of maximum usefulness to the owners of the business. It is further reasoned that the owners are primarily interested in obtaining an estimate of the normal earning capacity of the company. And, of course, it is a more reliable clue when presented on a basis which portrays only the recurring economic activities of the enterprise. Therefore, unusual gains or losses should be reported by a direct adjustment of the common stock equity and the appropriate assets of the company on the grounds that from a financial standpoint they are more properly evaluated as balance sheet transactions.

Because of the lack of uniformity, prudent analysis procedures include a brief examination of the income statement with a view to making appropriate adjustments if there are important gains or losses included in net income which are of historical significance only. It is of course a matter of judgment when an item becomes an "important" amount; as a rule of thumb, it might be suggested that it should increase or decrease net income for a given year by 10% or more (after an appropriate tax adjustment) before it would be worthwhile to make a quantitative adjustment.

There are other differences in accounting methods pertinent to the analysis at this point. First, companies may arbitrarily distort the pattern of earnings by the use of equity reserve transactions. Although these are infrequently found, it is probably desirable to understand the implications of such transactions. Second, it is very common practice to conduct a universe of business operations through subsidiary or affiliated corporations. As a result, it may be necessary to determine whether the reported earnings reflect the entire "group" of companies. Third, it might be necessary to adjust per share earnings for recent stock splits or accumulated stock dividends.

In addition, there are two other important areas of income accounting where alternative practices exist and where the differences may drastically affect the level of reported earnings. In these instances it is usually only possible to indicate the general effects of one approach as compared to another. Reference here is to inventory and depreciation policies, and it must be admitted that their analysis is often frustrating. But, since it is important to be aware of the major effects on earnings of different practices in these areas, the following chapter will be devoted to their specific consideration.

Special Income and Loss Items

Special income and loss items should usually be excluded from income when estimating future profit potentials of the enterprise. The assumption is that they will not be experienced again and, therefore are not relevant to the determination of the earnings potential. But, unfortunately, the problems are not quite as simple as might be expected at first glance. For example, sometimes a gain or loss may be an unusual transaction outside the normal activities of the business, but because it may recur at irregular intervals in the future, it may be a risk factor or a possible plus factor in determining the value of the securities. Because of the analytical problems, it might be useful to examine the major types of such transactions and indicate the interpretation which seems logical in the particular circumstances.

The major possibilities in this respect may be summarized as follows:

1. Special losses or gains may arise from the revaluation or disposal of assets consequent to an audit, change in the nature of the operations, or a catastrophe not covered by insurance.
2. The company may receive or have to make large payments as the result of litigation on income taxes, patents, government renegotiations on contracts, or damages for other causes.
3. The income tax deduction may be reduced or increased by special factors that are not likely to be operative in future years.

Revaluation or Disposal of Assets. Viewed as isolated transactions, gains or losses derived from the revaluation or sale of assets should be excluded from the past earnings reports when used as a clue to future earning power. The reasoning is rather self-evident; it is assumed that these are incidental and random transactions arising from decisions to modify the asset structure. However, if they are due to management problems or negligence, they may be regarded as reflecting on the ability of management to control the enterprise. In other instances, they may reflect to the credit of management by indicating an alertness to the need for eliminating unprofitable operations.

Examples. In 1963, the Whirlpool Corporation, consequent to an audit of its subsidiary finance company, showed a special deduction of $9.2 million on the income statement net of related taxes. According to the annual report, the deduction represented a revaluation of the receivables of its captive finance company.[3] It could be argued that the need for the charge indicated that the subsidiary had understated its provision for bad debts in prior years and thus overstated its earnings over a period of years. But as the company stated that the conditions which produced the need for the revaluation had been eliminated, an allocation of the item against the earnings of prior years would seem to be unnecessary. In any case, it should have been excluded from the 1963 earnings when estimating the earning power indicated from the operations of that year. Before the deduction, earnings amounted to $4.41 a common share as compared with $2.68 a common share shown in the annual report as "net earnings"; the former amount was clearly the appropriate measure of the results for 1963.

Property disposals, including the complete liquidation of a division of the company, gave rise to losses before taxes of some $1.12 million in 1961 for the Hoover Ball and Bearing Company. The result was that reported earnings before income taxes decreased from $3.03 million in 1960 to $1.13 million in 1961. However, because the losses gave rise to substantial tax savings, the entire amount should not have been added back to net earnings reported after taxes. Instead, as the tax rate then was about 50%, one half of the gross losses ($.56 million) represented the appropriate amount to add back to net earnings to indicate the actual earnings arising from the operations in 1961.

Litigation Settlements. Large gains or losses resulting from lawsuits or tax settlements on prior years' income ordinarily may be regarded as special items because they are unlikely to have any effect on future earnings. Therefore, appropriate procedure is to exclude them completely from the earnings results. Renegotiation settlements on specific government contracts which have been terminated are certainly of this character.

But there is one common type of gain and loss from corporate litigation that may be difficult to interpret—damages received or paid under patent infringement claims and license agreements. For example, in 1958 Merck & Co. indicated that $2.7 million was included in royalty income under such settlements. One interpretation of the gain is that it represented prospects for larger royalties in the future. But because the amounts to be received in the future (if any) are unknown, it would seem acceptable practice to disregard gains of this nature when estimating earning power.

[3] Whirlpool Corporation, *Annual Report for 1963*, pp. 1–2. Before taxes, it might be noted, the gross revaluation was $20.8 million.

Tax Adjustments. The interpretation of tax refunds and assessments depends upon the specific circumstances of the particular case. One major source of tax adjustments is the provision of the Internal Revenue Code which allows a company to carry losses forward or backward against income of future or past years. Thus, if a company has an operating loss in one year, it may apply immediately for a refund of taxes paid on prior years' income. Also, under some circumstances the company may allocate the loss to subsequent profits and thereby reduce the tax on such profits. The intent of the provision is to provide equitable tax treatment for companies whose earnings are typically "feast or famine" because of variations in the level of general business conditions.

Viewed in this light, refunds of taxes paid in prior years as a result of current losses would clearly be a legitimate addition to the income stream for purposes of determining average earnings. It merely makes the tax period longer than one year by allowing the company to average earnings in determining its tax liability. However, at the same time these refunds tend to distort year-to-year comparisons. For instance, it may appear that a company is considerably more stable in its economic operations than is actually the case. Therefore, for the purpose of estimating the effects of a recession on operating earnings, these tax refunds might logically be excluded. If a recession is extended, earnings cannot be bolstered indefinitely by tax refunds; only temporary financial relief can be afforded by this feature in the tax law.

When losses are carried forward for tax purposes, then refunds are not involved, but subsequent earnings are relieved of taxes for five years to the extent of the losses so realized. In some instances relief has been obtained from income taxes for a substantial number of years via mergers with companies having tax-loss carry-overs and then disposing of the properties at further book losses deductible for tax purposes.

Example. Dayco Corporation sold its Dayton Tire division to Firestone at a loss of $4.4 million in 1961. In addition, as the consequence of unsatisfactory results in this division, the company incurred large operating losses in both 1960 and 1961. Since then, concentration on the manufacture and sale of various mechanical and consumer rubber products has restored earnings to respectable levels, as shown in Table 9-1. However, because of the previous losses, no income taxes of any significant amount were payable during 1962–64. However, if pretax earnings continue at these levels, they will be subject to a tax rate of 48% in future years. Therefore, although the annual report reported earnings

TABLE 9–1
DAYCO CORPORATION
EARNINGS AND INCOME TAXES: 1960–64
(in millions of dollars)

Year	Net Income before Taxes	Reported Income Taxes	Net Income Adjusted for Taxes and Special Items†
1960	$(7.4)	$1.5 (cr.)	$(7.4)
1961	(7.0)*	—	(2.6)
1962	3.3	.3	1.7
1963	4.1	—	2.1
1964	5.0	.6	2.6

* Includes $4.4 million of loss on sale of assets of tire division.
† As suggested for use as potential earning power; applies 48% tax rate to 1962–64 earnings and excludes special loss in 1961.

per common share of $3.22 for 1964, the investment analyst might have considered that $1.67 per share reflected the prospective earning power generated from 1964 operations (52% of $3.22).

To generalize, the reported earnings, when used as an indication of future earning power, should be subjected to the appropriate tax rate if there have been unusual elements which have lowered the tax burden on a nonrecurring basis.[4] Particularly if earnings of any one or two years are used to project future earning power, then the appropriate income tax rate should be applied to such earnings if for any reason this has not already been done.

Finally, the application of the investment tax credit, as set forth in the Revenue Act of 1964, may distort the year-to-year recognition of income taxes. The credit has allowed an industrial company to deduct 7% of the cost of new equipment from the taxes otherwise payable in a given year, but the company can still depreciate 100% of such cost against taxable income in future years. Some companies have spread the tax savings resulting from the credit over the estimated useful life of the equipment, in which case it would not be a significant distorting item. Others, however, have considered that the entire 7% should be deducted from taxes in the year the equipment is acquired. Under this procedure if a company acquired a substantial amount of fixed assets in any one

[4] In industries where percentage depletion allowances are deductible for tax purposes, as in oil and other extractive operations, the effective tax rate must be estimated from the percentage of income taxes to pretax income.

year, its tax liability might be reduced substantially.[5] Again the application of the appropriate tax rate against pretax income might be used to estimate the effective earnings of a given year.

To summarize, although pertinent only to a minority of companies, it is possible to find significant extraordinary charges and additions to the income stream which are unrelated to the future economic activities of the company. Although they might have qualitative implications, these items should be excluded from any estimates of earning power. In addition, nonrecurring deductions for tax purposes may result in an understatement of the potential tax liability if earnings are maintained or increased from existing levels.

Equity Reserves: Interpretation

Definition. Equity reserves are defined as allocations of income or surplus for the purpose of absorbing indeterminate future losses. Indeed, the loss may never arise. Therefore, the amounts accrued in such reserves are usually considered part of the ownership equity; thus the name *equity reserve.* This means that in computing the book value of the common stock these reserves are included as part of the earned surplus of the company.

The terminology used to identify the allocation on the income statements and balance sheets may be quite varied, but by and large they are labeled *general reserves, contingency reserves,* or *reserve for inventory.* In most cases it is reasonably clear that the allocation does not represent an actual current expense of the business, and it is often an arbitrary amount decided upon by management.

Interpretation. The interpretation of equity reserves depends largely upon the method followed in establishing it and its subsequent disposition. There are several possibilities at this point, and a brief mention of each should suggest the implications of a given case.

First, most publicly owned companies have adopted the procedure recommended by the Committee on Accounting Procedure of the American Institute of Accountants. Their recommendation is that charges or

[5] Pan American World Airways, Inc., reported net income increased from $33.6 million in 1963 to $37.14 million in 1964. However, an investment credit of $6.9 million was taken against taxes in 1964 as compared to $.5 million in 1963. As it seemed highly doubtful if equipment purchases would continue on the scale indicated by the investment credit of 1964, it would have been logical to conclude that a large part of the growth in 1964 was the result of a nonrecurring factor.

credits to these reserves should not enter into the determination of net income. Consequently, they should be created only by an appropriation of earned surplus on the balance sheet; only unusual losses should be charged to them, and no part should be transferred to income in any way; they should be returned to earned surplus when no longer considered necessary.[6]

In effect, the rigorous following of this procedure would make the use of these reserves entirely innocuous. It would mean that a company could from time to time decrease earned surplus and set up a reserve for contingencies, or for any other purpose, but that it could never be used to increase or reduce the normal expenses charged against the revenues. In brief, the investment analyst would only have to add the reserve back into retained earnings when ascertaining the capital-structure breakdown and the book value of the common stock.

However, a few companies may follow other policies with respect to establishing and extinguishing equity reserves. One possible policy is to use equity reserves as a means of inducing a greater stability of earnings than would otherwise be the case. During very favorable earnings years, the company deducts an "expense" on the income report such as a "provision for contingencies" or "provision for price declines on inventory," and credits the reserve account, which is then a liability or equity item on the balance sheet. Then in a later year when sales and profits show a decline, a debit to the accumulated reserve is made, and a credit is shown on the income statement offsetting some loss or expense. This, of course, has the effect of increasing earnings in that year by the amount charged to the reserve. If the transactions are substantial, appropriate practice would be to restate the net income to eliminate the effects of the credits and charges to any equity reserves.

Earnings Analysis: Consolidation Practices

Nature of Problem. For a number of reasons the business activities of many corporations are carried on through the use of subsidiary or affiliated companies.[7] For example, Standard Oil Company (New Jersey), the largest oil-producing and refining complex in the world, is in

---

[6] Committee on Accounting Procedure, *op. cit.*, pp. 42–43.

[7] A company is usually considered a "subsidiary" when 50% or more of the voting stock is held and an "affiliate" when less than a mathematical majority of such stock is owned, even though effective control might be exercised with less than 50% control.

effect nothing more than a holding company in the sense that its assets consist largely of common stocks of other corporate entities that in turn carry on various phases of the oil business in various parts of the world. Although perhaps an extreme example, it is likely that most of the corporations listed on the New York Stock Exchange have one or more subsidiary or affiliated corporations operating under their control.

The investment analysis problem arising from these legal arrangements can be quite complicated in some instances. The problems result under one or both of two sets of circumstances. First, a company may have important affiliates that are not owned in their entirety, and as a result, the financial data may or may not be shown on a consolidated basis. Second, some of the affiliates or subsidiaries may be foreign companies whose earnings and assets may be subject to the risk of currency devaluation or governmental restrictions.

When either or both of these circumstances exist, two alternative policies for the recognition of the earnings of the affiliated companies may be followed. First, it is possible that the parent company will show in net income only the dividends actually received from certain subsidiaries and affiliates. The second alternative in effect ignores the legal separation of the companies and brings together the results of all the separate entities on the financial statements as if they were a single operating firm. Due allowance is made, of course, for any "minority interest" in the assets and earnings of companies that are only partially owned. This is known as the method of full consolidation.

As a general proposition, the latter procedure is preferable because it may usually be presumed that the parent company and its subsidiaries operate as an integral group and will continue to do so in the future. If this premise seems reasonable on the basis of the available information, then the investor in the corporate complex is essentially interested in the earning power prospects of the entire economic entity rather than in any particular legal component. For example, the Inland Steel Company itself is engaged primarily in the business of turning iron ore, limestone, and coke into steel of various kinds. However, it owns certain subsidiaries which mine or quarry the raw materials. And, in addition, the company owns Joseph T. Ryerson and Son, Incorporated, which is the largest distributor of industrial steel from warehouse stocks in the United States, although it produces no raw steel. As these several companies are all concerned with the manufacture or distribution of steel and related products, the fully consolidated results seem to be the best indication of the earning power which would be obtained by an investment in the securities of the Inland Steel Company. And as Inland's reports are on a full consolidation basis, there is no analytical problem.

Adjustment Technique. However, when the parent's equity in the earnings of affiliated companies is not included in reported income, proper accounting practice dictates that such earnings and the amounts of the dividends paid the parent be disclosed in a footnote ot the statements or in the body of the report.[8] Because both the amounts of the earnings of affiliates and the proportion paid to the parent company may vary widely from year to year, the adjustment procedure shown in Table 9-2 for Kimberly-Clark Corporation may be useful in these cases to obtain a more penetrating insight into the performance of the corporate group. This company, a producer of tissue and book papers, has several Canadian affiliates that produce pulp and other raw materials mainly for the parent company but also for sale on the open market.

TABLE 9-2
KIMBERLY-CLARK CORPORATION
(in millions of dollars)

	Fiscal years ended April 30				Percentage Increase, 1961–64
	1961	1962	1963	1964	
Affiliate dividends to parent	$ 1.9	$ 1.9	$ 1.9	$ 2.3	
Equity in earnings of affiliates	2.1	.8	1.2	1.1	
Excess (or deficiency) of earnings over dividends	0.2	(1.1)	(0.3)	(1.2)	
Reported earnings, including affiliate dividends	$31.4	$31.5	$33.9	$35.8	14.2
Add (or deduct) difference between earnings of affiliates and dividends received	0.2	(1.1)	(0.3)	(1.2)	
Adjusted earnings	$31.6	$30.4	$33.6	$34.6	9.4

In 1961, Table 9-2 shows that dividends received by Kimberly-Clark from affiliates were $0.2 million less than the earnings attributable to

[8] The equity of the parent company in the earnings of affiliates is determined from the percentage of the common stock owned by the parent. If 40% of the common is owned, then the equity of the parent would be 40% of the total net earnings of the affiliate.

Kimberly-Clark, whereas in 1962–64 the parent company caused dividends to be paid to it in excess of the related earnings. Therefore, to reflect the actual earnings of the corporate group, $0.2 million was added to net income in 1961; but in 1962–64 it was necessary to subtract from reported net income the excess of the dividends paid over the earnings of the affiliates. After these adjustments, it was apparent that the actual growth in earnings between 1961 and 1964 was only 9.4%, instead of 14.2% as reported. In short, the adjustment technique brought out the fact that there was a significant difference between the real growth rate and that indicated by the trend of reported earnings. As a result, the adjustments shown in Table 9-2 although not large as a percentage of total earnings in any given year, gave an insight into the actual earnings progress that was not apparent from the reported statements of income.

Reporting of Foreign Earnings. Because both the growth rates and the risks may have different dimensions, it would seem desirable to have the earnings generated from overseas operations reported separately from domestic activities. However, when the statements are prepared on a consolidated basis, this information may not be available. Therefore, complete consolidation may actually be a drawback for purposes of investment analysis when a substantial proportion of the earnings are derived from foreign operations. For example, because Chas. Pfizer and Company, a leading ethical drug firm, reported foreign income taxes of $15.5 million in 1963, it was clear that foreign operations were important, but no breakdown in either sales or earnings according to geographic origin was given in its annual report.

A second analytical problem may arise from differences in the treatment of unremitted foreign earnings. Within the office equipment industry, for example, Burroughs Corporation has followed the policy of including all foreign earnings, whether remitted or not, in its reported income, whereas National Cash Register Company deducts the unremitted portion before arriving at net income as shown in Table 9-3. Therefore, to compare the performance of Burroughs and National Cash Register, it would be necessary to add back the unremitted foreign earnings of the latter in order to put both on a comparable basis. The adjustment is also useful, as in the case of Kimberly-Clark, to show the trends of the combined operations more effectively. In the National Cash Register case, the data in Table 9-3 show that the fluctuations were greater and the trend was more adverse between 1961–64 on a fully consolidated basis than indicated by reported net income.

TABLE 9-3
NATIONAL CASH REGISTER COMPANY
SOURCES AND ADJUSTMENT OF EARNINGS
(in millions of dollars)

	1960	1961	1962	1963	1964
Reported net income					
Foreign subsidiary dividends	$10.3	$10.0	$ 8.7	$10.8	$10.5
Domestic and Canadian companies	9.7	11.7	11.9	9.3	12.0
Total reported income					
(on income statement)	$20.0	$21.7	$20.6	$20.1	$22.5
Unremitted earnings of foreign					
subsidiaries	3.8	8.4	2.6	2.3	3.6
Total including all subsidiary earnings	$23.8	$30.1	$23.2	$22.4	$26.1
Consolidated earnings					
Foreign earnings	$14.1	$18.4	$11.3	$13.1	$14.1
Domestic earnings	9.7	11.7	11.9	9.3	12.0
Total consolidated earnings	$23.8	$30.1	$23.2	$22.4	$26.1

Source: Annual Reports, National Cash Register Company, 1960–64.

Interpretation of Capitalization Changes

So far attention has been concentrated on the interpretation of matters which relate to the determination of total earnings. The objective was to portray the quantitative performance on the basis most indicative of future earnings prospects. Although this aspect is most important, one further consideration is of vital importance in the case of a common stock analysis: to ascertain that per share earnings reflect the appropriate number of outstanding shares. The necessity should be reasonably obvious; the investment decision must be based on the prevailing price of one share in the market; therefore, earning power per common share is the only relevant data which can be related to price.

On the surface the computation of earnings per share of common stock would seem very simple. Indeed, in many cases no special attention to this matter is necessary. When the number of shares outstanding remains constant for a long period of time, it requires merely dividing the total profits after taxes for each year by the total shares outstanding. But many companies find it expedient for one reason or another to change the number of shares from time to time. Then it becomes necessary to decide whether earnings per share should be stated on the basis of the shares outstanding at the end of each past year, or whether, alternatively, the number of shares currently outstanding should be divided into the earnings of the respective years. Two factors might be considered in reaching a practical decision on this point: (1) the nature of the transaction which resulted in a change in the number of common shares, (2) the magnitude of the change in the common shares.

Stock Dividends or Splits. With respect to the first factor, the general principle is that any transaction which had the effect of diluting the equity of one share in the earnings stream requires adjustment of earnings per share for all prior years. The most common situation requiring adjustment of prior earnings per share is when there has been a substantial stock split or stock dividend. Many companies have increased their common shares in this manner with the objective of broadening the market for the stock. The process merely involves increasing proportionately the number of shares held by each stockholder. Although the total equity of the common stock in the earnings remains the same, it is divided among a greater number of common share units.

The appropriate analytical procedure consequent to a stock dividend or split requires dividing the recorded earnings per share for the earlier years by the multiple by which the stock was increased. Thus, if there had been a two-for-one split, or a 100% stock dividend, earnings per share for years prior to this action would be divided by 2. Ordinarily the investment services, Standard and Poor's and Moody's, make the appropriate adjustment in their statistical analysis, but sometimes it is not very well presented. Also, in the year in which the stock dividend or split was effected the investor is obliged to make the necessary adjustments of the earnings data for past years.

For example, the McGraw-Edison Company split its stock in the spring of 1965 on a two-for-one basis. Table 9-4 shows the summaries of earnings per share for the years 1959–64 in the annual report of the company for 1964. An investor appraising the stock in the middle of 1965 and using the 1964 annual report as the source of quantitative data might be confused unless the necessary adjustment set forth in Table 9-4 was made. After the split the stock sold for about 34, whereas before the split its price was about 68. The stock, of course, at 34 might have seemed cheap when related to unadjusted per share earnings, but unfortunately such unadjusted earnings were not attributable to each share after the split was consummated. Therefore, it was necessary to divide the past per share earnings shown in the 1964 annual report by 2 to establish the appropriate earnings per share in terms of the common stock outstanding in 1965.

TABLE 9-4
Earnings per-Share Data: McGraw-Edison Company

Year	Per 1964 Annual Report	Shares Outstanding	Adjusted for 1965 Split
1959	$2.69	5,603,000	$1.34
1960	2.15	6,421,000	1.07
1961	2.10	6,427,000	1.05
1962	2.57	6,431,000	1.28
1963	2.40	6,440,000	1.20
1964	3.45	6,450,000	1.72
1965	—	12,900,000	—

Table 9-4 also shows that the outstanding shares increased by over 800,000 in 1960. Investigation indicated that these shares were issued to acquire the American Laundry Machine Company. As these shares represented the acquisition of assets with earning power, presumably no dilution of the existing equity was involved. When shares are issued pursuant to mergers or acquisitions, therefore, no adjustment of past reported earnings per share is required. Of course it is pertinent to appraise whether the merger or acquisition seems generally in the interests of the stockholders.

Sale of Shares. When shares are increased pursuant to a sale of stock for new capital purposes, the assumption is the same as for mergers or acquisitions: that the new shares should be able to "pay their way" via earnings from the new assets. Therefore, no adjustment of the past earnings per share is required in this case.

However, if the additional funds are used primarily to retire senior securities, then the only "earnings" contributed to future operations are the savings in interest or preferred dividends on the eliminated senior issues. This, in effect, is leverage in reverse, and it may involve a significant dilution which would justify a restatement of past earnings per share. The analytical technique involves two steps. First, the preferred dividends or interest (less related taxes) are added back to the past reported earnings available to the common stock. Second, the total earnings so adjusted are divided by the approximate new number of shares.[9]

[9] The word *approximate* is used to indicate the desirability of rounding off the quantities in order to simplify and expedite the arithmetic computation. Because the purpose of computing past earnings per share is merely to obtain a rough guide to future expectations, precise accuracy is not required in adjustments of this kind.

Potential per Share Dilution: Convertibles. A somewhat similar computation may be desirable if a company has a large convertible senior security outstanding which if converted to common stock would significantly increase the number of shares. Here the dilution of the common stock earnings per share is only potential: the senior-security holders have the option of exchanging their bonds or preferred stock for common, but until they do so they have no actual equity in the earnings available for the common stock. Nevertheless, if the terms of the conversion privilege are such that exercise of the option appears likely, then it would seem prudent to consider this factor when estimating the per share earning power. The techniques for determining whether a convertible issue is likely to be exchanged for common stock were discussed in some detail in Chapter 3. In general, the analysis can be summarized by stating that if the price of the convertible divided by the number of shares into which it is convertible is close to the market price of the common stock, then it is reasonable to assume that conversion will ultimately be consummated.

In the majority of companies with convertible senior securities outstanding, the potential increase in common shares arising from conversion is not large enough to warrant a supplementary computation. It may be suggested that at least a 10% increase in the number of shares should be indicated. But the increasing popularity of convertible securities as a financing device suggests that an investment analyst should be able to measure the magnitude of the potential earnings dilution of the common stock. Therefore, Table 9-5 shows such a computation applied to the Sinclair Oil Corporation as of the end of 1963.

The mechanics of the computation may be described as follows. First, by dividing the total amount of the outstanding convertible issue by the conversion price, the number of the additional common shares potentially resulting from complete conversion was obtained. The computation showed conversion of the Sinclair 4⅞% Subordinated Debentures would have increased the number of outstanding common shares by 2.4 million, or 16.1% of the common shares outstanding. Second, one half of the interest charges on the debentures was added to the earnings reported on the common stock. This amount represents the additional earnings which would have accrued to the common stock if the debentures were completely converted. Only half the interest was added because any increase in earnings arising from a saving on interest charges would be taxed at a rate of about 50%. However, if the convertible security was a preferred stock, then the entire amount of the preferred dividends would pass through to the common if conversion took place.

TABLE 9–5
EARNINGS PER SHARE OF SINCLAIR OIL CORPORATION
ADJUSTED FOR POTENTIAL CONVERSION

Capitalization Data, 12/31/63:			
Number of common shares outstanding			14.9 million
Amount of convertible 4⅜% subordinated debentures			$167.2 million
Conversion price			$70.
Number of shares possible from conversion (167.2 ÷ 70)			2.4 million
Per cent increase in shares (2.4 ÷ 14.9)			16
Earnings Data:	*1961*	*1962*	*1963*
Net income to common stock	$35.9	$47.3	$62.7
Per common share—			
14.9 million shares	2.40	3.15	4.20
Computation of potential dilution:			
Earnings reported to			
common	$35.9	$47.3	$62.7
Add: One-half interest			
charges on debentures	3.7	3.7	3.7
Earnings to common if			
debentures are converted	$39.6	$51.0	$66.4
Number of common shares			
if converted	17.3 million	17.3 million	17.3 million
Earnings per common share	$ 2.25	$ 2.94	$ 3.83

Third, total earnings so adjusted were divided by the common shares which would be outstanding if the debentures were completely converted. The per share earnings so computed represented the earnings for the specified years if the debentures should exercise their option and convert to common stock.

However, when a convertible security has just been issued for cash or other assets, it is not proper to consider that the common stock earnings per share will be reduced by this action. Presumably additional earnings will be forthcoming from the new assets. Perhaps a year or so will pass before the proceeds are entirely invested in productive assets. Therefore, a computation of potential per share earnings dilution is appropriate only when a convertible has been outstanding for at least a year.

Summary. To summarize it might be helpful to list the circumstances wherein adjustments are desirable in the per share earnings for the prior years to take account of actual or potential changes in the capital structure:

1. When a stock dividend or split results in an increase in the common stock of 10% or more.
2. When a convertible senior security has been outstanding for at least one year and ultimate conversion seems to be a possibility. The same percentage increase in the number of common shares should be evidenced in this instance as in (1) above.

However, if new common shares are issued for cash, in exchange for other assets, or pusuant to mergers, no adjustment in the past per share earnings is required, as it is presumed that the earnings from the assets so acquired will be roughly equal to those on the existing assets.

CHAPTER 10

Inventory and Depreciation Policies

Introduction

With respect to the matters considered in the preceding chapter specific quantitative adjustments can be made from information contained in the annual reports. For instance, certain items of reported income may not be relevant to future performance. Therefore, a specific exclusion of these items is appropriate when evaluating the prospective level and trend of earnings for subsequent years. In contrast, the problems involved in interpreting the significance of inventory and depreciation policies are not usually subject to precise quantitative solution.

In fact, the question might well be raised if an investigation of such policies is not beyond the practical scope of an investment appraisal. The main difficulty is that alternative computations cannot be made on any practicable basis. Moreover, even if sufficient data were available, there is no reason to believe that one theory of allocating plant and inventory costs to the revenue stream is unqualifiedly correct and that others are wrong. Unfortunately, certain arbitrary assumptions are inherent in the process of determining the appropriate amount of depreciation and cost of goods sold assignable to the revenues of a given accounting period. Therefore, despite the appearance of a high degree of accuracy in reporting earnings (usually income statements are shown down to the last dollar of income), the process of income determination is essentially one of approximation for any given period of years.

Depreciation, for example, involves estimates of the economic life of the various depreciable assets which are subject to the indeterminate forces of obsolescence as well as to ordinary wear and tear. Even if technically qualified, it is hardly possible to make a thorough review of these estimates with the aim of arriving at a more accurate expression of the depreciation expense. And even supposing such a review could be expeditiously made, what would be accomplished? At the most, the result would be substitution of one set of indeterminate assumptions for another.

In view of the inherent limitations, what analysis purposes are served by a review of the depreciation and inventory policies of a given company? The answer to the question is not easy; even experienced analysts do not agree on the scope of the analysis at this point. However, the following purposes of general importance to an investment appraisal might be suggested.

First, it would seem desirable to appreciate the general impact on earnings resulting from the alternative principles in determining costs of materials consumed and depreciation charges. The knowledge may prevent erroneous conclusions in forecasting potential earning power and in comparing the records of different companies. Second, in the interest of stimulating economic growth, the rates at which depreciable assets may be charged off against taxable income have been revised from time to time and further revisions may well occur in the future. The result has been that some companies have changed their depreciation rates each time the tax rules have been changed, with the consequence that the basis for determining the depreciation deduction on the income statement has not been consistent. Therefore, when this expense item is considerable and inconsistent policies have been followed, some means to obtain comparability for trend analysis purposes may be quite desirable even though it may not be possible to decide which depreciation rate (among the several used in the past) is actually the most appropriate.

Significance of Inventory Methods

Lifo vs. Fifo.   Unless one is exposed to a course in accounting concepts, it is difficult to understand the issues posed by alternative methods of inventory valuation. The source of the trouble rests in the fact that the problem is defined and discussed in terms of determining the values of the inventories on hand at the end of the year for position statement purposes. But, paradoxically, the principal effects of different inventory valuation methods are on the determination of income. Because of the possible confusion, the relationship between inventory values on the position statement and the determination of net income might be briefly reviewed. The connection rests in the technique for computing cost of goods sold, which is often a major item of expense. This technique in general terms is as follows:

Inventory on hand beginning of year—	Quantity x "Price" = xxx
Add:	
Purchases during year—	Quantity x "Price" = xxx
Less:	
Inventory at end of year—	Quantity x "Price" = xxx
Cost of Goods Sold	xxx

It should be readily apparent that the only figures in the above computation which are subject to discretionary determination are the "prices" of the inventory on hand at the beginning and end of the year. All the others are determined by physical counting or from actual invoices (in the case of purchases during the year). But what are the "prices" of the inventory remaining on hand? One theory holds that the oldest goods are normally sold first and therefore the "price" of the goods on hand at the end of the year is what was paid for the most recent additions to the stocks. Another theory holds that the purchase prices of new materials received during a year should be charged as expense against sales for the same year. This view would mean that goods received during the year are considered disposed of in the same year. The former theory is technically called *first-in first-out,* or *fifo;* the latter is termed *last-in first-out,* or *lifo.*

If prices remain relatively constant, the difference between the two methods is not of great significance. However, during periods when prices are moving upward or downward, different results for cost of goods sold will be obtained (and in consequence the reported earnings might vary to a substantial degree), depending upon which theory is being applied. To illustrate with a somewhat simplified example, assume that a company purchased materials during a period of rising prices, and consumption of inventory exactly equaled purchases, as shown on page 156.

Beginning inventory—January 1	10,000 × .05 = $ 500
Add: Purchases during year:	
1st — 5,000 × .10 = 500	
2nd—10,000 × .15 = 1,500	2,000
1. *Value of original inventory and purchases*	$2,500
Deduct: Ending inventory—December 31—shown on balance sheet	
2. *Fifo:* 10,000 × .15 (most recent price)	1,500
3. *Lifo:* 10,000 × .05 (oldest price)	500
Equals: Cost of goods sold—shown on income statement	
Fifo: (1 minus 2)	1,000
Lifo: (1 minus 3)	2,000

This illustration suggests that different methods of inventory valuation may have important consequences to the amount and interpretation of the earnings reported by a given company. First, it may be noted that under the lifo procedure cost of goods sold shown as an expense item more nearly represents the replacement costs of the inventory. Therefore, the revenues for the year, which are presumably also affected by the movement of prices, are matched with costs that reflect the price changes. As a result, greater stability of earnings, both when prices are increasing and when they are decreasing, is obtained under the lifo technique of valuing inventories.

Inventory Profits. Second, the source and meaning of *inventory profits*, a widely used expression during inflationary periods, is indicated by the illustration of the fifo method. Under the assumed sales pattern involving steadily rising prices, reported profits under fifo would be $1,000 greater than under lifo; this is because the 10,000 units on hand at the beginning of the year are considered sold and are charged to expense at their low unit cost price of $.05. The source of inventory profits is obvious: the sale of goods on hand acquired at low cost before the rise in the price level took place. To replenish the inventory, these goods must then be replaced at much higher unit prices. The rate of turnover is significant in this process, because there must be sufficient time for prices to rise before disposition; thus, up to a point the slower the turnover, the larger the inventory profits are likely to be during an inflationary period.[1]

The reason many regard these profits as illusory can also be indicated. It will be noted that the expense item *cost of goods sold* was

---

[1] This does not mean total profits are necessarily greater when turnover is low, but only that the profits arising out of price changes are likely to be greater.

exactly $1,000 less under the fifo procedure and, therefore, earnings were greater by this amount. Then it may be noted that $1,000 was precisely the amount by which the *value* of the inventory on the balance sheet has increased, although the *quantity* of inventory has remained constant. It is clear, therefore, that a substantial proportion of the earnings shown under the fifo method would not be available for distribution to the owners of the business, because they were automatically absorbed into an additional investment in inventories. As there is no reason to believe the company can operate with a smaller quantity of inventory at high prices than at low, these "profits" become permanently frozen in the business so long as prices remain at the higher level.

Interpretation. What is the practical significance of all this to the investment analyst? In the first place, it becomes a significant problem only when a substantial proportion of costs is represented by the consumption of materials which fluctuate widely in price. Companies engaged in such activities as meat packing, food processing, or the manufacture of vegetable oils or soap show this type of cost pattern. In the second place, it is not ordinarily feasible for the analyst to restate profits to eliminate those arising from an increase in inventory values, because sufficient information is not usually readily available. But this does not mean the problem should be ignored where it appears to be of some importance. As a practical compromise the following recommendations might be suggested:

1. When companies of this type are using the first-in first-out method of determining inventory values, their levels and trends of earning power should *not* be based on a sequence of years wherein substantial advances or declines in the price level are known to have occurred. Periods of stable prices or years of both increasing and declining prices of the same approximate magnitude should be used.
2. If several major companies are employing different methods in this respect, comparisons of performances are likely to be misleading when price levels have advanced or declined throughout the several years included.
3. When the fifo procedure is used, an artificial element of instability may be introduced into the earnings pattern. The source of instability may be considered less serious than when it is caused by variations in the sales of the product, as it is the result only of a failure to match current costs with current revenues. The average

earnings, therefore, have more significance as an indication of past earning power, assuming the earnings variations seem to be largely due to recurrent movements in inventory prices. The use of average earnings merely implies that the accounting period of a year is itself an arbitrary measurement. If the direction of change in price levels is persistent for a number of years, the trend of earnings may also be distorted by the first-in first-out method.

4. When large quantities of inventories are required and they are valued on a lifo basis that was adopted many years ago, their actual value at current price levels may be considerably different than book values. In such cases an intelligent appraisal of the short-term financial position may have to depend almost entirely on the "quick" ratio, as the current ratio which includes inventory values cannot be regarded as a significant indication of this position.

Depreciation

Nature of Problem. Depreciation is the other major expense determined by applying certain principles and theories instead of being computed from tangible cash outlays definitely assignable as costs to the particular accounting period. And although the necessity of recognizing depreciation as a normal operating expense is no longer a matter of controversy, considerable difference of opinion exists about the basic theories which should control the computation of these charges. The issues involved are highly complex and in many respects highly controversial. An estimation process is inherently involved. Moreover, because of the complex nature of the alternative methods of computing this expense, it is not feasible to discuss the many possible ramifications of depreciation accounting.

Therefore, the modest objective is to review a few of the major problems and to show how differences in depreciation concepts have affected the earnings reports of companies in certain industries where this expense is of significant proportions. First, a distinction might be made between the conventional accounting concept of depreciation and its theoretical significance to investors. In ordinary accounting usage, depreciation is the regular allocation to the revenue stream of the cost of an asset whose economic life extends beyond one accounting period. Strictly interpreted, there is no relationship between the charge and providing cash funds to replace the depreciated assets. However, cash in excess of reported net income should be generated by the process as long as revenues cover total expenses and the depreciation charges exceed outlays for fixed-asset expansion and replacement. But from the investor's standpoint depreciation can be theoretically viewed as the method of recognizing the gradual consumption of invested capital represented by plant and equipment and the means whereby productive capacity can and should be maintained intact without additional investment on the part of the security holders. But to evaluate the depreciation charges on this basis is impossible in practice except within very broad limits, because the prices of capital assets, their productivity, and their useful economic life are among the vital considerations which cannot be determined accurately.

Depreciation and Earning Power. In considering the problem, it is necessary to keep in mind that the calculation of depreciation involves two conceptually separate problems: (1) a determination of the value of the assets to be depreciated, (2) an estimate of the rate at which such values are to be written off against income. With respect to the first problem, the rise in the price level during and after World War II precipitated a violent controversy among accountants concerning the appropriate method for determining asset values subject to depreciation. One side is illustrated by the official viewpoint of the American Institute of Certified Public Accountants. This group specifically recommends using original cost as the value base, largely on the grounds that the concept has been the firmly established practice and that a radical change in practice would not be acceptable to all companies. Thus to have advocated appraisal value or replacement cost as the value base would have caused some companies to adopt the recommendation while others would have adhered to original cost. The result, it was felt, would have been a chaotic situation both for management and for investors who desire to compare the results of their companies with others in the same general line of business.[3] It is possible to be sympathetic with this viewpoint, because many analytical techniques involve comparison of one company with another, and their usefulness might be seriously impaired when important expenses are determined by radically different means in various companies. Therefore, unless a new basis of values is generally accepted, there is much to be said for adhering to the original cost as the asset value subject to depreciation.

On the other side, it has been argued that depreciation based on the original cost of plant and equipment, acquired when the price level was

[2] American Institute of Accountants, *Restatement and Revision of Accounting Research Bulletins*, New York, 1953, pp. 67–71.

significantly lower, results in an overstatement of earnings and because of high corporation tax rates, confiscation of capital.[3] The principle is relatively simple: when plant assets are depreciated on the basis of original cost, sufficient deductions will not be made to allow for their replacement at the inflated price levels. Therefore, new investment will be required merely to maintain intact the productive capacities of the company. For certain companies, in which plant and equipment investment is very large and depreciation charges are an important cost element (public utilities are a prime example) there seems to be special force to this argument. If depreciation is measured on the basis of original cost and the price level has advanced considerably, a fair proportion of reported net earnings may indeed represent additional plant investment that has not improved the basic productive capacity of the company.[4]

But it should be emphasized that in the typical industrial company the problem has undoubtedly been exaggerated for several reasons. First, specific plant assets are not replaced in exact kind, but new types of equipment are often installed whose productivity is greatly above the items retired from use. Second, even if depreciation deductions were based on replacement costs, the effects on earnings may not be substantial. This would be true for companies whose fixed assets have been largely acquired in recent years or whose plant assets are moderate in relation to the revenues and earnings.

Third, there has been little evidence that the adverse effects which presumably should have ensued from inadequate depreciation charges have actually been incurred. According to the proponents of the theory, additional capital investment in plant and equipment is inevitably necessary merely to make possible the same level of physical output, revenues, and earnings. The result, therefore, should be a declining ratio of sales and earnings to the investment in fixed assets. But despite very large capital outlays during the 1947–56 period of pronounced inflation, most companies in the "heavy industries" did not suffer a significant decline in this respect. For example, a leading company in the steel industry, Inland Steel, had sales revenues of about 3.15 times net fixed

[3] Paton, "The Depreciation Deduction—A Neglected Aspect," *Michigan Business Review*, University of Michigan, Ann Arbor, November 1953, p. 23.

[4] In its *Annual Report* for 1958 (p. 7) Inland Steel Company stated the problem as follows: "because of inflation the costs of machinery and equipment have been rising so rapidly that the replacement cost may be two or three times the original cost, and sometimes even more. Under present tax laws depreciation is calculated on original cost and, consequently, owners and managers must obtain a substantial amount of additional money for replacement of facilities by borrowing or by retaining earnings in the business which could have been paid out as dividends."

assets in 1947, whereas in 1956 they were only modestly lower at 3.0. However, a decline in profit margins from 9.4% to 7.3%, due largely to an increase in income tax rates, produced a modest reduction in net earnings as a percentage of investment in plant assets.

The predicted adverse effects did not take place because these industries were able to raise prices sufficiently to maintain the rate of sales on invested capital. This explanation appears most reasonable, because it was quite evident that productive capacity grew at a much less rapid rate than plant investment; revenues, however, more or less kept pace with plant investment. In addition, it may be observed that the rate of net earnings as a percentage of invested capital was higher for Inland Steel in the post-inflation year of 1956 than in 1947. Since then, however, prices of steel have not increased and the rate of return has declined.

Accelerated Depreciation. Assuming, however, that there was a problem, the logical remedy would have been to restate the value of plant and equipment on a replacement cost basis and then to have based the depreciation rate on the remaining useful life. But, because of special features in the tax laws, companies have been inclined to increase the rate of depreciation and continue to use historical cost as the value base for determining depreciation charges. The departure from conventional practice is known as *accelerated depreciation*.

The tax statutes have established two types of acceleration: (1) the new "guidelines," issued in 1962, reducing the number of years over which most assets may be depreciated for tax purposes, (2) the general privilege of depreciating plant assets much more rapidly in the early years of use than in the later years.[5] The result has been that a number of companies have followed highly inconsistent policies with respect to the rates at which depreciable properties are written off against earnings, although there is no evidence that the economic lifespan of the properties has varied accordingly.

Effects on Earnings. In industries where depreciation is a major expense, the inconsistencies in depreciation rates have sometimes had a significant impact on earnings. The companies in the steel industry can be cited as an example. To illustrate, an analysis of the depreciation expenses of Inland Steel Company for the 1957–64 period in Table 10-1

---

[5] In technical terms these are known as the *sum of the digits* and the *double declining balance* methods. Although some differences exist between the two methods, both have the effect mentioned in the text.

TABLE 10-1

INLAND STEEL COMPANY

ANALYSIS OF DEPRECIATION CHARGES: 1957-64

(in millions of dollars)

	1957	1959	1960	1961	1962	1963	1964	1957–64 Per Cent Increase
Depreciation charges	$ 26.0	$ 35.2	$ 41.0	$ 42.0	$ 60.7	$ 60.6	$ 62.5	140
Gross plant assets	$642.9	$822.5	$881.2	$896.7	$935.1	$1,017.3	$1,139.9	77
Depreciation as per cent of plant assets	4.0	4.2	4.6	4.6	6.5	6.0	5.5	
Sales	$763.9	$705.1	$747.1	$724.6	$760.1	$ 808.1	$ 873.7	14
Net Income	$ 58.9	$ 48.3	$ 47.0	$ 54.7	$ 52.5	$ 56.1	$ 71.1	22
Depreciation:								
Per cent of net income	44	73	87	76	114	108	88	100
Per cent of sales	3.5	5.0	5.4	5.8	6.0	7.5	7.1	100
Per share earnings	$3.45	$2.77	$2.68	$3.08	$2.94	$3.11	$3.91	

shows that a significant proportion of the very substantial increase in depreciation charges ($26 million to $62.5 million) was due to an increase in the annual rate of from 4.0% of plant assets to 5.5%. In short, the depreciation rate used in 1957 suggested at twenty-five-year average life of depreciable assets as compared to an eighteen-year average life in 1964.

Although technology undoubtedly changed in the industry over these years, it would seem highly doubtful if the service life of the asset mix was reduced by these proportions during this seven-year period. Whether rates were too low in 1957 or too high in 1964 cannot be determined. However, in its annual reports the company has repeatedly claimed that postwar advances in technology have shortened the economic life of steelmill equipment.[6] Although these claims may be partially discounted as attempts to secure more favorable tax treatment (which the stockholder might applaud), they are at least an indication that depreciation rates had been excessively low prior to 1962.

But in either case the important fact was that the earnings of 1957–61 were not comparable with those reported in 1962–64 because of the discretionary increase in depreciation rates engendered by changes in the tax rules. Therefore, for purposes of estimating the long-term growth performance, it could be argued that the same depreciation rates should have been applied against earnings in the base year as in the terminal year. Assuming the validity of this argument, the appropriate technical procedure would have been to adjust earnings of the base year to about a 6% depreciation rate and allow for the decrease in income taxes that would be applicable.

In the illustrative example, assuming 1957 appeared to be an appropriate base year for measuring the growth trend, a 6% depreciation rate applied to the gross plant assets of $642.9 million of that year would have resulted in depreciation charges of about $38.6 million as compared to the $26.0 million actually recognized. At a tax rate of about 50%, one half the $12.6 million difference, or $6.3 million, would be subtracted from 1957 earnings. With about 17 million shares outstanding in 1957 (adjusted for subsequent splits), the reduction would amount to $.35 per share. Therefore, the actual growth in earnings per share might have

[6] The annual report for 1963 contained the following statement: "It is encouraging that the Treasury Department through the guideline rules issued in 1962, recognized that numerous and rapid changes in technology in recent years have shortened the average economic life of steel mill equipment. Certain of the guideline lives, however, are still excessively long. . . ." Inland Steel Company, *Annual Report for 1963*, p. 5.

been computed as from $3.10 to $3.91 rather than from $3.45 to $3.91, an increase of 26% rather than 13%.[7]

Depreciation and Deferred Federal Taxes.   A number of companies have decided to maintain depreciation rates at a consistent level for purposes of reporting to shareholders, but of course claiming the maximum deduction for tax purposes as allowed by the successive changes in the tax regulations. This policy can be strongly defended on the grounds that the depreciation deductions allowed for tax purposes may have absolutely no connection with the estimated economic life of the assets concerned. As the economic life should control the rate of depreciation for the determination of income to the stockholders, taxable earnings may justifiably diverge from the earnings shown in the annual reports.

When properties are charged off more rapidly for tax purposes than on the income statement, the result is merely a postponement of taxes rather than a net saving. Only the actual cost of depreciable assets can be charged against taxes in total, so on given assets accelerated depreciation will reduce taxes in the early years but increase them in later years. For example, assume a plant facility with a cost of $10,000 can be depreciated in five years for tax purposes, but its estimated economic life is ten years. Tax amortization will be $2,000 per annum for the first five years and zero thereafter, whereas the conventional "straight-line" depreciation charge would be $1,000 per annum for ten years, as per Table 10-2. The result is that taxable income will be less than reported net income before taxes for the first five years. But once the asset is fully amortized for tax purposes, then the conventional depreciation deduction cannot be shown as an expense on the tax return. Therefore, taxable earnings become greater than reported earnings, so far as accounting for these particular assets is concerned.

Table 10-2 assumes that earnings before depreciation and taxes will be $10,000 for the next ten years. At a 50% tax rate, the actual taxes payable and net earnings after taxes (if no additional assets in this category are acquired) will be $4,000 during the first five years and $5,000 during the second five years if earnings are determined on the basis of tax-allowed depreciation (Inland Steel). But when earnings in the an-

---

[7] Because much of this growth resulted from cost reductions rather than an increase in sales revenues (sales increased by only 15% over the 1957–64 period), a projection of the 1957–64 adjusted increase in earnings per share into the future might have been questioned, but this question represented another issue which is discussed in the chapter on the analysis of growth rates.

TABLE 10-2
Tax-Return Earnings versus Annual Report Earnings
(five-year tax amortization versus ten-year economic life)

		Years 1–5		Years 6–10
Tax Return				
Earnings before depreciation (assumed)		$10,000		$10,000
Depreciation (five years)		2,000		0
Taxable earnings		8,000		10,000
Taxes payable @ 50%		4,000		5,000
Net earnings after taxes		4,000		5,000
Per Annual Report				
Earnings before depreciation		10,000		10,000
Depreciation (ten years)		1,000		1,000
Net before taxes		9,000		9,000
Income taxes:				
Payable as above	$4,000		$5,000	
Deferred taxes	500	4,500	(cr.) 500	4,500
Net earnings after taxes		$ 4,500		$ 4,500

nual report are determined by conventional depreciation methods, then the $9,000 earnings before taxes is considered subject to the regular 50% rate and a tax accrual of $4,500 will be established in each year. Net earnings after taxes, therefore, remain constant at $4,500 for each of the ten years. But for the first five years the total tax expense shown in the annual report will exceed taxes payable by $500, and for the second five years taxes payable will exceed the reported annual tax expense by a like amount. Over the entire ten years, the accelerated depreciation will not result in a net reduction in the tax liability, but the company will have the use of the money represented by the deferred tax accrual for a considerable period of years.

Example. The Air Reduction Company, a chemical company specializing in the production of industrial gases, reported its tax expenses as follows for the years 1962–63:

	1962	1963
Income before federal and foreign taxes	$32,205,000	$32,618,000
Provision for taxes:		
Currently payable	8,190,000	8,346,000
Deferred to future years	7,661,000	7,537,000
Net income for year	$16,354,000	$16,735,000

Then on the consolidated balance sheet an equity item of $24.4 million was shown under the heading *Deferred Income Taxes,* which represented the total past accruals of the deferred taxes deducted on the income statements. It may be noted that the item was given a separate classification on the balance sheet, or in short, was not considered as either debt or stock equity.

The separate status was based on the proposition that deferred taxes may be considered a contingent liability which will have to be met in future years under two conditions: (1) if depreciation claimed for tax purposes falls below that deducted for income determination purposes and (2) if future tax rates and earnings levels require the payment of income taxes on about the same basis as in 1962–63. If the expansion of plant facilities continues, giving rise to new assets subject to accelerated depreciation, the contingent deferred-tax liability may remain unpaid indefinitely. In a sense, therefore, it represented an interest-free investment of the federal government in the company for an indeterminate period.

Concept of "Cash" Earnings. To cope with the inconsistencies between companies in the determination of depreciation charges, the practice has emerged to restate earnings to a so-called "cash basis" which adds back to earnings stream *all* of the charges for depreciation and amortization. Although the adjustment might be useful for comparison of one company's performance with another, it is entirely misleading as a means of estimating the earning potential. Depreciation is, after all, one of the economic costs of operating a business, and ignoring it as an item of expense would imply that plant assets are not subject to the forces of wear and obsolescence. Assuming a profitable level of operations, it is true that a company can build up cash in excess of reported earnings by neglecting to maintain plant replacement expenditures equal to depreciation charges, but over a longer period of time these replacements will necessarily have to be made if productive capacities are to be kept intact. Therefore, it should always be recognized that these so-called cash earnings are highly misleading as evidence of the long-term earning potential.

Summary. The foregoing discussion of depreciation and amortization practices has necessarily been somewhat technical. However, perhaps the following summary of the conclusions might help in the analysis of companies where unusual depreciation policies have been practiced.

1. When a company has been taking accelerated depreciation for tax purposes but following conventional depreciation methods in its regular income statements, this results in a deferred-tax charge or credit on the income statement. Where this item is found on this statement, it may be concluded that earnings have been consistently determined through time, and no further question of earnings on this score is required.

2. When over a period of years a company has changed depreciation rates because of changes in the tax rules and the practice has materially affected the level of reported earnings, good analytical practice would suggest restating the depreciation expense to a consistent rate in order to estimate the trend performance or growth rate in earnings.

CHAPTER 11

Analysis of Financial Policies

Objectives of Analysis

Corporations, of course, have several options at their disposal to finance their asset requirements. These include the sale of bonds, the sale of preferred and common stock, and the retention of earnings. In addition, trade debt and other current liabilities may finance a substantial proportion of the assets. The analytical issues that emerge from the use of the various options may be summarized as follows. First, a brief inquiry into the short-term liquidity position is desirable, although it is quite unlikely to find a large corporation with any serious liquidity problem. Second, an analysis of the risk implications of a financial policy incorporating the use of senior securities may be pertinent in many companies. Third, the implications to the common stock of the alternative financing options might be appraised.

However, in many industrial corporations this phase of the analysis can be almost completely eliminated. For example, some have deliberately avoided the use of senior securities or have employed them in such modest quantities that it becomes immediately evident both that the risk is minimal and that other implications are not significant. And as is typical, if accompanied by adequate short-term liquidity, then the financial policy aspects of an investment analysis merely becomes a conclusion that no risks exist because of the financial structure and that the common stock will probably not benefit in the future through the use of financial leverage. But it might also be noted that an excessively liquid position might suggest undue retention of earnings which might better have been distributed to the stockholders. This point will be discussed further in the section on the appraisal of management.

To a very large extent, the analysis of the financial policy should reveal the inherent quality of the fixed-income securities for investment purposes. A strong financial position can be defined as one where the risk of default on the senior securities and other debt appears minimal. In this case, of course, the bonds and preferred stock, if any, would promise to achieve the objectives of investors in purchasing such securities: continuance of income payments under all reasonably conceivable economic conditions.

The common stock is also interested in maintaining the risk within reasonable proportions. But the assumption of some financial risk may be desirable because the use of senior securities may result in a higher level of per share earnings than would otherwise be possible. Moreover, the periodic use of additional senior securities may improve the growth rate in per share earnings, and as a result, the associated risks may appear worthwhile. To the senior securities, however, because they do not participate in such growth, highly aggressive financial policies are usually undesirable.

Financial Analysis: Short-Term Liquidity

The Current Ratio. The liquidity position of a firm has been traditionally measured by relating the short-term obligations to the amount of cash and other assets which in the ordinary course of business are likely to turn into cash within a reasonably short time. For the most part these other assets, classified as current assets on the balance sheet, are made up of accounts and notes receivable and inventories. Because of the obvious functional relationship, the conventional measure of a company's short-term financial position is the current ratio: the current liabilities divided into the total current assets. A current ratio of 2 to 1 was regarded for many years as the minimum standard for a satisfactory credit position. Such a ratio would mean that current assets could shrink to one half of their balance-sheet amount in the process of being converted into cash before there would be an inability to cover the current obligations.

But although a satisfactory current ratio may still be held desirable, there has been a notable tendency to subordinate its importance, because it fails to distinguish between the liquidity of the several types of current assets. This can best be shown by means of a hypothetical illustration. Assume a company showed the following figures on its balance sheet:

Current Assets		*Current Liabilities*	
Cash	$ 10,000	Accounts payable	$ 40,000
Accounts receivable	40,000	Bank loans	20,000
Inventories	300,000	Taxes payable	40,000
Total	$350,000		$100,000

Although the current ratio in this illustration is a reasonably satisfactory 3.5 to 1, the very heavy preponderance of inventories in the current assets creates a definite question about the immediate financial liquidity of the company (in the absence of any additional information). In the first place, it may take some time to turn the inventories into cash. In the meantime the current obligations may fall due and actually go into default, with consequent pressure or legal action by the creditors. In the second place, the book figures for inventories are typically based on cost or estimated market value at the time the statement is prepared. There is, therefore, no real assurance that they can be sold at the book figures under adverse conditions.

The Quick Ratio. In contrast, receivables represent actual contractual claims against customers which should be realized within a reasonable time. The customers can use their discretion as to whether they will purchase additional goods, but they have no such discretion with respect to debts owed for past purchases. Therefore, the receivables are regarded as much more liquid—i.e., close to cash realization at indicated balance sheet amounts—than are inventories. In consequence, a strong or weak working-capital position is often better indicated by the *quick ratio*—the relationship of cash and receivables to current liabilities. If the ratio is equal to or greater than 1 at a given time, the working-capital position is usually regarded as satisfactory even though the current ratio is substandard. Trends in the ratios would only have to be considered if the position appeared marginal at the time of analysis.

Turnover Ratios. In the usual case it is only necessary to ascertain if the current financial situation is adequate on the basis of both the current and quick ratios. Only if one or the other is substantially weak would further attention be required. If weakness is indicated, then additional techniques may be advisable. For example, the turnover of receivables may be estimated by dividing their balance-sheet amount into sales for the year; similarly, inventories can be divided into cost of goods sold to see how rapidly these items are turned into cash or receivables on the average. If there is a very rapid turnover, then the liquidity is improved. Therefore, a rapid turnover may offset to some extent an unfavorable showing in the basic tests. Also, if the company is likely to be quite stable in the demand for its products, a poor working-capital position may be regarded as less serious. Under these circumstances there is less need for a substantial cushion of working capital to finance either operating losses or involuntary backing up of inventories, or both.

Financial Policy Analysis: Long-Term Debt

Investment Significance of Leverage. It is axiomatic that the introduction of senior securities into a capital structure carries financial risk. But assuming a company has need of additional capital funds, then it may be to the advantage of the *then existing stockholders* to acquire the funds with a bond or preferred stock issue rather than to sell more common stock to share in the profits of the company.

But once senior securities are outstanding, risks are increased in two respects. In the first place, the senior-security charges siphon off a part of the earnings ahead of the common stock, thus necessitating cash earnings year after year that are at least equal to the senior-security charges in order to avoid default or a drain on working capital. In the second place, even though the prospects of actual default may be negligible, the introduction of senior claims will result in a greater variation in the residual earnings than would be the case otherwise.

To illustrate these propositions, a hypothetical case of two companies similar in all respects except capital structure is shown in Table 11-1. The difference in *past* financial policy between Company A and Company B may be summarized as follows: whereas Company B has seen fit to provide 40% of its long-term capital with bonds, Company A has restricted its capitalization to common stock and retained earnings. It is assumed, therefore, that to obtain equivalent capital funds, A has sold twice as many common shares and also has retained a larger amount of past earnings.

Because the rates of earnings assumed on the invested capital have

TABLE 11–1
EFFECTS OF FINANCIAL LEVERAGE

	Company A			Company B		
	20% on Inv. Cap.	10% on Inv. Cap.	5% on Inv. Cap.	20% on Inv. Cap.	10% on Inv. Cap.	5% on Inv. Cap.
Capital Structure:						
4% debentures	—			$20,000,000		
Common stock, $10 par	$20,000,000			10,000,000		
Surplus	30,000,000			20,000,000		
Total capital	$50,000,000			$50,000,000		
Net earnings before interest and taxes	$10,000,000	$5,000,000	$2,500,000	$10,000,000	$5,000,000	$2,500,000
Bond interest	—	—	—	800,000	800,000	800,000
Net after interest before taxes	10,000,000	5,000,000	2,500,000	9,200,000	4,200,000	1,700,000
Income tax—50% rate	5,000,000	2,500,000	1,250,000	4,600,000	2,100,000	850,000
Net to common stock	5,000,000	2,500,000	1,250,000	4,600,000	2,100,000	850,000
Earnings per share	$2.50	$1.25	$.625	$4.60	$2.10	$.85
Per cent decrease in earnings per share as total earnings decline in 50% stages	100	50	50	119	54	60
Per cent increase in earnings per share as total earnings increase in 100% stages	100	100	—	147	—	—

in each instance been in excess of the 4% paid on the bonds, the earnings per share on B's common stock have been consistently greater than on A's.[1] As there is a tax saving to Company B, because interest is deductible for tax purposes, earnings can decline to somewhat less than 4% on invested capital before the per share earnings of A will exceed those of B. Moreover, the use of bonds has enabled Company B to distribute over the years a larger proportion of past earnings in the form of dividends. Therefore, the past decision to finance part of its capital requirements by issuing debt obligations has resulted in some definite advantages to the stockholder of B over A.

But the realization of these advantages has also involved the assumption of the risk elements mentioned previously. First, if total pretax earnings at some later date decline to less than $800,000, there could conceivably be some difficulty in meeting the interest payments on the bonds and receivership could possibly result. Second, Table 11-1 shows that the earnings per share of Company B increase and decline more in both absolute amount and percentagewise with a given increase or decrease in total earnings before taxes. For example, if earnings before taxes move up 100%, from $2.5 to $5 million, earnings per share of Company B's common increase by 147%; a further doubling to $10 million results in a 119% increase in per share earnings. Therefore, the use of senior securities typically means that any increase in the rate of earnings on total invested capital will show up as an even greater percentage increase in the earnings on the common equity, but the magnification effect is gradually lessened as earnings go to higher levels. On the other hand, if total earnings before taxes decrease from any given level, the earnings per share of common will decline at an *increasing* rate. Per share earnings went down 54% when total profits went from $10 to $5 million but then decreased 60% when an additional 50% decrease was assumed in total profits. In brief, Company B, so far as the common stock is concerned, will be more unstable because of its use of fixed-income securities.

Thus although the value per share of B common may exceed A because of its higher per share earnings, *each dollar* of earnings per common share of Company B may have somewhat greater risk attached to

[1] It also should be noted that additional *new* bond issues will increase the earnings available to the common stock to the extent that the rate of return on the capital so obtained exceeds the rate of interest paid on the bonds. However, it cannot be presumed that a continuous growth in earnings can be achieved in this way; ultimately the capital structure will become top-heavy and the market will refuse to accept new bonds at a reasonable rate of interest.

it than would Company A. If the past earnings record is largely marked by boom periods, then the risk of decline in the rate of return earned on invested capital may appear greater than the prospects of a further increase in this rate. Under these conditions, each dollar of Company A earnings should be valued more highly than a dollar of Company B earnings. Conversely, however, if it appears that the prospects are favorable for a future increase in the rate of return on invested capital, then it is possible that the value attached to each dollar of per share earnings may be greater for a company with leverage in its capital structure than for the company without such leverage.

Times Fixed Charges Earned. The hypothetical example in Table 11-1 implicitly suggests the principal technique designed to indicate the quality of the senior securities and the possible risks associated with the financial policy: a comparison of earnings under various economic conditions with the amount of interest and equivalent payments. The arithmetical computation is simple; net earnings available for fixed capital charges are divided by interest and other contractual charges for capital. This ratio is called the *times fixed charges earned.* Its analytical significance is really expressed by its reciprocal: if the times fixed charges earned is, say, six on the average, then total earnings can decline to one-sixth of this level and it would be possible to pay these requirements without causing a deficit in the income account. Ordinarily it is desirable to view the coverage ratio for a considerable number of years to obtain some indication of the *average* performance along with its *minimum* and its *trend* if any.

Although the basic concept is relatively simple, there has been some controversy as to whether it is more appropriate to relate these charges to earnings before or after income taxes. Second, it is sometimes difficult to reach a decision on the amount of contractual capital charges which in fact have been incurred by a company.

Determining Earnings Available for Interest Charges. Because interest and equivalent items are tax deductible, a technically accurate computation is indicated by using earnings before taxes. To illustrate, assume that earnings from the actual operating activities of Company B in Table 11-1 have averaged $5 million although after taxes (at a 50% rate) earnings before interest charges are reduced to $2.9 million. With $.8 million of interest requirements, coverage on a before-tax basis is 6.25 (.8 divided into 5); on an after-tax basis it is 3.62. Now it is literally true that earnings from the productive operations of the company can decline to slightly less than one-sixth of their assumed average level of $5 million and the remainder will still be sufficient to meet interest requirements. The income-tax liability will disappear under such conditions. Therefore, it may be legitimately argued that the after-tax coverage ratio of 3.62 considerably understates the margin of earnings protection for the bonds.

On the other hand, it is also true that the tax liability has a legal prior claim to interest accruals once earnings are sufficient to make the tax accrual necessary. In view of the legal precedence, it is sometimes maintained that the tax collector siphons off his share of the cash earnings prior to the bondholders and, as a result, the coverage ratio is more appropriately stated on an after-tax basis. However, against this argument it can be pointed out that the legal precedence of taxes is in reality a balance-sheet ranking of an accrued liability against the income of the past. As already indicated, if the *future* income from operations is just sufficient to meet interest charges, then the bondholders actually will have a prior claim to such income in the sense that taxes on this amount of income will be zero.

Determining Amount of Capital Charges. The problem of deciding upon the *amount* of charges to be divided into earnings arises out of the fact that the amount of funded debt and resultant interest thereon is quite likely to change throughout time. The question is: Should the "historical" amount (that actually paid in each year) be used to evaluate the risk implication of the financial policy, or should the most recent "current" charges, which are presumably the best indication of the future burden, be related to past earnings?

Depending upon the nature of the financial developments, a decision may be quite clear-cut, but in other instances it may be quite controversial, with cogent arguments in favor of both procedures. The decision would seem clear when a company has recently eliminated all or a substantial proportion of its senior securities. In this case there would be very little significance in a series of coverage ratios which showed inadequate earnings coverage of debt that is no longer in existence. It would obviously be misleading to conclude that the previous coverage inadequacy implied financial risk with respect to future operations. The financial burdens no longer exist. Therefore, the coverage of prevailing interest charges, if any, would be a much more appropriate measure of the investment quality of the company.

However, the reverse has been more typical—a substantial increase in fixed charges resulting from issuing new debt. Here the analysis

TABLE 11–2

GEORGIA-PACIFIC CORPORATION

SELECTED INCOME AND BALANCE-SHEET ITEMS

(in millions of dollars)

	1957	1958	1959	1960	1961	1962	1963	1964
Income items								
Sales	$147.6	$152.4	$192.0	$222.0	$238.3	$325.0	$451.0	$481.0
Expenses	130.1	132.8	165.0	195.4	213.8	291.1	401.4	412.5
Operating profit	$ 17.5	$ 19.6	$ 27.0	$ 26.6	$ 24.5	$ 33.9	$ 49.6	$ 68.5
Other income	.3	.5	.1	2.5	2.2	4.2	9.0	(Not Reported)
Total income	$ 17.8	$ 20.1	$ 27.1	$ 29.1	$ 26.7	$ 38.1	$ 58.6	$ 68.5
Interest paid	5.7	5.5	6.7	6.9	7.4	9.6	14.4	13.3
Balance	$ 12.1	$ 14.6	$ 20.4	$ 22.2	$ 19.3	$ 28.5	$ 44.2	$ 55.2
Income taxes	3.6	4.5	6.3	7.0	5.5	9.3	15.7	19.0
Net income	$ 8.5	$ 10.1	$ 14.1	$ 15.2	$ 13.8	$ 19.2	$ 28.5	$ 36.2
Times charges earned (pretax)	3.1	3.7	4.1	4.2	3.6	4.0	4.1	5.1
Balance-sheet items								
Long-term debt	$135.8	$117.6	$138.6	$138.4	$131.7	$244.9	$244.1	$293.6
Preferred stock	1.2	1.1	10.0	10.0	10.0	20.0	23.2	13.2
Common equity	52.7	71.5	84.7	113.1	131.7	157.0	222.9	257.4
Total	$199.7	$190.2	$233.3	$261.5	$273.4	$421.9	$490.2	$564.2

is often quite difficult, as two alternative conjectures are possible. To illustrate the problems, Table 11-2 shows the developments in Georgia-Pacific Corporation for the years 1957–64.

On the one hand, the modest increase in the pretax coverage of interest charges during 1957–64 showed that despite the large increase in the debt since 1957, the company was able to expand earnings commensurately. As a result, one possible view is that the policy of substantially increasing the debt and interest burden did not impair the financial position of the company. On the other hand, one might argue that part of the increase in earnings between 1961 and 1964 might prove to be cyclical rather than permanent. Therefore, to show only modest improvement in the coverage ratio during these years might be interpreted as a sign of an excessive rate of debt assumption. To support the point, the fact that earnings in 1958 were only moderately in excess of interest charges in 1964 might have been emphasized.

The latter argument would seem particularly plausible if the preponderance of evidence suggested that the company was either highly vulnerable to cyclical downturns in business activity or had below-average long-term growth. In the case of Georgia-Pacific Corporation, although sales and earnings growth of significant proportions had been consistently realized over the entire 1957–64 period, the nature of the product line suggests considerable vulnerability to a downturn in the level of business activity. Therefore, the fact that the company had more than doubled its debt and interest charges between 1961 and 1964 suggests some increase in the financial vulnerability of this company, despite the fact that its coverage ratios actually improved modestly as a result of a strong earnings performance.

Coverage on Specific Bond Issues. The preceding analysis of Georgia-Pacific related the *total* interest charges on *all* outstanding bond issues to the earnings available for such charges. The question may be raised whether this procedure is appropriate when considering the investment quality of a "senior" bond, secured by a lien on particular property, which is followed by a substantial amount of "junior" debt. As an alternative, the earnings coverage of the senior bond interest could be determined independently in appraising its merits.

As a general proposition, the latter approach seems unrealistic, because it necessarily assumes that a default on junior debt and the consequent receivership would not seriously affect the investment status of the senior security. The past record of bankruptcy proceedings tends to justify the opposite assumption—a company in bankruptcy is quite likely to suspend all interest payments regardless of lien position until an equitable reorganization can be achieved, because foreclosure on mortgaged property has not been practical in most instances. As a consequence, it is usually advisable to attach considerable risk to a senior issue if there is any real prospect of default on *any* debt. In brief, the investment status of all outstanding bond issues should be primarily determined by the relationship of earnings to the total charges on both junior and senior debt.[2] And, of course, for the common stock a default on any bond issue is equally serious.

Earnings-Coverage Analysis: Preferred Stock.   When the senior securities include preferred stock, the evaluation of the earnings protection of the preferred dividend involves essentially the same procedures. But inadequate coverage of preferred dividends does not imply possible insolvency, as in the case of bonds. However, it would have adverse implications to the common stockholders, because preferred dividends have first claim on income after interest and taxes. Therefore, if the preferred-stock coverage ratio shows a narrow margin of protection, the dividends on the common are more likely to be suspended.

If there are no bonds outstanding preceding the preferred stock, the earnings protection is easy to measure; it is only necessary to divide net earnings after taxes by the amount of the preferred-dividend requirements. After-tax earnings are used in this case because preferred dividends are not deductible for tax purposes. However, when both bonds and preferred stock are outstanding, the earnings protection *must* be measured by one or the other of the following ratios:

1. $$\frac{\text{Net Earnings after Taxes but before Interest}}{\text{Interest} + \text{Preferred Dividends}}$$

2. $$\frac{\text{Net Earnings before Taxes and Interest}}{\text{Interest plus } \dfrac{\text{Preferred Dividends}}{1 - \text{Tax Rate}}}$$

If these methods are not followed, an entirely erroneous conclusion would result. The problem can best be explained by a hypothetical ex-

[2] This method is known as the *overall coverage* technique as contrasted to the *cumulative deductions* method, which includes only the interest on the senior issue in computing its earning protection after which a separate computation including both senior and junior bond interest is made to ascertain the protection afforded the junior debt issues.

TABLE 11–3
Hypothetical Illustration: Preferred Dividend Coverage

Net earnings before taxes	$5,000,000
Interest charges	1,000,000
Net earnings subject to taxes	$4,000,000
Federal income tax—50% rate	2,000,000
Net earnings to stockholders	$2,000,000
Preferred-stock dividends	400,000
Net to common stock	$1,600,000

Coverage Computations
Earnings before taxes/interest charges

($5 million ÷ $1 million)	5.0

Earnings before interest, after taxes/interest and preferred
dividends ($3 million ÷ $1.4 million) — 2.1

$$\text{Interest plus} \ \frac{\text{Earnings before taxes} \ \text{preferred dividends}}{1 - .50} \ \text{($5 million ÷ $1.8 million)} \qquad 2.8$$

Earnings to stockholders/preferred dividends ($2 million ÷ $4 million)   5.0*

* This is improper method. See text.

ample. Assume that a company has capital charges and earnings as shown in Table 11-3. The times-interest-earned ratio is 5; therefore, net earnings before taxes can decline to one-fifth of the assumed level, and just be sufficient to pay the interest charges on the bonds, with nothing left for either the tax collector or the preferred stockholders. Although this eventuality might result in deferring payment of preferred dividends, it would not produce receivership or otherwise disturb the enterprise as a going concern from the standpoint of the creditors. However, it is safe to observe that any default on the preferred dividend would be quite onerous to both the preferred and common stock.

Yet by relating net earnings to the stockholders to the amount of the preferred dividends, an earnings coverage of 5 would again be indicated. It would appear that the preferred stock is just as well protected as the bonds which rank ahead of it—a manifest impossibility. Therefore, *it is always misleading to relate preferred dividends to net earnings after interest charges have been deducted,* because it may imply that the company's operating income can decline by a much larger proportion before the preferred dividends are in jeopardy than is actually the case. Exactly the same delusion about the protection of a preferred stock results from a comparison of the per share dividend requirements with the indicated per share earnings on the preferred. Therefore, it is advisable for investors *never to pay any attention whatsoever to earnings per share on preferred stock when there are bonds outstanding.* This word of caution needs special emphasis, because the statistical investment services typically show earnings per share of preferred as a separate item even though the firm also has long-term debt.

The traditional measure of the earnings protection afforded preferred stock is to relate earnings after taxes (but before interest) to the cumulated total of interest charges and preferred dividends (Method 1). The ratio shows roughly the proportion by which operating earnings can decline before there is just enough left to meet the requirements on both the bonds and preferred stock. In the hypothetical illustration (Table 11-3) this computation shows a coverage of interest and preferred dividends of 2.1 (3 million divided by 1.4 million).

Theoretically, however, the method is not quite accurate, because it fails to allow for the tax savings produced by the bond interest. The somewhat more complicated technique shown in Table 11-3 has been devised to correct this inherent error. It merely amounts to using *before-tax* earnings in the numerator and then including in the denominator the interest charges plus both preferred dividends and the related corporate income tax—that tax which must be paid when earnings are just sufficient to meet the preferred dividend requirements. For example, in the hypothetical illustration it would take $800,000 of taxable earnings to be able to meet the preferred dividends of $400,000 when the tax rate is 50%. Therefore, the technique considers $800,000 as the effective dividend requirement on the preferred stock. By dividing preferred dividends by the fraction (1 − tax rate), the proper amount of such dividends and related taxes can be obtained for any level of corporate levies. However, as the coverage ratio will always be higher under the latter technique, it need not be used if the simpler, although less precise, traditional method shows adequate protection for the preferred stock. Only in a borderline case might it be desirable to make at least a rough computation according to the more precise formula.

To illustrate, Table 11-4 shows the application of the alternative coverage techniques to the preferred dividend requirements of the Georgia-Pacific Corporation. Because of the special depletion deduction allowed natural resource companies (in this case timberlands), the estimated tax rate was reduced to 30%, about the ratio of income taxes to taxable income through the years. In most companies, as of 1965, the applicable tax rate would have been 48%.

TABLE 11-4
GEORGIA-PACIFIC CORPORATION
EARNINGS COVERAGE OF PREFERRED DIVIDENDS

		1963
Method 1		
Earnings after taxes, before interest		$42,930,000
Senior-security charges:		
Interest on debt	$14,390,000	
Preferred dividends	1,140,000	15,530,000
Earnings coverage indicated		2.7
Method 2		
Earnings before taxes		$58,630,000
Senior-security charges:		
Interest on debt	$14,390,000	
Preferred dividends divided by $(1 - .30)$	1,630,000	$16,020,000
Earnings coverage indicated		3.6

Treatment of Rentals under Long-Term Leases. Appraising financial policies involves a "special case" problem when assets are financed by a long-term lease obligation rather than by outright purchase. In such an arrangement, which is very common in retail store operations, part of the rental charge is analogous to interest on capital funds. The legal owner has supplied the funds for the purchase of these assets, and as a result, the rent would normally include a return on the capital so committed. Moreover, in the usual case the rental charges are in the form of a fixed contractual obligation which must be paid by the company leasing the assets.[3] In some instances, some of the rental is contingent on sales volume; then only the fixed minimum rentals need be considered, within the scope of the problem.

In most cases the firm leasing the property is required to pay taxes, insurance, and maintenance in addition to rent, and then the entire amount of such rent may be considered the equivalent of interest on long-term debt capital.[4] Strictly viewed, however, a part of the lease

[3] Although a contractual obligation, the legal remedy for default on lease payments differs from that on debt. The lessor can only sue for damages in case of default, and these may be less than the total future rentals specified in the contract, whereas in a debt arrangement the entire amount of accrued interest and principal can legally be claimed in case of default.

[4] If taxes, insurance, and maintenance must be paid by the lessor, then about one-third of the total lease rental is usually considered the equivalent of interest charges.

rental under these conditions could logically be considered the equivalent of depreciation. But as it is not really possible to separate the depreciation component out of the rental charge, it seems preferable to consider the entire amount of the minimum contractual rentals as an effective interest charge.

To illustrate the major difference in the indicated financial policy that results when long-term lease rental commitments are added to fixed charges, Table 11-5 shows coverage ratios of S. S. Kresge Company on two bases. One computation is based on reported interest charges alone, and the other on the basis of adding to interest charges the annual minimum lease rentals. In the second computation, as reported earnings were shown after the deduction of rentals, their amounts were added back to income.

TABLE 11–5
S. S. KRESGE COMPANY: COVERAGE COMPUTATIONS
(Income statement amounts in millions of dollars)

Year	Earnings Before Taxes	Interest Charges	Times Interest Earned	Minimum Long-Term Rental Charges	Earnings Before Rentals and Taxes°	Times Rentals and Interest Earned
1961	$20.7	$ .7	28.7	$17.7	$38.4	2.1
1962	19.6	.9	21.8	19.7	39.3	1.9
1963	21.1	1.0	21.1	23.0	44.1	1.8
1964	34.1	1.3	26.2	30.0	65.4	2.1

° Adds back long-term rental charges to earnings.

The indicated financial policy which emerged from including the minimum contractual long-term lease rentals as fixed charges was clearly much different than shown by the coverage of interest charges alone. As Kresge enjoys a considerable degree of stability, the degree of risk because of the contractual obligations did not seem excessive. However, when interest charges alone were considered, the company appeared absolutely impregnable financially, and it seemed that future financial needs could be largely met with an increase in debt. These conclusions were not entirely justified in the light of the substantial minimum annual obligations on store leases.

Cash-Flow Analysis. The use of borrowed capital also typically requires cash outlays to discharge part or all of the principal of the debt in future years. Serial maturities or sinking funds are the typical contractual covenants that indicate cash requirements for this purpose. And although payments on debt principal may represent a regular flow of cash out of the company, they are not reflected on the income statement. The accounting transaction is related to the balance sheet only —a decrease in cash matched by an equivalent decrease in debt. Therefore, the total yearly cash requirements for debt principal can be determined only by an inspection of the balance sheet and possibly the terms of the senior-security contracts.

For the purpose of indicating any potential problems, the amounts to consider are future maturities and mandatory sinking-fund requirements. Also, it would not be reasonable to assume that the net earnings represent the sole source of cash to meet these payments. From a short-term financial standpoint, depreciation and depletion expenses charged on the income statement are not compulsory cash outlays. Moreover, there would seem to be a functional relationship between charging off of fixed assets by depreciation or depletion and the retiring debt which presumably helped finance their acquisition.

If the company is expanding rapidly, net outlays for fixed assets may exceed the depreciation charge, which would mean in effect that no funds are normally generated from this source. However, in periods of adverse economic conditions it seems logical to presume that expenditures on such assets can be suspended to a considerable extent. Of course net income after taxes and interest is also available to meet such mandatory principal payments. Therefore, average net income plus the indicated current level of depreciation and depletion may be related to future maturities and sinking funds to indicate the cash-flow protection of debt maturities and sinking funds.[5] The nature of the computation is indicated in Table 11-6 for Georgia-Pacific Corporation. The coverage ratio of 1.9 so computed did not indicate a strong position. Most leading industrial companies ordinarily show coverages of 4 or more on this basis, especially if they are subject to cyclical propensities.

Financial Policy Analysis: Interpretation. It has become increasingly evident that there is a strong commitment to a national economic policy oriented toward producing greater stability and growth in the economy even at the expense of some inflationary bias. Therefore, the risk to corporate solvency associated with the use of senior securities in the capital structure has clearly diminished as a result. However, even so,

---

[5] If it appeared that the company was likely to enjoy a highly stable performance, then the most recent earnings might have been used, rather than average earnings, in the computation. For Georgia-Pacific, however, the stability features did not appear particularly favorable.

TABLE 11-6
GEORGIA-PACIFIC CORPORATION
CASH-FLOW ANALYSIS: FUTURE MATURITIES AND SINKING FUNDS

	Annual Requirements 1966–70
Serial Maturities:	
$188,570,000 5¼% term loan	$15,700,000
50,000,000 4¾% term loan	10,000,000
7,225,000 4⅞% term loan	1,300,000
6,500,000 4% term loan	500,000
1,965,000 5½% notes	180,000
Total maturities	$27,680,000
Sinking funds (mandatory amounts):	
Subordinated debenture 5's	769,400°
5½% cumulative preferred stock	1,000,000°
Total sinking funds and maturities	$29,449,400
Depreciation and depletion: 1964	$33,950,000
Average net income after interest: 1960–64	22,590,000
Total	$56,540,000

$$\text{Cash-flow coverage of debt principal payments} = \frac{\$56.54}{\$29.45} = 1.9$$

° To begin in 1967.

financial policies leading to excessive debt assumption have caused problems from time to time. The financial difficulties of several highly levered real estate companies in the 1963–65 period can be cited as cases in point. Moreover, some industries and companies have continued to show considerable cyclical fluctuations in earnings despite the improved stability performance of the economy as a whole.

Therefore, adequate earnings coverage ratios of senior-security charges, based on the techniques outlined above, are still important to the determination of the investment quality of both senior securities and common stock. As companies differ greatly in their stability and growth characteristics, it is difficult to establish absolute standards for "adequacy." But the following rough bench marks, covering an eight-year period or so, might be suggested based on the performances of industrial companies considered to be of good investment quality.

Type of Company	Times Charges Earned		Times Charges and Pfd. Div. Earned	
	Average	Minimum	Average	Minimum
Cyclical	8	3	5	3
Stable	4	2	3	2

These standards, it might be noted, are considered applicable to an appraisal of the financial policy in general and to the quality of the bonds and common stock in particular.[6] When the special objective is the appraisal of a preferred stock, some modifications in these standards could be justified. Although the risk to corporate solvency is less when the senior securities take the form of preferred stock, the very fact that the obligation is less pressing on the corporation would be grounds for requiring equal, if not higher, earnings protection on a preferred stock than on a bond. Therefore, the coverage bench marks for bonds shown above might well be substituted in the special case where a preferred stock is under consideration.

Classifying Georgia-Pacific Corporation as subject to about average cyclical exposure, the bonds and preferred stock did not meet the standards indicated above. In addition, the heavy serial maturity and sinking-fund obligations of future years (1966–70) had a minimal cash-flow coverage. Of lesser importance, but also notable, was the fact that senior securities amounted to more than 50% of total long-term capital funds. It was not surprising, therefore, that these bonds were rated Ba by Moody's Investment Service, or low-medium grade, as of 1965.[7] It is quite possible that the company will continue to grow and meet all future obligations, but the lack of a substantial protective margin against potential adversity suggested that the debt obligations and the preferred stocks were not of adequate quality for long-term investment purposes.

However, although indicating a definite risk to the common stock, these conclusions did not necessarily mean that the common stock should have been automatically rejected for long-term investment. There are possible advantages of a large debt position to a common stock which are not available to senior securities per se. The nature of these advantages is illustrated by the comparative data in Table 11-7 for Georgia-Pacific and United States Plywood Company, a competitor in a major sector of the product line.

First, it can be observed that Georgia-Pacific showed a rate of return

---

[6] The decade ended with 1965 by and large enjoyed above-average economic stability based on historical precedents. For this reason, the minimum coverage of the fixed-charges of a cyclically vulnerable company should probably have been better than indicated by these standards in order for the fixed-income securities to be ranked as high-quality.

[7] Described as follows: "Bonds which are rated Ba are judged to have speculative elements; their future cannot be considered as well assured. Often the protection of interest and principal payments may be very moderate and thereby not well safeguarded during both good and bad times over the future. Uncertainty of position characterizes bonds in this class." Moody's, *Industrial Manual*, 1964 Edition, p. vi.

TABLE 11-7
GEORGIA-PACIFIC vs. U.S. PLYWOOD
CAPITAL STRUCTURES AND RATES OF RETURN: 1963
(in millions of dollars)

	Georgia-Pacific	Percent of Total	U.S. Plywood	Percent of Total
Long-term debt	$244.1	49.8	$ 62.0	29.9
Preferred stock	23.2	4.7	3.6	1.4
Common equity	222.9	45.5	141.2	68.7
Total capital	$490.2	100	$206.8	100
Earnings after taxes, before interest	$ 42.9		$ 16.3	
Rate of return, total capital	8.7%		8.0%	
Earnings to common equity	$ 27.4		$ 12.9	
Rate of return, common equity	12.3%		9.1%	

on the common equity investment in 1963 of 12.3% as compared to
9.1% for U.S. Plywood, although the rate of return on total capital (including all senior securities) was only moderately higher, 8.7% compared to 8.0%. Even though the rates paid on the debt and preferred
stock averaged about 5.5% for Georgia-Pacific, as compared to about
4.5% for U.S. Plywood, the leverage factor operated to the *relative* advantage of the former because of the much higher percentage of senior
securities in its capital structure. Therefore, although considerably more
exposed to adversity, the common-stock equity, based on book values,
of Georgia-Pacific has enjoyed a higher rate of return. Also, assuming
that the alternatives to the past increases in senior capital would have
been larger retention of earnings or the issuance of more common shares,
the shareholder in Georgia-Pacific has enjoyed greater dividends and less
dilution of the per share earnings as the company expanded its facilities.

Second, and perhaps of more importance, a given percentage increase in the rate of return on total capital would generate a larger increase in the rate of return on the common equity for Georgia-Pacific
than for U.S. Plywood. Assume that a 1% increase in the return on total
capital is achieved in both instances. This would mean $4.9 million of
additional earnings to Georgia-Pacific and $2.068 million to U.S. Ply-
wood (1% of total capital in Table 11-7). The result would be an 18.1%
increase in the earnings available to the common stock of the former as
compared to 15.9% increase for the latter.[8] Thus, an inflationary trend

[8] Computed by dividing the amount of the assumed increase in earnings by the
1963 earnings to the common equity shown in Table 11-7.

or a general improvement in industry conditions usually tend to produce greater increases in the per share earnings of the more highly levered situation. The reverse is also true of course; an economic decline would hurt the equity earnings of Georgia-Pacific to a larger extent.

Third, one other factor deserves emphasis. These comparative effects would be realized only on the assumption that the same relative proportions of senior securities in the capital structure continues to exist. Such an assumption may not be valid, and it should be evident that U.S. Plywood should have less difficulty in placing additional debt than Georgia-Pacific. As a matter of fact, U.S. Plywood did increase its long-term debt by some $45 million in 1964, whereas Georgia-Pacific found it necessary to issue more common shares in addition to increasing its debt. In short, a negative implication of high debt ratios and inadequate earnings coverage of the senior securities is the possible inability to finance a large proportion of future expansion with senior capital at favorable rates.

CHAPTER 12

~~~~~~

Appraisal of
Management Performances

Introduction

Because of natural advantages or favorable economic conditions, a company with mediocre management may show adequate results for a number of years. But in a highly competitive economy, it is more than likely that management atrophy will ultimately result in a deterioration of earnings, with consequent adverse effects on both the fixed-income securities and the common stock. On the other hand, strong management may offset generally unfavorable industry conditions. For example, the coal industry has experienced considerable problems, mainly because of severe interindustry competition, yet a few companies, such as Consolidated Coal, have been able to adjust their operations to the new conditions and show remarkable progress in every respect. Therefore, the quality of management is highly important both to maximize the opportunities available within an industry and to minimize the effects of adversity.

It also must be recognized that the "outside" investor, even though endowed with the legal right to vote for corporate directors, is not really in a position to influence the composition of management. Realistically viewed, there is an effective separation of ownership and management in most publicly owned corporations. These firms are usually large and have a large number of shares outstanding, spread among many relatively small stockholders. Each year the proxy machinery, financed at corporate expense, enables the existing management to continue in power. Although certain large interests have now and then successfully turned out management, it must be assumed that it would be very difficult for the individual investor to influence management selection to any material extent.[1]

From the standpoint of the "outside" stockholder, the quality of management has two dimensions which are usually entirely separate from one another. The first dimension, and of most importance, is the ability of management to compete successfully in its industry and generate a favorable earnings record for the corporation. The second is the question of whether management, defined as the board of directors, treats the stockholders with reasonable equity in matters in which there may be a conflict of interest between the stockholders and operating management. In theory, it would be desirable to be personally acquainted with top management of the concerns in which investments are contemplated. In practice, however, this is not feasible, except perhaps for the large institutional investor.

Therefore, as a practical substitute, indirect indications must be used. First, there may be qualitative appraisals of management in some of the financial journals. Although such information may have considerable value, it usually tends to emphasize favorable elements, perhaps because of a natural reluctance to condemn publicly the personal capacities of an important group of individuals. Second, it might be logically reasoned that indications of managerial competence and fairness to stockholders should be reflected in the crucial facts of past performance revealed by the financial statements and related statistical data.

In the analysis, as in most uses of the past record, a certain degree of continuity is assumed; more specifically, in the case of management there should be no indication that the past results depended upon the abilities of one or two individuals and that there is a lack of appropriate successors of equal ability. In a few instances one or two men may dominate a company and there may be some doubt about the availability of capable replacements. But in the typical publicly owned enterprise this state of affairs is undoubtedly the exception. In the great majority of

[1] This is not to say that stockholders should automatically approve all proposals instituted by management and requiring stockholder approval that are submitted for vote on the proxy. If a proposal does not seem to be in the interests of the owners as a whole, a negative vote should be registered as a strong minority opposition may have a salutary effect on subsequent policies. Cf., Graham, *Intelligent Investor*, New York: Harper & Row, 1965, Chapters 14 and 15.

corporations the past results probably reflect the abilities of a managerial group whose composition will change relatively slowly; perhaps the major reason is the sheer inability of one or two men to direct effectively the complex activities of a large corporation.

Measuring Operating Efficiency. There are perhaps three tests that are typically used to measure the operating efficiency of management —(1) the rate of return on net worth over several years as compared to that of competitors, (2) the sales trend as compared to that of competitors, (3) the comparative profit margin, or the ability to produce the maximum amount of profits per dollar of sales. For reasons indicated later, however, the profit margin test is usually considered less significant than the other two.

The logic of the first ratio is based on the hypothesis that the principal task of management is to maximize the profits on the ownership equity within the constraints of the industry. In a free-enterprise economy this is the acid test of the effective management of capital resources.[2]

There is, however, one technical problem that arises in connection with the analysis of the comparative return on the stockholder's equity— the use of financial leverage, in the form of bonds and preferred stock, can increase the return on the common-stock equity if the rate of earnings on total invested capital exceeds the interest rate or preferred dividend that must be paid to acquire senior-capital funds. In short, the rate of return on the equity can reflect differences in financial structures as well as differences in operating performance. And of course the use of senior capital introduces a prior claim on income and thereby increases risk.

As a consequence, if senior capital has been used in a given instance, it is necessary to consider the potential risk as well as the advantages. But as management discretion extends to the judicious use of senior se-

---

[2] Corporate officials have tended in recent years to use the rate of return on invested capital as the most important measure of corporate performance. The following remarks of the President of Socony-Mobil Oil Company are illustrative: "What is the best measure of performance? I do not believe we should use sales volumes, even though our sales volume increased 5% in 1960. We could build up our volume simply by giving away products. What about net income as a measurement of performance? It is a good measure, and we have already seen how our net income rose from 1959 to 1960. But, again, net income is not the best measure, because it does not take into account the amount of money that you and all the other shareholders have invested in the company. The best measure, in our opinion, is the rate of return on investment; that is, the net profits as a percentage of the amount of money we have to invest in order to earn them." *Report of Annual Meeting for 1961*, Socony-Mobil Oil Company, 1961, p. 18.

TABLE 12-1
1963 FINANCIAL DATA: BRISTOL-MYERS AND CHAS. PFIZER & CO.

	Bristol-Myers	*Pfizer and Co.*
Sales	$238.8 million	$414.3 million
Costs (including taxes)	219.7	374.
Net earnings	19.1	40.3
Stock equity	95.6	244.1
Sales ÷ stock equity	2.48	1.68
Net earnings ÷ sales	8.0%	9.8%
Rate of Earnings Return on Equity	2.48% × 8.0% = 19.8%	1.68% × 9.8% = 16.3%

curities, it seems only reasonable to incorporate the financial management policies into the performance record. This is accomplished by focusing attention on the return obtained on the stockholder's equity. The risk, if any, surrounding such policies is then considered as a separate element in the analysis.

Relationship of Measurements. The relationship between the volume of sales, profit margin, and the rate of return on the equity can be expressed in an arithmetic expression as follows: the amount of sales per dollar of common-stock equity multiplied by the profit margin (after deduction of all expenses, taxes, and senior-security charges) gives the percentage rate of return on the equity. An example of the computation is shown in Table 12-1 for two large drug companies, Bristol-Myers and Chas. Pfizer & Co. It will be noted that although Bristol-Myers showed net earnings on each sales dollar of only 8% (costs and taxes absorbed 92%) as compared to 9.8% for Pfizer, Bristol-Myers was able to obtain $2.48 of sales for each dollar of stock equity, whereas Pfizer obtained only $1.68 in sales per dollar of equity.[3] As a result, Bristol-Myers enjoyed a higher rate of return on the stock equity (19.8%) than did Pfizer (16.3%), despite the fact that profit margins were lower for Bristol-Myers.

The functional relationship between sales volume, profit margin, and

[3] Both companies produce ethical and proprietary drugs although Bristol-Myers is considered to be much more heavy in the proprietary area of toiletries and cosmetics. The differences in product lines may be responsible for the ability of Bristol-Myers to generate a larger volume of sales per dollar of stock equity, but it may also be argued that the development of profitable proprietary lines may be regarded as an effective managerial achievement.

rate of return suggests the possibility of alternative managerial strategies. Some may emphasize large volume at low margins and others may concentrate on obtaining higher margins at the sacrifice of some sales volume. In most cases the rate of return on the equity should indicate which has been the better strategy for the shareholders.

Therefore, the main technique suggested to evaluate management is the comparison of the rate of return on net worth with that obtained by major competitors or for the industry as a whole. But it is desirable to examine the trend of sales in addition to the rate of return on net worth, because it may be possible for a company to improve earnings for a few years by reducing expenditures on such discretionary expenses as research, advertising, and new product development. Revenue dollars generated from the sales of existing products are thus not burdened by expenses directed to the development of new products and markets. Such activities are often quite necessary to maintain a satisfactory competitive position. Of course, the failure to keep up with product development would be a shortsighted policy, and it would be desirable to be aware of the possibility as soon as possible. Therefore, even though a company has shown a favorable rate of earnings on its equity capital, if accompanied by a declining sales volume relative to its major competitors, then there may be some question as to the aggressiveness of management.[4]

Example.   To illustrate the use of these techniques, Table 12-2 shows an analysis of the sales and rate of return performances of three major ethical drug companies for the period 1957–64. The percentage increase in sales was shown on a per common share basis as well as on a total basis because investigation revealed that Pfizer had in fact made several acquisitions of end-product companies via exchange of stock during these years. However, even on an adjusted per share basis, the sales trend of Pfizer was moderately better than Merck and substantially better than Parke-Davis. On the other hand, Merck was able to show a somewhat higher average rate of return on net worth and also was the only company to match its 1957 performance in 1964. Between Pfizer and Merck, therefore, the differences were not substantial, yet on balance a modest preference might have been given to the manage-

---

[4] When a company has engaged in mergers or has made numerous acquisitions of other companies by exchanging stock, the comparative sales trends are less significant. In this case, sales per share of common stock, adjusted for all splits and stock dividends, can be used to suggest the comparative trend of sales achieved by several companies when some have engaged in mergers and acquisitions and others have not.

TABLE 12-2
COMPARATIVE MANAGEMENT PERFORMANCES
(Sales in millions of dollars)

	Parke-Davis		Merck & Co.		Chas. Pfizer & Co.	
	Sales	Rate of Return	Sales	Rate of Return	Sales	Rate of Return
1957	$162.3	23.9%	$189.9	19.2%	$207.1	18.8%
1958	172.6	21.6	206.6	17.7	222.7	18.0
1959	191.5	22.1	216.9	18.1	253.7	16.6
1960	200.0	20.3	218.1	15.6	269.4	16.0
1961	184.3	14.3	228.6	14.4	312.4	15.3
1962	181.7	11.9	240.3	14.9	383.6	15.7
1963	189.1	13.2	264.6	17.2	417.8	16.3
1964	204.6	14.6	286.7	19.3	480.0	16.2
Sales, per cent increase 1957–64:						
Total	26		51		130	
Per common share	26		50		85	
Rate of return:						
1957–64 average		17.7%		17.1%		16.6%
1964 as % of 1957		61		100		86

ment of Merck for the superior rate of earnings obtained on the share-holders' equity.

In contrast, the management performance of Parke-Davis was definitely disappointing over the period. Although the average rate of return had been above the other companies, the trend was clearly adverse, and since 1961 it had been well below its competitors.[5] Moreover, the company actually suffered a decline in sales between 1960 and 1962 and the sales growth over the entire period was less than half of the other companies. Difficulties with a major antibiotic, chloromycetin, were held to be responsible for some of the problems in 1960–62, but such problems are not uncommon in the ethical drug industry. Therefore, although perhaps Parke-Davis was unfortunate to some extent, its management record appeared clearly less attractive as of 1965 than either Merck or Pfizer.

Because discretionary research expenses, directed to the development of new products aimed at generating revenues in future years, are very significant in the ethical drug industry, the profit-margin test

[5] The possible misleading impression sometimes derived from the use of long-term averages is well illustrated by this case. An average derived from time-series data where there is a clearly defined trend in one direction or another must be interpreted with considerable care.

TABLE 12–3

COMPARATIVE MANAGERIAL PERFORMANCES: INLAND STEEL vs. U.S. STEEL

(Sales in millions of dollars)

	Inland Steel			U.S. Steel			Steel Industry		
	Sales	Rate of Return	Profit Margin	Sales	Rate of Return	Profit Margin	Sales*	Rate of Return†	Profit Margin†
1957	$763.9	14.5%	7.7%	$4,378	14.0%	9.6%	$13,803	13.2%	7.4%
1958	656.0	11.0	7.3	3,438	9.7	8.8	11,158	8.2	6.3
1959	705.1	10.5	6.9	3,598	7.8	7.1	12,281	8.4	6.0
1960	747.1	9.7	6.3	3,649	9.2	8.3	12,342	7.8	5.8
1961	724.6	10.6	7.6	3,302	5.8	5.8	11,486	6.4	5.1
1962	760.1	9.6	6.9	3,469	5.0	4.7	12,136	5.4	4.1
1963	808.1	9.7	6.9	3,599	6.0	5.7	12,644	7.3	5.2
1964	883.0	11.5	8.1	4,129	6.8	5.7	14,500 (est.)	9.2	6.0
1964 as % of 1957	115	79	105	94	49	59	105	70	81
1957–64 average	—	10.9%	7.2%	—	8.0%	6.8%	—	8.2%	5.7%

* As reported in Moody's, *Industrial Manual*, 1964 edition, Special Features Section, p. a17.
† Per Monthly Letter, *First City Bank of New York*, April issues, 1958–65.

did not appear particularly pertinent to the determination of managerial performances; a lower profit margin might well be due to a more aggressive research program, which ultimately might prove highly beneficial to the shareholders.

Comparative Profit Margins. However, in industries where the products are sold largely on a competitive price basis (no product differentiation) and major innovations from research expenditures are unlikely, profit margins become a more important indication of comparative managerial performances. These same circumstances also suggest that composite industry data may be more useful as another measure of comparative performance.

The steel industry, still a large factor in the economy, might be cited as an example of where these conditions prevail, and Table 12-3 presents an analysis of Inland Steel, U.S. Steel, and the steel industry in general for the years 1957–64. Inland Steel, it is clear, outperformed both U.S. Steel and the entire industry in all respects. Although Inland's rate of return declined over this period, the important point, so far as the appraisal of management is concerned, is that there was a lesser decline than for the industry and U.S. Steel.[6] Moreover, the average rate of return enjoyed by Inland Steel was well above both. But perhaps the most impressive evidence revealed by the data was the ability of Inland Steel to generate a larger percentage growth in sales than U.S. Steel and at the same time maintain both higher average profit margins and a better trend in such margins. It could be argued that the favorable location of Inland Steel in the Chicago area might have been responsible for the above-average performance, but whether due to location or management, the company clearly showed greater achievement of the essential managerial objectives than its counterparts.

The record of U.S. Steel, on the other hand, was not particularly reassuring during these years. Although, except for 1964, it consistently maintained a somewhat higher profit margin than the industry, the trends of both sales and the rate of return on the equity were comparatively unfavorable. On balance, it would seem more desirable to show above-average results on the latter items than on profit margins. A declining share of the market, coupled with a greater than average reduction in the rate of return, suggests the possibility of continued problems for U.S. Steel. Greater volatility in addition to a less favorable trend

[6] The decline in the rate of return, however, would be pertinent to an estimate of the growth potential offered by Inland Steel. See Chapter 13.

performance also marked this company in relation to the industry and Inland Steel. The volatility factor, however, might well produce an above-average recovery in earnings under strong boom conditions in the steel industry. It is perhaps for this reason that the common stock of U.S. Steel has often been recommended to implement cyclical timing strategies in the stock market.

Treatment of the Outside Stockholder. This second dimension of management's performance ordinarily has considerably less importance and is often more difficult to evaluate than operating efficiency. For these reasons it is often ignored in an investment analysis, except perhaps by implication. However, because conflicts of interest might arise between management and stockholders, at least a brief review of the possible problems is desirable. But by and large, the managements of large publicly owned corporations seem to accept the proposition that their policies and actions should conform to the long-term interests of their shareholders.

The two major areas in which conflicts of interest might arise are compensation of management, including bonuses and stock options, and dividend policy. Judgment on the first of these is particularly hard to resolve, because standards for compensation are difficult to establish. Put another way, a highly efficient and aggressive management is difficult both to obtain and to retain. Therefore, unless extreme greediness is evidenced, one might reasonably prefer a good operating management at high cost to a mediocre management at low cost. A second difficulty is that information on managerial compensation is usually found only in the proxy statements; neither the annual reports nor the statistical investment services typically include the required data. But assuming the proxy material is available, total salaries and bonuses should not be markedly out of line with competitors of approximately equal size and profitability. Also, if large bonuses continue to be paid even when earnings decline, some question about the reasonableness of such compensation might be raised.

The fairness of stock options granted to executives also represents a difficult problem. On the one hand, it might be argued that management will work more diligently in the interests of all stockholders if they also own a substantial amount of common stock. Also, compensation by options on common stock at a price close to the market should give a direct incentive for management to adopt policies which will maximize its value, because the future value of the options is directly proportional to the subsequent appreciation of the stock. On the other hand, large options may dilute the earnings per share on the stock if it is assumed the capital contributed could have been obtained at lesser cost to the company by other means. And even if new common-stock money did appear desirable, obtaining it by the take-up of stock options means that the existing stockholders are precluded from subscribing to new stock on a preemptive rights basis.

On balance, moderate options to management not already owning large stock interests would seem reasonable. This view suggests two tests about the fairness of management in this respect. First, the amount of stock granted under the options should be moderate in relation to the number of shares already outstanding. Perhaps about 5% would be a rough bench mark of a reasonable maximum. Second, if options are granted to officers or directors who already have substantial stock interests, a legitimate question of equity may be raised, even though substantial detriment to the outside stockholder is not involved.[7]

Most outside investors of moderate means are concerned with obtaining a reasonable amount of dividends on their common-stock commitments. However, if a company requires substantial retained earnings for expansion and the earnings potential thereon seems favorable, then a small payout of earnings in the form of dividends cannot be interpreted as inequitable treatment of stockholders. But when earnings seem to be retained beyond the needs of the corporation, then the equity of dividend policies must be questioned. Careful analysis, therefore, should precede a conclusion on this factor.

There are perhaps two reasons why some managements retain an excessive amount of earnings. First, if the controlling management also owns substantial blocks of stock, then it is possible that because of taxation, a company will have a propensity to declare low dividends. These individuals may be subject to very high marginal tax rates on their incomes, and additional dividend income may be largely taxed away. However, if retained by the corporation, the earnings may somehow add to the value of the stock. To individuals in a high tax bracket, long-term capital gains are much more preferable than returns in the form of current income.

Second, some managements may be oriented toward an excessively conservative financial position. A large amount of cash or its equivalent

---

[7] Some companies follow the practice of having all stock options and bonuses recommended by a committee of the board of directors made up from nonmanagement members who are not eligible to receive either bonuses or options. To some extent this practice removes the possibility of alleged self-dealing on the part of the recipients.

coupled with almost no debt represents the maximum degree of security and simplifies the financial management. Although the investor is also concerned with maintaining the financial solvency of the company, he is penalized by an excessively large retention of earnings if they are diverted to assets on which earning power is negligible. These observations suggest the major quantitative test as to management's fairness on dividend distributions. If cash plus marketable securities substantially exceed all the current liabilities and no major expansion program is indicated, then retention of any significant proportion of earnings would seem questionable.

Example. At the end of 1964 the Champion Spark Plug Company showed cash and short-term marketable securities of $50.7 million as compared to current liabilities of $23.4 million and total operating assets (receivables, inventories, and net plant) of $57.8 million. Moreover, the same comparative proportions had existed for several years. Although the record of operating efficiency had been quite favorable, the rate of growth in sales did not suggest the need for future capital investment in an amount nearly equivalent to the large holdings of liquid assets. Therefore, although the percentage of earnings distributed in the form of dividends (the payout ratio) had approximated 70% in the years 1960–64, the need to retain even 30% of earnings could be questioned in view of the more than adequate liquidity position. However, it must be admitted that any adverse conclusion would have to be tentative, as management's plans for acquisitions or expansion could not be clearly determined from the available evidence.

CHAPTER 13

Analysis of
Corporate Growth Rates

Introduction

The American economy has clearly achieved an outstanding record of long-term growth in most sectors, and corporate earnings have shared in the upward trend. Data on the growth pattern and its significance to investment strategies in common stocks were discussed in Chapter 5. But although the data suggested a reasonably favorable rate of growth of per share earnings and dividends as a whole, the use of average data obscured great disparities between individual situations. Therefore, a highly important task of common-stock analysis is to develop procedures to estimate the potential growth rates of individual companies.

There are perhaps three major dimensions to this phase of an investment analysis. First, there is the problem of selecting bench marks for comparison and isolating long-term growth from interim fluctuations. Second, techniques must be developed for estimating growth rates in a useful form for comparative valuation purposes. Third, it is necessary to examine the dynamic causes of growth in earnings; the purpose is to appraise whether the factors producing growth in the past are likely to be operative on a similar scale in the future. To reiterate, the past results are only useful to the extent that they appear relevant as an indication of the future range of probabilities.

Interpretation of Past Record: Isolating Growth

Bench Marks for Comparison.   For most analytical purposes, growth is a relative concept. In other words, the investigation attempts to determine if a given company is likely to show a growth in earnings and dividends per share at a more rapid rate than the average company. For comparative purposes, therefore, data on average corporate performances are quite useful, preferably restricted to corporations which are publicly owned and thus are available to outside investors.

Professional investors, who have access to an extensive research staff, may find it expedient to prepare their own data for this purpose. However, the average investor can hardly be expected to devote the time and effort which would be required to prepare aggregate measurements of corporate performance. Fortunately, however, the statistical investment services provide reasonably adequate material on groups of companies through the compilation of information on their stock indexes.

For example, the special-features section of *Moody's Industrial Manual* shows long-term data for the book value, earnings, and dividends on an index of 125 industrial stocks. From this information it is possible to obtain an indication of the average growth rate in earnings and dividends which has been realized by a cross-section of large industrial companies. By relating the book values to earnings, the level and trend of the rate of return on the equity capital of these firms can be estimated. In addition, in the same section of the *Industrial Manual*, total gross sales of goods and services of 425 industrial companies are published. By measuring an individual company against such data, it should be possible to determine whether the company has been above or below average in its long-term performance. A compilation of this information for the Moody's Industrial Stock Average is shown in Table 13-1 for the years 1953–64.[1]

Isolating Long-Term Growth.   The major problem is the choice of an appropriate past period that might best represent the future long-term potential. The general rules would be as follows: (1) a period of sufficient length should be selected to show the long-term performance,

---

[1] It may be noted that 1964 data represented Moody's estimates published near the end of that year. As the most up to date information is obviously desirable, such estimates must often be used because a considerable lag exists in the publishing of the actual results for the year in question. In the case of a stock average, the information in a final form is not available until six months or so after the end of the year.

TABLE 13-1
SELECTED DATA: MOODY'S INDUSTRIAL STOCK AVERAGE

Year	Sales†	Book Value	Earnings	Dividend	Return on Equity	Dividend Payout
1953	n.a.	$ 57.6	$ 7.71	$4.19	13.3%	54.4%
1954	n.a.	63.7	8.38	4.46	12.1	53.1
1955	$144.1	68.4	10.51	5.13	15.4	48.8
1956	149.0	72.2	10.35	5.81	14.3	56.4
1957	156.0	78.0	10.27	5.91	13.1	57.4
1958	145.1	81.1	8.31	5.75	10.2	69.2
1959	158.2	84.9	9.85	5.81	11.6	59.2
1960	162.3	88.7	9.62	6.03	10.8	62.8
1961	164.3	91.8	9.61	6.07	10.4	63.8
1962	180.0	95.1	11.10	6.43	11.7	58.0
1963	193.0	100.0	12.43	6.98	12.4	56.3
1964	208.0(E)	107.0(E)°	14.50(E)°	8.10(E)°	13.1	55.8
Increase:						
1955–64	—	$ 38.6	$ 3.99	$2.97	10.3%	—
Average:						
1955–64	—	—	—	—	12.3%	58.8%

° (E) means estimated as of year-end 1964.
† In billions of dollars for 425 industrial corporations.

Source: Moody's *Industrial Manual*, 1964 edition and *Moody's Stock Survey*, 12/7/64.

usually between seven and ten years is required, (2) the state of business conditions of the terminal year should be similar to those prevailing in the base year, (3) if possible, at least one downturn in business activity should be included.

As of 1965, when results for 1964 represented the most currently available data, the terminal year (1964) represented a period of generally favorable business conditions. Earnings on the Moody's Industrial Average, it can be noted, reached a new historical high in that year, and had increased about 50% since 1961. A similar upswing took place for the years 1953 through 1955. Therefore, the period of 1955 through 1964 appeared to be appropriate for evaluating the long-term trend performance of the Moody's Average.

However, it would be highly inappropriate to consider the percentage improvement in earnings between 1958 (or 1961) and 1964 as a growth performance, because the base year would then be a recession period quite different in its economic characteristics from the prosperous terminal year. More refined statistical techniques, such as a least-squares trend line, are sometimes used by professional analysts to isolate the

TABLE 13–2

Condensed Compound-Interest Table: 3 to 25% Rates

Years	3%	4%	5%	6%	7%	8%	9%	10%	12%	14%	16%	20%	25%
1	1.03000	1.04000	1.05000	1.06000	1.07000	1.08000	1.09000	1.10000	1.12000	1.14000	1.16000	1.20000	1.25000
2	1.06090	1.08160	1.10250	1.12360	1.14490	1.16640	1.18810	1.21000	1.25440	1.29960	1.34560	1.44000	1.56250
3	1.09273	1.12486	1.15762	1.19102	1.22504	1.25971	1.29503	1.33100	1.40493	1.48154	1.56090	1.72800	1.95313
4	1.12551	1.16986	1.21551	1.26248	1.31080	1.36049	1.41158	1.46410	1.57352	1.68896	1.81064	2.07360	2.44141
5	1.15927	1.21665	1.27628	1.33823	1.40255	1.46933	1.53862	1.61051	1.76234	1.92541	2.10034	2.48832	3.05176
6	1.19405	1.26532	1.34010	1.41852	1.50073	1.58687	1.67710	1.77156	1.97382	2.19497	2.43640	2.98598	3.81470
7	1.22987	1.31593	1.40710	1.50363	1.60578	1.71382	1.82804	1.94872	2.21068	2.50227	2.82622	3.58318	4.76837
8	1.26677	1.36857	1.47746	1.59385	1.71819	1.85093	1.99256	2.14359	2.47596	2.85259	3.27841	4.29982	5.96046
9	1.30477	1.42331	1.55133	1.68948	1.83846	1.99900	2.17189	2.35795	2.77308	3.25195	3.80296	5.15978	7.45058
10	1.34392	1.48024	1.62889	1.79085	1.96715	2.15892	2.36736	2.59374	3.10585	3.70722	4.41144	6.19174	9.31323
11	1.38423	1.53945	1.71034	1.89830	2.10485	2.33164	2.58043	2.85312	3.47855	4.22623	5.11726	7.43008	11.64153
12	1.42576	1.60103	1.79586	2.01220	2.25219	2.51817	2.81266	3.13843	3.89598	4.81790	5.93603	8.91610	14.55192
13	1.46853	1.66507	1.88565	2.13293	2.40984	2.71962	3.06580	3.45227	4.36349	5.49241	6.88579	10.69932	18.18989
14	1.51259	1.73168	1.97993	2.26090	2.57853	2.93719	3.34173	3.79750	4.88711	6.26135	7.98752	12.83918	22.73737
15	1.55797	1.80094	2.07893	2.39656	2.75903	3.17217	3.64248	4.17725	5.47357	7.13794	9.26552	15.40702	28.42171
16	1.60471	1.87298	2.18287	2.54035	2.95216	3.42594	3.97031	4.59497	6.13039	8.13725	10.74800	18.48843	35.52714
17	1.65285	1.94790	2.29202	2.69277	3.15882	3.70002	4.32763	5.05447	6.86604	9.27646	12.46768	22.18611	44.40892
18	1.70243	2.02582	2.40662	2.85434	3.37993	3.99602	4.71712	5.55992	7.68997	10.57517	14.46251	26.62333	55.51115
19	1.75351	2.10685	2.52695	3.02560	3.61653	4.31570	5.14166	6.11591	8.61276	12.05569	16.77652	31.94800	69.38894
20	1.80611	2.19112	2.65330	3.20714	3.86968	4.66096	5.60441	6.72750	9.64629	13.74349	19.46076	38.33760	86.73617

trend from interim variations, but the effort involved in these procedures seems excessive when it is realized that the data are only a rough clue to the future.

These data clearly suggest that corporate earnings growth is not likely to be a continuous affair. The failure of earnings to recover to their 1955 levels until 1962 suggests that economic problems may inhibit growth for periods up to several years. Therefore, for the majority of companies, and for cyclically vulnerable situations in particular, it would seem prudent not to expect a consistent rate of growth but only a potential long-term rate that will proceed at an irregular pace from year to year. One great virtue of stability, such as is witnessed for the electric power utilities, is that their growth is less dependent upon the cyclical fortunes of the economy during intermediate periods of several years in duration.

Measurement of Growth: Annual Compound Rates

Use of Compound-Interest Tables. Assuming that appropriate base and terminal years are selected so that the earnings increase seems representative of long-term growth rather than cyclical recovery, then a rapid computation followed by reference to a compound interest table will measure the annual compounded growth rate for the period. Dividing the earnings per share of the base year into the earnings per share of the terminal year converts the growth into a ratio which in effect shows the increase applicable to $1 of earnings in the base year. For example, the earnings in 1955 on the Moody's Industrial Average were $10.51 and were estimated at $14.50 for 1964. Dividing the $10.51 into $14.50 resulted in a ratio of 1.38, or in other words, each dollar of earnings in 1955 had grown to $1.38 over the nine-year period ended with 1964.[2]

The compound annual rate of growth associated with $1 becoming $1.38 over a nine-year period can be estimated from a condensed compound interest table (Table 13-2). For nine years, 1.38 falls between 3% (1.3048) and 4% (1.4233), although slightly closer to 4%, so a reasonable estimate of the compound annual growth rate realized on the Moody's Industrial Average between 1955 and 1964 would be about

[2] In simple mathematical terms it can be expressed as follows:

$$\frac{14.50}{10.51} = X = 10.51X = 14.50 \text{ and } X = 1.38.$$

3.6%.[3] It should be emphasized again, however, that although this growth rate is useful as a rough long-term estimation of the average annual growth potential (assuming no drastic change in the structure of the economy), for periods of several years or more the actual realized growth rates may be considerably different than the long-term average. Because American economic history has been characterized by inconsistent rates of short-term growth, considerable caution would seem advisable with respect to projections based on experience of a few years.

Use of Rate of Return and Dividend Payout. Although the compound interest method of determining the past growth rate has the great virtue of being easy to compute, it does not point up the dynamic financial process which has produced growth in the majority of large industrial companies. By and large these companies have financed a large proportion of this expansion internally or in other words have used the capital markets infrequently. Under these conditions, the financial process of growth can be considered to be a function of the rate of return obtained on the common equity and the proportion of earnings retained in the business.

For example, if a company earns a constant 10% on its net worth, there will be $1 of earnings per share for every $10 of book value per share. If the company retained all its earnings, then book value would grow by 10% annually and at a constant rate of return, earnings per share would also grow by 10% annually. However, complete retention of earnings is not probable; if 50% of the earnings were distributed in dividends, then book value would increase by 5% annually and earnings would grow, again assuming a constant rate of return of 10%, at the same rate as the annual increase in book value (5%).[4]

The formal relationship between these two variables which will re-

---

[3] The following interpolation method may be used:

    1.4233 less 1.3048 = .1175 = 1%
    1.38   less 1.3048 = .0732 = X
    X = .0732 ÷ .1175 = .6

[4] The assumption that increases in per share book values are entirely a function of retained earnings seems valid for most large industrial companies. Minor influences can be cited which modify this assumption, such as nonrecurring gains and losses outside of the earnings stream. More importantly, the issuance of new shares at prices above or below existing book value may affect the growth rate. This factor is particularly important in public utilities which have recurring capital needs beyond the amounts available from retained earnings. Therefore, in the chapter on public utilities the effects on the growth rate of the sale of new shares are considered specifically, and the several variables in such sales which react on the growth rate are discussed.

flect the growth rate over a period of time can be expressed in the formula $Rg = Re (1 - PO)$, where Rg = rate of growth in earnings per share; Re = rate of return on book value per share; PO = percentage of earnings distributed in dividends (payout ratio).[5]

Unfortunately, in most cases the rate of return on the common-stock equity does not remain constant over a period of years. Therefore, there are often several alternative rates which might be extracted from the past record as possible evidence of the future potential. One is the average rate that has been obtained over the entire period. For example, Table 13-1 showed that annual earnings as a percentage of the year-end book value of the Moody's Industrial Stock Average have varied between 15.4% in 1955 and 10.2% in 1958, with an average for the entire period of 12.3%. Use of the average rate of return would be based on the theory that it was obtained over a significant span of years, which includes both prosperous and recession years, and therefore would be the best evidence of the average future potential.

However, the average rate of return does not take account of any trend which may have been shown during the period. In the case of the Moody's Stock Average, there was evidence of a modest downward trend in the rate of return during the 1955–64 period. (In 1955–56 the companies constituting the average earned about 14.8% on the common equity as compared to 12.8% for 1963–64.) The decline in the rate of return may have reflected either of two possibilities: (1) the earnings rate obtained on the additional assets represented by the successive increments to book values (by retained earnings) was lower than that on the existing asset structures, (2) the rate of earnings on both new and old assets declined to some extent from prior levels. Without recourse to the details of divisional and project earnings, one would not be able to decide which possibility was in fact correct. But in either case the investment results were the same; the rate of return obtained on retained earnings for that period and the actual rate of earnings growth were actually (and might continue to be) less than that suggested by the average rate of return on net worth.

Recognition of the trend can be achieved by computing the rate of return as follows: divide the total increase in earnings (between 1955 and 1964) by the total addition to book value per share. Book value per share of the Moody's Average increased from $68.40 to an estimated $107, or by $38.60, whereas earnings increased by $3.99. During these

---

[5] This formula was originally expressed in H. C. Sauvain, "Common Prices in the Sixties," *Business Horizons,* Bloomington, Indiana. Indiana University, Fall, 1960, p. 36.

years, therefore, reinvested earnings were actually employed at a 10.3% rate of return ($3.99 divided by $38.60).[6] This rate, is might be noted, was significantly below the 12.3% average return on total equity for these years.

With an estimated dividend payout of earnings of 60% (slightly above the 1955–64 average), the earnings growth rate of the Moody's Average would then be computed as follows: rate of growth = 10.3% (1 − 60%) = 10.3 times .4 = 4.12%. As an alternative, the 12.3% average rate of return might be used which would suggest a possible growth rate of 4.92%. Use of this rate of return, however, would imply that successive increments to net worth will in the future generate somewhat larger increases in earnings per share than were achieved in the 1955–64 period. Although it may be possible, it would require a more favorable operating environment for industrial corporations than in these years of reasonably favorable economic conditions.

Because there are factors affecting book values other than retained earnings, such as new stock issues and unusual gains or losses, the growth-rate computation based on the financial factors differs modestly from that obtained by using compound-interest tables. But as the purpose of the computations was to obtain rough clues to the future potential, there would be little point in attempting to achieve an arithmetic reconciliation. Instead, the results from both methods might be used to suggest a spectrum of possibilities; in short, under conditions similar to 1955–64 the growth rate on the Moody's Average might well range from 3.6 to 4.5%.

Growth Rates: Analysis of Causation

Cause of Growth: Balanced Increase in Sales and Earnings. Although techniques for isolating and measuring the past rate of growth are obviously essential, it would seem equally essential to appraise the dynamic trends shown by a series of financial statements. The purpose is to obtain some insight into the possible reasons for the indicated rate of growth and from an interpretation of these reasons to evaluate whether the probabilities indicate a different *future* potential than that shown in the past. Although the qualitative conclusions on a company

[6] In terms of economic theory, this rate of return may be defined as the marginal rate of return as it reflects the increments to earnings which can be associated with increments to net worth.

are relevant to such an evaluation, the performance trends revealed by the significant items on the income statement are usually of primary importance. Several alternatives may be indicated with respect to the performance trends. First, the optimum situation would be roughly balanced increases in all the pertinent data that are related to the increase in per share earnings.

Under these conditions, as book value per share increased, there would have been proportionate increases in sales and costs; in other words, the turnover of net worth (sales per dollar of book value) and profit margins would have been reasonably constant. The result should have been a fairly constant rate of return on the equity, and as a consequence, only a modest difference between the average and marginal rates of return. Preferably cyclical fluctuations in sales and profit margins should also have been modest, but this factor would not be essential, assuming that the beginning and terminal years represented roughly the same general level of economic conditions. The computed growth rates would then seem more assured, because the data would not reflect disparate trends in the causative factors that may not be repeated in future years. However, in a dynamic economy the normal expectation is that companies will change their financial and operating characteristics to some extent over long periods of time. Therefore, it is doubtful if any company can show a completely balanced rate of growth in book values, sales, profit margins, and earnings. But at the same time, if such a performance can even be reasonably approximated, there is usually more reason to have confidence in the continuation of the indicated growth rate.

Example. Table 13–3 shows the operating pattern for Chas. Pfizer and Co., a leading ethical drug manufacturer and distributor, for the years 1955–64. In this instance sales increased at a reasonably consistent rate with 1964 sales about 2.9 times the level of 1955. Because profit margins remained fairly constant, total net earnings available to the common stock increased proportionately to sales. Therefore, unless some serious qualitative problems concerning continued sales growth faced the ethical drug industry and this company in particular, continued increases in total sales and earnings appeared probable at about the same rate.

However, the growth rates in earnings per share and book value per share were moderately lower than for total sales and earnings. In this respect, therefore, the rates of change in the essential financial factors

TABLE 13–3

Selected Financial Data: Chas. Pfizer & Co.

	Sales (in millions)	Net Income (in millions)	Percentage of Net Income to Sales	Per Share Earnings	Per Share Book Value	Per Share Return	Payout Ratio
1955	$163.8	$15.3	9.4%	$ .98	$ 5.80	16.9%	52%
1956	178.3	18.3	10.2	1.12	6.75	16.7	50
1957	207.2	22.9	11.1	1.41	7.48	18.8	50
1958	222.7	24.0	10.8	1.48	8.19	18.0	51
1959	253.7	24.8	9.8	1.51	9.10	16.6	53
1960	289.8	28.3	9.7	1.57	9.85	16.0	51
1961	332.5	32.7	9.8	1.74	11.37	15.3	49
1962	386.2	36.8	9.5	1.92	12.24	15.7	49
1963	414.3	40.3	9.7	2.07	12.75	16.3	51
1964	480.0	44.7	9.3	2.27	13.80	16.4	55
1964/1955	2.92	2.92	—	2.316	2.37		
1955–64 average						16.7%	51%
Increase in book value 1955–64					$ 8.00		
Increase in earnings 1955–64				$1.29			
Increase in earnings to increase in book value						16.1%	

Growth-rate computations:

Marginal rate of return: 16.1% (1–51%) = 7.9%

Average rate of return: 16.7 (1–51%) = 8.2%

Compound interest method: 2.316 for nine years = 9.7% (Table 13–2) were not absolutely proportionate. But in a growth situation some disparity can be expected. The lower rate of growth in per share earnings than in total earnings indicated that retained earnings did not entirely finance the growth in sales, but that additional shares also were issued to a moderate extent.[7] As a matter of fact, the increase in the total book value of the common equity (number of shares times book value per share) was about 3.2 times, or actually exceeded the growth in sales.

It would be logical to presume that future financial policies will also involve some additional modest increments in the number of outstanding shares. If so, then the growth rate in earnings per share might continue to be less than for total sales and earnings. However, in a sense the indicated need for equity capital in excess of that provided by retained earnings may be interpreted as a favorable indication. It suggests that the opportunities for profitable investment of capital (including retained earnings) have been considerable.

On balance, therefore, an analysis of the several pertinent income statement items of Pfizer for the 1955–64 period did not yield any significant evidence that the past rate of return on equity capital overstated the future potential. Therefore, a spectrum of possible growth rates seemed reasonable based on the average and marginal rates of return and the compound-interest method applied to per share earnings. In other words, a growth rate of between 8% and 9.5% in per share earnings appeared possible based on the quantitative evidence for the years 1955–64.

Cause of Growth: Wider Profit Margins. In some cases it might be found that the growth in earnings had exceeded that of sales revenues. Such a divergence could result only from an increase in profit margins—in other words, a reduction in the proportion of each sales dollar absorbed by operating expenses and other deductions from gross income. Under these circumstances, although the company's management may deserve a commendation for its improved efficiency, that portion of the earnings growth obtained from the increase in profit margins may be difficult to duplicate in the future. The reason is basically one of common

[7] In this instance over one million new shares were issued to acquire other companies whose sales and earnings were then consolidated into the company. When there have been several mergers of this kind, the total figures for sales and earnings may be considered less significant as an indication of the future growth potential of the company because they would assume a continuation of acquisitions.

TABLE 13-4
SELECTED FINANCIAL DATA: MUNSINGWEAR INC.

	Sales (in millions)	Net Income (in millions)	Total Common Equity* (in millions)	Percentage of Net Income to Sales	Per Share Earnings	Per Share Book Value*	Rate of Return	Payout Ratio
1955	$28.6	$ .75	$10.4	2.6%	$ .90	$14.30	6.3%	65%
1956	27.7	.65	10.6	2.3	.76	14.60	5.2	80
1957	33.1	1.14	10.8	3.4	1.43	14.70	9.8	43
1958	37.7	1.36	11.4	3.6	1.70	15.50	11.1	35
1959	43.8	1.61	12.3	3.7	2.01	16.50	12.4	41
1960	44.7	1.65	13.3	3.7	2.06	17.50	11.8	46
1961	46.8	1.70	14.2	3.6	2.10	18.60	11.5	48
1962	49.7	2.15	15.3	4.3	2.62	19.70	13.6	40
1963	51.9	2.24	17.1	4.3	2.69	21.50	13.1	41
1964	57.4	2.85	19.1	4.9	3.28	23.00	14.3	37
1964/1955	2.0	3.8	1.9	—	3.64	1.6		
Average, 1955–64							10.9%	48%
Increase in book value, 1955–64						$ 8.70		
Increase in earnings, 1955–64					$2.38			
Rate of return on increase in book value ($2.38 ÷ 8.70)							27.3%	

Growth-rate computations:
Marginal rate of return: 27.3% (1–.48) = 14.2%
Average rate of return: 10.9 (1–.48) = 5.7%
Compound-interest method:
Earnings per share: 3.64, nine years = 15.6%
Sales revenues: 2.0, nine years = 8.1%

* Beginning of year.

sense: cost reductions, or alternatively, price increases greater than cost increases, cannot usually be continued indefinitely in a competitive economy. Ultimately expenses should reach a basic minimum level or competitive forces preclude additional price increases.

Example. Munsingwear, Inc., manufactures a diversified line of apparel products with emphasis on lingerie and sports clothing. The financial record of this company for the 1955–64 period is shown in Table 13-4. It is quite evident from these data that the company enjoyed an exceptional growth in earnings during this period; the more than threefold increase in earnings per share is well in excess of that obtained by industrial companies in general as evidenced by the Moody's Stock Average. A significant proportion of the growth, however, was because of an increase in the profit margin from 2.6% in 1955 to 4.9% in 1964, as the growth in sales was substantially less than the growth in earnings per share. The rapid growth in earnings also produced a significant improvement in the rate of return on equity, with the result that the indicated marginal rate of return (increase in per share earnings related to the increase in per share book value) was an astounding 27%.

Because a continuation of the same rate of improvement in profit margins hardly seemed to be a realistic expectation, it seemed quite doubtful if the growth rates computed by the compound-interest method applied to earnings per share or by the marginal rate of return had much significance as an indication of the future potential. The more logical alternatives were to compute a range of possible growth rates from the compound-interest method applied to sales and the rate-of-return method applied to the average rate. The consequent indicated growth rates of between about 6% to 8% were based on the view that long-term repetitive increases in profit margins were unlikely; instead the average profit margins realized in the past seemed more likely to indicate future long-term conditions.

Sales Growth: Reduced Profit Margins. But increased profit margins were rather unusual during the 1955–64 period. In fact, that data on the Moody's Industrial Stock Average suggested that average profit margins narrowed slightly, because they showed that sales for a broad group of industrial companies increased by 45%, whereas earnings advanced by only about 38%. Under these conditions a conservative expression of the growth-rate potential should be obtained from either (1) the compound-interest method applied to earnings per share, or (2) the

TABLE 13–5
SELECTED FINANCIAL DATA: J. C. PENNEY COMPANY

Year*	Sales (in millions)	Net Income (in millions)	Net Income to Sales	Per Share Earnings	Per Share Book Value	Rate of Return	Payout Ratio
1955	$1,220.1	$46.14	3.8%	$1.87	$10.00	18.7%	70%
1956	1,291.9	46.78	3.6	1.89	10.50	18.0	75
1957	1,312.3	49.41	3.8	2.00	11.10	18.2	71
1958	1,410.0	46.88	3.3	1.90	11.70	16.2	75
1959	1,437.5	51.52	3.6	2.09	12.40	16.0	68
1960	1,468.9	44.99	3.1	1.82	12.80	14.2	82
1961	1,553.5	51.74	3.3	2.10	13.30	15.8	71
1962	1,701.3	54.80	3.2	2.20	14.20	15.5	68
1963	1,834.3	55.29	3.0	2.22	15.10	14.8	68
1964	2,079.9	68.27	3.3	2.74	16.10	17.0	65
1964/55	1.70	1.48	–	1.44	1.61	–	–
1955/64 average	–	–	3.4	–	–	16.5%	71%
1958–64 average	–	–	3.2	–	–	15.7	70

Increase in book value, 1955–64

Increase in earnings, 1955–64 = $ .87 $ 6.10

Earnings increase to increase in book value = 13.3%

Growth rate computations:
Average rate of return, 1958–64 = 15.7% (1–.70) = 4.7%
Marginal rate of return = 13.3% (1–.70) = 4.0%

Compound interest method:
Sales, 1.70 for nine years = 6.1%
Per share earnings, 1.44 for nine years = 4.1%

* Fiscal year ended January 31 of following year.

marginal rate-of-return method. Use of either would imply that the pressure on profit margins might continue or alternatively, that the company must settle for a reduced growth rate in sales in order to inhibit a further decline in margins.

On the other hand, the expression of the growth rate through the sales performance would imply that the sales would continue to grow at the same rate, the profit-margin erosion would cease, and the capital needed to finance the future growth in sales could be obtained without diluting the position of the common stock (or in other words, without issuing more common shares). As a compromise, the average rate of return on the equity for a period of both high and low margins might be used to estimate the future growth-rate potential. The implicit assumption would be that continued variations in profit margins will take place rather than a continuation of the downward trend and that sales growth will proceed at about the same rate.

Example. Table 13-5 shows selected financial data for the J. C. Penney Company, a nationwide department-store chain, for the decade of 1955–64. In 1955 the company enjoyed a net profit margin of 3.8%, which in comparison with most manufacturing firms was quite low. But as is characteristic of large retail chains, annual sales amounted to 4.9 times equity capital, with the result that the rate of return on the stock equity was a quite respectable 18.7% (3.8% x 4.9).

However, although the equity turnover remained reasonably constant at slightly less than five times, profit margins declined to average levels of about 3.2% for the years 1958–64. In absolute terms, the decline of .6% did not appear serious, but it represented a percentage erosion of about 16% in the profit margin. As a result, the rate of return on the equity dropped to approximately 15.7% for the 1958–64 period as contrasted to 16.5% for the entire 1955–64 period. The result also was that the indicated marginal rate of return on reinvested earnings was about 13.3%.

The annual compound growth rate in per share earnings, computed from the compound-interest table, turned out to be 4.1% as compared to an annual growth rate in sales of 6.1%. As a range of the potential growth rates, these percentages may be of some use. But a more reasonable approximation might be obtained from the 1958–64 average rate of return on the equity of 15.7%, when profit margins averaged close to their 1964 levels. Using the 15.7% rate of return and an expected payout ratio of 70%, a growth rate of about 4.7% could be estimated. This rate would suggest that if profit margins fluctuate around 3.0% to 3.3%, retained earnings would probably yield an earnings return of between 15% and 16% on the average. Therefore, the long-term financial data on the J. C. Penney Company as of 1965 indicated a range of potential growth rates of between 4.0% and 6.0% with perhaps about 5% as a compromise figure.

Growth Evaluation: Extreme Cases. It should be clear from these illustrations that several dynamic elements affect the rate of return on the equity and the related growth rate in earnings per share. In summary, they are (1) the rate of growth in sales, (2) variations and trends in profit margins, (3) the ability of the company to finance the growth without issuing new shares, (4) the ratio of sales per share to book value per share, and (5) the dividend policy as reflected in the level and trend of the payout ratio. In some cases the trends or levels of these elements show evidence of remaining fairly constant. As a result, a reasonable approximation of the growth-rate potential appears to be possible. In more numerous instances, one or more of these elements moves in such a way that the interpretation of growth rates computed from the past record becomes a problem. At best under these conditions, a range of potential growth rates can be computed, as was done for J. C. Penney and Munsingwear. However, these have a definite value to the investor, as they suggest the spectrum of possible growth in earnings per share and thus greatly contribute to a decision on the comparative attractiveness of these common stocks.

However, there are those cases where the past record has shown such extreme changes that it becomes very difficult to estimate even a range for prospective growth in earnings per share. On the one hand, the changes may have been adverse. Then unless supplementary information indicates a probable reversal, it can only be concluded that a growth factor does not apply to the company. Indeed in extreme cases the adverse trends may suggest that the risk of continued adversity should completely eliminate its consideration for investment purposes. On the other hand, the variables may have shown such a rapid upward trend, especially in unseasoned companies, that projecting the past trends and the consequent growth rate on a geometric basis (percentage rate of change) would result in a modest-sized company exceeding the size of General Motors within a decade. As such extreme growth rates have always moderated, reasonable prudence would suggest that it would be highly questionable to project the past indicated growth rate very far into the future.

Examples. In 1955 Borg-Warner Corporation, a diversified producer of auto parts and durable appliance products, showed sales revenues of $552.2 million, net earnings of $41.1 million, and earnings per share of $5.17. In 1964, sales were $719.2 million, net earnings were $41.8 million, and earnings per share had decreased to $4.64. Thus although sales increased modestly, a decline in profit margins and an increase in the number of shares outstanding had resulted in significant reduction in per share earnings over the entire period. In the interim years, earnings had fluctuated erratically between $4.36 per share in 1959 to $2.34 in 1958. Considerable sensitivity to changes in the level of business conditions was thus indicated, and even using 1956 or 1959 as base years resulted in no apparent growth trend through 1964.

The quantitative record of Borg-Warner, therefore, did not provide any tangible basis for computing even a spectrum of potential long-term growth rates for per share earnings. A similar performance, it may be added, typified the record of many producers of durable products or their components; many of the leading steel and aluminum companies, for example. Prospective long-term growth under these conditions becomes essentially a qualitative conjecture, and as such, should be heavily discounted in appraising the values of the related common stocks. At the same time, the absence of growth does not support a conclusion that companies such as Borg-Warner are necessarily unattractive for long-term investment. The possibility remains of acquiring the indicated earning power without any growth at a favorable price (a low price-earnings ratio). In short, it is possible for a common stock to be attractive for some investment purposes at a zero growth rate.

At the other extreme, the dramatic performance of Xerox Corporation can be cited. This company produces machines for the rapid duplication of all kinds of paper records without special mats or developing processes, and it has become the leading source of copy service in all areas of paperwork systems such as engineering prints and office documents. Rapid market acceptance of its new technology for document reproduction produced a fantastic growth over the 1955–64 period, as shown in Table 13-6. (Even more impressively in some respects, the growth rate actually accelerated slightly in the last half of the period.) Sales increased by more than twelve times from their 1955 levels. Moreover, profit margins advanced also, with the result that net income increased by more than thirty-two times. Earnings per share increased at a less rapid rate than total net income because of a persistent increase (about 40%) in the number of outstanding shares. Even so the percentage rate of growth in all respects was clearly phenomenal.

TABLE 13–6
SELECTED FINANCIAL DATA: XEROX CORPORATION

	Sales (in millions)	Net Income (in millions)	Book Value per Share	Earnings per Share	Rate of Return	Payout Ratio
1955	$ 21.4	$ 1.2	$ .52	$ .08	14.6%	37%
1956	23.6	1.3	.69	.08	11.8	50
1957	25.8	1.5	.77	.09	11.9	44
1958	27.6	1.6	.89	.10	11.1	40
1959	33.3	2.1	1.05	.12	11.7	33
1960	40.2	2.6	1.56	.13	8.9	38
1961	66.2	5.7	1.79	.28	15.8	22
1962	115.2	13.9	2.50	.71	28.5	20
1963	176.0	23.0	4.19	1.13	27.0	22
1964	268.0	38.5	6.00	1.88	31.2	21
1964/55	12.5	32.1		23.5		
1964/60	6.7	14.8		14.4		
1962–64 average					28.9%	21%

The inherent problem in a case of this kind is that by virtue of its own success the company changed its nature entirely from a relatively small operation to one of comparatively large size. As a result, future increases in sales and earnings must be continuously greater in absolute amounts to maintain the same percentage rate of growth. Typically, it may be presumed that ultimately the rate of growth must diminish in such a situation. The Xerox data may be used to illustrate the point. Over the past ten-year period, sales and earnings increased in the absolute amounts of about $220 million and $35 million, respectively. Similar *absolute* increases in the future would result in a percentage growth of less than 100%; to achieve the same *percentage* rate of growth in the following decade would require absolute increases in sales and earnings of about $2.4 billion and $950 million, respectively. The scope of the market for products of this type hardly makes such increases probable; also in these situations competitive forces have a tendency to become more intense.

Certainly the past record of Xerox as of 1965 indicated a very favorable prognosis for continued growth, but to find a logical basis for expressing the prospective rate in quantitative terms was quite difficult.[8]

---

[8] Because the available compound interest tables do not go beyond a 25% growth rate (a ratio of 5.16 to 1 for nine years), the growth rate in earnings per share applicable to the Xerox ratio of 23.5 cannot even be computed. As a guess, it looks like it might have been between 60% and 80% per annum.

However, assuming the average rate of return realized in the 1962–64 period (29%) could be continued for several years and assuming the payout ratio remains at about 21%, the application of the rate of return method would yield a growth rate of about 23% [29% (1 — .21)]. These assumptions, of course, could be very wide of the mark, but any alternatives appear equally problematical.

SELECTION OF
CORPORATE SECURITIES

PART III

SELECTION OF
CORPORATE SECURITIES

CHAPTER 14

Selection of
Common Stocks

Approach to Selection Process

Quality Determinants. In the preceding several chapters attention
has been directed at the means of obtaining clues to the desirability of
an industry and company for investment purposes. The investigation
should have led to conclusions along the following lines:

1. Economic characteristics of products and costs.
2. Competitive position in the industry and the economy.
3. Capacity of management.
4. Soundness of financial policies.
5. Potential growth rates in earnings and dividends per share (if any).

These elements can be regarded as the essential determinants of overall
investment quality. In short, they indicate whether a company should
be classified as a "blue chip" or a "leading" firm or should be down-
graded to a lesser ranking for one reason or another. For example, such
industrial giants as Texaco, General Motors, and General Electric are
generally conceded to represent top-flight investment quality. As a matter of fact, because their quality features are clearly superior on practically every count, data on these companies are not particularly useful
analytical problems.

Of the several companies used to illustrate various appraisal techniques in the preceding chapters, perhaps only Merck, Pfizer, and J. C. Penney could be rated, as of 1965, close to blue-chip quality. Xerox lacked a long-term seasoned record and, therefore, its vulnerability to adversity had not been tested. (However, if its remarkable growth rate were to continue, it might well achieve such a rating within a few years.) Georgia-Pacific had a top-heavy debt structure; the steel companies and Borg-Warner had shown erratic and below-average growth rates; finally, despite its favorable growth record, Munsingwear occupied a modest role as a specialty producer in the textile industry.

Subjective Judgments Required. It is inevitable that the assignment of investment-quality ratings to companies involves subjective judgments about the comparative importance of the favorable and unfavorable qualitative and quantitative evidence. These judgments are inherent in a selection process which of necessity requires some conclusions on the possible future performances in a dynamic economy. Because such judgments are necessary, there is one extreme view that it is undesirable to evaluate equities in quantitative terms and that decisions should be based purely on the general quality conclusions.[1] At the other extreme, there is the view that common stocks should be selected through the application of highly precise present-value mathematical formulas, in which subjective decisions are presumably replaced by the "scientific" procedures of mathematical logic.[2] It is found, however, that subjective decisions translated into quantitative terms are invariably required in the application of these formulas. These decisions include such matters as the duration of growth rates, the choice of appropriate discount rates, and "normal" market capitalization rates for earnings and dividends of common stocks.[3]

The controversy between the qualitative approach and the scientific

[1] Bell, "Compound Interest and Annuity Tables and Their Use in Equity Valuation," *Financial Analysts Journal*, May–June, 1964, p. 115.

[2] See, for example, Burrell, "A Mathematical Approach to Growth Stock Valuation," *Financial Analysts Journal*, May, 1960, pp. 69–76.

[3] An excellent comparative discussion of the various mathematical approaches incorporating present-value theory and other mathematical techniques to stock valuations can be found in Paul F. Wendt, "Current Growth Stock Valuation Methods," *Financial Analysts Journal*, March–April, 1965, pp. 91–101. Professor Wendt concludes as follows: "It is apparent that widely different values can be assigned to growth stocks by varying the assumptions concerning future growth rates and duration of growth and by applying different discount rates to future dividend returns." (pp. 99–100). In short, the subjective decisions remain highly significant in the determination of stock values even where it appears that precise mathematical logic is being applied.

or mathematical approach will undoubtedly continue indefinitely. However, a compromise would seem practical and desirable. A compromise position would first accept the view that subjective decisions are required to establish the general investment-quality rating of a company within a broad comparative spectrum. Basically the subjective quality rating might represent a consensus "confidence factor" as to whether the firm (and perhaps its industry) will be able to meet successfully the challenges of future economic problems, take advantage of future opportunities, and continue to show the same rate of progress as in the past with the minimum of interim variations.

But in addition, the compromise approach would take the view that the quantitative data on the past and projected per share earnings and dividends represent the only tangible expression of the prospective value elements that are embodied in a common stock. In short, it would hold that investment decisions should not be predicated solely on quality conclusions (for example, General Electric is a top-flight company so purchase the stock) or on the basis of set formulas which incorporate rigid subjective decisions and static "norm" concepts either explicitly or by inference. Rather, it is held that a selection decision includes several dimensions: (1) the estimated size of the value elements as ratios of the price, (2) a comparison of these ratios with alternatives available in the securities market at the time, and (3) an explicit decision as to whether the comparative ratios are favorable or unfavorable in view of the quality rating assigned to the company under consideration.

The Probability Approach. Because it is necessary to make subjective decisions about future potentials, the selection of common stocks inherently is subject to considerable uncertainties. It is only realistic to admit that rational appraisals may not yield satisfactory investment results. Some unexpected development might occur in the future that would reduce the level of profit expectation. And it is entirely possible that such an event would leave the position of the senior securities undisturbed. They might retain their investment standing because even a lower level of earnings would still be adequate in relation to the claims of the senior issues. On the other hand, unanticipated events can also be highly favorable and greatly increase the earning power and resultant value of a common stock.

To a considerable extent much of the greater "risk" traditionally associated with common stocks as an investment medium may be traced to this fact. It is implied in many analyses which purport to differentiate between "conservative" and "speculative" common stocks. For instance, when the earnings of a company seem to be relatively impervious to cyclical or technological developments within the economy (the basic food companies are examples), then, unless inadequate management or financing exists, the common stock is likely to be characterized as "conservative" or "investment grade." On the other hand, when a company is likely to experience substantial variations in its earnings in response to changing levels of business activity, its stock is quite often labeled "speculative," although it may have shown good average earnings over a number of years. Because there is no other plausible explanation, the real source of the "speculative risk" in the latter case seems to boil down to the inherent difficulty of predicting the future earnings and dividend performance with any degree of confidence.

But in spite of the lack of preciseness which inherently surrounds the selection of common stocks, it is not wise to exaggerate the problem and thereby lose perspective. Some indication of comparative value, even if tenuous, is usually better than a completely uncritical acceptance of market price. Experience has shown that commitments which are made regardless of price may prove to be unsuccessful long-term investments. And it should be evident that one cannot evaluate common-stock prices unless some attempt is made to determine their long-term values on a reasonably objective basis.

It may be of some help to observe that investment operations in common stocks can be related to the statistical concept of probabilities. Because their intrinsic nature makes their value depend upon quantities which are unsolvable (earnings and dividends in the future) it is only possible to express the merits of a given common stock in terms of the comparative probabilities. Where the probabilities seem to be in the investor's favor, overall results from a series of such investments should be favorable.

This observation suggests two points in the practical selection of common stocks for long-term investment. First, the decisions must be based on the apparent range of probabilities. Sometimes the probabilities seem fairly easy to determine, and sometimes they may be quite difficult. Experience and competence in appraisal techniques, however, should be of assistance in this task. Second, when stocks are not available at bargain prices, then an adequate diversification of commitments should be part of the investment strategy in the common-stock area. This is necessary because statistical theory shows that an adequate sample of cases is required in order to achieve the indicated probabilities. In other words, some stocks may inadvertently turn out to be worth less than the facts indicated at the time of analysis, but these results may be offset by the possibility that others will prove to be worth more.

Therefore, it does not seem reasonable to accept the conclusion that selection decisions involve such an excessive degree of intangible elements that it is desirable to place more emphasis on a technical study of the economy and the market as a whole. A knowledge of current trends in the market and in business conditions may be helpful in reaching a decision about whether the selection conclusions should be aggressively implemented. But the results of general market analysis, at least with respect to known techniques, have not been sufficiently consistent to recommend that common-stock investments should be largely predicated on forecasts for the market as a whole.

Quantitative Value Elements

For most common stocks it has been shown that the basic quantitative value elements are the prospective flow of earnings and dividends per share. Dividends of course represent the current income return, whereas retained earnings are an important means of financing the asset needs necessary to achieve growth in both dividends and earnings. The specific value elements, therefore, which are usually applicable to the selection of a common stock would usually be as follows:

1. The current level of earnings per share for companies demonstrating consistency in earnings.
2. The prevailing dividend rate both on a regular basis and with recent year-end "extras" (if any).
3. The average level of earnings per share over a complete cyclical swing for companies with erratic earnings records.
4. The projected earnings and dividends per share as indicated by the range of the computed growth rates for companies with a positive growth record.

As of 1965 these several elements are represented in Table 14-1 for the several companies considered in the preceding chapter, assuming the analyses of the potential growth rates were accepted as reasonable.

The current annual dividends and earnings represent the most recently reported actual or estimated data; estimates are particularly useful in the last half of a given year when results for the first six or nine months are available. Then projections of the remainder of the year can

TABLE 14-1
QUANTITATIVE VALUE ELEMENTS: EARNINGS AND DIVIDENDS PER SHARE

Company	Current Earnings (1964)	Average Earnings (1960–64)	Estimated Growth Rates	1965 Dividend Rate	
				Regular	Extra†
Chas. Pfizer and Co.	$ 2.27	Not applicable	8 to 9.5%	$1.00	$.25
Munsingwear	3.28	$ 2.55	6 to 8%	1.20	none
J. C. Penney	2.74	2.22	4 to 6%	1.50	.225
Borg-Warner	4.46	3.54	none	2.20	none
Xerox Corporation	1.88	Not applicable	20 to 25%	.50	none
Moody's Stock Average	$14.50	$11.45	3.5 to 4.5%	$8.22°	none

° Estimated by Moody's Stock Survey in April of 1965.
† Paid in 1964.

usually be made on the basis of the percentage of total annual earnings usually obtained in the latter part of a year.

Use of Value Elements: Comparative Selection Decisions

Use of Current Earnings and Dividends. As an indication of value, current dividends and earnings per share reflect the established dividend rate and the level of earning power that has actually been realized by the company as it now exists. The advantage of current dividends and earnings as value elements is that they represent the most recent tangible evidence of achievement derived from the past managerial policies of the company. In a very real sense, therefore, they constitute the established base from which future dynamic developments must take place. As a result, a *tentative* indication of the comparative attractiveness of common stocks can often be obtained from a comparison of their prices as ratios of current earnings and dividends. Similar ratios prevailing on common stocks in general, as reflected by data on a broad market average, are also useful as bench marks for measuring the status of a given stock. For example, Table 14-2 indicates that Munsingwear was available at a lower price-earnings ratio and a higher dividend yield than were prevailing in the general market as reflected by the Moody's Industrial Stock Average. As the stock had shown consistency of earnings and as the estimated range of the potential growth rate had been found to exceed that of the Moody's Average, on a *quantitative comparative basis,* the stock appeared clearly attractive.

TABLE 14-2
PRICE-EARNINGS RATIOS AND DIVIDEND YIELDS

Company	Stock Prices (April, 1965)	Price-Earnings Ratios		Dividend Yield	
		Current Earnings	Average Earnings	Regular Yield	Including Extra
Pfizer	$ 56	24.6	–	1.8%	2.3%
Munsingwear	39	11.9	15.3	3.1	–
J. C. Penney	70	25.5	31.8	2.1	2.5
Borg-Warner	51	11.3	14.5	4.4	–
Xerox	123	64.7	–	0.4	–
Moody's Stock Average	273	18.8	23.7	3.0	–

Final Decision Criteria. A final selection decision, however, would have depended upon (1) whether the overall quality of the company, based on an interpretation of the other pertinent qualitative and quantitative evidence, was adequate to recommend the stock for long-term investment, (2) the character and needs of the particular portfolio (income, aggressive or defensive), (3) a subjective evaluation of whether the lower price-earnings ratio and the superior growth-rate potential adequately compensated for any possible quality differential between Munsingwear's common stock and those represented by the Moody's Industrial Average.

At this point it might be useful to consider briefly a controversial issue: whether the decision criteria should also include a judgment on the prevailing attractiveness of the stock market in general for long-term investment. The position taken herein is that this factor should be regarded as pertinent to a decision on the appropriate investment strategy that should be followed at a given time (Chapter 5), and not to the selection process once a strategy decision has been made to seek out common stocks for long-term investment.

However, if selection decisions are considered properly oriented to *absolute* rather than *comparative* values, then it can be argued that individual stocks should be appraised in relation to an "appropriate market norm" rather than in relation to its prevailing level.[4] Historical

[4] For example, it has been suggested that historical precedents, adjusted for postwar developments in national economic policy, justify a "market norm" bench mark of 15 times current earnings on an appropriate market index of industrial stocks, and 13 times estimated average future earnings for a seven year period. This would mean using a rigid P/E ratio bench mark of 15 for current earnings rather than the 18.8 actually used as per Table 14-2. Graham, Dodd, and Cottle, *Security Analysis*, New York: McGraw-Hill, 1962, pp. 507–512.

precedents certainly suggest that the general market may reach over-valued levels in relation to corporate earnings and dividend prospects, and, therefore, the "norm" concept should be explicitly or implicitly considered at some point in the investment decision process. The issue is not the *need* to consider the general level of stock prices but *when* and *where* it should be considered: in the selection of individual stocks or in a strategy decision on the appropriate composition of the portfolio as between types of securities at a given time. Alternatively, the decision might relate to the proportion of new funds that should be committed to common stocks. Logically, it would seem that an evaluation of the existing level of the market would be more useful in the general portfolio strategy decision than in the decisions on individual stocks.

If this view is accepted, then once a conclusion is reached that *any* common stocks are currently needed for the portfolio the only appropriate bench marks become the alternative values available within the common-stock area at the time. And such alternative values may be at least roughly indicated by the price of a market index in relation to the earnings and dividends indicated thereon. To use a static maximum or normal level of the general market as a bench mark of value would imply alternative choices for common-stock selection decisions that might not in fact exist at the time.

Use of Average Earnings. Under certain conditions, the comparative quantitative values might be largely predicated on current earnings. To repeat, these conditions would be: (1) an indicated growth rate equal to or in excess of that estimated for the general market (Moody's, Standard and Poor's, or the Dow-Jones industrial indexes), (2) an earnings record marked by consistency of the upward trend: no interim declines of any magnitude for a decade or so, (1) the price in relation to current earnings and dividends produces a price-earnings ratio and dividend yield that compare favorably with those prevailing on the index. It may be noted that all these conditions were met by Munsingwear.

However, for the common stocks of the other companies whose earnings, dividend, and price data were shown in Tables 14-1 and 14-2, these conditions did not apply. The first two conditions were met by Pfizer, J. C. Penny, and Xerox, but in these cases the price-earnings ratios were markedly higher and the dividend yields lower than on the market index. Therefore, the decision problem that emerged on these stocks was whether the higher price-earnings ratios and lower yields were justified by the greater estimated growth potential. Alternative techniques to resolve this issue are considered later (pp. 230–38).

In contrast, Borg-Warner did not meet the first two conditions but it did meet the third. The price-earnings ratios of 11.3 (based on current earnings) and 14.5 (based on average earnings of 1960–64) were well below the 18.8 price-earnings ratio prevailing on the Moody's Industrial Average. In addition, its dividend yield of 4.4% based on the established dividend rate ($2.20 on price of $51) was well above the yield of 3% available on the average good-quality industrial common stocks. The stock, it may be noted, appeared particularly attractive in comparison to the Moody's Average on the basis of its current earnings price-earnings ratio of 11.3.

However, the earnings record had been marked by great sensitivity to even moderate fluctuations in business conditions, and partly as a consequence, there had been no measurable long-term growth of any significance. In view of these facts, average earnings over a complete cyclical swing seemed to be a more logical basis for an estimate of long-term earning power than current earnings of a highly prosperous year in the economy, such as 1964. In short, the erratic earnings record brought into serious question the ability of Borg-Warner to show average earnings equal to 1964 results.

On the other hand, the company had shown positive earnings of varying amounts throughout the entire previous decade, and there was no evidence of an actual secular decline. Therefore, although the pronounced volatility and the lack of growth were reasons to lower the subjective quality rating of the stock, they did not seem sufficient to warrant a conclusion that it was inherently unsuitable for long-term investment purposes. As the price-earnings ratio, based on average earnings, was below that prevailing on the Moody's Stock Average (using favorable 1964 earnings) and the dividend yield was well above average, compensation for the quality differential was obtainable. Therefore, income-oriented accounts requiring protection against possible future inflation might have been willing to consider the probable compensation sufficient to justify acquisition of the stock. However, as before, the decision should have included a subjective interpretation of the entire framework of qualitative and quantitative evidence (financial policies, management record, etc.).

Use of Projected Earnings. It is now pertinent to consider the vexing decision problems posed by common stocks of companies, such as

TABLE 14-3

PRICE-FUTURE EARNINGS RATIOS (PAYOUT PERIODS)

Price-Earnings Ratio (Current Earnings)	Estimated Annual Growth Rate of Earnings Per Share													
	1%	2%	3%	4%	5%	6%	7%	8%	9%	10%	12%	15%	20%	25%
12	11.4	10.9	10.4	10.0	9.6	9.3	9.0	8.7	8.5	8.3	7.9	7.4	6.7	6.2
13	12.3	11.7	11.1	10.7	10.3	9.9	9.6	9.3	9.0	8.7	8.3	7.7	7.0	6.5
14	13.2	12.5	11.9	11.3	10.9	10.5	10.1	9.8	9.5	9.2	8.7	8.1	7.3	6.7
15	14.0	13.2	12.6	12.0	11.5	11.0	10.6	10.2	9.9	9.6	9.1	8.4	7.6	7.0
16	14.9	14.0	13.3	12.6	12.0	11.5	11.1	10.7	10.4	10.0	9.5	8.8	7.9	7.2
17	15.8	14.8	13.9	13.2	12.6	12.1	11.6	11.2	10.8	10.4	9.8	9.1	8.1	7.4
18	16.6	15.5	14.6	13.8	13.2	12.6	12.1	11.6	11.2	10.8	10.2	9.4	8.4	7.6
19	17.5	16.3	15.3	14.4	13.7	13.1	12.5	12.0	11.6	11.2	10.5	9.6	8.6	7.8
20	18.3	17.0	15.9	15.0	14.2	13.5	12.9	12.4	11.9	11.5	10.8	9.9	8.8	8.0
21	19.2	17.7	16.5	15.5	14.7	14.0	13.4	12.8	12.3	11.9	11.1	10.2	9.0	8.2
22	20.0	18.4	17.1	16.1	15.2	14.4	13.8	13.2	12.7	12.2	11.4	10.4	9.2	8.4
23	20.8	19.1	17.8	16.6	15.7	14.9	14.2	13.6	13.0	12.5	11.7	10.7	9.4	8.6
24	21.6	19.8	18.3	17.2	16.2	15.3	14.6	13.9	13.4	12.8	12.0	10.9	9.6	8.7
25	22.4	20.5	18.9	17.7	16.6	15.7	15.0	14.3	13.7	13.1	12.2	11.1	9.8	8.9
26	23.2	21.1	19.5	18.2	17.1	16.1	15.3	14.6	14.0	13.4	12.5	11.4	10.0	9.0
27	24.0	21.8	20.1	18.7	17.5	16.5	15.7	15.0	14.3	13.7	12.7	11.6	10.2	9.2
28	24.8	22.5	20.6	19.2	17.9	16.9	16.0	15.3	14.6	14.0	13.0	11.8	10.4	9.3
29	25.6	23.1	21.2	19.6	18.4	17.3	16.4	15.6	14.9	14.3	13.2	12.0	10.5	9.5
30	26.4	23.7	21.7	20.1	18.8	17.7	16.7	15.9	15.2	14.5	13.5	12.2	10.7	9.6
32	27.9	25.0	22.8	21.0	19.6	18.4	17.4	16.5	15.7	15.1	13.9	12.6	11.0	9.8
34	29.4	26.2	23.8	21.9	20.4	19.1	18.0	17.1	16.3	15.5	14.3	12.9	11.3	10.1
36	30.9	27.4	24.8	22.7	21.1	19.7	18.6	17.6	16.8	16.0	14.7	13.3	11.5	10.3
38	32.4	28.5	25.7	23.6	21.8	20.4	19.2	18.1	17.2	16.5	15.1	13.6	11.8	10.5
40	33.8	29.7	26.7	24.4	22.5	21.0	19.7	18.6	17.7	16.9	15.5	13.9	12.1	10.7
45	37.3	32.4	28.9	26.3	24.2	22.5	21.0	19.8	18.8	17.9	16.4	14.7	12.6	11.2
50	40.7	35.0	31.0	28.0	25.7	23.8	22.2	20.9	19.8	18.8	17.2	15.3	13.2	11.7
60	47.2	39.8	34.8	31.2	28.4	26.2	24.4	22.8	21.5	20.4	18.6	16.5	14.1	12.4
70	53.3	44.2	38.3	34.0	30.8	28.3	26.2	24.5	23.1	21.8	19.8	17.5	14.9	13.1

Source: Bell, The Price-Future Earnings Ratio, *Financial Analysts Journal*, August, 1958, p. 28 formula:

$$x = \frac{(1+i)^n - 1}{i}, \text{ where } x = \text{price-earnings ratio, current earnings}$$

n = price-future earnings ratio

i = growth rate in per share earnings

Pfizer and Xerox, where both the estimated rates of growth and the prevailing price-earnings ratios are significantly above average, and the prevailing dividend yields are much lower than average. One approach to the problem, which has the great virtue of simplicity of application, is to consider the price-earnings ratio as a payout period or the number of years required to recover the price from the flow of earnings. With given estimated rates of earnings growth, the payout periods (or number of years required for estimated future earnings to equal the prevailing price) can then be computed.[5]

To illustrate, it may be noted that as of early 1965, the common stock of Chas. Pfizer and Company was selling at 24.6 times 1964 per share earnings. This fact may be interpreted to mean that it would take 24.6 years to recover the price through annual earnings if the earnings remained (or averaged out) at 1964 levels. But previous analysis had indicated that the potential growth rate in per share earnings might be estimated to range between 8 and 9.5%. Therefore, at least an approximation of whether Pfizer was markedly overvalued or undervalued might be indicated by the number of years it would take to recover the price with earnings growing at 8 to 9.5% as compared to the Moody's Stock Average at 18.8 times current earnings with an estimated growth rate of 3.5 to 4.5%.

The estimated payout periods, also termed *price-future earnings ratios*, can be computed by a laborious hand process through the use of compound-interest tables; it would require adding up the amount of $1 compounded annually at the estimated growth rates until a total is reached equal to the price-earnings ratio based on current earnings.[6] Fortunately, however, by a general formula programmed on a computer, Table 14-3 could be constructed to show the ratios of prices to future earnings (payout periods) when estimated growth rates are between 1 and 25% and when the current earnings price-earnings ratios are between 12 and 70.[7] To use the table, interpolation will usually be required. But because the applicable data represent estimates, it is recommended that the payout period be computed only to the nearest

---

[5] This concept was first set forth in Bell, "The Price-Future Earnings Ratio: a Practical Aid to Stock Valuation," *Financial Analysts Journal*, August 1958, pp. 25–28.

[6] For example, for Pfizer at an 8% rate from Table 13–2, 1.08 + 1.1664 + 1.25971 + 1.36049 + . . . until the sum is 24.6; the *number* of individual entries so totaled would be the payout period for Pfizer selling at 24.6 times current earnings with a growth rate of 8%.

[7] Formula contained in Bell, *op. cit.*, p. 28.

TABLE 14-4
EARNINGS AND PRICE DATA
(as of April, 1965)

Company	Stock Price	1964 Earnings Per Share	Growth Rates	1970 Projected Earnings†	Ratio of Stock Prices to: Current Earnings	Ratio of Stock Prices to: Projected Earnings	Ratio of Stock Prices to: Future Earnings (Payout Period)	Projected Dividend Yield*
Chas. Pfizer	$ 56	$ 2.27	9%	$ 3.80	24.6	14.7	13–14	3.4%
J. C. Penney	70	2.74	5%	3.70	25.5	18.9	16–18	3.8
Xerox	123	1.88	25%	6.00	64.7	20.5	13–14	1.0
Moody's Average	273	14.50	4%	17.50	18.8	15.6	14–15	3.5

* Price in 1965 divided into estimated 1970 dividend based on 1970 projected earnings and average past payout ratio.
† Computed via multiplying 1964 earnings by compound interest factor determined by estimated probable growth rate for six year period, i.e. J. C. Penney, 5% for 6 years equals 1.3401 times $2.74 or $3.67, rounded off to $3.70.

232

complete year in order to avoid a false impression of probable accuracy. If, in fact, a payout period worked out to within a year or so of the estimate, it could be considered a highly successful analysis. As an example in the use of Table 14-3, assume that a stock is selling at twenty times current earnings and has an estimated growth rate of 8%, then by finding 20 in the first column and proceeding across to 8%, a payout period of 12.4 years is indicated, which might be rounded off to twelve years.

In addition to estimating the payout periods which typically cover a period of ten years or more, intermediate estimates of possible per share earnings and dividends five to seven years hence are often quite useful in making selection decisions. The reason is that achievement of the potential growth rates would seem more probable for such an intermediate period than for a decade or more. Mechanically, projected earnings, once the growth rates have been estimated, are easy to compute. It is only necessary to multiply current earnings by the appropriate compound-interest coefficient. For example, in Table 14-4 earnings were projected for 1970 from 1964 results, or for six years hence. Concluding that Pfizer's most probable growth rate appeared to be 9%, then multiplying the 1964 earnings of $2.27 by the compounded amount of $1 at 9% for six years (1.677 from Table 13-2) resulted in projected earnings of $3.80 per share for 1970. (Rounding out to the nearest $.10 amount seemed appropriate to indicate clearly that estimates rather than demonstrated amounts were involved.)

The payout periods and the existing stock prices in relation to projected earnings and dividends, shown in Table 14-4, suggested that except for a slightly higher projected dividend return, J. C. Penney was less attractive than alternative common-stock commitments. On the other hand, the results for Pfizer compared quite favorably with those for the Moody's Industrial Average. Therefore, unless the subjective conclusions about Penney were highly favorable, it seemed to be somewhat overvalued on a comparative basis. Pfizer, however, even at a current price-earnings ratio of 24.6 seemed attractive for long-term investment on the basis of the projected approximations again assuming the appraisal of management, financial policies, and so forth did not indicate serious problems of one sort or another.[8]

[8] In actual selection decisions, the comparative values of other ethical drug company stocks probably would also be considered as well as the desirability of the industry for portfolio representation. The same approach, however, could be used for several companies in the same industry area.

The evidence on Xerox suggested a very difficult decision problem. On the adverse side, even if a compounded growth rate of 25% per annum was realized for six years, the prevailing price in 1965 was more than twenty times projected earnings for 1970, or well above alternatives. In addition, the prospective dividend yield associated with this growth rate for the next several years seemed likely to average considerably less than 1% (.4% in 1965), and it probably would not reach 1% of the 1965 price until about 1970.

On the positive side, the payout period at the indicated growth rate was actually below the Moody's Average. Moreover, as indicated in the preceding chapter, the growth rate in the past several years had actually been well above the 25% computed rate. So long as the highly dynamic growth period continued, the stock might well continue to advance in price proportionately to the increase in earnings, and thus give appreciation results equal to the highly favorable growth rate. However, the low dividend yield and the premium price-earnings ratios suggested the stock was quite vulnerable to any retardation in the rate of increase in per share earnings. On balance, both the opportunities and the risks seemed considerable in Xerox, which suggested that only highly aggressive investors might have considered this stock for long-term investment.

Use of Growth Yields. Although a comparison of the payout periods and the prices to projected earnings and dividends in relation to alternatives should provide a reasonable approximation of the comparative quantitative values embodied in common stocks; for some portfolio decisions the concept of growth yields may be quite useful. The growth yield can be defined as that yield which equates the present value of a rising dividend stream with the present market price.[9] The assumptions on which growth-yield computations are based are: (1) the estimated growth rate in dividends, (2) the expected duration of the growth rate in years, (3) a constant level of dividends after growth has been completed.

The concept is based on the principle that the dividend yield can also be considered to be a discount rate applied to a future stream of dividend payments. For example, when the dividend rate is $2 and the market price of a stock is $50, the current dividend yield is 4%;

[9] Soldofsky and Murphy, *Growth Yields on Common Stock: Theory and Tables,* Bureau of Business and Economic Research, State University of Iowa, Iowa City, Iowa, 1961, p. 8.

it also could be considered that $50 is the present value of a $2 stream of income received annually in perpetuity discounted at a 4% rate.[10] However, if the dividend is expected to increase in the future, it can be argued the actual discount rate or true yield is really greater than the 4% suggested by the current dividend of $2 per share. To allow for dividend growth in yield computations, a series of tables have been prepared to show the time-discounted yields which result from various rates of dividend growth for specified future periods.[11]

Their use might be illustrated from the cases of Pfizer and J. C. Penney; unfortunately the tables do not extend to extreme cases such as Xerox, where the price was 246 times the dividend rate in effect in 1965. As illustrated in Table 14-5, the growth yields are presented in terms of a $1 dividend at the beginning of the growth period. For example, if a stock sells at 70 with a $2 dividend per share, so that its price per dollar of dividend is $35, and the estimated dividend growth rate is 7%, then the growth yield from Table 14-5 would be 5%. Therefore, it was first necessary to divide the price by the existing annual dividend to obtain the price per $1 of dividend as follows:

> Pfizer 56 ÷ 1.25 = $44.80, growth rate, 8–9.5%
> J. C. Penney 70 ÷ 1.725 = 40.46, growth rate 4–6%
> Moody's Stock Average, 273 ÷ 8.22 = 33.29, growth rate 3.5–4%

The growth yield can then be estimated from the complete tables for various periods of projected dividend growth.[12] In general, about a decade of potential growth at the indicated rate might usually be reasonable. The reason is that as the assumed future growth period becomes longer the uncertainties surrounding the realization of the projections increase; on the other hand, a short period would not incorporate the concept of growth as a long-term phenomenon. Therefore, considering a ten-year growth period to be reasonably appropriate, the growth-yield was obtained by locating in the tables the above prices per $1 of dividend under the appropriate growth rates for ten years.

For Pfizer, with a price per dollar of prevailing dividend of $44.80 and a growth-rate estimate of 8 to 9.5%; the growth yield estimates obtained from Table 14-5 were between about 4.3 and 4.8%; for Penney they were between about 3.5 and 4.1%, and for the Moody's Stock

[10] *Ibid,* p. 6.

[11] *Ibid,* pp. 85–141.

[12] In the Soldofsky and Murphy complete tables, growth yields for intermediate dividend growth rates are given as well as the yields for various periods of projected dividend growth.

TABLE 14-5
ILLUSTRATIVE GROWTH YIELDS
DIVIDEND GROWTH PERIOD OF TEN YEARS

Estimated Dividend Growth Rate	Growth Yields*												
	2%	3%	4%	5%	6%	7%	8%	9%	10%	12%	15%	20%	25%
3%	64.4	43.2	32.7	25.3	21.0	17.8	15.6	13.7	12.3	—	—	—	—
4	70.4	47.1	35.0	27.4	22.7	19.3	16.7	14.7	13.2	—	—	—	—
5	77.0	51.4	38.1	29.8	24.6	20.8	18.0	15.8	14.1	11.5	9.0	6.5	5.0
6	84.2	56.0	41.4	32.3	26.6	22.5	19.4	17.0	15.1	12.2	9.5	6.8	5.3
7	92.0	61.0	44.9	35.0	28.7	24.3	20.9	18.3	16.2	13.1	10.1	7.2	5.5
8	100.4	66.4	48.8	37.9	31.1	26.2	22.5	19.6	17.4	14.0	10.7	7.6	5.8
9	109.5	72.3	53.0	41.1	33.6	28.2	24.2	21.1	18.6	14.9	11.4	8.0	6.1
10	119.4	78.7	57.6	44.5	36.3	30.5	26.1	22.7	20.0	16.0	12.2	8.5	6.4
11	130.1	85.6	62.5	48.2	39.3	32.9	28.0	24.4	21.5	17.1	12.9	9.0	6.7
12	141.8	93.1	67.8	52.2	42.5	35.5	30.3	26.2	23.0	18.2	13.8	9.5	7.1

* Rounded to nearest .1; complete tables to nearest .01

Source: Soldofsky and Murphy, *Growth Yields on Common Stocks: Theory and Tables*, Bureau of Business and Economic Research, State University of Iowa, Iowa City. (Selections from complete tables reprinted by permission.)

Average they were between about 3.9 and 4.3%.[13] These comparisons suggested that if the estimated growth rates in earnings do in fact materialize for the subsequent decade and the payout ratios do not change significantly, the time-discounted dividend yield expectation on Pfizer compared favorably with the average stock available in the market in 1965, whereas the comparison was unfavorable for J. C. Penney.

The growth-yield estimates derived from these tables might be particularly useful to selection decisions in pension fund and insurance company portfolios, where long-term actuarial compound-interest assumptions are applied to the security portfolios in order to determine the appropriate annual contributions (premiums) necessary to meet a prescribed level of payments to beneficiaries in future years. For instance, the indicated current dividend yield of about 2% on Pfizer as of 1965 probably was below most portfolio actuarial yield assumptions. But incorporating the potential dividend growth into the time-discounted yield computation, the result of 4.3 to 4.8% might well have suggested the future current income rate of return would probably cover the actuarial assumption. Of course a subjective interpretation of whether the risk surrounding the achievement of the projected return was within tolerable limits would also be involved in the final decision.

Growth Yields: Drawback. The major drawback to the use of growth yields, besides the uncertainties involved in the dividend projections, is that they assume an indifference to the *timing* of the anticipated income receipts. For accounts oriented to obtaining maximum income returns immediately, this assumption would be invalid. For example, the flow of anticipated dividend income from Pfizer at a growth rate of 9.5% for ten years reflected an estimated discounted yield expectation of 4.8% on a price of $56 per share as contrasted to only 4.4% for Borg-Warner with no anticipated growth. However, for the *immediate* future, the actual income yield on Pfizer will be well below that on Borg-Warner, as indicated by the comparative existing dividend yields of 2.3 and 4.4%, respectively.

The fact that a substantially higher income return was immediately available on Borg-Warner may have been quite important for some investors. For example, those at retirement age may be unwilling to sacrifice income now even for the promised probability of substantially larger income five or ten years hence. While these instances may be

---

[13] Interpolations were estimated in accordance with the view that reasonable approximations of the growth yields suffice for comparative selection decisions.

considered special in nature, they are of sufficient importance to suggest that the comparative income yield attractiveness of several common stocks cannot always be evaluated in terms of the growth yield concept.

Use of Present-Value Theory. In the case of high-quality bonds, appropriate values are logically determined by the rigid application of present-value theory to the known income receipts and known repayment of the principal at a specified date in the future. For example, when the coupon rate is 4%, the maturity is ten years hence, and the prevailing interest rate for such maturities is 4.5%, the appropriate price is determined by computing the present value, at a 4.5% discount rate, of the series of $4 income payments for ten years and the $100 to be received at the end of ten years. All bond yield-to-maturity tables are based on the application of this concept.

Perhaps in order to develop a consistent system of security-valuation theory, it has become fashionable to apply the techniques of present-value theory to the valuation of common stocks. The projected dividend payments are made equivalent to the coupon rate on bonds and an "appropriate" discount rate is made equivalent to the prevailing interest rates in the market. As common stocks have no maturities, some present-value methods regard the dividend stream as a perpetuity and thereby ignore the appreciation element in common stock returns.[14] Other methods, however, introduce the appreciation return (the equivalent of the repayment of bonds at maturity) by adding the present value of an "estimated" selling price at some finite future date to the present value of the projected dividends.

An example of the application of present-value theory to the appraisal of a common stock, International Business Machines in this case, is shown in Table 14-6. The assumptions leading to the final estimated value of $462 per share as of 1963 were as follows: (1) the annual dividend to grow at a 25% rate for fifteen years, (2) the growth rate in dividends to decline from 25% gradually after fifteen years to 4% after thirty years (transitional period), (3) the original discount rate to be 5% on a very high-quality stock such as I.B.M., (4) the discount rate to increase by .0375% a year to reflect the greater risk involved as divi-

---

[14] If all returns are assumed to be obtained through the corporation (no secondary market), then the approach would be plausible. This assumption was the basis for the earliest treatise on the subject: Williams, *The Theory of Investment Value,* Cambridge, Mass.: Harvard University Press, 1938.

TABLE 14-6
COMPUTED PRESENT VALUE: INTERNATIONAL BUSINESS MACHINES (1963)

Year	Future Yearly Dividend†	Yearly Discount Rate	Yearly Discount Factors*	Present Value Future Dividends‡
1	$ 1.25000	.050000%	.95238095	$1.19047
2	1.54500	.050375	.90638198	1.40036
3	1.88799	.050750	.86198923	1.62742
4	2.28064	.051125	.81918612	1.86831
5	2.72314	.051500	.77795360	2.11848
.				
.				
.				
13	7.26730	.054500	.50164283	3.64559
14	7.76148	.054875	.47335418	3.67392
15	8.18060	.055250	.44634408	3.65136
16	8.50782	.055625	.42057702	3.57819
17	8.84813	.056000	.39601680	3.50401
.				
.				
.				
140	1,101.4165	.102125	.00000122	.00134
141	1,145.4371	.102500	.00000106	.00121
142	1,191.2920	.102875	.00000091	.00108
143	1,238.9436	.103250	.00000079	.00097
143, value per share	81,741.9696**	.103250	.00000079	.03492

Total of present values = $142.26
1963 dividend rate = $3.25
Computed value of stock = $3.25 × $142.26 = $462

* Yearly discount rate applied for appropriate number of years; example: discount rate of .0515% applied for five years against expected dividend five years hence.
† Based on $1 of dividends in original year.
‡ Future yearly dividends multiplied by the discount factor.
** Based on assumption that the stock will sell at thirty-six times the dividend rate 143 years from now or at $1,238.9436 × 36. The multiplier of 36 was chosen as it reflected the price-dividend ratio of very high-quality stocks with a growth rate of 4% in 1963.

Source: Bauman, *Estimating the Present Value of Common Stocks by the Variable Rate Method,* Bureau of Business Research, Graduate School of Business, University of Michigan, Ann Arbor, 1963, pp. 29–30.

dends are projected into the future.[15] Present values of dividends for the years 6 through 12 and 18 through 139 were included in the totals,

[15] Bauman, *Estimating the Present Value of Common Stocks by the Variable Rate Method,* Michigan Business Reports, No. 42, Bureau of Business Research, Graduate School of Business, University of Michigan, 1963, Ann Arbor, pp. 29–30.

but the computations were not shown to save space. Although these computations would be very laborious if done by hand, Bauman's book included tables to make possible the rapid determination of present values under various assumptions as to growth rates and discount rates.[16]

As a theoretical expression of the value of a common stock, the present-value concept cannot be questioned. Moreover, the application of present-value theory to the determination of common-stock values requires explicit estimates of future earnings and dividends and their comparative discounted total value at a given time. Unfortunately, because of the inherent nature of common stock, there are serious drawbacks to the practical implementation of present-value theory.

First, there are the problems associated with the choice of an "appropriate" discount rate. One view is that it "should be guided by returns on alternative investments and historical stock market returns."[17] On the other hand, Bauman's view is that the discount rate should have a base of 5% for high-quality stocks and then be increased subjectively in two ways: (1) increases in the original discount rate to levels above 5% to reflect quality differentials in stocks, (2) gradual increases from the original discount rate to reflect the greater uncertainty surrounding more remote dividend payments.[18] Still other "appropriate" discount rates have been suggested; ingenuity has certainly not been lacking in this area.

However, the cited views on the determination of discount rates should suffice to make two points. First, the present-value approach necessarily involves certain subjective decisions, and these may be both varied and quite complex when translated into quantitative terms. Second, the choice of the discount rate is a crucial factor in the computation of present values, and if these rates are derived from "historical returns on common stocks" or from "the rate of return an investor desires,"[19] the application of the method may well result not in a decision about *which* common stocks should be acquired but whether *any* stocks should be acquired. This may occur because the prevailing prices of

[16] Ibid., pp. 66–82.

[17] Molodovsky, May, and Chottiner, "Common Stock Valuation," *Financial Analysts Journal*, March–April, 1965, p. 104. Molodovsky has found the average long-term historical returns on common stocks including both dividends and appreciation since 1871 to be between 7 and 8% in "Stock Values and Stock Prices," *Financial Analysts Journal*, May–June, 1960.

[18] Bauman, *op. cit.*, pp. 11–12.

[19] *Ibid*, p. 10.

most common stocks may exceed present values computed from "appropriate" discount rates derived from historical experience or from subjective investor expectations of desired rates of return.

Second, the present-value methods as typically applied tend to give a misleading appearance of arithmetic accuracy to the determination of stock values; note that the present values in the illustration were carried out to five decimal places and that the sum of the present values of the estimated future dividends was shown as precisely $142.26. Third, as in the use of growth-yield tables, present-value techniques usually assume an indifference to the timing of dividend receipts, although this factor could be incorporated into the discount rate. Fourth, when the technique includes in its methodology the present value of the future selling price, additional highly uncertain subjective estimates are required: the expected growth rate of the stock at the time of sale and the market multipliers that will prevail on common stocks at that time.

Conclusion. As a consequence, it is concluded that comparative selection decisions for most industrial common stocks can usually be intelligently reached through the appropriate use of one or more of the following techniques, depending upon the nature of the stock and its prevailing price: (1) the price-earnings ratio and dividend yield based on current earnings and dividends (where consistency of earnings performance is demonstrated), (2) average earnings and current dividend yields on volatile nongrowth stocks, (3) the prevailing price in relation to projected earnings and dividends, including both the comparative payout periods and the relationship of the prevailing prices to estimated earnings and dividends several years hence, (4) the computation of growth yields where indifference to the timing of income returns is indicated. The data on individual common stocks derived from these techniques should ordinarily be compared with bench mark data for a representative stock market average or index to give an indication of the comparative values that are currently available in the market. In all cases, however, a subjective interpretation of the various quality features is inherently a part of the decision process.

As a final warning it might be noted that even the most sophisticated appraisal techniques cannot assure superior long-term investment results. Because results entirely depend upon the realization of future earnings and dividends, it is possible that they will be seriously affected by dynamic new developments. Such possibilities are one reason for portfolio diversification of reasonable proportions. But at the same time, it would seem only reasonable that selection decisions derived from a penetrating analytical process of the quality of the company and its earnings and dividend potential in relation to the price of the stock should substantially increase the probabilities of obtaining satisfactory long-term investment results.

CHAPTER 15

Selection of
Fixed-Income Securities:
Standards of Performance

Introduction

The investment implications of bonds and preferred stocks may be summarized as follows: the investor sacrifices all benefits ensuing from any future growth of a company in order to obtain a specified prior claim on income. The only major difference between bonds and preferred stocks is in the claim. Bondholders must be paid or the corporation suffers receivership, whereas the holders of preferred stock have only the right to receive their income before common dividends are declared. However, in the event of severe financial difficulties, experience indicates that both bonds and preferreds may incur substantial losses of principal.

The contractual implications suggest that the only purpose of investing in bonds or preferreds is to obtain safety of dollar income, and the investor is presumably willing to forego any significant prospects of appreciation to obtain it. The natural corollary of this proposition is that bonds and preferreds should be selected from the viewpoint of the pessimist. Analysis is not directed to an appraisal of the profit potential under favorable circumstances; instead emphasis is on what the position would be under unfavorable conditions within the industry and the economy.

The negative orientation suggests that the bond analyst should be a gloomy sort of person with a natural inclination to look on the worst side of things. And to some extent there seems to be this tendency in practive. Most specialists in bond analysis are likely to take a very cautious attitude toward the level of the stock market and the outlook for business conditions. They generally can find more reasons why the stock market is vulnerable to a severe decline than why its upside prospects are favorable. Actually, the Cassandra-like attitude may be commended so far as the approach to fixed-income securities is concerned, although its carry-over into the common-stock area is of course questionable.

The techniques discussed in Chapter 11 on the analysis of financial policies represent the principal measures of the safety of a fixed-income security and its investment quality. Therefore, at this point a summary review of the qualitative and quantitative indications of a strong credit position should suffice. But in addition, the intelligent selection of bonds and preferred stocks involves some evaluation of the specific indenture provisions which set forth the rights and responsibilities of the investor and the corporation. Finally, it is necessary to appraise the reasonableness of the indicated yields based on the prevailing price.

Standards of Performance: Qualitative

Role in Selection. The various aspects of the qualitative appraisal were previously discussed in some detail. But it might be useful to relate the possible conclusions emerging from this analysis to decisions on the investment attractiveness of fixed-income securities. Occasionally the qualitative picture is sufficiently dismal to eliminate the company from any serious consideration. It is more likely, however, that the qualitative indications are not entirely conclusive in themselves. They usually suggest either that the quantitative standards should be very rigorous (when, qualitatively, the company is not entirely favorable) or that they can be relaxed to some modest degree.

Importance of Stability. From the standpoint of bonds or preferred stock the qualitative analysis should clearly point to a conclusion that the company is very likely to remain a continuously profitable entity over the long term. In other words, the secular trend should not be unfavorable. The stability factor is also of primary importance. Therefore, the analysis of sales potential for the products should indicate at least a neutral trend and prospects for maintaining a level of sales sufficient to avoid losses under unfavorable business conditions. Moreover, as instability can sometimes be caused by cost elements, it is similarly desirable to find a cost structure subject to reasonable control. For example, the need to maintain large inventories which are subject to wide price swings would be an undesirable qualitative feature.

The Size Factor.   Although the basic economics of the company's product line and cost structure are of great importance, the competitive position of the company is perhaps of equal significance. By and large there is good reason to have much greater confidence in the long-term continuity of companies that are of substantial size and are competitive leaders in their industry. Although size alone, of course, does not guarantee a profitable level of operations, seasoned firms that are dominant in their industry area naturally tend to be better able to withstand adversity,[1] This does not necessarily mean that only the relatively few real industrial giants are satisfactory for bond or preferred-stock investment, but it does mean that the company should be of reasonably large size and have a long record of demonstrated performance. The mortality rate of unseasoned firms has always been significantly greater, and therefore, one can categorically recommend avoidance of fixed-income securities of such companies. To be more specific, it is suggested that the company (or its antecedents, when mergers are involved) should have been a profitable entity for at least twenty years and should have reached levels of both assets and sales of about $50 million as a minimum before its fixed-income securities are considered for investment purposes.[2]

The Management Factor.   The attainment of a major position within an industry usually implies that the management factor is reasonably favorable. Now and again, however, there can be signs of management atrophy in a well-established company. The major signs are usually either a declining share of the market or a decline in the rate of earnings on invested capital. Where this situation exists it usually is a good and

[1] An empirical study of the rate of return on net worth of manufacturing companies for the years 1951–60 showed that companies of less than $5 million in assets had average annual fluctuations in the rate of return of more than 28%, whereas companies with $100 million of assets showed average annual fluctuations of about 11%. Graham, Dodd, and Cottle, *Security Analysis*, New York: McGraw-Hill, 1962, p. 329.

[2] For the 1900–43 period, which included the Great Depression, the default record on bond offerings of industrial companies of more than $100 million in assets was 17% as opposed to 25% for companies with assets between $5 and 99 million and 38% for companies with assets of less than $5 million. W. B. Hickman, *Corporate Bond Quality and Investor Experience*, Princeton, N. J.: Princeton University Press, 1958, p. 495.

sufficient reason to reject the fixed-income securities, because, as has already been indicated, the objective is to avoid trouble over the long term and this is not achieved when there are managerial difficulties.

But a word of caution is necessary here. Sometimes highly aggressive managements have been guilty of a very liberal use of senior securities to finance growth requirements. The discussion of the financial policies of Georgia-Pacific Corporation showed that during periods of prosperity the aggressive assumption of debt may well result in more favorable management indications than would have been produced by a more conservative course of action. Therefore, it is imperative that both financial management and managerial capacity from an operating standpoint be appraised. The quantitative tests of financial integrity should suggest the nature of such management. But the effects are mentioned to caution against becoming enthusiastic about a company's fixed-income securities because of a favorable managerial showing which, in fact, may have been accomplished by eroding the quality of the senior obligations. Financial conservatism is a highly desirable attribute of a management when considering a company's fixed-income securities.

Desirable Qualitative Features: Summary. These brief comments should be suggestive of the type of firm that is most attractive for bond and preferred-stock investment. First, it should have a stable demand for a diversified group of products that show no evidence of being drastically affected by interindustry competition. Second, competitive conditions within the industry should be orderly and new firms would find it difficult to enter the field. Third, the company should be of substantial size and occupy a dominant competitive position. Fourth, the management tests should be favorable, but these should not be attained at the cost of a reduction in the financial soundness of the company. Fifth, there should be no significant cost problems except as are inherent in any large productive unit under modern conditions. Sixth, the products should be able to compete effectively without any help from the government in the form of tariffs, subsidies, or governmental purchases.

It is, of course, almost impossible to find all these desirable characteristics embodied in a single company. In practice the analyst must weigh conflicting evidence and decide whether on balance any qualitative weaknesses are sufficient to eliminate a company from further consideration. In this connection, a distinction might be made between the elements which would be disqualifying and those which could conceivably be offset by a very strong quantitative showing. It would seem logical to disqualify immediately any small company, one that lacks a strong position in its industry, or is undergoing a definite long-term decline for any other reason. On the other hand, those elements which imply only some degree of instability might well be offset by an extremely modest amount of debt and preferred stock on which the charges are quite nominal relative to the average flow of earnings.

Quantitative Performance: Analysis and Standards

Importance. The point has been made previously that the analysis of quantitative data is based on the presumption that the past financial statements provide a reasonable clue to future performance. When the qualitative facts about a company indicate that the hypothesis is highly questionable, then all its securities become somewhat speculative, because of the lack of any tangible basis for measuring performance and estimating values. But quantitative evidences of value are particularly important to selection decisions on fixed-income securities. The rewards for a favorable resolve of the speculative elements are small for the fixed-income securities, but the penalties consequent to their turning out unfavorably may be considerable.[3]

But when the subject company has a seasoned record over a number of years and is of substantial size, it is more likely that the past record will be at least roughly indicative of future performance. Such a company has become "socially acceptable"; its management and products have been tested against the several forms of competition; it has developed close relations with suppliers, customers, and bankers. In brief, it has proved itself in the economic world, and it would be surprising if there was not a considerable degree of continuity in an established firm of this type.

The point is emphasized because when the past performance seems to be a more reliable guide to the future, the quantitative factors have greater importance in determining the investment merits of the securities. It is not an exaggeration to suggest that in the selection of bonds and preferred stocks the major purpose of the qualitative review is to obtain assurance of reasonable confidence in the past financial statements as a clue to the future, and the major reasons for accepting or rejecting such securities are then based on quantitative standards derived from the past financial data.

[3] We are using the term *speculative* here as equivalent to a substantial amount of uncertainty as to the future. The outlook need not necessarily be unfavorable, but only that it is very difficult to have any basis for estimating the future potential. New companies are a good example of this case.

Stability. As the prospective stability of a company is of considerable importance in determining the quality of its fixed-income securities, it is particularly desirable to appraise its vulnerability to a cyclical downturn in business activity. The vulnerability of sales, earnings, and cash flow would seem relevant. The technical measurements might be termed *stability ratios* and would represent the percentage declines in these items from a prosperous year to a subsequent adverse year.[4] For example, the effects of the recession of 1958 on the Inland Steel Company would be indicated as follows:

	1957	1958	Percentage Decline
Sales (in millions)	$763.9	$656.0	14
Earnings before taxes	124.8	96.7	23
Cash flow (earnings plus depreciation)	150.8	125.4	17

As that recession did not represent a major downturn in business activity based on historical precedents, the declines in sales and earnings of 14 and 23%, respectively, indicated considerable vulnerability to cyclical disturbances. However, the fact that the percentage decline in cash flow was considerably less than that of pretax earnings was reassuring as an indication of an ability to meet temporary adversity. It might be added, as a technical note, that if 1955 or 1956 had shown higher sales and earnings figures than 1957, then they would have been the appropriate base years for measuring the cyclical exposure.

As of 1965, however, a quantitative estimate of potential future stability posed a vexing problem. The past decade had witnessed only moderate cyclical variations yet the "pessimist approach" would imply the desirability of a more drastic test. The argument for a more rigorous test of stability would not be that a more severe recession is likely or even reasonably probable, but only that long-term economic history suggests such a possibility. On the other hand, one must go back about twenty-seven years to 1938 to find a severe downturn in business activity, and many if not most companies were entirely different in size and product line in 1965 than in 1938. In a very real sense, therefore, a rigorous quantitative measure of potential stability was not possible as of 1965, although where the nature of the company had not completely changed, the "stability ratios" based on the experience of 1936–38 might have been of some use.

---

[4] It would not be appropriate to work backward from a prosperous year to a recession year, say from 1964 to 1958, because in this case any company with a strong growth performance would appear to be highly unstable. Xerox Corporation would look very poor if such a measurement were made as of 1965.

An example was the steel industry, which had not greatly changed the nature of its product line and customers since 1938. Therefore, the declines in sales and earnings of Inland Steel of 33 and 61%, respectively, in 1938 as compared to 1937 might have been regarded as the potential exposure to very unfavorable cyclical conditions. The fact that such percentage declines applied to 1964 sales and earnings would still result in an earnings coverage of four times interest charges as of 1965 could be used as evidence that the fixed-income securities were well protected against even a severe downturn in business activity.

Earnings Protection. Because fixed-income securities must look to earnings for the payment of interest or preferred dividends, the most significant test of their investment quality is the size of these charges in relation to the indicated flow of earnings. As brought out in chapter eleven on financial policies, this relationship is measured statistically by the *times fixed charges earned for bonds and times fixed charges and preferred dividends earned* for preferred stock. The significance of these ratios can be expressed in terms of their reciprocals: a coverage ratio of, say, 6 means earnings can decline to one-sixth of that year's level and there then will just be sufficient earnings to meet the particular charges under consideration. The technical problems involved in the computation of these ratios are considered at some length in that chapter and need not be repeated at this point.

In measuring the general financial quality of a company it was necessary to suggest standards of performance with respect to earnings and "cash flow" protection of the interest and principal payments on fixed-income securities. These were as follows:

Type of Company*	Coverage Ratio: Interest Average	Coverage Ratio: Interest Minimum	Coverage Ratio: Interest and Pfd. Dividends Average	Coverage Ratio: Interest and Pfd. Dividends Minimum	Cash Flow Coverage†
Cyclical	8X	3X	5X	3X	4
Stable	4X	2X	3X	2X	4

* Trend is assumed neutral or good in all cases. Fixed-income securities of a company suffering a long-term decline should be avoided.

† Earnings (after taxes but before interest charges) plus depreciation to interest and preferred dividends plus maturities and contractual sinking funds.

As both holders of the common stock and the bonds would desire strong assurance that earnings will be adequate to meet interest payments under all reasonably conceivable conditions, these standards were considered pertinent to the determination of the investment quality of the debt obligations.

On the other hand, it was pointed out that the financial consequences of a default on preferred dividends are less serious. For this reason, so far as the common stock is concerned, the coverage standards on preferred stocks can be lower than demanded on bonds. The common stock, in brief, can afford to be less sure about the ability of the company to meet preferred dividends than it can about the ability to meet bond interest.

But from the standpoint of the preferred stock the lack of compulsion to pay preferred dividends is a cogent reason to insist on earnings coverage standards at least equal to that which would be required on bonds. As the only really logical reason for investors turning to preferred stocks is to obtain regularity of income payments during periods of adverse business conditions, it follows that only those preferreds which are most likely to pay full dividends at all times as a matter of course should be eligible for consideration. Very adequate coverage, especially by earnings during unfavorable periods (minimum), is therefore imperative. Thus, it would seem reasonable to suggest that the *minimum* earnings coverage of interest and preferred dividends combined should be at least 4 for a cyclical company and 3 for a reasonably stable company in order to qualify a preferred stock for long-term investment purposes.

Some might be concerned with the apparent paradox involved in suggesting slightly higher minimum coverage standards for preferred stocks than for bonds when within a given company the coverage of preferred dividends must be less than that of interest charges. However, from the standpoint of the preferred this is only tantamount to maintaining that when earnings are only marginally sufficient to qualify the bonds for investment purposes, the less well-secured preferred stock of the company is not adequately protected. The weaker contractual position of a preferred should be accepted only when it is clearly apparent that the company will not exercise its prerogative to omit preferred dividends.

Example. Standard Oil of Ohio for the 1955–64 decade showed a minimum coverage of its fixed-charges before taxes of 10.5 times and an average coverage of about 18 times, or well in excess of the suggested standards. The after-tax coverage of the combined preferred dividends and interest charges averaged about ten times, with a minimum of eight. As the trends were also quite favorable, the $3.75 preferred stock of this company clearly qualified for long-term investment purposes, but only because the bonds were protected by earnings to a much greater degree than would have been necessary to obtain a high-quality rating.

The Capital Structure: Going-Concern Value. For two reasons the balance-sheet breakdown of the capital structure into percentage components of bonds, preferred stock, and common stock does not appear particularly significant as a quality bench mark. First, the average earnings on invested capital vary widely between industrial entities, and where earnings on total capital are high, a much larger percentage of the capital structure can safely be committed to fixed-income securities. The conclusion is based on the following rather obvious hypothesis: that large earnings rather than large asset values are the means of avoiding financial difficulties. Therefore, the risk implications of a given capital structure are derived mainly from the size of the earnings and not from the size of the book value of the junior equity. Second, the stability characteristics of industrial enterprises are vastly different; a company that is reasonably stable can safely afford to acquire a much larger proportion of its capital by using fixed-income securities. And this factor again can be measured by the intelligent and rigorous use of the earnings-coverage concept, along with a qualitative evaluation of the nature of the company's operations.

However, some analytical significance might be attached to the going-concern value implied by the market price of the common stock in relation to the maturity or liquidating value of the senior securities. The purpose is to test the market's judgment of the values embodied in the company to protect the senior securities. If the coverage ratios are adequate, there should be a substantial amount of earnings available to the common stock. This condition in turn should mean an adequate total market value for the common relative to the senior securities, because such market values are normally related to the size of the earnings. But if this is not the case, the stock market must be placing a low value on each dollar of earnings. Unless the general stock market is at depressed levels, the situation would suggest a lack of confidence in the outlook for the company on the part of investors. Therefore, if the coverage ratios are adequate and the market value of the common equity is low in relation to the amount of outstanding senior securities, it may be interpreted as evidence that there are substantial qualitative uncertainties.

It has been suggested that the common equity should show an average total market value of at least 1.5 times the effective values of the senior securities. This particular figure seems reasonable as a standard because, assuming both an average coupon or dividend rate of 4% on the senior securities and an earnings coverage averaging about five times interest and preferred dividends after taxes, the common stock would be selling at less than ten times average earnings if the standard was not met. To illustrate, the following computation shows that when the coverage ratio after taxes is 4.75 and the common stock has a market price of ten times the remaining earnings, then the total market value of the common stock will be exactly one and a half times the par value of the senior securities:

$$
\begin{array}{llrll}
\text{Senior securities} & \$100 & \times & 4\% & = \$\ 4 \\
\text{Common stock} & 150 & \times & 10\% & = \underline{15} \\
\end{array}
$$

Total earnings before senior charges $= \$19$
Coverage is $19 \div 4 = 4.75$

Notice that if $15 of earnings are available to the common stock for every $4 of interest or preferred dividends (necessary if the after-tax coverage ratio is to be at least 4.75), then a market value for the common of $150 per $100 of senior securities would mean it is selling for ten times earnings. And it is generally conceded that a common stock valued at less than ten times earnings carries with it the supposition that the risk factors are substantial.

If the market value of the common is below this standard, then it would be advisable to review the entire appraisal of the company and either decide that the market valuation is unwarranted or that the uncertainties are sufficiently great to justify rejection of the senior securities. The burden of proof should be to show why going-concern value is not reflected accurately in the market appraisal. As has been continually reiterated, in the case of fixed-income securities the techniques are largely designed to indicate signs of weakness. When any significant adverse sign shows up, it is reason for rejection unless other evidence indicates that the results of a technique may be discounted.

The principal difficulty encountered in the practical application of the technique is to decide what market price reflects the typical opinion about the long-term worth of the junior equity. The most recent market price has the advantage of showing the most up-to-date opinion of the company's outlook. On the other hand, it has the disadvantage of reflecting only the current status of the stock market, which may be transitory and not indicative of more normal values. A straight average of the market-price range based on the past three or four years should eliminate the random circumstances of prevailing market opinion, but at the same time the average price does not reflect investor opinion based on the most current information about the company. The problem would be especially serious if the position of the company had deteriorated in the past few years. As a compromise, it is suggested that the *lower* of the current or average price be used and in that way the most conservative appraisal of going-concern value will be shown.

TABLE 15–1

GOING-CONCERN VALUE: GEORGIA-PACIFIC CORPORATION, DECEMBER 31, 1964

	Amount (in millions)
Long-term debt	$293.6
Preferred stock	13.2
Total senior securities	$306.8
Common-stock equity value (12,744,000 shares outstanding):	
1962–64 average price @ $40 per share	509.7
Current price, first quarter of 1965, @ $60	770.6
Equity value to senior securities:	
Average value of common stock	1.7
Current value of common stock	2.5

* Adjusted for 25% stock dividend in 1964.

Example. In Chapter 11 it was concluded that the senior securities of Georgia-Pacific Corporation were of low medium-grade quality, because large debt financing in the 1962–64 period resulted in coverage ratios at below minimum acceptable levels during these years of general economic prosperity. However, as shown in Table 15-1, the market value of the common equity consistently exceeded one and a half times the book value of the debt and preferred stock. The equity market, therefore, was apparently favorably impressed with the prospects for the company for several years. Indeed the growth record was quite favorable, but partly because of the heavy reliance on senior securities to finance the substantial expansion in assets. Therefore, although the considerable going-concern value was a plus factor to the status of the bonds and preferred stock, the ability of the company to withstand serious adversity with the debt structure existing at the end of 1964 remained somewhat uncertain.

CHAPTER 16

Selection of
Fixed-Income Securities:
Terms and Yields

Terms of Contract: General Significance

Senior-security investment contracts typically include a number of detailed provisions which set forth specific rights and privileges of both the company and the investor, and they also usually contain certain restrictions on the future financial policies of the company. One need only to examine a prospectus on a public offering of a bond or preferred stock to testify that these contractual terms are spelled out in great detail in language which can best be described as "legalese." Generally, most of these terms do not really add to or detract much from the investment quality of a bond or preferred stock. No combination of legal rights or restrictions can compensate for a lack of economic stature; on the other hand, there is no need for them when the company is manifestly of very good quality and will be able to meet its obligations to the senior securities as a matter of course.

However, although there is no substitute for a superior corporate performance, it is still desirable to find in the specific contractual terms some safeguards against discretionary practices that conceivably could reduce the investment quality of the security. Then again there might be some aspects of the contract that are generally undesirable or at least questionable from the standpoint of the investor. Therefore, a brief analysis of the significant contractual features is desirable when evaluating the attractiveness of senior securities for investment purposes.

Specific Terms: Investment Significance

Creditor and Cumulative Provisions. The basic legal right of a bond is its creditor position with respect to income and principal. Its creditor position assures that every effort will be exerted to maintain interest payments and meet maturities because the penalty for default is bankruptcy. The legal position of preferred stocks is limited to the right to receive the contractual rate of dividends in full before the common stock is entitled to any return.

The preference should always be cumulative: any dividends not paid in past years must be made up in full before dividends can be resumed on the common stock. Without the cumulative provision there is little reason to expect a company to maintain preferred dividends in any year when it may be inexpedient to pay a common dividend. Both the unqualified creditor relationship on bonds and the cumulative feature on preferreds are almost always found in the senior issues of the large, well-known industrial companies.

Future-Issue Limitations. Although not imperative, it would seem desirable that the contractual terms limit the ability of the company to market additional senior securities of equal or prior rank. A company could conceivably "trade down" the protection afforded its existing bonds and preferreds by selling large new issues with an equal or superior claim on the earnings stream. For example, the quality of the Georgia-Pacific preferred stocks was certainly not improved by an increase in the long-term debt from an amount of $134.1 million in 1961 to $283.6 million at the end of 1964. Therefore, some reasonable restrictions would seem appropriate. They would seem especially desirable in preferred-stock contracts, because the bond market might be perfectly willing to absorb new debt issues which would usurp a favorable senior position formerly occupied by the preferred. It was notable that no restrictions on debt assumption existed in the preferred-stock contracts of Georgia-Pacific Corporation. On the other hand, additional bond issues may run into market resistance if outstanding debt is already at a practical maximum.[1]

However, debt-limitation provisions have been more common in

[1] A possible exception to this observation may be additional borrowings from commercial banks. In order to retain the deposit relationship, many banks have been inclined to be less rigorous in their standards of credit quality than purely outside investors. In this connection, it is notable that most of Georgia-Pacific's debt expansion in 1963–64 was in the form of bank term loans.

bond 'indentures than in preferred-stock contracts. These may be phrased in a number of different ways, but perhaps the most typical are: (1) the so-called "equal security" clause in debenture issues, (2) limitations on total funded debt to a certain percentage of assets, (3) restrictions on total interest requirements to a percentage of the earnings stream for some defined past period. Of these three alternatives, the third would seem the most desirable from the standpoint of the existing bonds. The primary test of quality is a sufficient earnings coverage of the total fixed charges, and any requirement that it be maintained is a step in the right direction.

However, the restriction may not be very rigorous, and therefore, it may mean very little as a practical matter. For example, the Inland Steel bond indenture limited new bonds to a point where total interest payments both old and new will be covered 1½ times by earnings of the past year or by average earnings of the preceding three years. The provision seemed unduly lax in terms of both the size of the pro-forma coverage and the length of the earnings period. As an optimum, it is suggested that the contract might require a coverage of total old and new interest requirements of at least three by average annual earnings before taxes for about five past years. This pro-forma coverage standard is less than suggested as a standard for good quality industrial bonds, but it amounts to an allowance for some earnings potential on the capital supplied by the new issue.

The "equal security" clause states that new bonds cannot be issued which have a lien on assets prior to outstanding bonds. It is designed to insure that the relative claim of the existing bonds on the assets will be maintained in the future. It seems entirely reasonable and equitable, but it is of dubious practical significance, although it does no harm. Liens on specialized industrial assets do not usually add much to the ultimate soundness of a bond issue. In the absence of earnings and under liquidation or reorganization conditions, most fixed assets (on which liens are customarily granted) tend to have very little realizable value. Therefore, the actual workout of prior lien bonds is often not materially greater than the so-called unsecured debt. Moreover, the selection process on bonds is designed to obtain considerable assurance against any sort of financial trouble, because experience indicates that default on any debt seriously affects all of the bond issues regardless of priority to assets. It follows that indenture restrictions designed to prevent the company from incurring an unwieldy *total* debt structure are more significant than a clause which protects the priority to assets but which does not limit the size of the total obligations.

Limiting total funded debt to a percentage of total net assets is another means of attempting to prevent the development of an unwieldy debt structure. For example, an indenture provision for the American Brake Shoe Company, sinking fund debenture 4½s of 1982, specified that net tangible assets must be at least 300% of the total outstanding funded debt.[2] In effect, the provision limited long-term debt to 33% of the capital structure. A prohibition on sales and lease-backs was also included to prevent the company from incurring rental obligations in lieu of debt. However, the amount of earnings—not assets—represents the crucial protective factor. Therefore, a clause that relates the total pro-forma interest requirements (on both old and any contemplated new debt) to the amount of the past earnings stream is the most desirable method of limiting the debt structure.

However, the absence of an effective debt-limitation clause is not a sufficient reason in and of itself to reject a bond or preferred stock for investment purposes. Neither the debenture 4½s of 1982 nor the $3.75 preferred stock of Standard Oil of Ohio had a contractual provision limiting new debt issues in any way, yet these securities certainly deserved a prime investment quality rating based on the past record of strong earnings protection and prudent financial policies.

Dividend Restrictions. Many contracts contain a provision, usually quite complicated, limiting the dividend distributions which may be made on the common stock. The specific terms of the limitation take a variety of forms, but the purpose seems to be identical in all: to prevent the directors from declaring dividends which would reduce the assets of the firm below a certain level and in effect represent a partial liquidating dividend. While it is conceivable that a profligate Board of Directors might "milk" the company to the detriment of the bonds or preferred stock, it is hard to believe that well-established firms of long standing would resort to such practices, which border on the unscrupulous. Therefore, although there is no objection to these clauses, they do not seem to be imperative if the analysis has resulted in the rejection of all companies whose managements have shown any indication of following questionable practices.

By and large the directors of most large industrial firms restrict dividends to a proportion of the earnings of a given year. It is quite rare to find common dividends in excess of earnings for any significant period of time, although occasionally such distributions may be slightly

---

[2] Net tangible assets are usually defined as the book values of all assets less the usual intangibles, such as "goodwill" or "patent rights," and less current liabilities.

greater for a year or so. Special situations which are undergoing partial or complete liquidation are exceptions, but here the senior issues should be avoided unless there is complete assurance that full provision had been made for the senior claims.

Perhaps because many bank term loans are made to small family-owned companies, term loan agreements seem to invariably carry dividend restrictions. Georgia-Pacific, for example, was subject to a limitation that dividends could not exceed 70% of earnings in any year. On the other hand, the Standard Oil of Ohio contracts contained no limitation on dividend distributions. In general, such limitations would seem more necessary in closely held firms where a family that controls the Board of Directors may also be dependent upon dividends for its income.

Voting Rights on Preferred Stock. On the theory that preferred stock represents a limited ownership position interested only in a fixed rate of income (like bonds), the contract often contains a proviso which specifically disenfranchises the stock from participating in the election of directors. Usually, the provision makes little difference, as the number of outstanding common shares ordinarily greatly exceeds the preferred. Therefore, if management can control the common through the proxy machinery, the effective voice of the preferred as a group in determining corporate policy is negligible. In essence, whether the preferred is given an equal share for share vote with the common is of no practical significance.

There is another theory, however, whose principles have sometimes been incorporated into preferred-stock contracts, which may materially improve the strategic position of the preferred. According to this theory if preferred dividends are in default, then the residual values in the form of earnings, etc., to the common stock have temporarily disappeared, and the preferred is really the de facto residual equity for the time being. It would follow that under such circumstances the preferred should be endowed with the exclusive right to select a substantial proportion of the directors and preferably a majority. However, in most cases where the principle is recognized in the contract, the preferred is given the right to elect only a minority of the board.

But, assuming that the preferred stock when in default is given the sole right to choose a majority of the directors, its bargaining position would be substantially improved if exercised in an intelligent fashion. In some situations, an impasse has occurred when the preferred held out its arrearage rights to prevent dividends on the common, but it could not force the company to declare preferred dividends even though earnings improved. Compromise settlements for less than full arrearage claims, which were usually offered with the implied promise to resume current preferred dividends, have usually been accepted under such conditions.

However, the clause cannot be regarded as a panacea which by itself can offset the basic contractual weakness of preferred stocks. When a preferred dividend default occurs, someone must take the initiative to send out proxies to the preferred shareholders and convince them that management's solicatations for the existing directors should be rejected. On the surface the step would not appear too difficult, as it might be presumed that the preferred would be quite unhappy (to put it mildly) and ready for a change in management. However, many stockholders are notoriously apathetic with respect to their rights; in actual practice, control of the organized proxy machinery may enable existing management to withstand any attempt of the preferred stockholders to elect new directors that will specifically represent the preferred stock interests. But if this practical impediment could be overcome, many of the sacrifices demanded from the preferred stock in settlements of arrearage claims might be eliminated.

Possibly, the mere threat of loss of control may cause the directors to be less casual in passing preferred dividends. There has been some evidence in the past of a predilection to shut off preferred dividends rather quickly if earnings suffer a temporary lapse and a policy of conserving cash seems to be expedient. The uncertainty as to whether the preferred will actually act in an effective manner and replace a substantial portion of the board may cause that body to think twice about defaults.[3] After all, self-preservation is a strong human motivation.

The difference on this score between the 5¼% cumulative preferred and the 5% cumulative convertible preferred of the Georgia-Pacific Corporation was interesting. The former, as a straight fixed-income security, had the right to elect as a class three directors in case of default of six quarterly dividends and no voting power otherwise, whereas the con-

---

[3] The practical operation of the clause may be illustrated by the Penn-Texas Corp. action in May of 1959. In that month the directors of this company declared a $.40 dividend on the preferred after the stock had been in default since September, 1957. Asked the reason for this action, an officer of the corporation was reported as follows: "he remarked that the preferred is in arrears for five quarterly payments, and if another payment is passed preferred shareholders would have the right to elect two directors. Mr. Landa has said in the past he thinks this ought to be avoided, if possible." *Wall Street Journal*, May 5, 1959, p. 2.

vertible had one vote per share in either case. The theory apparently was that a convertible preferred should be treated like the common stock because of the contingent claim on the common stock.

Sinking Funds.   A plausible argument can be advanced that sinking funds as typically established in bond indentures or preferred contracts have been a mixed blessing to the investor. The argument is at odds with most opinion on the subject, which regards sinking-fund requirements as entirely beneficial to investors in fixed-income securities.[4] The sinking-fund provision as generally worded requires the company either to buy in the market or redeem at a set price a certain amount of the outstanding securities each year. The investment virtues of sinking funds are held to be twofold. First, if significant in annual amount, they represent a definitive program to handle the debt load and presumably enable the company to avoid any potential difficulty resulting from large debt maturities at a particular time. In brief, they are alleged to represent prudent financial planning as contrasted to a "drifting" policy that considers maturities when they are imminent but not before. Second, the operation of the sinking fund may tend to keep the market prices of the securities higher than they would otherwise be. As the company has the option of meeting sinking-fund requirements by open-market purchases, there is a special market demand introduced when the issue declines below the specified call price. It should be noted, of course, that the sinking-fund purchases do not set a price floor by any means, and such purchases operate as a market support only when prices are below the sinking-fund call price.

Although these virtues cannot be ignored completely, their importance can be exaggerated. For example, a good quality company can meet its maturities by means of refunding operations, either through private placements or public offerings. Moreover, a potential disadvantage of a sinking-fund requirement can arise when, because of a decline in money rates, the senior securities sell at substantial premiums in the market. In explaining this aspect, it should first be noted that sinking-fund call prices are usually below the ordinary redemption prices. This was true for the bonds of both Inland Steel and Standard Oil of Ohio, as shown in Table 16-1. Up to the amount of the sinking fund, therefore, the companies had the right to conduct a lottery to determine the specific bonds to be called for sinking-fund purposes. If the bonds at any time sold at a premium above these prices, those

---

[4] Cf. Graham, Dodd, and Cottle, *Security Analysis*, New York: McGraw-Hill, 1962, pp. 335–336.

TABLE 16–1
SCHEDULE OF REDEMPTION PRICES

Issue	Regular Redemption Price*	Redemption Price-Sinking Fund Only
Inland Steel Company		
1st 3½s, Series J, due 1981	102½	100.33
1st 4⅜s, Series K, due 1987	103½	100
1st 4½s, Series L, due 1989	103½	100
Standard Oil of Ohio		
Debenture 4½s, due 1982	102½	100
3¾ % Preferred Stock	100	100

* In each case the redemption prices decline in future years to par at maturity; also the Series K and Series L bonds could not be called until 1967 and 1969 respectively.

holders unfortunate enough to be drawn would sustain an effective loss by the amount of the difference between the market and the sinking-fund call price.

Therefore, the purchase or holding of a bond at a significant price premium above the sinking-fund call price involves a decision as to whether the "lottery risk" is negligible or not. This "risk" can be estimated roughly by relating the size of the bond issue currently outstanding to the amount of the annual sinking-fund. For example, the sinking-fund requirement on the Standard Oil of Ohio debenture 4¼s of 1982 was $1.25 million per year. At the end of 1964, there were $20 million of this issue outstanding. In 1964, therefore, the chances were 1.25 out of 20 (about 1 in 16) of a given bond being selected. In each year thereafter, the probability of a given bond being drawn increases as the amount of the outstanding issue declines due to the regular operation of the sinking fund. It should be reiterated that the risk is only operative when bond prices rise materially above the sinking-fund call price or during periods of low money rates. As of 1965, these bonds sold below par because prevailing interest rates were above the 4.25% coupon. Under these conditions, the sinking-fund operation tended to support the price through market purchases.

Redemption Price. It has been noted that the contractual provision giving the company the option to redeem a bond or preferred in whole or in part at a specified price is an undesirable feature. It limits the appreciation which might otherwise be enjoyed because of a decline in money rates or an improvement in the credit position of the company, but it does not limit a large decline in market price from the reverse of these circumstances. The absence of any redemption price whatsoever would be most desirable in this respect.

However, most contracts include a call provision, which makes it possible for the company to take advantage of low interest-rate periods through refunding operations. The best that can be expected is a reasonably high call price written into the contract, or alternatively, a "deferred call" provision which prohibits the company from redeeming the issue for five or ten years after its original sale. It should hardly be necessary to indicate that any bond or preferred selling materially above call price should be avoided at all times. The only possible exception would be when an issue is convertible and commands a value in terms of common stock about equal to its own market price; in this case, of course, the investor could convert his holdings to common instead of surrendering it at the call price when and if notice of redemption is given by the company.

From the standpoint of contractual call protection, the Inland Steel 4¼s of 1989 were the most attractive of the several issues shown in Table 16-1 as the issue was not subject to call until 1969. However, the prospects of redemption are also reduced by a low coupon rate. As a result, the Inland Steel 3¼s of 1981 were actually less exposed to call in the foreseeable future. Given a specified call price, the actual risk of redemption can be measured by the difference between market price and call price.

Prices, Yields, and Relative Values

Bench Marks of Yields. Thus far attention has been concentrated on the standards for appraising the intrinsic merits of a company's fixed-income securities both with respect to their credit quality and the terms offered in the contract. The final task in the actual selection of these securities for long-term investment portfolios would be to consider their prices and yields in relation to some bench mark of yields. Except for minor technical complications, this phase of the selection process is considerably easier for bonds and preferred stocks than for common stocks, because the exact amount of the future income is known and expected yields can, therefore, be measured precisely. Moreover, it is assumed that the investor is considering only high-grade securities (all others should have been rejected in the course of the analytical process), and subjective allowances for credit risk need not be considered to any appreciable extent.

When interest rates are at a low level, the primary bench mark against which yields on industrial bonds and preferreds might be measured is the yield offered by United States Savings Bonds. These are unquestionably riskless. Moreover, the terms of the contract are distinctly favorable in one important way, namely, that they are redeemable at the option of the holder instead of at the option of the issuer. This is the redemption feature in reverse, and it endows savings bonds which absolute recoverability of the principal invested, unlike industrial securities, which are exposed to a decline in price in case interest rates rise in the market. Yields of 3.75% can be obtained on these bonds if held to about a seven-year nine-month maturity and 3.53% if held for only five years.[5]

In view of the significant superiority in the terms on savings bonds, it is suggested that an individual should be interested in corporate fixed-income securities only if there is a material yield advantage obtainable on them. Although it is difficult to justify any particular yield differential which would be required at all times and under all conditions, as a rule of thumb it would seem reasonable that about .5 to 1% higher yield should be available on a corporate fixed-income security. In addition, the general market yields prevailing on good-quality bonds or preferreds are relevant to a decision on the attractiveness of a particular issue.

Comparative Yield Analysis. It has been established that the senior securities of both the Inland Steel Company and Standard Oil of Ohio deserved a high-quality credit status. Therefore, they might have been considered for that portion of an investment account on which continuity of income was the major objective. However, the comparative yield data, shown in Table 16-2 suggested that both the preferred stock and debenture bonds of Standard Oil of Ohio were not particularly attractive, because their prevailing yields were below those available on alternatives.[6] On the other hand, the yields on the Inland Steel obligations were equal to or above the several bench marks. Between the three Inland Steel issues, there were reasons to prefer either the 3⅛s of 1981 or

---

[5] Yields on savings accounts or certificates of deposits at banks or savings and loan institutions might also be considered as yield bench marks. These accounts offer recoverability similar to Savings Bonds, but the ability of the institution to change the rate at any time represents a possible disadvantage, especially when interest rates are currently high and may decline in the future. In other words, the prevailing rate paid on such accounts is subject to a "call risk" at any time.

[6] The fact that the preferred stock carried a lower yield than the bonds which preceded it might have seemed unusual. The probable reason for this paradox was that 85% of the preferred dividends were exempt from income taxes if received by another corporation whereas the bond interest was fully taxable. To taxable corporate investors, the preferred stock carried a significantly higher after-tax yield.

TABLE 16-2
SELECTED BOND PRICES AND YIELDS
(as of March 1965)

	Price	Current Yield	Yield to Maturity
Inland Steel Company			
First mortgage 3½s of 1981	88½	3.95%	4.50%
First mortgage 4⅜s of 1987	99⅞	4.38	4.40
First mortgage 4½s of 1989	100¼	4.49	4.47
Standard Oil of Ohio			
Debenture 4¼s of 1982	99	4.29	4.33
3¾% preferred stock	96	3.91	—
Comparative Yields:			
Savings accounts and certificates of deposit			4 to 4.50
U.S. Savings Bonds			3.75
Barron's high-grade bond yield			4.40

the 4½s of 1989. The considerable spread between the market price and call price gave attraction to the 3½s, and the yield to maturity was highest on this bond. However, the comparatively low current yield represented a disadvantage to accounts emphasizing cash income. The most favorable combination of current income and yield to maturity was available on the 4½s of 1989. In addition, the call protection was adequate—noncallable until 1969, and then at 103½.

These bonds were listed on the New York Stock Exchange but had been infrequently traded. Therefore, large institutional investors, such as pension funds that require the availability of large blocks of bonds before a commitment is practicable, would probably not have considered them. But for accounts satisfied with $10,000 to $20,000 of the bonds, the Inland Steel obligations might have had considerable appeal.[7]

Yield Analysis: First Step. Because the yield analysis phase is much less laborious, the selection process in practice can be more efficiently conducted by reversing the sequence of steps from that discussed previously. In other words, it probably would be more expeditious to review the relative yields obtainable on several bonds or preferreds at prevailing prices as the first step. The investment advisory and statistical services, and lists supplied by reputable brokerage houses can all be used to

[7] Alternative yields on tax-exempt municipal obligations would be a logical additional yield bench mark for taxable investors wherein the yields indicated would be reduced by the applicable taxation rate for purposes of comparison with tax-exempts. See chapter 28 on taxation and investment decisions.

obtain candidates for further inquiry. Then those which appear to offer the most favorable yield opportunities can be thoroughly appraised.

The final decisions would then be based on the comparative investment qualities and technical terms. In the actual construction of a fixed-income security portfolio, other considerations might also be relevant, such as an appropriate maturity distribution. These matters, however, are properly part of the portfolio planning process, which will be discussed fully in Part VII.

PART IV

ANALYSIS OF REGULATED INDUSTRIES

CHAPTER 17

Public Utilities

Introduction

Scope of Utility Operations. The major singular characteristic of public-utility companies is their regulated monopoly status. The companies are given the exclusive right to render the service involved to a prescribed geographic area and in return they are obliged to submit to public control of the prices charged for the service. The suspension of free-enterprise concepts is considered necessary under the following conditions. First, the service rendered must be highly essential to consumers. Second, a very large capital investment must be required, so that duplicating competitive facilities would be highly wasteful of economic resources. Third, even if competitive facilities were allowed, consumers would find it very difficult to change back and forth from one supplier to another. Finally, in many instances it is necessary to confer certain quasi-governmental powers on these companies, such as property condemnation rights or compulsory easements.

There are a considerable number of economic activities provided under these conditions, but for one reason or another many can be excluded from practical consideration. One major group, railroads, requires special consideration because of its several unique features. The sale of water services is technically a public-utility operation, but for the most part local governments supply this service directly to consumers and the operations are financed with municipal revenue bonds which are specifically considered in a later chapter.

By and large the interests of investors tend to be concentrated in the following areas: (1) electric-power companies, (2) telephone companies, and (3) natural-gas pipeline and distributing companies. Of these, the electric-power industry offers by far the most opportunities for investment in different geographic areas and types of securities.[1] Because of the predominant role of the electric-power companies, this chapter will be primarily concerned with the special factors pertinent to their analysis. For the most part, however, the same general techniques and concepts are applicable to the other activities mentioned above.

Reasons for Special Treatment. It should be emphasized that an investment analysis of a public utility has the same objectives as for industrial companies. Therefore, the selection process in many respects follows the same lines. The major objectives can be summarized as follows: (1) to obtain some absolute and comparative indications of the quality and stature of the company for investment purposes, (2) to appraise the safety, yields, and contractual attractiveness of the senior securities, (3) to obtain some reasonable clues to the potential earning power and dividends per share of the common stock, (4) to decide upon a reasonable price for the earning power and dividends in the light of the conclusions on the quality factors. As many of the specific analytical techniques used to implement these objectives are similar to those discussed at some length for industrials, repetition of the reasoning behind these techniques should not be necessary.

However, because of substantive differences in the economic nature of utility operations, there are many unique features involved in their appraisal. One of the major purposes, therefore, will be to illustrate how investment analysis techniques must adjust to the special characteristics of a given industry. A second purpose is to illustrate with specific cases the nature of a comparative appraisal of several companies in the same industry. This could be done only to a very limited extent in the preceding chapters because the primary objectives there were to develop an understanding of the basic principles applicable to the appraisal of a company regardless of special-industry features. The heterogeneous

---

[1] The common stocks of companies supplying electric power have often been the largest single industry representation in the portfolios of institutional investors. The large number of companies available and their desirable investment characteristics are the logical explanations for this fact.

nature of industrials made it difficult to select any one industry group as being particularly typical or appropriate for special treatment in terms of comparative analysis. Utilities, rails, and certain financial institutions represent reasonably homogeneous activities that are of sufficient importance to warrant special mention. Within each group it becomes possible to illustrate how relative investment preferences for certain companies might emerge from the appraisal of several similar companies at the same time.

Public Utilities: Economic Analysis

Special Economic Factors. The endowment of a monopoly to provide a given set of services to a defined geographic area in return for substantial governmental intervention eliminates some qualitative factors which are pertinent to the appraisal of industrials and creates others which are special to utilities. Some factors, however, are common to both. For example, an analysis of the sources of demand for utility services to determine the potential for growth and stability of gross revenues is equally important for utilities and industrials. Also, like industrials, a dynamic analysis of the cost structure in relation to the revenue features may give some useful indications of how earnings may behave under various conditions in the economy. Third, the capacity of management is a pertinent factor for consideration, but it usually is of less crucial importance in utilities than in industrials.

On the other hand, the legal monopoly condition eliminates the need in most instances to consider intraindustry competition. Moreover, in the case of electric-power companies, interindustry competition is not a problem of any consequence. To some degree, gas and electricity are competitive, but often the same company will supply both services. For illumination and many power needs electricity has no effective competition from other energy sources. However, the natural-gas pipeline and distributing companies are perhaps faced with slightly greater prospects of interindustry competition from oil with respect to the important use of gas for heating purposes.

There are, however, some additional qualitative factors unique to utilities. First, there is the question of whether the company operates within a favorable political jurisdiction. However, although an unfavorable regulatory environment would have unsatisfactory implications for investors, the relations of most state commissions and the utilities have been good since World War II. Second, unlike industrials, utilities are irrevocably committed to a given geographic market for their service. Detroit Edison, for example, cannot decide that it would be desirable to move its service market to the West Coast. It is necessary, therefore, to consider the general economic prospects for the geographic area. Third, there is a "special case" qualitative risk associated with a few utilities that operate in areas where federal power projects (usually under the guise of flood-control programs) are a possibility. This risk is almost impossible to appraise rationally because it depends essentially on the unknown future philosophy of Congress on the role of government with respect to providing power services to consumers.

Gross-Revenue Pattern: Electric-Power Industry. Electric power is used both as an indirect production component of other goods and services and as a final service to consumers. As a result, physical output and revenue statistics for electricity usage are classified into three major categories: industrial, commercial, and residential.[2] The pattern of physical output (measured by kilowatt hours) and revenues for selected years over the decade ended with 1963 is shown in Table 17-1 for all privately owned electric power companies in the United States. The remarkable growth of both output and revenues is immediately evident from this data.

The factors responsible for the growth are numerous and seem likely to have a continuing impact in the future. For example, in the industrial category the persistent trend toward automation of manufacturing processes has had very salutary effects on the sale of electric power, and there is every evidence that this trend will continue indefinitely. In addition, the continued development of new household electrical equipment and appliances indicates a continued favorable trend in demand by residential customers. The trend toward more intensive use of electric power per residence is shown by the fact that the average annual bill has increased from about $70 in 1953 to about $105 in 1963.[3]

The evidence, then, suggests a very favorable growth picture for electric power usage in the foreseeable future. From an economic point of view, it is entirely justifiable to conclude that at least one essential feature of growth companies is present: that of a favorable trend in demand and revenues. And if the trend in revenues can be effectively translated into a similar growth in earnings per share then a majority might deserve the growth-stock label.

---

[2] In some cases, individual companies combine the industrial and commercial categories. This is unfortunate because the demand characteristics are quite different in the two categories.

[3] Edison Electric Institute, *Statistical Yearbook for 1963*, New York, pp. 46–47.

TABLE 17–1
ELECTRIC POWER OUTPUT AND REVENUES
SELECTED YEARS 1953–63

Year	Industrial		Commercial		Residential	
	Kilowatt Hours (in billions)	Revenues (in millions)	Kilowatt Hours (in billions)	Revenues (in millions)	Kilowatt Hours (in billions)	Revenues (in millions)
1953	194	$1,932	71	$1,782	101	$2,777
1955	258	2,416	78	1,944	125	3,323
1957	292	2,754	92	2,241	152	3,909
1959	313	3,010	109	2,598	180	4,515
1961	347	3,370	134	3,168	209	5,116
1963	388	3,596	166	3,788	242	5,723
1963 as % of 1953	200%	190%	234%	211%	241%	204%

Source: Edison Electric Institute (Statistical Yearbook for 1963.)

The outlook for a high degree of stability in the revenue pattern is equally favorable for a number of reasons. First, and perhaps of primary importance, electric power can be classified as a low-priced consumer necessity so far as residential use is concerned. Therefore, even under adverse business conditions, household use tends to continue at about the same level. Second, a large part of commercial demand is also highly inelastic, because as long as stores or offices remain open for business about the same amount of electricity will be consumed. Third, the strong growth aspects undoubtedly contribute to stability. A strong upward trend in demand usually tends to show resistance to even temporary declines. Fourth, the "step-down" rate structure also contributes to stability because as customers use less power, the unit price increases and vice versa.[4] As a result, any decrease in physical demand has a less than proportional effect on revenue.

Few industries, in brief, have as desirable a combination of growth and stability in the demand for their products as the electric-power companies. These characteristics are probably the important reason why such a large number of these companies enjoy the status of "blue chip" investments, and both their bonds and stocks are heavily favored by institutional investors.

[4] The "step-down" rate pattern is characteristic of the electric-power industry and is usually explained in the following way: the first kilowatt hours used in any month carry a higher price than succeeding units, and rate brackets for successive units are established. The reason for this pricing system is that much of the costs associated with supplying power to a given user are fixed and marginal costs are low for the most part.

Gross-Revenue   Analysis: Specific   Company.   Although   continued
growth in population and new forms of electric-power application result
in a very bright outlook for the industry, the comparative revenue outlook for different companies may vary widely according to the character
of the service area. Some areas, such as Florida, California, and Texas,
have shown relatively rapid rates of population and industrial growth.
Companies in these locations, therefore, have enjoyed an especially
favorable revenue trend.

But by and large the companies serving large metropolitan centers
are regarded as representing the best overall investment quality. The
major reason is that the seasoned character of the large cities makes it
unlikely that significant long-term declines in population and industry
will occur. Moreover, the diversification of industry in most large city
areas tends to be greater. Finally, a dense population is desirable in the
service area, because important capital costs (e.g., distribution lines)
per customer decrease as density of usage increases.

Some of the older large cities, especially in the East, have shown
below average rates of growth in population and industry; consequently
the related utilities have demonstrated below average growth in revenues. Therefore, although the defensive characteristics of these companies are usually superior, more enterprising investors often prefer to
concentrate on utilities serving less densely populated areas which are
showing more rapid population and industry growth.

To show the substantial differences between companies in revenue
growth, Table 17-2 shows the index of gross revenues for three major
companies located in different parts of the country. Although all have
participated in the greatly increased usage of electric power, the dynamic development of Houston stands out quite clearly. The stable and
mature character of industry and commerce in Philadelphia and Detroit
suggests that Philadelphia Electric and Detroit Edison might appeal
largely to defensive investors. However, even these companies have
shown both a consistant and substantial growth in revenues.

Cost Factors.   Most electric power in the United States is generated
through steam-driven turbines, with hydro operations constituting a
distinctly secondary role. From a cost standpoint, there are major differences between the two methods of generating power. The major operating cost of steam power is fuel, largely coal, but also oil and some
natural gas. Hydro power eliminates fuel costs but requires much larger
original capital outlays for the dams and related facilities. Operating
expenses, as conventionally defined, are thus less for hydro operations,
but the savings are offset by the need for much more invested capital

TABLE 17-2
INDEX OF GROSS REVENUES: SELECTED YEARS (1957-59 = 100)

	Detroit Edison	Philadelphia Electric	Houston Lighting
1953	75	75	56
1955	76	84	69
1957	98	95	91
1959	105	106	110
1961	112	116	126
1963	122	125	163
1964	135	129	174

for each dollar of revenue produced. Because of these differences, it is not logical to compare operating performances of a hydro plant with a steam plant, but most of the major private utilities are essentially steam operations.

Even when steam turbines are the source of power, capital outlays are large in comparison with industrial companies. It is estimated that about $4 of plant investment is required for each $1 of revenues, whereas even a heavy industry operation like an integrated steel company ordinarily shows annual revenues about 1.5 times the net plant investment. As a result, from an economic standpoint "costs of capital" per dollar of revenue are relatively high, although these costs are not included in operating expenses. To illustrate, assuming an overall cost of money of 5% and $4 of plant investment per dollar of revenues, capital costs would be at least 20% of the total revenues ($.20 per $1). Under these conditions a utility would have to show an after-tax operating ratio (operating expenses and income taxes divided by revenues) of less than 80% in order to pay the interest and dividends on the outstanding securities with no reinvested earnings. In brief, because of the large capital outlays required to produce $1 of revenues, operating ratios must be much lower in utilities than in industrials.

To indicate more specifically the cost characteristics of the electric power companies, Table 17-3 shows the breakdown of the revenue dollar for 1962 and, for comparative purposes, the same breakdown for 1953. The cost record over the decade suggests that the electric power companies have been able to improve productivity considerably, because despite a reduction in the average prices of electric power and a drift upward in wage rates, labor costs per dollar of revenue have decreased. The reduction in fuel costs per dollar of revenues also indicates improved efficiency; the increase in taxes was of course outside of the control of the industry.

However, during the rapid inflation period of 1945-49, profit margins

TABLE 17–3
PERCENTAGE APPLICATION OF UTILITY REVENUES
(Private Electric Power Companies)

	1953	1962
Gross Revenues	100%	100%
Operating Expenses		
Fuel costs	16.4%	14.5%
Depreciation	9.1	11.0
Taxes°	21.6	22.6
Wages and salaries	18.8	15.1
Other	12.5	12.1
Total expenses	78.4%	75.3%
Operating Earnings	21.6%	24.7%

° Includes all kinds of taxes including income taxes.
Source: Edison Electric Institute.

of the electric power companies declined, and despite increases in revenues, earnings of many companies held steady or also declined slightly. The inability of the companies to obtain regulatory approval of rate increases fast enough to offset rapidly rising cost levels was responsible. Therefore, during a "burst" type of rapid inflation, utility common stocks were not desirable, but under the slow "cost-push" type of inflation they have shown good earnings results.

Built-in Stability Concept. In reviewing the revenue and cost characteristics of the electric-utility companies, there are reasons to believe that although the physical output of electric power may decline significantly during a recession, earnings may decline only moderately. This built-in stability arises from the combination of (1) the step-down rate structure, (2) the low unit price of industrial power, and (3) the varying efficiency of generating plants according to their age.

Any decline in power usage tends to be concentrated in the industrial category where unit prices per kilowatt hour are very low. Moreover, the step-down rate structure means that as customers reduce usage the unit price increases. Revenues thus automatically decline less than output. Furthermore, as physical usage declines a utility will shut down the oldest and least efficient plants. In fact, it is conceivable that the direct costs of generating power in the older and least efficient plants exceed the marginal revenue from the large industrial customers, which would mean earnings might actually increase if these customers took less power.

TABLE 17-4
RATE OF RETURN ON NET UTILITY PLANT

	1958–64 Average	1964
Detroit Edison	5.8%	6.8%
Philadelphia Electric	6.0	6.4
Houston Lighting	7.6	8.5
National average (1958–64)	6.1	6.5

Source: Annual Reports and Moody's *Public Utility Manual,* 1965 Edition.

The operating experience of Detroit Edison during the recession of 1958 clearly supported this view. In that year, kilowatt-hour sales declined by more than 10%, but total revenues decreased by only about 2%, and operating income declined by only slightly more than 1%. Therefore, a moderate recession in general business activity may have little effect on electric-utility earnings even though kilowatt-hour sales to industry decline significantly at such times.

Public-Utility Regulation. On the whole the state commissions have been reasonably sympathetic to the needs of utilities for adequate earnings. Perhaps in a very general sense the apparent political trends of the state in which the utility is located is some indication of the ultimate regulatory prospects. If left-wing elements seem to be increasing their political influence, then utilities of that state might be assessed with a long-range qualitative risk. But this factor is highly intangible and repeated prophecies of danger in some states have so far proven entirely unwarranted.

A possible indication of potential regulatory action to reduce rates is an unusually high rate of return on the book value of the assets. But careful interpretation of the data is required because some states, notably Ohio, allow reproduction cost or "fair value" to determine the rate base, and earnings may be high on original cost shown in the accounts yet moderate on the established rate base. Table 17-4 shows the seven-year average and the 1964 rate of return on net property for the three illustrative companies.

In the case of Detroit Edison and Houston Lighting, the 1964 rate of return on net plant assets was well above the seven-year average, which perhaps suggests two conclusions. First, there might be some exposure to voluntary rate reductions, or alternatively, some pressure from the regulatory authorities.[5] Second, that portion of the past growth in earnings which resulted from an increase in the rate of return must be viewed with some suspicion as an indication of the probable future trend. In a regulated industry, the probability of continued increases in the rate of return on invested capital would seem quite doubtful.

In summary, although the regulatory outlook is often difficult to appraise, it is usually reassuring to find the rate of return on net property more or less in line with the national average.[6] If it is not materially above the average, it may be presumed that the utility in question is not vulnerable to regulatory action to reduce rates. If the rate of return is well above the average, as for Houston Lighting, then the regulatory exposure might require further investigation. In this case, it can be noted that Texas has no state commission and rates are established by negotiation with municipal governments, which historically have condoned above-average rates of return.

Governmental Competition. The only significant competition facing the private electric-power utilities has been the special and sporadic problem of governmental power developments. In the past, only in those areas where federal hydro projects appeared feasible was this factor given any serious consideration. But the Rural Electrification Administration has in some areas, mainly outside the major metropolitan centers, granted loans at a 2% rate to expand both generating and transmission facilities of cooperatives in partial competition with private companies. By and large, however, the private companies by vigorous expansion of their own facilities have been able to prevent the widespread development of such cooperatives except in sparsely populated areas. Although a latent threat to some companies in these areas, the problem of government competition has not been a serious factor impeding the development and growth of most private utility companies.

Public Utilities: Financial Analysis

The analytical objectives here are the same as for industrials. To repeat, they may be summarized as follows: (1) to obtain evidence on

---

[5] In January of 1965 Detroit Edison did announce that "voluntary" rate reductions of modest proportions were to be made to residential customers.

[6] Note that a high rate of return on invested capital or net worth cannot be used as an indication of managerial competence in utilities as it is in industrials. Differences in regulatory attitudes and service-area characteristics make comparisons in this respect of no real significance.

the general investment qualities as revealed by the efficiency, earnings, and revenue patterns of the companies, (2) to appraise the financial position and the consequent quality of the fixed-income securities, (3) to obtain specific clues to the possible future amounts of earnings and dividends per common share, (4) to decide upon a reasonable price to be paid for the existing earnings and their possible projections. To a considerable extent the investment qualities should be suggested by the comparative economic appraisal of the companies. However, the past financial statements are useful not only to substantiate, or perhaps modify, the conclusions derived from the economic analysis, but also to provide the prime evidence on certain aspects of investment quality. For example, the measures of efficiency are primarily determined from balance-sheet and income-statement data.

Appraisal of Operating Efficiency. Because the operating characteristics of each public utility are in some respects unique, there are no completely satisfactory comparative techniques to measure comparative managerial capacities. But whether because of superior management or the characteristics of the area served, it is still reasonable to prefer those utilities which have produced revenues and profits at the lowest cost and with the least capital investment. Two ratios perhaps sum up the general operating efficiency. First, there is the operating ratio, computed by dividing operating expenses by revenues.[7] The ratio shows the ability to produce earnings from each dollar of revenues, and because competitive pricing policies are not used by utilities, it is a more conclusive test of efficiency than for industrials.

Second, there is the ratio of gross revenues to the gross investment in plant assets. This ratio represents a measure of the productivity of the utility's assets. More than 90% of total assets are typically committed to fixed assets in the form of generating and transmission facilities, and it is desirable of course to use these assets as intensively as possible. From an engineering standpoint "use intensity" might be measured by kilowatt hours generated per dollar of plant investment, but from an economic standpoint the revenues obtained from the investment are a more significant measure of efficiency, because the economic purpose of plant assets is to produce revenues.

Table 17-5 shows the level and trend of these ratios for the three companies during 1960-64. It is quite clear that Houston Lighting had an exceptionally efficient operation. Detroit Edison, on the other hand,

---

[7] Operating expenses normally include all deductions on the income statement except income taxes, interest charges, and dividends.

TABLE 17-5
EFFICIENCY RATIOS: 1960-64

	1960	1961	1962	1963	1964
Detroit Edison					
Operating ratio	71.6%	70.4%	69.6%	68.9%	68.8%
Gross plant to revenues	4.2	4.2	4.1	3.9	3.7
Philadelphia Electric					
Operating ratio	66.4%	64.9%	64.9%	66.2%	66.3%
Gross plant to revenues	4.7	4.6	4.6	4.6	4.6
Houston Lighting					
Operating ratio	54.4%	56.5%	53.9%	52.4%	53.8%
Gross plant to revenues	4.4	4.3	3.9	3.7	3.7

Source: Moody's *Public Utility Manual*, 1964 edition, and annual reports for 1964.

had a relatively high operating ratio, although the trend was favorable. Philadelphia Electric had enjoyed a satisfactory operating ratio, but the amount of plant investment required to generate a dollar of revenues was significantly greater than for the others.

Absolute standards for these ratios are difficult to establish. But it might be useful to construct a somewhat simplified illustration using some assumptions based on data for the entire electric-power industry. These assumptions are as follows: (1) a capital structure made up of 60% senior securities and 40% common stock, (2) an average cost of senior capital of 4%, (3) a 50% income-tax rate against earnings after deducting the charges on senior securities, (4) an average operating ratio of 70%, (5) gross plant of $4 for each $1 of revenues, and (6) invested capital, largely represented by gross utility plant investment.[8] On the basis of these assumptions, the balance sheet and income statement would show the proportions indicated in Table 17-6. The illustration indicates that the operating ratio should not exceed about 70%, and gross plant should not be much more than four times gross revenues if the utility is to earn a return on the common-stock equity of at least 6%.

Analysis of the Capital Structure. Because utilities require large amounts of capital and because their stability makes financing with senior securities expedient, the capital structures invariably include a high

[8] True invested capital at any given time is actually about 10% less than gross plant, because the accumulated allowance for depreciation should be deducted and net working capital added to obtain true invested capital. Normally the depreciation reserve greatly exceeds net working capital.

TABLE 17-6
RATES OF RETURN: ASSUMED FINANCIAL STATEMENT PROPORTIONS

Assets		Equities	
Plant, gross	$4	4% Bonds	$2.40 (60%)
		Common-stock equity	1.60 (40%)
Total	$4		$4.00 (100%)
Gross revenues			$1.00
Operating expenses (70% ratio)			.70
Net operating income			.30
Interest charges (4% × 2.40)			.10
Net taxable income			.20
Income taxes (50% rate)			.10
Earnings to common stock			.10
Percent earned on common-stock equity			6.25%

proportion of bonds and in some cases preferred stocks. It is necessary, therefore to appraise financial policies by the conventional techniques of computing the senior-security earnings coverage and inspecting the capital-structure breakdown.

There is also a more positive aspect of capital structure analysis in the special case of utilities. It arises out of the fact that these companies seem destined to need continued large amounts of capital in the future because of secular growth in electric-power usage. Therefore, if the analysis shows an existing conservative financial structure, it is possible that the proportion of senior securities could be safely increased in the future. The resultant greater leverage may significantly improve the per share earnings on the common stock. On the other hand, if investigation shows that senior securities are already being used to a practical maximum, then this source of growth may not be possible, although new issues of debt in combination with new sales of common stock may also increase earnings per share.

The favorable stability characteristics of electric-power companies suggest that the coverage standards may be much more liberal than for the average industrial. As it is very doubtful if earnings available for fixed charges would ever decline to less than one-third of the most recent five-year average in the case of an entrenched electric-power operation, an average fixed-charge coverage of 3 would seem to be a reasonable standard for demonstrating sound financial policies. This coverage can usually be obtained with 60 to 65% of the capital structure composed of senior securities.

TABLE 17-7
CAPITAL STRUCTURE: AND SENIOR-SECURITY COVERAGE

	1960	1961	1962	1963	1964
Detroit Edison					
Capital structure:					
Per cent bonds	53	52	51	50	49
Per cent preferred	—	—	—	—	—
Per cent common	47	48	49	50	51
Times charges earned°	5.1	5.3	5.8	6.4	7.1
Philadelphia Electric					
Capital structure:					
Per cent bonds	52	54	53	52	54
Per cent preferred	9	9	9	8	8
Per cent common	39	37	38	40	38
Times charges earned°	6.5	5.6	5.5	5.7	5.4
Times charges and preferred earned†	3.1	3.0	3.0	3.1	3.0
Houston Lighting					
Capital structure:					
Per cent bonds	54	53	54	52	50
Per cent preferred	3	3	2	2	2
Per cent common	43	44	44	46	48
Times charges earned°	7.1	6.2	7.8	8.5	9.6
Times charges and preferred earned†	3.8	3.4	4.1	4.7	5.1

° Before income taxes.
† After taxes.

Table 17-7 shows the capital structures and the fixed-charge coverage for the three utilities over the 1960–64 period. Although it would be preferable to include a period of economic adversity, the strong growth and stability characteristics of these companies makes the adversity test less essential. But there might be one technical accounting problem in computing the times-charges-earned ratio. This is the practice of showing on the income statement a deduction from interest charges entitled *interest charged to construction,* which represents an imputed interest cost (usually at a rate higher than actually paid on the debt) on the funds committed to construction in progress. The cost of the plant assets on the balance sheet is then increased by a like amount. The purpose of the procedure is to incorporate into the rate base all the economic costs involved in building new plant facilities. And interest on the money invested in plants under construction is logically one of the economic costs of the new facilities. However, the cash outlay for debt service is not reduced because of this book transaction. Therefore, because earnings on the new facilities when completed should at least equal the amount of *interest charged to construction*, an appropriate procedure is to add the imputed interest credit to the earnings and divide by the total actual cash outlays for debt service. However, in the case of the illustrative utilities, the amount of *interest charged to construction* was not an important amount in any of the years shown.

The computations in Table 17-7 indicate that all the companies have sound financial structures. Therefore, because of the strong earnings protection and the favorable stability prognosis, the senior securities of these companies are of high investment quality.[9] But whether these securities would be attractive to individual investors would also depend on their contractual terms and the prevailing yields in relation to alternative bonds and preferreds.

Both Detroit Edison and Houston Lighting seemed to be in a position to finance a substantial proportion of future expansion with an increase in their debt ratios because of their higher than average coverage ratios and common-stock equities as a percentage of total capitalization. Therefore, some growth in per share earnings might be obtained from this source. Philadelphia Electric, however, seemed to have more limited possibilities on this score. But the strong financial position of all three companies, measured by the reasonably favorable equity ratios and the good earnings coverage of senior-security charges, suggested that the future bond issues would be readily received by the market at the prevailing rates for high-quality issues.

Sources of Earnings Growth. As indicated previously, there is strong evidence that the future growth in electric-power consumption and in total gross revenues of the companies will be highly favorable. But it also appears probable that substantial investment in plant assets will be required to make possible the growth in revenues; about $4 of new plant for each additional dollar in revenues might be estimated, although a short-term downward or upward trend in this relationship may take place for several years, as indicated in Table 17-5.

Assuming, however, that capital needs will be heavy over a decade or so, and much greater than can be met with retained earnings, then

[9] It is interesting to note, however, that the bonds of Detroit Edison and Houston Lighting were rated Aa (high quality) by Moody's, whereas Philadelphia Electric's bonds were rated Aaa (highest quality), despite the fact that the coverage and capitalization ratios were more favorable for the former two situations. The reasons for the differences in the ratings were not explained; as a conjecture it might be that the greater instability characteristics of the Detroit and Houston areas were responsible.

considerable amounts of new issues of both senior securities and common stocks would be required from time to time. Thus it might be concluded that the growth in per share earnings might be much less than the growth in revenues and total net income, because of the dilution resulting from new sales of common stock.

However, if the conditions that have prevailed in the stock market during most of the 1960–65 period continue in the future, then considerable growth in per share earnings may result even though new stock issues or the equivalent (convertibles) are necessary from time to time. During this period the market prices of most utility common stocks were greatly in excess of book values. As a result, when and if new common stock is sold, the book value per share of all the outstanding stock is increased. Assuming a constant rate of return on total invested capital, which would appear reasonable in a regulated industry with growth characteristics, and a constant proportion of debt to equity, then as the consequence of new stock issues, earnings per share will increase by an amount equal to the increase in per share book value times the rate of return on the book value.

A quantitative illustration of the phenomenon is shown in Table 17-8. Here it is assumed that because of growth in the demand for electric power a 50% expansion in invested capital is required, and a proportion of 60% debt in the capital structure is constantly maintained. It is further assumed that existing book value per share of the 1,000,000 outstanding shares is $40 but that new stock can be sold at close to its prevailing market price of 2.5 times its book value, or at $100 per share. Under these conditions, 200,000 new shares will provide the $20 million of additional equity capital required. As a consequence of the sale of these shares, the total common-stock equity will increase to $60 million and the book value per share of the 1,200,000 outstanding shares will increase to $50 or by $10. Because of profitable leverage (a 6% allowed rate of return on invested capital but 4% paid on borrowed funds), the rate of return on the equity is 9%. The increase in earnings per share that results is $10 times 9% or $.90 (from $3.60 to $4.50).

Notice, however, that the 50% expansion in total assets and earnings under the assumed conditions resulted in only a 25% increase in earnings per share. Therefore, in the sense that earnings per share increased at a less rapid rate than total revenues and earnings, there has been some dilution in transmitting the revenue growth rate to earnings per share. But to a considerable extent, the dilution may be reduced by removing the inhibiting assumption that no additions to the common equity

TABLE 17-8
EFFECTS OF SALE OF COMMON STOCK: PREMIUM OVER BOOK VALUE

	Present	*50% Expansion*	*Pro-forma*
Balance-sheet data			
Invested capital	$100,000,000	$50,000,000	$150,000,000
4% senior securities	60,000,000	30,000,000	90,000,000
Common-stock equity	40,000,000	20,000,000	60,000,000
Number of shares	1,000,000		1,200,000
New shares—price $100	200,000		
Book value per share	$40		$50
Income-statement data			
6% return on capital	$ 6,000,000		$ 9,000,000
Prior charges—4%	2,400,000		3,600,000
Balance for common	$ 3,600,000		$ 5,400,000
Earned per share	$ 3.60		$ 4.50
Rate of return on book value	9%		9%

Assumptions
1. 6% return on invested capital
2. Constant capital structure of 60% debt and 40% common stock
3. 4% constant cost of senior capital
4. No reinvested earnings
5. New common stock sold at 250% of book value

will be made from retained earnings. Also a higher premium of market value over book value would reduce the dilution effect. However, the amount of the premium may be related to the payout ratio on the basis that a liberal dividend policy will produce a more generous market valuation of the stock. Therefore, although a reduction in the payout ratio may increase the growth rate in the absence of the need for sales of new stock, such action may reduce the growth rate if new stock issues are required and the premium of market price over book value is lower than it would be with a more liberal dividend payout.[10]

Some utilities in the rapid growth areas have been able to retain considerable proportions of their earnings, but even so the market prices of the stocks have sold at handsome premiums over book values. Houston Lighting, for example, paid out only about 47% of its earnings in the

[10] The apparent paradox of utilities requiring substantial amounts of new capital accompanied by earnings retentions of only 25% or so might be explained by this observation. Many utility companies have apparently concluded that policy should favor the payment of liberal dividends and thus encourage higher market prices for their common stocks in anticipation of new offerings rather than to obtain a larger proportion of their capital needs through retained earnings.

TABLE 17-9
EARNINGS AND DIVIDEND DATA: SELECTED YEARS

	1957	1960	1961	1962	1963	1964	1964 divided by: 1957	1960
Detroit Edison								
Gross revenues (in millions)	$250.6	$279.0	$285.7	$301.4	$319.5	$342.8	1.37	1.23
Net income (in millions)	32.7	38.4	39.7	42.9	46.2	51.7	1.57	1.35
Earnings per share	$1.31	$1.34	$1.38	$1.49	$1.60	$1.80	1.38	1.34
Dividends per share	1.00	1.00	1.10	1.10	1.20	1.225	1.225	1.23
Payout ratio	76%	75%	79%	74%	75%	68%	—	—
Book value per share	$13.62	$14.12	$14.41	$14.78	$15.18	$15.75	1.15	1.11
Rate of return	9.6%	9.5%	9.6%	10.1%	10.5%	11.4%	—	—
Philadelphia Electric								
Gross revenues (in millions)	$237.8	$276.0	$292.3	$303.2	$314.4	$323.8	1.37	1.17
Net income (in millions)	37.2	42.3	46.6	47.6	50.2	52.8	1.42	1.26
Earnings per share	$1.30	$1.42	$1.57	$1.61	$1.69	$1.79	1.38	1.26
Dividends per share	1.00	1.12	1.18	1.20	1.29	1.32	1.32	1.18
Payout ratios	77%	79%	75%	75%	76%	73%	—	—
Book value per share	$12.28	$13.79	$14.03	$14.44	$15.05	$15.52	1.25	1.12
Rate of return	10.6%	10.3%	11.2%	11.2%	11.2%	11.5%	—	—
Houston Lighting								
Gross revenues (in millions)	$87.1	$115.8	$120.5	$141.6	$155.2	$166.1	1.91	1.43
Net income (in millions)	18.5	22.1	21.1	27.0	31.1	34.4	1.86	1.56
Earnings per share	.92	1.09	1.04	1.33	1.54	1.70	1.86	1.56
Dividends per share	.52	.53	.535	.57	.69	.84	1.63	1.58
Payout ratio	56%	49%	52%	43%	46%	49%	—	—
Book value per share	$6.49	$7.98	$8.49	$9.26	$10.10	$10.96	1.69	1.37
Rate of return	14.1%	13.7%	12.3%	14.6%	15.2%	15.5%	—	—

years 1960–64, yet in 1965 its common stock sold for about $55 per share as compared to a book value at the end of 1964 of about $11 per share. Its rate of return on book has also been relatively high, 13 to 15% in this period. As a consequence of (1) a lower than average payout ratio, (2) a relationship of 5 to 1 of market to book, and (3) an above average rate of return, its growth rate in earnings per share should be much more favorable than the average utility, assuming these conditions continue to prevail in the future.

A second possible source of growth in per share earnings would be an increase in the rate of return on the equity either through (1) a reduction in the operating ratio, (2) a decrease in the amount of invested capital per dollar of revenues, or (3) an increase in the proportion of senior securities in the capital structure.[11] Indeed Table 17-9 shows that moderate increases in the rate of return did occur in the 1956–64 period for the three illustrative companies. In these instances, declines in both the operating ratio and in the ratio of invested capital to revenues were responsible as the data in Table 17-7 indicated that the proportion of senior securities in the capital structures had actually declined moderately for all three companies.

The impact of these elements can be illustrated from data in Table 17–9 related to Detroit Edison. Note that revenues increased by 1.37 times over the 1957–64 period, whereas book value increased by only 1.15 times showing an increase in the turnover of total invested capital as the debt ratio did not increase. Second, the fact that net income increased by a factor of 1.58, or by more than revenues, demonstrated the decline in the operating ratio. In this case some new shares were issued as a consequence of the gradual voluntary conversion of a convertible debenture bond sold in 1956. As a result, earnings per share showed a growth less than that of net income, although the practical identity of the percentage increase in net income and per share earnings in 1960–64 indicates that conversion was largely completed by 1960. However, the net consequence was an increase in the rate of return on the equity from 9.6 to 11.4%. Similar trends, except for the operating ratio in Houston Lighting, can be noted for the other companies.

But to forecast a long-term repetitive increase in the rate of return on

[11] Lower interest rates on new and refunding senior-security capital could also produce an increase in the rate of return on the equity, but as the companies have a number of senior issues outstanding which mature at different times in the future with various redemption terms and as there is no evidence that significantly lower interest rates will prevail in the future, this factor would seem to be merely a fortuitous possibility.

the equity would appear questionable for two reasons. First, although moderate improvement in the efficiency factors may continue for a few years, it would seem logical that ultimately the operating ratio and the ratio of invested capital to revenues will reach practical minimums. Second, the regulatory authorities would logically take a dim view of allowing a rate structure to persist which continually produced larger earnings returns on the equity; passing along to the customers a major part of the benefits of improved efficiency would seem to be their entirely tenable position. Therefore, that part of the growth which has been caused by an improvement in the rate of return might well be substantially discounted.

Nevertheless, other sources of growth which did not operate in the 1956–64 period to any appreciable extent may well operate in the future: greater leverage and the sale of new shares at a premium over book value. As a consequence, it would not be appropriate in the case of these utilities to use the formula based on the rate of return and the payout ratio to estimate their potential growth rate as was used for industrial companies. External financing is too important an element in their growth dynamics to assume a major reliance on retained earnings for this purpose. On balance after considering the several factors, it seemed appropriate to estimate the range of potential growth rates by using the compound-interest method applied to either revenues or earnings per share; revenues were used if their growth factor was lower than per share earnings because it did not seem probable that earnings could continue to achieve a growth rate above that of total revenues.[12]

Comparative Earnings Estimates. In view of their favorable stability and growth characteristics, it would not seem unreasonable in these instances to use current earnings per share as a conservative estimate of earning power. Moreover, in order to suggest the relative desirability of utility stocks, it is usually useful to project earnings at the computed growth rates and relate the projections to the prevailing market prices. Based on the data in Table 17-9 the following per share earning power and projections might be estimated:

[12] The resultant growth rate factors from Table 17-9 were as follows: (1) Detroit Edison, revenues, 1.37 for seven years and 1.23 for four years; (2) Philadelphia Electric, revenues, 1.37 for seven years and 1.17 for four years; (3) Houston Lighting, earnings per share, 1.86 for seven years, and revenues, 1.43 for four years. Refer to compound-interest table in appendix for growth-rate readings.

	1964 Earnings	Projected Earnings: 1969 *	Annual Compounded Growth Rate
Detroit Edison	$1.80	$2.25–$2.30	4.7–5.2%
Philadelphia Electric	1.79	2.15– 2.25	4.0–4.7%
Houston Lighting	1.70	2.65	9.3%

* Rounded to nearest $.05 per share. Computed via using compound interest table at indicated growth rates for 5 years. Range of projected earnings not required for Houston Lighting as growth rate consistent during 1957–64 period.

Comparative Valuations. For perhaps several reasons, price-earnings ratios on the common stocks of the leading electric power companies have usually been above those prevailing on industrial stocks in general.[13] First, the growth record of utilities has been better and more consistent than that of the widely disparate industrials. Second, the stability record has been outstanding, which means considerable confidence can be placed in the forecast of earning power and on the maintenance of dividend income. Third, these factors have particular attraction to trustee-type institutional investors, such as pension funds. And as is well known, the importance of these institutional investors in terms of funds available for investment has greatly increased during the past two decades or so.

It was not surprising, therefore, to find that the price-earnings ratios of the utility index and of the three utility companies, shown in Table 17-10, were above those prevailing on the industrial index. But the price-earnings data clearly showed that two different types of electric-power companies were represented. First, there were the large metropolitan companies represented by Detroit Edison and Philadelphia Electric. Second, there was the growth utility, represented by Houston Lighting. The former companies showed price-earnings ratios about in line with the utility index although the dividend yields were moderately higher which indicated above-average payout ratios.[14]

[13] In the decade 1955–64 the only exceptions to this general observation were found in recession periods, such as 1958 and early 1961, when the market apparently considered the prevailing depressed earnings on industrial shares non-representative of future prospects and the price-earnings ratios computed on the basis of such prevailing earnings moved above those reported for utilities. These exceptions merely indicate the drawbacks of making market comparisons on the sole basis of *current* earnings especially for industrial companies subject to cyclical fluctuations.

[14] The growth-yield concept explained in Chapter 14 might also be appropriately applied to those electric power utilities which have clearly positive growth rates.

TABLE 17–10
PRICE-EARNINGS RATIOS AND YIELDS: 1965

| | Price | Price-Earnings Ratios | | Payout Period* | Dividend Rate | Dividend Yield |
		Current Earnings	Projected Earnings			
Detroit Edison	38	21.1	16.5–16.9	14–15 years	$1.30	3.4%
Philadelphia Electric	37	20.6	16.8–17.2	14.5–15.5	1.32	3.6
Houston Lighting	54	31.7	20.4	15.5	.84	1.5
Standard and Poor's Utility Index		20.7	–	–		3.1
Standard and Poor's Industrial Index		18.3	16.2†	14.0†		2.9
High-grade bond yields						4.4

* Computed by using Table 2 (in appendix at back of book) on the basis of indicated growth rates.
† Based on assumption of 4% growth rate.

Between Detroit Edison and Philadelphia Electric, it was difficult to find a significant difference. The price-earnings ratio and dividend yield, based on the current earnings and dividend rate, were slightly more favorable for Philadelphia Electric, but the moderately better growth rate of Detroit Edison gave it a slightly lower price-earnings ratio based on projected earnings in 1969 and a shorter payout period.[15] In both cases, however, the prices to projected earnings and the payout periods were in line with the industrial index, and dividend yields were above that prevailing on the index. Therefore, both might have been considered eligible at the prevailing prices for investors interested in a combination of above-average income and moderate growth prospects.

The Houston Lighting situation was quite different. Its price-earnings ratio of almost thirty-two times current earnings was well above those on both the industrial and the utility indexes and its dividend yield was well below average. Although the very superior growth record and prospects clearly vindicated a premium price for this stock, a decision on this stock posed a vexing problem. On the one hand, if the growth rate continued to be highly salutary for the next five years and beyond, the premium price-earnings ratio might be maintained at close to its current level, in which case the appreciation return would be roughly equal in percentage terms to the growth rate. On the other hand, the price-earnings ratio based on projected earnings (which assumed full continuation of the growth rate for five years) was still well above those of the other companies shown and the indexes. And even if the high rate of growth demonstrated by this company in the 1960–64 period continued indefinitely, it would take as long for accumulated earnings to equal the 1965 price (payout period) as for the other companies. Moreover, the growth rate, from which the payout period was derived, depended upon a much larger retention of earnings, so a considerable sacrifice of dividend income was associated with the acquisition of this stock. Based on the comparative relationships, therefore, it appeared that Houston Lighting was relatively overvalued, and particularly vulnerable to any moderation in the indicated rapid rate of growth. But at the same time, appreciation prospects seemed favorable on the assumptions of a continued premium in the price-earnings ratio and of continuation in the past rate of growth. In short, the opportunities and risks in the common stock of Houston Lighting in 1965 seemed to resemble closely those embodied in Xerox Corporation, discussed in Chapter 14.

[15] For a discussion of the concept of the price-future earnings ratio or payout period, see Chapter 14.

CHAPTER 18

Railroads

Introduction

For perhaps two reasons technical publications on security analysis have in the past devoted considerable attention to railroads. First, up until about 1940 railroad securities were generally considered to be of great investment importance. This legacy of past importance has been slow to dissolve, but it has become increasingly evident that railroads have become a minor element in most investment portfolios. As evidence, it can be noted that the percentage of railroad securities in the portfolios of leading institutional investors has declined to very small proportions in recent years. For example, as of the end of 1963 the major fire and casualty insurance companies had only .8% of their common stock investments in railroad shares as compared to 52 and 26% in industrial and utility common stocks, respectively.[1] Railroad fixed-income securities also declined in significance to those institutions emphasizing bond investment; portfolio classifications of leading life insurance companies showed about 11% of their investments in railroad bonds in 1940 but only 2.6% in this category at the end of 1963.[2]

The second reason for the inordinate attention to rails has probably resulted from the sheer volume of data available. The Interstate Com-

---

[1] Standard and Poor's, *Industry Surveys: Insurance*, Basic Analysis, September 17, 1964, p. 13.

[2] Moody's Bank and Financial Manual, 1964 edition, pp. a41–a42.

merce Commission requires detailed statistical information on practically every possible physical and financial aspect of the business. Moreover, railroad accounting is completely standardized, so extensive comparative analyses can be made. In addition, the I.C.C. publishes collective detailed figures on the industry as a whole.

As a consequence, railroad analysis is often considered a "statistician's paradise." However, the tremendous volume of data creates a real problem of separating the significant from the immaterial. Although an excess of information is better than an inadequacy, the consequences are that innumerable analytical techniques can be developed. It is possible, however, that the economic principle of diminishing returns applies to investment analysis as well as to other fields. In short, additional refinements of technique become increasingly less important in reaching an intelligent decision on the securities.

This observation does not condone superficial appraisal procedures. But it does mean that an extension of analytical techniques merely because data are available (and there is an uneasy feeling that somehow they should be used) is not always desirable. A good question can be raised as to whether the importance of rails as an investment medium justifies the effort necessary to become highly qualified in railroad analysis. Therefore, only the most important factors bearing on the analysis of railroads shall be discussed.

The Railroad Industry: Economic Review and Analysis

Gross Revenue Pattern. Until 1930 railroads provided most of the common carrier transport service of both passengers and freight between cities. The demand for rail services then reflected the level of production and distribution of physical goods throughout the economy. Because alternative methods of transportation were highly limited, rail traffic and revenues had grown about in line with the economy as a whole. Moreover, during the latter part of the nineteenth and the first three decades of the twentieth century, cyclical fluctuations tended to be concentrated in the financial areas rather than in physical output, so reasonable stability was also enjoyed by the rails, although some experienced financial difficulties because of the highly levered capital structures fostered by the "free-wheeling" financiers of that era.[3]

---

[3] Because the rails required large amounts of capital to expand across the country, securities of all types were made available to "outside" investors in considerable quantity at a time when the supply of industrial securities was strictly limited because of the prevailing custom of family ownership.

TABLE 18–1

PERCENTAGE DISTRIBUTION OF INTERCITY FREIGHT AND PASSENGER TRAFFIC

	1940	1950	1960	1963
Freight				
Railroads	61.3%	56.2%	43.7%	43.1%
Trucks	10.0	16.3	22.4	23.8
Great Lakes	15.5	10.5	7.5	6.8
Rivers and canals	3.6	4.9	9.1	9.6
Pipelines	9.6	17.5	17.2	16.6
Air		Less than 0.1% throughout		
Passengers				
Railroads	64.5%	45.3%	27.2%	21.6%
Buses	26.5	37.7	25.5	25.3
Air	2.8	14.3	43.5	49.9
Waterways	3.6	1.7	3.4	2.9
Electric Rail	2.6	1.0	0.3	0.3

Source: *Yearbook of Railroad Information,* 1964 Ed., p. 4.

But Table 18-1 shows that the percentage of intercity freight and passengers moved by rail has drastically declined since 1940. From a position of unquestioned dominance the role of the railroads has consistently dwindled for over twenty years in relation to competing forms of transportation. Therefore, although growth in the economy and increases in rates have provided the means to approximately double revenues since 1940, the demand for rail freight services has suffered a considerable relative decline due to the impact of interindustry competition mainly from the trucking industry and pipelines. Passenger traffic has declined to an even greater degree; in fact, the absolute number of passengers carried by rail declined by about 35% between 1940 and 1963; the cause here, of course, was the great growth of the airlines and automobile. The composition of railroad traffic has also been affected by the growth of competitive means of transportation. By and large the rails can transport efficiently very heavy and bulky materials for long distances, whereas trucks are particularly adaptable to transporting light package freight and to making short-haul movements. Therefore, the traffic retained by the rails has been largely products of mines and heavy materials used in the durable-goods industries. As a consequence, the rails' earlier stability in revenues has changed to a condition of comparative instability.

As proof of this fact, Table 18-2 shows that in all of the postwar recessions the volume of rail carloadings and revenues has declined considerably more than general indices for the entire economy. It is clear,

TABLE 18-2
VARIATIONS IN RAILROAD VOLUME AND REVENUES
(postwar recession years)

Years	Revenue Ton Miles	FRB Production Index	Railroad Gross Revenues	GNP
1949, percentage of 1948	82%	93%	88%	100%
1954, percentage of 1953	90	93	88	99
1958, percentage of 1957	89	94	91	99
1961, percentage of 1960	97	100	96	103

Sources: *Yearbook of Railroad Information* and *Federal Reserve Bulletins.*

therefore, that the revenues and earnings of most railroads are quite vulnerable to a decline in business activity. The prognosis of instability suggests that: (1) standards for fixed-charge coverage should be stringent, (2) earning power must be cautiously appraised when based on a past record dominated by prosperous years, (3) fluctuations in dividend income and market prices will probably be extensive.

The Regulation Factor. It is paradoxical that the railroads, which have been subject to extreme interindustry competitive pressures, are still closely regulated on the theory that they have a monopoly on common-carrier transportation. However, to some extent the development of other transportation has complicated and indeed changed the concept of regulatory objectives. The monopoly theory suggests governmental limitation of maximum rates to prevent unreasonable profits from an exploitation of the monopoly position. Although this objective still prevails, the Interstate Commerce Commission has also felt obliged in recent years to rule on rate reductions as well and has refused to allow reductions when they may attract more than a "fair share" of competitive traffic.[4] The regulation process, in brief, has become highly complex and confusing; on the one hand it is designed to protect the public, and on the other it acts to prevent one group of carriers from competing with another even though higher rates to the public ensue as a consequence.[5]

However, a few comments on the significance of regulatory policies

[4] Wilson, *A Critical Appraisal of Regulated Rate Making of Common Carrier Transportation*, Washington, D.C.: The Federation for Railway Progress, 1956, p. 21.

[5] As of 1965, the Harris Bill (HR. 9903) had been pending in Congress for two years but the Rules Committee had so far refused to allow it to come to a floor vote. This bill would free the rails from regulation of *minimum* rates on most traffic.

can be suggested. First, it should be emphasized that public regulation does not mean an assured but limited earning power. This is a common misconception, because there is a natural assumption that regulation is only invoked in an industry where monopoly profits would normally occur. The very existence of regulation, therefore, by implication conveys the image of a highly essential service wherein the only problem is limiting profits that automatically would accrue to the companies. On the contrary, the competitive developments in transportation suggest that some railroads might not be able to show earnings even if regulation was completely removed.

Second, regulated industries often find it difficult to maintain earnings under inflation conditions. Prices for the service tend to move upward relatively slowly, because ordinarily any changes in rates require lengthy public hearings and other legal processes before a decision is rendered, whereas costs in the interim may advance rapidly. The rather poor earnings record of the railroads in the 1947–49 inflationary episode provides empirical evidence in support of this view. While freight revenues actually increased slightly in those years as compared with 1944–45, net railway operating income declined by more than 15% on the average.

Third, one of the most unfortunate aspects of regulation from the standpoint of the investor is the power of the regulatory agencies to require a railroad to continue unprofitable passenger service. Announcement of the intention to abandon certain runs because of dwindling patronage has brought quick protests from the cities concerned that service must be continued in the "public interest," and the regulatory agencies usually have been highly sympathetic to these claims. The losses on unprofitable passenger traffic in 1961 alone were estimated at $408 million or about 50% of total net income before fixed charges.[6]

Fourth, interstate railroad rate schedules, by far the most important, are regulated by the Interstate Commerce Commission on a regional rather than an individual road basis. For regulatory purposes there are three major districts subdivided into eight regions. Rate relief, therefore, can be expected only if the earnings performance in a given geographical area is unsatisfactory. It also means that some rails may obtain rather handsome earnings without pressure for rate reductions if poor performances by other roads make earnings in general only adequate or worse. Wide differences in earning power between railroads in a

[6] Bretey, "Railroads' Problem: 'A Compound of Several Brews,' " *Financial Analysts Journal*, Sept.–Oct., 1962, p. 91.

TABLE 18-3
MAJOR OPERATING EXPENSES OF CLASS I RAILROADS

Year	Maintenance of Way and Structures Amount (in millions)	Percent of Revenue	Maintenance of Equipment Amount (in millions)	Percent of Revenue	Transportation Expenses Amount (in millions)	Percent of Revenue
1956	1,403.6	13.3	1,891.6	17.9	4,040.3	38.3
1957	1,430.5	13.6	1,913.0	18.2	4,094.8	39.0
1958	1,223.4	12.8	1,720.4	18.0	3,834.3	40.1
1959	1,236.5	12.6	1,797.9	18.3	3,887.7	39.6
1960	1,191.7	12.5	1,759.8	18.5	3,832.9	40.3
1961	1,117.7	12.2	1,683.4	18.3	3,710.8	40.4
1962	1,154.8	12.2	1,743.6	18.5	3,755.1	39.8
1963	1,182.5	12.4	1,731.7	18.1	3,771.3	39.4

Source: *Moody's Transportation Manual,* 1964 edition, p. a27.

given area can be maintained indefinitely under this scheme of rate regulation.

Finally, although many regulatory practices have operated to the disadvantage of investors, there is one aspect which has generally operated to the investor's advantage. This is the I.C.C. insistence on detailed information on each railroad's performance on a consistent and comparable basis. However, in recent years the control over accounting methods has been a mixed blessing, because some of the prescribed accounting methods have resulted in questionable earnings reports as will be shown.

Analysis of Cost Factors. The major operating expenses of Class I railroads for selected years in total and as a percentage of gross reven .es are shown in Table 18-3. One of the pecularities of railroad reporting is that depreciation is included in "maintenance" expenses along with direct cash outlays for ordinary maintenance items. In 1963, for example, depreciation on way and structures amounted to $161 million, or slightly more than 13% of the total maintenance charges in this category. Depreciation charged on equipment during 1963 amounted to $507.8 million, or about 30% of total equipment maintenance.

Transportation expenses are all costs directly associated with the actual make-up and movement of trains. These include wages of train and yard crews, fuel, and dispatching costs. Although the proportion of revenues absorbed by these expenses has been 36 to 40% for all railroads, there have been wide differences between roads in the incidence of these costs. The ratio of transportation expenses to gross revenues of the Norfolk and Western, for example, averaged about 27% for the years 1956–64, whereas for the Pennsylvania Railroad, burdened with substantial passenger operations and short hauls, transportation expenses absorbed about 46% of gross revenues during the same period. The ratio, in brief, tends to show both efficiency and the inherent "economic advantage" of a given road; where it consistently averages about 37% or less, adequate profit margins usually result.[7]

From a cost standpoint the major problem that has been faced by the railroads in the postwar years is that wage rates have increased much more than productivity. As a result, labor costs as a percentage of revenues have averaged about 50% of revenues in 1961–64 as compared to about 45% in 1939–41. Both management and labor practices have been held responsible, but in any case the need to increase productivity is clearly evident in the railroad industry.

The high incidence of transportation expenses might infer that costs are largely variable and could be reduced significantly if traffic volume declines. The nature of rail operations, however, indicates this is not so. The number of trains moving per day does not vary proportionately with changes in traffic volume; by and large only the length of trains is affected by these fluctuations. As it does not cost much more to move a long train than a short one, decreases in physical volume do not result in a proportionate decrease in expenses, and vice versa. Moreover, most of the maintenance expenses continue regardless of the intensity of use of way and equipment, although temporary deferral is possible in times of stress.

In brief, the rails typically operate on a decreasing unit-cost basis. As equipment and roadways are used more intensively, operating expenses increase at a less rapid rate and average costs per unit of traffic decline. The result has been that during boom periods of heavy traffic, such as in 1964–65, the rails show favorable earnings, but even a moderate decline in traffic results in a large decline in earnings. For example, in 1958 total railroad revenues declined to $9.5 billion from $10.5 billion in 1957 or by about 10%, whereas net operating income

[7] The "all rail" average for the transportation ratio of almost 40% for 1956–63 was weighted adversely by the unsatisfactory performances of the very large New York Central and Pennsylvania systems, although the implication given thereby that the average railroad was not of adequate investment quality is perhaps not far from the truth.

TABLE 18–4

TON MILES AND TOTAL REVENUE COMPARISONS: SELECTED YEARS

Year	Sante Fe		Pennsylvania		Denver and Rio Grande	
	Ton Miles (in billions)	Revenues (in millions)	Ton Miles (in billions)	Revenues (in millions)	Ton Miles (in billions)	Revenues (in millions)
1956	33.9	$590.1	53.4	$991.1	5.8	$81.4
1957	33.8	610.7	50.6	987.3	5.8	85.2
1958	33.2	595.3	41.5	844.2	5.3	76.9
1959	36.0	633.8	43.4	887.7	5.3	75.4
1960	36.6	614.0	42.8	843.7	5.4	76.3
1961	36.0	604.5	42.1	820.1	5.4	77.2
1962	36.1	612.3	45.2	850.6	5.3	75.8
1963	37.2	616.1	46.4	840.1	5.6	78.8
1964	39.6	637.8	49.8	873.2	6.1	79.1
Percent increase: 1956–64	17.8%	8.1%	−6.9%	−12.0%	5.1%	−2.8%

declined from $922 million to $762 million, or by 17%, despite a substantial reduction in maintenance outlays.

Railroads: Individual Company Analysis

Appraisal of Service Area. Despite the unfavorable trend of the railroad industry, there are some individual companies that have maintained a respectable earning power. The wide disparity in performance is due to the fact that each road is committed to a specific geographical service area. The area characteristics differ widely, and the result is that some roads have been able to maintain or increase their traffic, while others have borne the brunt of the competitive difficulties. Some have been blessed with the rapid growth of their areas (the Southwest, for example), and, despite a decline in the percentage of traffic carried, in absolute terms they have enjoyed a slow upward trend of both revenues and earnings.

For example, Table 18-4 shows that both revenues and the physical volume of freight for the Santa Fe have increased moderately since 1956. The Pennsylvania railroad system has not been so fortunate. The rate of industrial growth in the eastern section has been slower. Moreover, the distances between major terminal points are much shorter and short-haul traffic has been extremely vulnerable to truck competition. These conditions have not been propitious for rails, and the effects are shown in an absolute decline in both ton-miles and revenues over the 1956–64 period.

The Denver and Rio Grande represents an intermediate situation. Its service area, largely in Colorado and Utah, has enjoyed substantial growth, but traffic and revenues have merely maintained a flat pattern over the 1956–64 period. However, as about 60% of its traffic is represented by the bulk movement of mining products which the rails can transport more effectively than trucks, it appeared less vulnerable to competitive pressures than many railroads.

In summary, the character of the geographical service area and the type of traffic are the major qualitative factors in railroad analysis. It is desirable to find a combination of the following characteristics: (1) a rapidly growing industrial, mining, or agricultural area, (2) long distances between major terminal points, (3) a major part of the revenue derived from transporting heavy bulk commodities such as mining products or other items where the rails have a cost advantage.

Measurement of Efficiency.   Because maintenance expenses are subject to some managerial discretion as to their level from year to year, conventional practice measures operating efficiency excluding maintenance expenses. In the short run a low operating ratio may be due to a conscious policy of deferring maintenance outlays. The other major costs are transportation expenses. Therefore, although there are other minor expenses, the ratio of revenues to transportation expenses (transportation ratio) is conventionally used as the index of efficiency.[8] This ratio also has the practical advantage of being published in the statistical investment manuals.

Table 18-5 shows the transportation ratio for the three railroads whose revenue and traffic characteristics were previously discussed. In appraising any time series, it is of course desirable to note (1) the long-term average, (2) the indicated trend, and (3) the relation of the performance to some estimated benchmark. The entire railroad industry showed an average transportation ratio of almost 40% in the 1956–64 period. But as the railroad industry as a whole has not been attractive for investment purposes, a ratio somewhat below the average would seem desirable to qualify a given road for investment consideration. It

---

[8] There are other tests of physical efficiency and productivity, such as gross ton-miles per freight-train hour, but it is considered more significant to investigate "cost" efficiency: the ability to minimize cost of operations in relation to revenues.

TABLE 18-5
TRANSPORTATION RATIO: 1956-64

Year	Santa Fe	Pennsylvania	Denver and Rio Grande
1956	34.2	45.0	29.9
1957	34.9	45.7	30.4
1958	35.3	47.4	31.4
1959	35.5	45.4	32.1
1960	37.4	46.1	32.1
1961	36.5	46.1	31.9
1962	36.9	45.3	33.0
1963	36.9	45.1	32.9
1964	37.4	45.2	34.0

is suggested, therefore, that a transportation ratio of not higher than about 37% on the average should be indicated. When using this criterion, both the Santa Fe and the Denver and Rio Grande seemed reasonably attractive, although the trends have not been reassuring. The Pennsylvania, on the other hand, was a distinctly marginal situation.

Importance of Financial Risk. The fluctuations and trend of the revenues and ton-miles along with a review of the transportation ratio ordinarily provide a good first indication of the prospective quality of a railroad as an investment. But the appraisal of the financial position is also of crucial importance. By and large the railroads have large amounts of senior securities in their capital structures. The historical reasons are perhaps twofold. First, very large amounts of capital investment are required, and it was necessary in the period of construction and expansion (1850–1900) to tap every possible source of capital funds. Second, during this period the rails had a virtual monopoly on intercity transportation and, therefore, were regarded as highly essential and rather stable operations. As a result, the bond market was willing to absorb railroad obligations on a relatively narrow coverage margin.

However, as previously explained, one of the major consequences of the competitive problems has been to increase the cyclical vulnerability of revenues and earnings. The adverse result of the heavy debt burden was forcefully demonstrated during the Great Depression when about one-third of all Class I railroads went into receivership.[9] The impact of the consequent reorganizations on the subsequent investment quality has been ironical. Some that managed to weather the adversity have

[9] Freight operating revenues declined from $4.9 billion in 1929 to $2.5 billion in 1932, or by about 50%, as compared with a decline in the industrial production index of about 47% during the same period. In brief, railroad revenues proved slightly more vulnerable to cyclical setbacks than industrial output generally.

continued to be saddled with large fixed charges and, as a consequence, evidence considerable financial problems. The New York Central and the Pennsylvania may be offered as illustrations.

On the other hand, the drastic scaling down of debt by the reorganization process has materially improved the quality of others. The Denver and Rio Grande, for example, emerged from a long period of receivership in 1947 with a tarnished reputation but with fixed charges reduced from $6.46 million to $2.5 million plus $1.8 million of contingent charges which have since been reduced to $2.3 and $1.4 million, respectively.[10] It is arguable, therefore, that a previous drastic reorganization instead of reflecting on the investment status of a railroad might have improved it, at least from the standpoint of financial position.

Financial Risk: Coverage Ratio. The primary indications of any possible financial difficulty arising from the use of senior securities are of course the average, trend, and minimum showing of the "times fixed charges earned" ratio. The determination, however, of railroad fixed charges can be rather complicated. In the first place, contractual long-term rental charges on leased roads are common; these ordinarily should be added in full to interest charges because all maintenance, taxes, and depreciation must be borne by the lessee. Therefore, they represent the equivalent of interest charges on a bond issue to acquire these roads.

TABLE 18–6
SENIOR-SECURITY EARNINGS COVERAGE

Year	Santa Fe Fixed Charges	Santa Fe Total Senior Securities	Pennsylvania Fixed Charges	Denver and Rio Grande Fixed Charges	Denver and Rio Grande Total Senior Securities
1957	12.5	4.2	1.5	11.2	7.0
1958	12.8	4.6	1.2	9.3	5.8
1959	12.9	4.5	1.4	8.4	5.3
1960	10.1	3.1	1.0	8.4	5.3
1961	10.8	3.9	1.2	8.6	5.4
1962	10.2	4.8	1.0	8.2	5.1
1963	9.8	4.6	1.3	8.1	5.4
1964	10.1	4.7	1.5	9.5	5.6

Second, there is the troublesome problem of interpreting charges or credits against net income for "equipment rents" and "joint facility rents."

[10] *Moody's Transportation Manual*, 1964 edition, pp. 82–83.

Such rental charges presumably include a depreciation-and-maintenance component in addition to an implied interest charge on the capital investment in the facilities and equipment. In part, therefore, they are the equivalent of fixed charges, and in part they are similar to normal operating expenses. There can be no really accurate breakdown of the total rental charge, but, as a rather arbitrary estimate, one-half of the net rental payments (or receipts) are usually added (or subtracted) from fixed charges. The result represents an estimate of the minimum interest component in these charges.

Table 18-6 shows the before-tax coverage ratios wherein charges have been so adjusted.[11] The after-tax coverage of total senior security charges, including preferred dividends, is also shown in the table.[12]

The results clearly showed an adequate financial position for the Santa Fe and the Denver & Rio Grande system, but a rather weak position for the Pennsylvania both with respect to the average and trend of the coverage ratio. The volatile nature of railroad earnings suggests the need for a large earnings coverage of fixed capital charges in order to obtain adequate investment quality. An average before-tax coverage of 8 for contractual charges in the case of cyclical companies and an after-tax coverage of preferred dividends plus charges of 4 have been previously suggested. Of the three illustrative rails, only the Pennsylvania failed to meet the indicated benchmarks.

Financial Risk: Margin-of-Safety Concept. The discussion of railroad cost characteristics concluded that rails have found it difficult to reduce expenses when traffic and revenues decline. On the assumption that operating expenses are quite rigid, a supplementary indication of financial risk has been developed by railroad analysts. It is called the "margin of safety," and it is computed by dividing the earnings after fixed charges by gross revenues. It expresses the percentage amount by which revenues can decline (with expenses assumed absolutely constant) and still provide just enough earnings to meet the fixed charges.

A hypothetical example can perhaps best illustrate the potential use-

[11] The described procedure represents the most accurate technique for measuring potential protection of fixed charges and the consequent financial risk in practice. But if rentals on leased roads and net equipment and facility rents are nominal, the coverage ratios shown in the statistical manuals would be acceptable as a substitute. The drawback to this technique is the considerable statistical computations required.

[12] A substantial reduction in the amount of income-taxes recognized in 1963 as compared to 1961 produced the strange result that before-tax coverage was higher in 1961 than in 1964 for the Santa Fe, yet after-tax coverage was lower on all senior securities including preferred stock. The earnings distortion produced by accelerated depreciation lowering income tax recognition in certain years is considered later.

fulness of this computation. Assume that two railroads show the following income-statement relationships:

	A	B
Gross revenues	100	100
Operating expenses	90	70
Earnings before charges	10	30
Fixed charges	2	10
Balance after charges	8	20
Fixed-charge coverage (3 ÷ 4)	5x	3x
Margin of safety (5 ÷ 1)	8%	20%

In the example, the coverage ratios would indicate that *A* was less vulnerable to adversity then *B*; the small amount of fixed charges in *A* produced this result even though operating expenses absorb considerably more of each dollar of revenues in *A* than in *B*. But it is arguable that *B* is really in a better position in the event of a decline in revenues, assuming that operating expenses would not change materially under such conditions. In brief, it can be argued that the relative vulnerability is measurable by the margin-of-safety percentage, *B* can incur a 20% decline in revenues with expenses and charges remaining constant before the coverage ratio would be exactly 1, whereas *A* can only stand an 8% revenue decline and still have earnings equal to fixed charges.

TABLE 18-7
MARGIN OF SAFETY FOR FIXED CHARGES

	1958	1959	1960	1961	1962	1963	1964
Santa Fe	18.1%	16.9%	13.3%	14.5%	13.6%	12.4%	13.0%
Pennsylvania	.54	.94	Negative	.56	Negative	1.03	3.3
Denver & Rio Grande	25.1	23.3	23.8	24.3	22.4	21.5	22.0

Source: *Moody's Transportation Manual* 1965.

The margin-of-safety percentages for the three illustrative rails for the years 1958–64 are shown in Table 18–7. The results indicated that the Denver and Rio Grande could suffer a decline of 22% from 1964 revenues and still meet fixed charges. On the other hand, despite its more favorable general coverage ratios, a decline of only 13% from revenue levels in 1964 might put earnings levels of the Santa Fe close to the amount of fixed charges. The margin-of-safety test also emphasized the narrow earnings protection afforded the fixed charges of the Pennsylvania, especially in 1960 and 1962.[13]

Analysis of Reported Earnings. There have been two problems with railroads in ascertaining whether reported earnings have been realistically presented. First, maintenance expenditures may be partially controlled by management, and thereby the long-run burden of these expenses could be materially different than shown for any short span of years. Second, the deduction for income taxes may be seriously overstated or understated because of the curious treatment of accelerated amortization for tax purposes.

TABLE 18–8

RATIO: MAINTENANCE EXPENSES TO GROSS REVENUES

	1958	1960	1961	1962	1963	1964
Santa Fe	31.9%	33.5%	33.5%	33.9%	35.5%	34.4%
Pennsylvania	29.8	29.2	28.3	29.1	28.1	27.4
Denver & Rio Grande	25.5	25.5	25.1	25.7	25.6	25.8
Class I Rails	30.6	31.0	30.5	30.7	30.5	30.2

Source: *Moody's Transportation Manual,* 1965 edition.

Substantial distortions of earnings, which may be difficult to detect, have arisen through chronic undermaintenance of way and, to a lesser extent, of equipment. One conventional indication of the adequacy of maintenance is the comparative percentage of gross revenues absorbed by these expenses. As shown in Table 18-8, Class I railroads as a whole spend about 30% of revenues on maintenance per year. On the assumption that the entire industry has over the years maintained its properties in reasonable condition, the 30% ratio is often used as a rough guide to test the maintenance expenditures of a given road.

It would seem logical to expect the maintenance ratio to increase as revenues decline and vice versa, because a good share of these expenditures are fixed regardless of traffic volume. This type of fluctuation has consistently marked the performance of the Denver and Rio Grande, despite the fact that its maintenance ratio has been consistently below average. The Pennsylvania, however, showed declines in its mainten-

---

[13] The negative margin of safety was produced by the fact that "nonoperating income" made possible coverage of charges; before such income, coverage was less than one.

ance ratio in 1961 and 1963, when revenues were at a low point, which is the opposite of what might have been expected.

The distortion of earnings arising from unusual treatment of accelerated amortization for tax purposes has been much more important. Most industrial companies, when using normal depreciation rates in their annual reports, deduct from earnings a reserve equal to the amount of tax savings from accelerated depreciation. The procedure thus eliminates from the determination of earnings the temporary reduction in taxes resulting from depreciation of plant and equipment at a more rapid rate for tax purposes than on the income statements submitted to shareholders.

The railroads, however, have followed the highly misleading practice of deducting from reported income only normal depreciation and taxes actually paid.[14] They do not establish a reserve to cover the larger tax liability that will result when the accelerated depreciation is completed and the normal depreciation on the related assets cannot be deducted in determining the tax liability.

However, the effects of the unusual accounting practices are reported in the form of supplementary information to the financial statements, and Table 18-9 shows earnings as reported and then as adjusted for appropriate tax recognition.[15] The adjustments were not consistent from year to year and did not have an equal impact on the several roads, because the annual rates of expenditures for new equipment and other depreciable facilities determined the amount of accelerated depreciation allowed for tax purposes. In summary, the adjustments were rather substantial for the Santa Fe, moderate for the Denver and Rio Grande, and hardly worth recognizing for the Pennsylvania, except possibly in 1964. In a nongrowth industry, which certainly would seem to characterize the railroads, the rate of expenditures for depreciable facilities probably will not increase. If so, then within a few years the pretax income should be subject to a much higher tax rate as properties become fully amortized for tax purposes but are still subject to depreciation for income-determination purposes. Therefore, adjusted earnings

---

[14] The ICC accounting rules apparently require the reports to the Commission to be made of this basis, but there is no reason why reports to the stockholders could not be made in accordance with recognized accounting practices.

[15] No adjustments were made for the Pennsylvania Railroad because its pretax earnings in the 1958–63 period were not sufficient to give rise to any significant tax savings especially on a per share basis. If pretax earnings can be maintained at 1964 levels in the future, then the same problem will emerge. In 1959 and 1961, it can be noted, income taxes were paid because prior accelerated depreciation had reduced the depreciation allowed for tax purposes to below that recognized for statement purposes.

TABLE 18–9
EARNINGS: REPORTED AND ADJUSTED FOR TAX EFFECTS OF ACCELERATED DEPRECIATION

Santa Fe In millions:	1958	1959	1960	1961	1962	1963	1964
Net income before taxes	$107.9	$105.6	$79.0	$85.8	$81.4	$75.0	$81.5
Income taxes (reported)	40.7	39.8	28.4	31.0	10.7	7.5	5.7
Reported net income	$ 67.2	$ 65.8	$51.6	$54.8	$70.7	$67.5	$75.8
Estimated tax adjustment	12.5	11.9	8.3	6.2	25.3	24.8	26.8
Net after adjustment	$ 54.7	$ 53.9	$43.3	$48.6	$45.4	$42.7	$49.0
Preferred dividends	6.2	6.2	6.2	6.2	6.2	6.2	6.2
Net to common stock	$ 48.5	$ 47.7	$37.1	$42.4	$39.2	$36.5	$42.8
Per share, reported	$ 2.51	$ 2.45	$1.87	$2.00	$2.65	$2.52	$2.84
Per share, adjusted	2.00	1.97	1.53	1.74	1.65	1.51	1.74
Dividends per share	1.40	1.45	1.45	1.45	1.45	1.45	1.60
Denver & Rio Grande In millions:							
Net income before taxes	$ 17.8	$ 16.1	$16.7	$17.3	$15.5	$15.3	$16.5
Income taxes (reported)	7.4	7.4	8.1	8.5	6.4	5.3	5.8
Reported net income	$ 10.4	$ 8.7	$ 8.6	$ 8.8	$ 9.1	$10.0	$10.7
Estimated tax adjustment	1.5	.6	.4	.2	1.1	1.4	1.6
Net to common after adjustment	$ 8.9	$ 8.1	$ 8.2	$ 8.6	$ 8.0	$ 8.6	$ 9.1
Per share, reported	$ 1.64	$ 1.37	$1.35	$1.37	$1.43	$1.56	$1.65
Per share, adjusted	1.38	1.26	1.28	1.35	1.24	1.35	1.41
Dividends per share	.83	.91	1.00	1.00	1.00	1.00	1.00
Pennsylvania In millions:							
Net income before taxes	$ 4.6	$ 8.4	$(6.6)	$ 4.6	$(2.1)	$ 8.7	$28.7
Income taxes	1.1	1.1	1.2	1.1	1.1	(.5)	(.4)
Reported net income	$ 3.5	$ 7.3	$(7.8)	$ 3.5	$(3.2)	$ 9.2	$29.1
Per share	$ .27	$ .55	$(.59)	$ .27	$(.24)	$ .68	$2.12
Dividends per share	.25	.25	.25	.25	.25	.50	1.00

seem to be the logical basis for estimating the future earning potential of these railroads.

Price-earnings Ratios and Dividend Yields. Because the railroads have shown a volatile earnings performance and in addition have shown no significant growth characteristics, average earnings would seem logical as the major valuation criterion; in short, as of 1965 there was no evidence to support a growth-rate computation. Moreover, because of the lack of growth potential, it seemed reasonable to place considerable

TABLE 18–10
PRICE-EARNINGS RATIOS AND DIVIDEND YIELDS: 1965

	Stock Price	1958–64 Average Earnings*	Indicated Dividend Rate	Price-Earnings Ratio	Dividend Yield
Santa Fe	33	$1.73	$1.60	19.1	4.8%
Denver & Rio Grande	21	1.32	1.00	15.9	4.9
Pennsylvania	45	.43	1.00	100.4	2.2
Standard and Poor's Composite Index				18.5	2.9

* Based on adjusted earnings data in Table 18–9.

emphasis on the comparative dividend yields. However, because of their volatility features, some of the lower-quality rails, such as the Pennsylvania, have often been used as devices to implement cyclical timing operations. In 1965 this road also attracted considerable speculative attention because of publicity given to various merger opportunities. But as Table 18-10 indicated, at a price of $45 per share in 1965, it hardly qualified for consideration as a long-term investment. In fact, in view of the adverse trends and heavy debt position, the Pennsylvania Railroad common stock could reasonably have been rejected at almost any price.

Between the Santa Fe and the Denver and Rio Grande, the latter on balance seemed more attractive as of 1965. The Santa Fe had the advantages of being a major railroad system in a strong financial position and of enjoying an above-average revenue trend. On the other hand, the Denver and Rio Grande had maintained a lower transportation ratio, with the result that adjusted earnings per share had a more favorable relative trend. Moreover, on the basis of the prevailing prices, the stock was available at a lower price-earnings ratio and slightly higher dividend yield than the Santa Fe. For income purposes, coupled with the possibility of some improvement in railroad earnings through improved productivity, the Denver and Rio Grande common stock seemed moderately attractive as of 1965.

PART V

ANALYSIS OF FINANCIAL INSTITUTIONS

CHAPTER 19

Investment Companies

Investment Concept of Financial Institutions

From an investment point of view, financial institutions are those companies that obtain most of their earnings from interest and dividends on security or loan portfolios.[1] The definition is useful because it identifies some of the unique technical procedures pertinent to the appraisal of financial institutions. For example, the amount of portfolio assets per share is usually an important element to consider in estimating the values of the common stocks, because the assets are stated at prevailing market prices or at amortized cost for bond holdings. Therefore, by dividing the net portfolio assets (after deducting liabilities) by the number of common shares outstanding, the investor can determine the amount of portfolio assets per share that can be acquired through the purchase of the common stock.

However, certain companies which have a large proportion of their assets in securities or loans are not included. The major exclusions are in the insurance area. Life insurance companies, for example, obtain most of their earnings from pure underwriting activities. This means that they collect in premiums more than claim losses and expenses, and the bal-

---

[1] Appreciation on common-stock portfolios may also represent sources of returns for investors in some financial institutions, but such appreciation is not reflected in earnings until actually realized through market sales of particular securities.

ance is profit. Investment earnings are secondary or are distributed to policy holders. Moreover, analysis of underwriting operations is a highly complex and specialized procedure. In essence these activities represent the competitive sale of a service, similar to many industrial companies, rather than a financial operation.

Besides investment companies and banks, both of which obtain almost all their revenues and earnings from interest or dividends, the other major group is the fire and casualty insurance companies. Although underwriting is an essential feature of their business, the great majority of their earnings result from income on security portfolios. Therefore, fire-insurance common stocks are legitimately included in the category of financial institutions.

There are also other companies which are properly a part of this area. The finance companies, for instance, obtain most of their earnings from consumer loans. Their source of funds are the stock equity plus a great amount of borrowed funds. But in most respects the techniques for their appraisal are similar to commercial banks. Therefore, these companies will not be separately considered.

Investment Companies: Nature and Purpose

Nature of Investment Companies. Investment companies, also known as *investment trusts*, have as their corporate purpose the investing of funds collected from many individual investors. In essence this is accomplished by selling the common stock of the investment company to the public and then investing the proceeds in a diversified list of securities selected by management. The portfolio so acquired is then subject to continuous management.

The logic behind the investment-company device is as follows. First, the prudent management of an investment account demands a level of diligence, training, and experience which many individuals cannot hope to attain. Second, a pooling arrangement is the only expeditious means of bringing the costs of professional investment management to a reasonable level for small accounts. Third, limited portfolio size makes it difficult for the small investor to achieve adequate diversification. Again, the pooling of many small accounts into a large diversified portfolio can overcome this obstacle to good investment practice.

It would follow, therefore, that investment companies should appeal primarily to (1) small investors and (2) those with an inadequate training in financial analysis. These two groups tend to be more or less identical but not necessarily so. The first classification may include some individuals highly competent to select their own securities yet unable to obtain adequate diversification because of the small amount of funds available. The second may include some with adequate funds to acquire a diversified portfolio—say, $20,000 to $40,000—but for whom costs of investment counseling service on an individual basis would still be prohibitive.

A paradox, however, is involved in the recommendation of these companies for individuals lacking training in security analysis, because the investment policies and performances of these companies vary widely. Therefore, some knowledge of investment principles would seem necessary in order to select a company whose investment policy fits the needs of the specific individual. In addition, as management is of crucial importance, managerial competence should be appraised, but this again requires considerable analytical ability.

To solve the problem, these investors must rely on certain practical avenues. First, there are a number of large and seasoned investment companies, such as Massachusetts Investors Trust. The investor need only be wise enough to insist on one of these organizations and bad mistakes can be avoided. Second, the brokerage firms selling investment-company stocks are well versed in their characteristics and performances and can offer competent advice.

There are, however, some possible conflicts of interest. The investor would desire, other things being equal, to secure the company with the lowest fees for sales commissions, whereas it might be expected that a broker would naturally tend to favor the company offering a large commission. In addition, some brokerage firms may be closely related in one way or another to the management of particular investment companies.[2]

Classification of Investment Companies

Open End vs. Closed End. Although investment companies use the corporate form of organization (or the related trust form), some have the right to sell continuously new shares to the public, and also these companies agree to redeem shares at the shareholder's option. Where

---

[2] For example, a study of the investment company industry showed that brokerage business on purchases and sales of portfolio assets may be directed in part to those firms which are most active in selling the investment company shares to the public. Report of the Committee on Interstate and Foreign Commerce, *A Study of Mutual Funds* (prepared by the Wharton School of Finance and Commerce), U.S. Government Printing Office, Washington, D.C., 1962, pp. 32–33.

these rather unique features exists, they are known as "open-end" companies. The name probably derives from the fact that the common-stock equity is "open-end" in the sense that it increases or decreases from day to day as new shares are sold on the one hand or redeemed on the other.

Under this arrangement, the company itself creates the market for the stock. Dealers and brokers continuously sell new shares, and by the redemption process, shares already outstanding are sold back to the company. The *asset value* determines both the sale and redemption price. It is computed two or three times a day by adding up the total market value of all the securities held in the portfolio and dividing by the shares then outstanding.

For example, if the market value of the secruities in the portfolio amounted to $24 million at 1 P.M. on a given day, and if there were 1 million shares of the investment company held by the public, then the asset value would be $24 per share. Until recomputed at perhaps 3 P.M., the offering price of the investment company's common stock would be $24 plus a "load" charge of between 5 and 10% to cover the salesman's commission and other costs of issuing the stock. At a 10% load charge the price would be $24 plus $2.40, or $26.40. The redemption price is typically the asset value, although a few companies charge a redemption fee. Therefore, so far as the public is concerned, the investment-company stock is offered at $26.40 and bid at $24.

In popular jargon, the open-end companies are conventionally known as *mutual funds,* and they constitute by far the largest dollar value of investment-company shares. As of December 31, 1963, it was estimated that the total value of mutual-fund shares held by the public was more than $25 billion.[3] As recently as 1948, total mutual-fund assets amounted to only $1.5 billion. The tremendous increase in these dollar values represented both a large number of new shares and the increase in the market values of individual securities held in the portfolios.

The closed-end investment company has the usual type of corporate organization. It has a fixed capitalization consisting of common stock and occasionally senior securities. Shares can be purchased only on the stock exchange or in the over-the-counter market from existing shareholders offering the stock for sale. In this case, there is strictly an auction market, and the per share price is determined by supply and demand conditions. Although asset value may affect the price through its impact on the decisions of buyers and sellers, there is no necessary relationship.

[3] Wiesenberger, Investment Companies, 1964 edition, New York: Arthur Wiesenberger & Company, p. 18.

Therefore, closed-end shares may sell at a "discount" below asset value or at a "premium" above asset value, depending on market conditions at the time. In the 1953-64 decade, however, shares of closed-end companies as a group have generally sold at discounts between 5 and 10% from indicated asset values. In a few exceptional cases premiums have existed from time to time, especially when the stock market in general is at a high level and investors are in an exhuberant mood.

The advantage of the closed-end form is that it offers some opportunity for seeking out possible undervalued situations. There may be opportunities of obtaining an equity in the security portfolio at a substantial discount from its indicated market value because of temporary market conditions. Typically, as previously suggested, discounts from asset value tend to widen during declining stock market conditions and to narrow or even disappear during rising markets; in brief, closed-end shares are usually more volatile than the stock market in general.

But although more aggressive investors may be inclined to closed-end companies, it is possible to become confused by the irregular movement of the price in relation to asset value. As a general proportion, therefore, closed-end shares are usually more attractive to sophisticated investors, whereas open-end shares appeal to the general public.

The great growth in the investment-company area has been in the open-end category, this is probably because of effective merchandising techniques, among which are the high commissions offered security salesmen and a great amount of attractive literature. The divergence in growth trends suggests that there is an inherent advantage accruing from a constant sales effort to sell new shares.

The discount, which is in itself desirable to new investors, in effect inhibits the growth of the close-end companies, because it means the per share asset value of existing shareholders would be diluted by new issues of stock. Moreover, there actually may be some benefits to the remaining shareholders if a closed-end company contracts in size by buying its own shares at sizable discounts in the market.[4] The remaining shares thus increase their asset value per share solely by the stock-retirement process.

Classification by Investment Policy. Distinctions among investment companies according to alternative investment policies are of consid-

[4] In the years 1955–63 net new stock offerings by closed-end companies exceeded retirements of their outstanding securities by $323 million, but in the years 1930–54 the securities of these companies in the hands of the public had persistently declined through liquidations and the repurchase of outstanding shares. *Ibid.*, p. 30.

erable importance in the selection process, because they determine which companies fit the needs of a specific investor. The conventional classification along these lines shows the following types: (1) common-stock funds, (2) balanced funds, (3) bond funds, (4) specialty funds, and (5) nondiversified funds.

Common-Stock Funds. Common-stock funds are the most prevalent. Their policy, as implied by the name, is to keep their assets fully invested in common stocks. A good example is the Massachusetts Investors Trust, with assets at the end of 1964 of more than $2 billion. This company has made the following statement, "It is the policy of the Trustees to keep the assets of the Trust invested in common stocks except for working cash balances."[5] From the statement of policy it appeared that the underlying investment strategy was to obtain dividend income and appreciation from long-term growth. But there is some opportunity to engage in a cyclical timing strategy even when fully invested in common stocks. Shifts may be made to "defensive" stocks when, in the opinion of management, the economic and market outlook is unfavorable and to "aggressive," cyclical stocks when the reverse is predicted.[6]

Balanced Funds. Because common-stock portfolio decisions are the most difficult, and also because diversification needs are greater in this area, common-stock funds would seem to have more general appeal than the other types. The bond component of a portfolio can take the form of government bonds, which, of course, are easy to select and do not require diversification. Even high-quality corporate or municipal obligations can be selected with a minimum of analytical training.

Perhaps it is for this reason that the balanced funds, which ordinarily include significant proportions of fixed-income securities as well as common stocks in their portfolios, have shown a less rapid rate of growth.

---

[5] Massachusetts Investors Trust, *Annual Report* for 1963, p. 1.

[6] The quarterly report dated July 31, 1957, of Affiliated Fund, Inc., a common-stock fund, contained the following statement: "We believe that in the months ahead there will continue to be wide divergence in the price changes of individual securities. The impact of such things as rising interest rates and shifts in defense policies varies considerably from industry to industry and from company to company. We have been giving weight for some time to the possibility that the economic trends currently in evidence would develop and have been selecting our portfolio holdings accordingly." Although perhaps not conclusive, this statement suggests a policy to switch holdings to profit by (or limit market losses from) cyclical movements in the economy. It is on the basis of such evidence that clues to basic investment philosophy are obtainable.

The balanced fund attempts to offer a complete investment portfolio. Balanced funds have appeal to those desiring complete freedom of care from all investment decisions, except the job of selecting and buying the appropriate investment fund. However, there is a legitimate question of whether the investor should incur the expenses of investment management for the bond section of the portfolio in view of the simpler dimensions of bond selection.[7]

At first glance it might be presumed that the investment policy of balanced funds would be more conservative than that of common-stock funds. The bond section, in brief, should provide a stable balance wheel to the more erratic common-stock operations. But the policy of holding varying proportions of bonds and preferreds may make cyclical timing operations even more tempting to investment management. For example, the Commonwealth Investment Company, a balanced fund, made the following policy statement in an annual report. "From time to time, as economic conditions change, the proportion of assets invested in each kind of security is changed. If, for instance, the outlook for common stocks seems especially favorable, the investment in common stocks may be increased. Should the outlook be less promising for common stocks, the proportion might be decreased."[8]

It may then be noted that in the decade 1955–64 the percentage of common stocks in the Commonwealth portfolio varied between 54 and 69%.[9] However, because the cyclical timing strategies are usually not carried to extreme, balanced funds show less volatility of asset value than common-stock funds.

Bond and Preferred-Stock Funds. There are few of these, and on balance there would seem to be less logical use for them than the other types. As pointed out above, bond selection is a much less difficult process. However, there is a theory that wide diversification of medium-grade bonds will produce total returns greater than high-quality obligations over a number of years. Most of the bond funds seemed to be based on this theory. For example, the National Securities Bond Series as of the end of 1964 had a portfolio consisting of 46% medium-quality railroad

---

[7] Investment management fees charged against the investment company's income are expressed as a percentage of total asset value. Fee schedules vary but there seems to be a trend toward using a sliding fee scale starting at ½% of asset value and declining to ¼% or ⅛% on assets over a certain amount. The fee, of course, applies against the bond component as well as the common-stock component of a balanced fund.

[8] Commonwealth Investment Company, *Annual Report*, December 31, 1956, p. 9.

[9] Wiesenberger, *op. cit.*, p. 206.

bonds, such as New York Central, and another 46% in similar industrial bonds.[10] However, the net yields in 1963 and 1964 were 4.8 and 4.6%, respectively, and as high-grade corporate bond yields were about 4.4% in those years, the net advantage hardly seemed to justify the possible risks involved.

Specialty Funds. Specialty funds include investment companies which limit their operations to a particular industry or geographic area. In theory at least they are designed to appeal to the sophisticated investor, as they do not pretend to offer a complete investment account. These funds allow a wider diversification within a particular industry than might be practical by direct investment. Such diversification might be particularly desirable in industries dominated by a large number of companies which have not shown seasoned performances of profitability yet show qualitative promise. For example, as of 1965, such funds might have been desirable in the aerospace and electronics areas. To a lesser extent they may be useful to obtain some investment representation in unusual types of companies which are very difficult to analyze. Several funds concentrating in life insurance stocks were based on this view, as were others concentrating on Japanese and European securities.

Some investment companies construct their portfolios on the basis of unusual selection procedures, and these are included within the specialty classification. For example, there is the Value Line Special Situations Fund, which according to its prospectus, is intended only for those who wish to devote part of their investment capital to obtain capital appreciation and can also assume greater risk. *Special situations* were defined as companies experiencing unusual developments, such as mergers, liquidations, litigation, or discoveries, which might add significantly to the value of the stock.[11] This type of fund would presumably only appeal to experienced investors who are familiar with the nature of the risks and opportunities afforded by such a selection approach but who lack the time or inclination to carry out the process themselves.

Nondiversified Funds. Nondiversified funds are in essence a type of specialty fund, but their close resemblance to holding companies justifies special mention. Here the operation is partly investment management and partly business management. In the 1960–64 period, real estate participation syndicates became a popular device along these lines. A

[10] Moody's *Banks and Finance News*, December 8, 1964, p. 1372.
[11] The Value Line Special Situations Fund, Inc., *Prospectus*, August 15, 1956, p. 1.

number were organized shortly after an amendment to the federal income tax allowed such companies to receive tax treatment as regulated investment companies. It was also possible for these companies to take large depreciation deductions for tax purposes against the receipt of rental incomes and thus give tax-free distributions to their shareholders from the cash flow. However, several of these companies assumed large debt obligations and have had financial difficulties; others were accused of fraudulent activities. Therefore, it has become apparent that the risks to investors in these operations have been considerable, to say the least.

There are also a few nondiversified funds whose holdings represent concentrations in several different types of companies which may be in fact subsidiaries or affiliates. For example, the Equity Corporation, as of 1965, had 50% of its assets in the common stocks of four affiliates in the life insurance and electronic industries and another 29% in the common stock of the Singer Company. In purchasing the shares of such a company, the commitment is more nearly comparable to that in an industrial company. In Equity Corporation the long-term prospects for the several major operating areas plus the indicated ability of the management to operate the *de facto* subsidiaries effectively were the major problems.

Types of Companies: Investment Implications. The preceding classifications of investment companies suggest that the first problem is to select from the entire area a list of candidates suited to the individual investment requirements. Perhaps the greater number of investors would find common-stock funds, either the open-end or the closed-end type (when selling at a discount), most appropriate. However, under some circumstances balanced or specialty funds might offer some appeal. By and large, bond and nondiversified funds are much more limited in their general appeal as investment media.

Selection of Individual Companies: Analytical Factors. Once a decision as to the appropriate type of company has been reached, the next task is to select the particular situation which appears to offer the greatest opportunity for investment success at the minimum cost. There are really three major analytical factors pertinent to a decision in this respect: (1) the indicated capacity of management, (2) the level of management expenses in relation to income and asset value, (3) the price of the investment-company share as compared to asset value.

Of the three, unquestionably the most important is the indicated capacity of management. As noted, the only service these companies have to offer is their competency in managing investments. The costs of obtaining the management service, although they cannot be ignored, are of secondary importance. Other things being equal, they may influence a decision, but the indicated managerial capacities are of dominant importance.

Qualitative Appraisal. Management's general investment strategies might first be appraised in qualitative terms. The various alternatives and their possible virtues and shortcomings were discussed in some detail in Chapter 5. At this point it might be useful to repeat the major strategies set forth in that chapter. They are: (1) trading for short-term market fluctuations, (2) attempting to "buy-low sell-high" by predicting the major cyclical swings of the market over several years, (3) obtaining long-term appreciation and income through a buy-and-hold strategy. However, the latter strategy has some definite subclassifications, which include the acquisition of a cross-section of leading stocks, emphasis on growth stocks, and attempts to seek out so-called undervalued issues.

A detailed review of the major investment companies described in the 1964 edition of Weisenberger's *Investment Companies* reveals none wherein the strategy was short-term trading. All the other strategies were represented in part or in whole. Combinations of approach are frequent. To illustrate, the policies of the Investment Company of America were described as follows: "Long-term growth of capital and income are the primary objectives of this fund with current income a secondary consideration. While predominantly a widely diversified common stock fund, it may hold substantial sums in cash and Government obligations at times."[12] This statement implied combining growth stocks with cyclical switching as the basic strategies of investment operations. This quotation suggests that it is desirable to evaluate the underlying investment policies because wide differences exists. Some might prefer aggressive strategies despite the risks involved, and some might consider defensive operations more suitable to their personal needs.

Quantitative Appraisal of Management. As in industrial companies, the long-term comparative performances are the major quantitative clue to managerial capacity. The comparisons are based on the hypothesis that there is likely to be a direct relationship between past

[12] Wiesenberger, *op. cit.,* p. 243.

performance and future performance. Unquestionably, it is more plausible to assume continuity in performance between the past and the future than to assume complete discontinuity.

However, the nature of the operations makes the assumption less reliable for investment companies. Superior management of an industrial company tends to generate a certain amount of momentum which carries forward into the future. An entrenched competitive position generated by more efficient productive, marketing, and research activities is not easy to dislodge. But investment companies do not compete in this sense. At any given time each has a list of marketable securities which can be held or sold at the discretion of management. The past investment decisions have no necessary impact on future decisions, although of course it would be difficult to liquidate most of the portfolio overnight and place it elsewhere. But to a considerable extent, each investment company is starting from scratch at any given time.

In spite of these unique features, however, the past record of management would still seem to be some indication of future prospects. The investment decisions were not made in a vacuum; they represented conclusions derived from the philosophy, security-research activities, and general intelligence embodied in the organization. These factors do not change overnight. Although the results for a single year or two might be accidental, a consistently superior performance over a number of years cannot be casually dismissed.

The measurement of management results involves a few contrived statistical calculations. Over a period of years three types of returns may be obtained from an investment portfolio, and each must be taken into account in the calculation. First, there is regular dividend and interest income; second, realized capital gains; third, unrealized capital gains. The total of all these make up the aggregate investment returns produced by management, recognizing, of course, that these returns can be negative if capital losses are incurred.

Unrealized capital gains or losses are automatically taken into account by comparing changes in asset value per share from one year to the next. For any one year, then, total investment returns can be measured by adding the dividends paid from ordinary income and realized capital gains to the year-end asset value per share and then dividing by the asset value at the beginning of the year. The result is the performance "relative" for that year, which can be compared with others.[13] To illus-

---

[13] It might be noted that a similar technique could be used to measure the investment performance of any individual's portfolio for any given period of years.

trate, the calculation of the performance of Massachusetts Investors Trust for the year of 1963 would be as follows:

	Per Share
Asset value—year end 1963	$15.25
Add	
Dividends paid from investment income—1963	.42
Dividends paid from realized capital gains—1963	.31
Total adjusted asset value—12/31/63	$15.98
Asset value—December 31, 1962	$13.32

$$\frac{\text{Adjusted asset value, December 31, 1963}}{\text{Asset value, December 31, 1962}} = \frac{\$15.25}{\$13.32} = 114\%$$

Of course, the comparative performance over a period of five to ten years is more indicative of relative managerial ability than the results for any one year, which may be influenced by circumstances peculiar to that particular period. However, the results must be interpreted with considerable care, especially when the stock market as a whole is much higher or lower at the end than at the beginning. For instance, any common-stock fund should show up better than a balanced fund during a period when the stock market has advanced. All the result shows is that, by hindsight, the investor was wise to concentrate in common stocks when the market subsequently went up. Therefore, only similar types of funds can logically be compared.

To illustrate, Table 19-1 shows the pertinent long-term data for four large open-end common-stock funds for the eight-year period 1956–63. The analysis shows that Massachusetts Investors Trust provided the greatest total returns of the four companies. However, its margin over two of the others was not significant. But it can be noted that although the Investment Company of America showed results for 1956–63 closely approximating those of M.I.T., its performance was considerably more erratic, perhaps because of its avowed policy of engaging in cyclical timing operations. For example, in the ten years ended with 1958, I.C.A. showed by far the worst results. Its record suggests that past results may be a doubtful clue to the future when a cyclical timing strategy dominates investment policy. In any event, other factors equal, there appeared to be some reason to prefer Massachusetts Investors Trust among the companies compared above.

Some analysts, in addition to comparing the investment results of

TABLE 19-1
RELATIVE INVESTMENT PERFORMANCE: 1956–63
OPEN-END COMMON-STOCK FUNDS

	Asset Value 12/31/55	From Income	*Dividends: 1955–63* From Capital Gains	Asset Value 12/31/63	Management Relative*
Incorporated Investors	$ 9.53	$1.53	$3.90	$ 7.39	135
Massachusetts Investors Trust	10.95	3.23	2.07	15.25	187
Investment Company of America	9.42	2.03	4.50	10.90	185
Fundamental Investors, Inc.	7.81	1.91	2.08	10.05	180

* Total of all dividends added to asset value at end of 1963, the result divided by asset value as of end of 1955.

several companies, also measure the management performances against a selected common-stock index wherein all dividends paid on the component stocks are added to the index. A performance better or worse than this index indicates whether investment managements added or detracted from total investment returns as compared with those derived from an arbitrary holding of the index. However, the comparison really tends to indicate the general desirability of investment companies as a group rather than their relative attractiveness. Assuming the need for the services of an investment company, the added technique does not seem really necessary.

Statutory Regulation. Brief mention might be made of the statutory regulation of management. After several years of detailed study by the Securities and Exchange Commission, the Investment Company Act of 1940 was passed by Congress. It was primarily aimed at preventing certain abuses and unethical practices that a minority of these companies had followed to the detriment of investors. The statute is highly detailed, but the following provisions may be of some interest to potential investors in these companies.

1. Leverage is limited by a provision that any funded debt must be covered three times by assets and preferred stock twice.
2. Investment companies cannot purchase more than nominal amounts of securities of other investment companies.
3. Companies must state the nature of their investment policies, and they cannot be changed without stockholder approval.

4. Regular reports on operations and security portfolios are required.
5. Inside dealings between investment banking sponsors and the in-investment company are restricted.[14]

Although the statute, if enforced diligently, operates to the advantage of investors, its effects are largely negative. It prevents certain fraudulent or unsound practices, but it cannot in a positive sense insure a successful investment management. Competent management cannot be legislated into existence. Therefore, positive indications of managerial performances are still necessary.

Analysis of Management Expenses.   Although the investment policy and the past management record are undoubtedly the most significant factors in selecting an investment company, the amount of expenses incurred in performing the management function should also be given some attention. It is, of course, desirable to have the maximum amount of the gross investment returns available for distribution, although reasonable costs should be expected for the services rendered.

There are two conventional techniques for appraising managerial expenses. One is to relate expenses to total assets, on the theory that these expenses should relate to the size of the portfolio managed. The second is to compare expenses to the level of gross income received in the form of dividends and interest; the concept is that investors are interested in the proportion of regular current income that is siphoned off to meet recurrent operating expenses. The application of these ratios to the four companies whose management results were examined previously are shown in Table 19-2; it may be noted that as these ratios do not change significantly, their levels in the past two years or so give sufficient indication of their probable future magnitude.

It is imperative to use these ratios in conjunction with each other, as either one alone may be inconclusive. For example, a high ratio of expenses to gross income is not conclusive of an unfavorable expense performance, because the company may be emphasizing investment for appreciation rather than current income. Growth stocks, of course, carry

[14] However, a detailed study of the practices of the "open end" companies in 1962 revealed that a few companies were open to criticism on the grounds of conflicts of interest. Excessive turn-overs of portfolios to generate brokerage fees for affiliated brokerage firms and excessive fees for portfolio management were among the abuses cited. The S.E.C. has apparently tightened its rules as a consequence of the study, but as of 1965, no new legislation had resulted. Committee on Interstate and Foreign Commerce, *A Study of Mutual Funds*, (prepared by the Wharton School of Finance and Commerce), Government Printing Office, Washington, D.C., 1962, pp. 15–36.

TABLE 19-2
COMPARATIVE EXPENSE RATIOS: 1963–64
OPEN-END INVESTMENT COMPANIES

	Ratio of Expenses to Net Assets		Ratio of Expenses to Gross Income	
	1963	1964	1963	1964
Incorporated Investors	.55%	.58%	20.4%	20.7%
Massachusetts Investors Trust	.17	.18	5.9	6.3
Investment Company of América	.55	.56	19.3	19.6
Fundamental Investors, Inc.	.56	.52	19.2	19.5

low current-income yields, but it is expected that greater than average appreciation will compensate for the lower than average yields. As gross income only includes dividends received, a growth-stock fund may well have a high ratio of expenses to gross income, although its management fees may be low in relation to the total value of the assets managed.

But where both ratios are high or low there is some indication of a relatively unfavorable or favorable performance. Massachusetts Investors Trust, for example, showed up very well with an exceptionally low ratio of expenses to both assets and gross income. The others are roughly equal and do not seem to be markedly favorable or unfavorable. As a rough standard, it has been suggested that the ratio of expenses to net assets should not exceed 0.5%. Because the level of available yields in the market fluctuates considerably, it is more difficult to establish a specific standard for the ratio of expenses to gross income, although in the 1963–64 period the average was between 15 and 20% for most companies.

Price to Asset Value. Because the purchase of an investment-company share represents the indirect acquisition of a diversified list of marketable securities, the relationship between the market prices of the shares and the asset value per share is a significant factor in its appraisal. For example, if the market price of the shares were twice the underlying asset value, it would be a prima facie case of overvaluation, even assuming a highly favorable management performance. It would mean that the investor would be paying twice as much for the portfolio as the constituent stocks were worth in the open market.

On the other hand, if the shares are selling for materially less than asset value, it would represent evidence of a possible bargain situation. Of course, if management has been exceptionally poor, then caution might still be advisable, because a continued poor performance might

TABLE 19–3
SELECTED OPEN-END INVESTMENT COMPANIES
SCALE OF SALES CHARGES
(as of 1964)

	Sales Charge: % of Asset Value for Purchases of:			
	0–$10,000	*$10,000– $25,000*	*$25,000– $50,000*	*$50,000– $100,000*
Incorporated Investors	8.5%	8.5%	6.0%	4.5%
Massachusetts Investors Trust	8.5	8.5	5.75	4.0
Investment Company of America	8.5°	8.0	5.5	4.0
Fundamental Investors, Inc.	8.75	7.5	5.75	4.0

° Charge reduced to 8.0% at $5,000.

erode asset value in the future to a level even below the current price of the shares. Perhaps an analogy can be drawn with the appraisal of industrial common stocks. There the final question is whether the projected earning power in relation to the current market price is reasonable in the light of the quality of the company. In the case of an investment company, the question is whether the market price in relation to asset value seems reasonable after taking account of the apparent managerial capacity and expenses.

Prices: Open-End Companies. This phase of the appraisal, however, is much less important for open-end companies than for closed-end companies, as the price of open-end company shares is always at least equal to asset value. However, the purchase price also includes a "load" charge which varies slightly from company to company and is scaled down as the amount of each purchase increases. Table 19-3 shows the "load" charges for the several companies.

The main purpose of the charge is to pay a commission to the dealer or broker handling the transaction, although other incidental expenses, such as the costs of issuing new shares, are also involved. In a sense the load charge may be compared to the brokerage and incidental costs of acquiring any security. On very small transactions they only slightly exceed brokerage costs on the acquisition of listed securities, but on purchases of $300 or more the load charge is ordinarily significantly greater.[15]

[15] There are a few open-end companies which impose no load charge and sell directly to investors. Other things being equal, of course, this is preferable to investors.

TABLE 19-4
SELECTED CLOSED-END INVESTMENT COMPANIES;
ASSET VALUE IN RELATION TO PRICE OF SHARES

	Per Share Asset Value 12/31/64	Common-Stock Market Price	Percent Discount from Asset Value
Lehman Corp.	$32.01	31.375°	1.9%
Dominick Fund	24.14	21.5°	10.9
Niagara Share Corp.	21.01	22.375°	6.5 (premium)

° Closing price on N.Y. Stock Exchange as of 2/5/65.

Prices: Closed-End Companies. Closed-end situations, however, are an entirely different story. As the secondary market determines the price of the shares, there is no consistent relation of price to estimated asset value. It is pertinent to note that the phrase *estimated asset values* must be used for closed-end companies, because they customarily publish asset values only quarterly, with perhaps a week or so lag from the end of the quarter to publication date. During a given quarterly period, therefore, the prevailing market price of an investment company's shares is compared to the asset value reported as of the end of the preceding quarter.

To illustrate the nature of a comparative price analysis, Table 19-4 shows the asset value at the end of 1964 for three closed-end companies and the closing market prices of their shares on February 5, 1965. By dividing the asset value per share into the difference between asset value and market price, the percentage premium or discount prevailing on the stock is obtained. Niagara Share, for example, was selling at a 6.5% premium and Dominick Fund at an 11% discount on the illustrative date, whereas Lehman Corp. was available at a small discount from asset value.

If there has been a material change in the general level of stock prices since the last reported asset value, then it may be desirable to make an approximation of the current asset-value level. This can be done roughly by assuming that asset values will move up or down proportionately to the movement of a selected stock market index. For example, the Dow-Jones Industrial Average increased from about 875 on December 31 of 1964 to about 901 on February 5, 1965, or by about 3%. A rough estimate of asset values on February 5, 1965 might have been obtained by adding 3% to the reported year-end amounts. In view of the relatively modest change in stock prices between these dates, the

TABLE 19-5
SELECTED CLOSED-END INVESTMENT COMPANIES
MANAGEMENT AND EXPENSE PERFORMANCES

	Management Relative 1956 through 1964	Expense Ratios: 1962–64	
		Expenses/ Gross Income	Expenses/ Net Assets
Dominick Fund	166	16.2%	.41%
Lehman Corp.	192	16.3	.37
Niagara Share Corp.	209	19.5	.50

adjustment did not seem necessary in this instance. However, if the stock market had advanced or declined by perhaps 10% or more between these dates, then a more useful indication of the prices of these stocks in relation to prevailing asset values would be obtained by adjusting the indicated asset values.

The less favorable management performance of Dominick Fund, shown in Table 19-5, explains why this stock sold at a larger discount from asset value than the others. In this connection, it is interesting to note that Dominick had done more switching of its portfolio through the years than the others.[16] Niagara Share had an excellent management record for the indicated period; it had concentrated in a few growth areas which proved very successful during these years. However, its price was above asset value, whereas Lehman Corp., with almost as good a performance, could have been acquired at a 2% discount from asset value. Moreover, Lehman's expense ratios were significantly below those for Niagara Share in recent years. Therefore, Lehman Corp. seemed to be the preferable stock, although aggressive investors might have been inclined to Niagara Share, despite the price premium.

Taxation Factors in Investment-Company Analysis. Most investment companies qualify under the Internal Revenue Code as regulated investment companies, which exempts them from all corporate taxes. There are several requirements the companies must meet in order to obtain this exemption. Perhaps of primary interest is the fact that "regulated"

---

[16] The portfolio turnover ratio shows the amount of switching that has taken place. It is computed by taking one-half of the combined purchases and sales of securities for a year and dividing by asset value at the beginning of the year. This ratio averaged about 27% for Dominick Fund in the years 1957–63 inclusive as compared to average ratios of 11% and 12% for Niagara Share and Lehman, respectively. Wiesenberger, *op. cit.* p. 68.

companies are obliged to pass on to their shareholders substantially all of their net income exclusive of realized and unrealized long-term capital gains. When dividends are declared to shareholders from realized capital gains, they are taxed as long-term gains at one half of the regular rate, with a maximum rate of 25%.[17]

When realized capital gains are retained, the company must pay a 25% tax on them for the account of their shareholders. The stockholders are then required to include their share of these gains in their income-tax returns and can take credit for the tax paid for their account. If their effective tax rate on long-term gains is less than 25%, a tax credit is obtained. Moreover, the cost basis of the investment-company stock for tax purposes can then be increased by 75% of the realized capital gains retained by the companies. The tax effects are exactly as though the realized gains had been distributed as dividends and taxed at a 25% rate and then the remaining 75% of such gains reinvested in the company by the shareholders.

Because the tax law requires the complete payout of net earnings exclusive of capital gains, there is no need to appraise dividend policy. In effect, all net income is turned over to the investor as though the portfolio of the company was owned outright. The only difference is that expenses of management must be assumed, and decisions on when capital gains are to be realized are not made by the investor.

Because capital-gains dividends represent irregular distributions of past appreciation which has finally been realized at the discretion of management, it is customary practice to define the dividend yield as the relation between market price and dividends derived from the net dividend and interest income on the portfolio. For example, Massachusetts Investors Trust in the years 1963–64 paid about $.42 in annual dividends from investment income and irregular amounts from realized capital gains. With its offering price at about $19 per share in early 1965, the estimated current yield was 2.2%.

Investment Companies: Summary. Investment companies are designed to provide professional investment management and portfolio diversification to small investors. However, the numerous types and diverse management records of these companies suggest the need for

[17] The majority of open-end companies allow capital-gain dividends to be reinvested without "load" charge at the option of the investor on an automatic basis. Automatic reinvestment of regular dividends is also typically allowed, although some impose the "load" charge in this case.

considerable investigation before investments are made in the area. In
summary, the following suggestions may be offered to guide investors in
this area:

1. Common-stock funds are the most logical type, because management is more difficult and diversification more necessary in the
common-stock section of an investment account.
2. As the investor is essentially purchasing management, an appraisal
of probable managerial capacity is of primary importance. A qualitative review of the investment strategies used by management
and the comparative quantitative performance in the past are the
techniques used, although continuity of a successful performance
is probably less assured in an investment company than in an industrial company.
3. An evaluation of the costs of management is also desirable. Management fees and miscellaneous expenses typically amount to about
.5% of total assets, or between 15 and 20% of gross income. It is
useful to compare similar types of companies on both these expense ratios. These expenses are the primary drawback to investing in these companies.
4. The market prices of open-end companies are always equal to asset
value based on market prices of the portfolio on a given day. When
they are purchased, a load charge is added which may vary slightly
from one company to another. But the price factor is of minor
significance in open-end-company evaluations.
5. Closed-end companies may sell at a premium or discount from
estimated asset value. Therefore, the relationship between price
and asset value is of greater significance. The investment decision
boils down to weighing the advantages of a large discount, on the
one hand, and management and expense performance, on the
other. Because the appraisal process is usually more complex,
closed-end shares tend to attract the more sophisticated investor.
6. Under existing tax laws, investment companies declare dividends
about equal to net income from dividends and interest on the
portfolio.
7. Most companies also distribute realized capital gains on the sale
of any portfolio assets as special dividends taxable to the investor
at the capital-gains rate.

Although these companies undoubtedly perform a useful service to a
special group of investors, they do not seem to be the major answer to
the individual investor's problems. Intensive promotion by brokers and

dealers has resulted in a rapid growth of open-end companies, and this growth has focused considerable attention on them. But as the costs of management are by no means negligible, those individuals with adequate background might do better with direct portfolios or with the closed-end companies, when available at relatively large discounts from asset values.

CHAPTER 20

Commercial Banks

Economics of the Banking Industry

Scope of Activities. Like investment companies, commercial banks also obtain a dominant proportion of their earnings from investing or lending money. However, in several important respects banking operations are fundamentally different. First, with the possible exception of the New York and Chicago banks, their earnings potential is closely related to the economic characteristics of a particular geographical area. By and large, banks do not operate on a nation-wide scale. Therefore, the analysis of a commercial bank usually includes a general appraisal of the economic characteristics of the area served. In this respect, the analysis is similar to that required for utilities.

Second, the investments and loans of banks are restricted by statute solely to creditor instruments. No preferred or common stocks can be voluntarily acquired, and only on the relatively rare occasions when foreclosure occurs on a loan secured by stocks will such securities become temporarily a part of the assets. This fact suggests that portfolio appreciation of a bank's assets is not likely to be an important source of returns on a bank stock in contrast to investment companies.

Third, the traditional financial function of commercial banks is not the acquisition of securities for investment purposes. Although variations in policy undoubtedly exist, it is safe to generalize that banks purposely emphasize direct loans to customers in preference to security investments. There are several reasons for this policy. First, loans on the average usually give higher yields. Second, borrowing customers are also usually depositors and therefore must be accommodated in order for the bank to retain their deposits. Finally, because the growth of a bank is dependent upon the progress of the local community, it stands to benefit by encouraging through financial assistance the activities of local enterprise.

Liquidity and Solvency Concepts. The normal liability and capital structure of a bank present some unusual problems. These liabilities take the form of deposits, which are to all intents and purposes demand obligations. Moreover, the total deposit liabilities are usually ten to twenty times the equity of the stockholders. The demand nature of the liabilities creates what is commonly known as the liquidity problem. Primary reserves of cash items and secondary reserves (investments which can be quickly converted into cash at any time without loss) must be maintained in sufficient quantity to anticipate demands of depositors. But as these assets usually tend to give lower yields than alternatives, excessive liquidity adversely affects earnings. Maintaining appropriate but not excessive liquidity is, therefore, a major managerial problem in banking, and the result is that only a modest yield can be obtained on a significant share of the assets.

The large size of deposits in relation to the stock equity creates what is sometimes known as a solvency problem. In essence, the problem is that a very small percentage loss on the total loans and investments can entirely wipe out the stock equity, and, of course, this would mean insolvency. To illustrate, it has not been uncommon for banks to have $20 in deposits for every $1 of capital. Assuming that 25% of the deposits are maintained in cash and the balance loaned or invested the balance sheet would roughly show the following proportions:

Assets		Liabilities	
Cash	5	Deposits	20
Loans and Investments	16	Stock equity*	1
	21		21

* In general the stock equity consists of the capital stock, surplus, and undivided profits accounts, although nominal amounts of equity reserves might also be included.

In the assumed relationship, the stock equity amounts to slightly more than 6% of the total loans and investments on the asset side. The result is, then, that a 6% loss experience on these assets would wipe out the stock equity and the bank would be insolvent.

As a result, banks find it necessary to be reasonably conservative in their loan and investment policies. There is, moreover, a general rule of thumb followed by the examining authorities that "risk assets," usually defined simply as all loans and investments except government bonds, should not be more than eight to ten times the stock equity. In the hypothetical example, following the rule would mean that roughly half the earning assets would be committed to governments or similar nonrisk assets, even though liquidity needs per se may not require this amount. Therefore, although banks normally give priority to customer loans for reasons indicated previously, a bank may be effectively "loaned up" even when it still holds a sizable portfolio of government bonds which are held either because of its liquidity or solvency situation.

Sources of Income.   Banks typically obtain about 85 to 90% of their revenues from interest on loans and investments, but certain corollary activities produce a modest amount of income. Table 20-1 shows the breakdown of the major revenue sources for banks which are members of the Federal Reserve System, and these include almost all banks whose stocks are publicly owned. It is apparent from these data that banks depend upon their loan and security portfolios for the great majority of their income. Therefore, it is reasonable to conclude that their gross income will be largely determined by the size of and available yield on these portfolios. Other revenues include charges for trust services, safety deposit boxes, foreign exchange, and miscellaneous services of this kind. Because of their nominal amount, no special analytical attention of these items is necessary.

Variations in Interest Rates.   In a very real sense banks are engaged in the business of "selling" immediate money for future money and charging a fee (interest) for this service. The structure of interest rates at any given time, therefore, represents a sort of price index for the product which banks are offering for sale. As a consequence, it might be expected that bank earnings would fluctuate directly with the movement of interest rates, earnings rising when interest rates increase and vice versa. In general, a direct correlation between fluctuations in interest rates and earnings tends to prevail, but there is a corollary relation which tends to produce the opposite result.

TABLE 20-1
MEMBER BANK REVENUES: 1960–63
(in millions of dollars)

Source	1960	1961	1962	1963
Interest on				
U.S. governments	$1,414	$1,537	$ 1,687	$ 1,726
Other securities	467	513	629	773
Loans	5,730	5,870	6,435	7,200
Total interest revenues	$7,611	$7,920	$ 8,751	$ 9,699
Other Revenues	1,316	1,297	1,403	1,471
Total Revenues	$8,927	$9,217	$10,154	$11,170

Source: Federal Reserve Bulletins, May, 1964, and May, 1962.

To explain this paradox it is necessary to distinguish between the effects of interest rate changes on new loans and investments and on the existing investment portfolio. When rates advance, it obviously means that yields on new commitments will be greater, and as loans and investments mature and are reinvested, revenues will increase. However, the advance in interest rates also means that the prices of securities already held in the portfolio will decline. The extent of the decline in the prices of securities held, of course, will be governed by the amplitude of the change in rates and the maturity schedule of the portfolio. These "losses" will show up in the income statement only if actually realized by sale of the securities, because banks, unlike investment companies, are permitted to carry these securities at amortized cost rather than at market value on their statements.[1] Even so, the possibility of large paper losses deters most banks from acquiring any large amount of long-term bonds. Most banks seem to limit maximum maturities to about fifteen years, and average maturities are usually only three to five years on their holdings of marketable securities.

As the general practice is to maintain reasonably short maturity schedules on loans and investments, market losses because of an advance in interest rates are ordinarily modest. Moreover, the shorter the maturities, the more rapidly funds are released for new commitments

[1] For tax reasons banks have some incentive to realize gains and losses on their security portfolios as values change due to interest rate fluctuations, because under existing income tax laws banks can deduct losses on the sale of securities from ordinary income (which was taxed as of 1965 at 48%) while long-term gains are taxed at half that rate. Banks are thus encouraged to realize gains and losses in different years as they must be offset against each other if realized in the same year.

at a higher level of rates and the more immediate the rise in revenues in response to this event.

If interest rates decline, the effects are precisely the opposite. A short maturity schedule means revenues decline more rapidly as a greater proportion of the total earning assets is "rolled-over" at the lower yields. Moreover, the price appreciation on the existing portfolio is more limited under these conditions. Because of these diverse effects, many banks attempt to lengthen maturities somewhat when, in the opinion of management, interest rates seem destined to decline and to shorten maturities when rising interest rates seem to be in prospect.

It is not suggested that these operations will be extreme; in fact, many banks, especially those of smaller size, prefer to maintain an evenly spaced maturity schedule on their investment portfolio and thereby obtain the average yields available over a period of time.[3] Furthermore, it is important to recognize that the amplitude of interest-rate fluctuations is controlled by the Federal Reserve authorities to a very substantial degree. In general, the effects of Federal Reserve monetary policy have been in the direction of preventing large swings in interest rates over short periods of time. It is probable, therefore, that the stability of bank earnings has been enhanced somewhat by the concepts of monetary policy that have emerged in the postwar years.

Variations in Deposits. For the banking system as a whole, the level of deposits is determined by (1) the supply of reserves (Federal Reserve deposits) available to the banks and (2) the utilization of the reserves by the acquisition of loans or investments. In order to execute monetary-policy objectives, the total supply of bank reserves is controlled by the Federal Reserve, and its stated policy is to encourage "stable growth" although temporary decreases in bank reserves might take place if the Federal Reserve feels it essential to restrict inflationary pressures at certain times. But wide cyclical variations in bank reserves, such as occurred under gold standard conditions, are unlikely, although slow growth over a period of years is a reasonable probability.

Total bank deposits have also shown a favorable trend because of the growth in suitable instruments for loans and investments. The basic change has been the tremendous growth in the size of the government debt. In earlier eras if private loans were reduced because of adverse

---

[2] When a portfolio of bonds has an evenly spaced or staggered maturity schedule, it means that a constant proportion will come due for reinvestment each year or so, and thus such investments should obtain a return equal to the average interest rate prevailing through time.

business conditions, banks were often unable to find suitable substitutes to replace these assets. It is now possible, however, for the bank to replace any decline in loans with short-term government bonds rather than hold idle reserves. There is no doubt that both the growth and stability of bank deposits have been improved by active monetary and fiscal policies aimed at promoting stable growth of the economy. The deposit experience of member banks since 1951, when monetary policy was relieved of restraints imposed during World War II, strongly supports this observation. Total deposits of these banks increased from $155.3 billion at the end of 1950 to about $241 billion at the end of 1964, or buy about 54% and interim variations have been very limited.[3]

The Individual Bank: Specific Analysis

Deposit Trends. Although reasonably stable and slowly growing deposit levels for the entire banking system appear probable, the rate of growth of any given bank may vary widely from the systemic outlook. Here the controlling factor is predominantly the economic characteristics of the area served. Perhaps the statistical record of deposits in the past ten years or so provides the best tangible clue to the growth potential. The year-to-year changes in deposits also indicate the performance under moderate fluctuations in the economy such as have been witnessed in the 1955–64 decade. However, a complicating factor is that many banks have participated in mergers during the postwar period, which means (assuming that growth by future mergers is likely to be more limited) the past deposit record may overstate the growth potential for the future.[4]

Even with these limitations, a rough idea of potential deposit experience can be indicated by an index of deposit movement through the years. Table 20-2 shows such an index for three large banks in different areas of the country. All these banks appear to have enjoyed satisfactory trends in their deposit performance, although the deposit growth of Morgan Guaranty is overstated by the merger of J. P. Morgan and Guaranty Trust in 1959; adjusting 1954 to include the deposit totals of

[3] *Federal Reserve Bulletins*, Data on Assets and Liabilities of Member Banks, various issues.

[4] When the merger has been between two or three relatively large banks, this distortion can be corrected by including all the banks in the data for the entire period. However, there have also been numerous instances of a large bank taking over a number of small banks from time to time. In this case, adjusting the data would be too laborious to be practicable.

TABLE 20–2
INDEX OF DEPOSIT MOVEMENTS (1947–49)

Year End	National Bank (Detroit)	Bank of America (California)	Morgan Guaranty (New York)
1954	95	83	92
1955	105	88	96
1956	104	90	90
1957	101	95	87
1958	99	103	94
1959	100	106	120
1960	107	108	130
1961	111	115	147
1962	122	121	156
1963	129	132	159
1964	141	140	171
Percent increase 1954–64	48%	68%	86%

Source: Standard & Poor's, *Industry Surveys.*

both banks would result in an index of 110 for that year and a growth percentage of 55% rather than 86%.

The data also suggest that Morgan Guaranty might be more exposed to a deposit decline during tight money periods, as indicated by the decline in their deposit index between 1955 and 1957. As a major money market bank in New York, a modest deposit decline might well occur under similar conditions in the future, although the higher interest rates during such periods should alleviate the effects on earnings.

Asset Analysis per Share. Traditionally, book value per share has been regarded as an important bench mark of the investment value of a bank stock. The reasoning is that since bank assets and liabilities are largely fixed-dollar instruments subject to realization at their stated amounts, book value represents an approximation of the actual investment of the shareholders in the loan and investment portfolio. In brief, this argument is similar to that advanced for other financial institutions, such as investment companies. But in fact there is good reason to question the significance of book value per share as a major indication of value. In the case of banks, earnings are obtained from the investment of deposits as well as from the capital funds supplied by the shareholders. The book-value concept in effect ignores the variations in the earnings potential arising from large differences in the relation of deposits to book value (the deposit-capital ratio).

TABLE 20-3
COMPARATIVE EARNING ASSET ANALYSIS
DECEMBER 31, 1964

	National Bank (Detroit)	Bank of America (California)	Morgan Guaranty (New York)
Earning Assets (in millions)			
U.S. governments	$ 603	$ 2,022	$ 491
Loans and other securities	1,566	10,439	3,765
Total earning assets	$2,169	$12,461	$4,256
Percent loans of total	71	83	87
Liabilities (in millions)			
Total deposits	$2,508	$14,000	$4,788
Capital funds	199	860	631
Number of common shares (in thousands)	4,000	28,480	8,294
Price: common stock, January, 1965	70	63	120
Book value per share	45	30	76
Comparative ratios			
Deposits to capital	12.5	16.3	7.6
Risk assets° to capital	7.9	12.6	5.9
Earning assets per share	$ 542	$ 437	$ 514
Price to book value	1.55	2.1	1.58
Earning assets per dollar of market price	$7.74	$6.93	$4.28

° Risk assets defined as all earning assets other than government obligations.

A very high level of deposits in relation to capital funds may demand correction through obtaining additional capital, but even so, extensive differences between banks in this respect continue to exist. It is also argued that a high deposit-capital ratio will require a greater utilization of deposits in liquid assets to protect the solvency position, and, therefore, the earning power per dollar of assets will be lower under such conditions. There probably is some tendency in this direction, but even relatively liquid earning assets can contribute a great deal to earnings on the common stock when, because of a high deposit leverage, there is a large amount of such assets per share of stock.

A better indication than book value of the comparative value of a bank stock is the total amount of loans and investments attributable to each share. When banks are compared on this basis, there is the implicit assumption that the quality and rate of return on all loan and investment portfolios are roughly the same, and, therefore, that earnings per share will be proportionate to the amount of loans and investments per share. For example, Table 20-3 shows that National Bank of Detroit had about 71% of its total portfolio in loans and other securities at the end of 1964, whereas Bank of America and Morgan Guaranty had about 85% in this category. These proportions suggest that the earning power per dollar of earning assets should be modestly lower for National Bank of Detroit than for the others. On the other hand, the intrinsic quality of the portfolio is improved by a high proportion of government obligations, and also N.B.D. enjoyed greater "elbow room" to increase earnings through shifts from governments to higher-yielding assets.

But it is not enough to know which bank has the greatest indicated portfolio values per share. The market prices of the shares must be brought into account to determine which bank offers the greatest amount of asset values per dollar of common-stock market price. To make several banks comparable, it is only necessary to divide the total earning assets per share by the market prices of the stocks; the result shows the amount of portfolio assets working for each dollar invested in the stocks at the prevailing market prices.

Assuming the quality of the several banks to be roughly identical, the comparative results (computed for the three banks, at the bottom of Table 20-3) should be a good indication of which common stock was most attractively priced on an asset-value basis at a given time. It is interesting to note that although Bank of America sold at a higher price in relation to book value (2.1) than did Morgan Guaranty (1.58), the investor obtained $6.93 of loans and investments per dollar of market price with Bank of America as compared to $4.28 with the Morgan Guaranty. But National Bank of Detroit, with $7.74 of earnings assets per dollar of market price, offered the greatest value of the three in this connection.

Importance of Earnings Record. Although the comparative amount of portfolio assets that can be acquired per dollar of market price is one useful technique to appraise the attractiveness of several bank stocks, an analysis of the earnings records, their potentials, and the relation of the earnings and the dividend rates to the stock prices is more important with banks than with other financial institutions for two reasons.

First, net earnings as a percentage of asset values in banks may vary considerably as a consequence of (1) differences in the proportion of income derived from other activities, such as trust services, (2) differences in the nature of the deposit structure and consequent costs thereon, such as the proportion of time deposits and small commercial accounts to the total, (3) differences in operating efficiencies.

Second, banks, unlike most investment companies, do not include large amounts of common stocks in their investment portfolios. As a result, long-term capital gains on common-stock holdings outside of the earnings stream are not a factor in bank operations as they are in the other financial institutions. For these reasons the comparative price-earnings ratios are more important in the selection of bank stocks than in financial institutions in which common-stock portfolios are an important factor in their investment operations. In addition, because most banks have well-established dividend rates, the dividend yield may also be an important element in a selection decision.

Earning Power: Problems in Determination. There are, however, some problems in evaluating the earnings of commercial banks. It is quite clear that most of the earning power is derived from interest on loans and securities from which operating expenses are deducted to obtain "net operating earnings." But as the banks have large amounts of marketable bonds in their portfolios, it is inevitable that there will be some capital gains or losses in connection with the management of this portfolio. The question arises as to whether these capital gains or losses should be included or excluded from earnings in arriving at estimates of earning power.

Because banks are limited to fixed-income securities any capital gains would have to arise either from a secular downward trend in interest rates or from an ability to forecast interest rate fluctuations correctly or, in other words, to buy bonds low and sell high. From about 1935 through 1951 many banks did show significant net capital gains on balance due to a continued downward drift in interest rates. But since 1951 interest rates have in general moved upward. Although the long-term trend in rates may again move downward sometime in the future, it is not at all clear when and to what extent this may take place. Therefore, repetitive future capital gains on bond portfolios would seem to be a very doubtful prognosis. In fact, many banks credit all capital gains to an equity reserve and charge all capital losses against the reserve, so that these transactions are shown separately and are eliminated from the net earnings. For analysis purposes, the practice seems quite desirable.

There are no special problems in connection with expense determination. Salaries and interest paid on savings deposits are by far the major expense items. As the proportion of deposits represented by savings and certificates of deposit have increased greatly in recent years and as rates paid thereon have also moved upward substantially, the profit margins of many banks have declined in the years 1959–64 and the growth of bank earnings may continue to be inhibited by this expense item.

TABLE 20-4
EARNINGS AND DIVIDEND ANALYSIS: 1956-64
(000 omitted on earnings totals)

	1956	1961	1962	1963	1964
National Bank of Detroit					
Revenues	$ 58,823	$ 77,726	$ 85,137	$ 93,781	$103,905
Operating expenses and taxes	44,855	60,490	68,292	75,720	83,638
Net operating earnings	$ 13,968	$ 17,236	$ 16,845	$ 18,061	$ 20,268
Net per share	3.49	4.31	4.21	4.52	5.07
Dividends per share	1.45	1.75	1.80	1.80	1.95
Payout ratio	41%	41%	43%	40%	40%
Rate of return on equity	10.3%	10.0%	9.3%	9.5%	10.7%
Bank of America					
Revenues	$368,626	$522,231	$601,303	$656,321	$718,088
Operating expenses and taxes	294,660	464,448	518,176	565,812	618,463
Net operating earnings	$ 73,966	$ 87,783	$ 83,127	$ 90,509	$ 99,625
Net per share	2.89	3.08	2.92	3.18	3.50
Dividends per share	1.75	2.00	2.00	2.00	2.00
Payout ratio	60%	65%	69%	66%	57%
Rate of return on equity	13.3%	11.3%	10.4%	11.0%	11.2%
Morgan Guaranty*					
Revenues	$115,946	$170,746	$183,826	$188,444	$212,703
Operating expenses and taxes	78,471	121,475	133,533	139,764	158,130
Net operating earnings	$ 37,475	$ 49,271	$ 50,293	$ 48,680	$ 54,573
Net per share	4.51	5.94	6.06	5.87	6.58
Dividends per share	2.77	3.61	3.64	3.91	4.00
Payout ratio	61%	61%	60%	66%	60%
Rate of return on equity	7.8%	8.6%	8.5%	8.1%	8.7%

* Pro-forma for 1956 based on combined totals of Morgan and Guaranty Trust,

Earning Power: Quantitative Estimates. Because wide variations in bank deposits are not likely to be tolerated under accepted concepts of national economic policy, bank earnings are likely to be fairly stable. However, earnings may vary to a modest degree in accord with movements in interest rates and in the effective demand for loans, both of which are likely to be high or low at the same time. In addition, many banks have shown moderate growth in per share earning power as deposits have increased, with retained earnings providing most of the resultant capital needs. The growth factor, however, has varied widely between different geographic areas and will probably continue to be more favorable in those areas where population and industry have been increasing most rapidly. Therefore, there is likely to be considerable differences between banks with respect to earnings growth.

The preceding comments suggest the following observations as to the appropriate means of estimating a bank's potential earning power: (1) the net operating earnings are the most reliable indication, (2) a past period including both high and low interest rates should be used, on the assumption that moderate fluctuations in rates are probable in the future, (3) the estimation of growth rates should be based on beginning and terminal years of roughly the same level of interest rates.

Table 20-4 shows the pertinent earnings and dividend data for 1961–64 of the three illustrative banks. In addition, the earnings for 1956, the rates of return on the equity, and the payout ratios were shown for the purpose of estimating the comparative values of retained earnings and the potential growth rates. The base year of 1956 was chosen because the level of interest rates was roughly similar in 1956 and 1964.

Although its deposit trends have been less favorable, National Bank of Detroit demonstrated the most favorable rate of growth in earnings per share over the 1956–64 period and also during 1961–64. With a rate of return on net worth of 10% (the 1961–64 average) and a payout ratio of 42% this bank enjoyed a growth rate of 5.8% annually.[5] As another measure, it may be noted that over the eight-year period 1957–64 earnings per share increased by a factor of 1.45, or at a compound rate of 4.9% per annum. Bank of America's rate of return approximated 11% in the 1961–64 period, and with a payout ratio averaging 65%, a growth rate of about 3.9% was indicated. Its actual realized growth rate, however, in earnings per share was only about 2.5% (a factor of 1.21 for eight years) because of a modest decline in the rate of return since 1956.

[5] Computed from the formula: Rate of growth = Rate of return (1 − payout ratio)

Finally, Morgan Guaranty had the lowest growth rate; a rate of return of about 8.5% and a payout ratio of 62% resulted in a growth rate of about 3.2%. The 1956–64 increase was not considered significant for Morgan Guaranty because the 1956 results were based on a pro-forma combination of the two large banks (Morgan and Guaranty Trust) that merged in 1959, and any economies resulting from the merger would have been realized in 1964 but not in 1956. In the 1961–64 period its earnings growth was less than the others, 11% as compared to 18 and 14% for National Bank of Detroit and Bank of America, respectively. Therefore, the ranking for growth would be as follows: (1) National Bank of Detroit, (2) Bank of America, (3) Morgan Guaranty.[6]

The earning power per share, based on the reasoning set forth above, might be estimated as follows from the data in Table 20-4:

	1961–64 average	*1964*	*1965 Dividend Rate*
National Bank of Detroit	$4.50	$5.10	$2.00
Bank of America	3.20	3.50	2.00
Morgan Guaranty	6.10	6.60	4.00

Comparative Valuations. Table 20-5 gives the comparative price-earnings ratios and dividend yields for the three banks as of the first part of 1965. For purposes of comparison with general stock market alternatives, the price-earnings ratio and the prevailing dividend yield on the Standard and Poor's 500 Composite Index are also shown. As these banks represent major institutions with favorable stability and average growth characteristics, it appeared that the stocks were reasonably priced relative to alternative common-stock commitments at that time; all were selling at lower prices in relation to existing earning power than the Standard and Poor's Index. For immediate current income they did not appear particularly attractice. However, Bank of America and Morgan Guaranty provided yields slightly above those prevailing on good-quality common stocks in general.

Having established that the stock prices in relation to the stock market in general were reasonably favorable, although not indicative of bargain levels, there remained the question of selection within the group. In this connection, the comparative price-earnings ratios and growth rates indicated a relative preference for National Bank of Detroit assuming no substantive differences in the qualitative elements. With a price-

[6] The increase in the rates paid on savings accounts and certificates of deposits in early 1965 would be a qualitative factor which would suggest some problems in maintaining the growth rate in the next year or so. The effects, however, could not be estimated specifically.

TABLE 20-5
Price-Earnings Ratios and Dividend Yields

| | Price | Price-Earnings Ratios | | Dividend Yield |
		1961–64 Av. Earnings	1964 Earnings	
National Bank of Detroit	70	15.5	13.5	2.8%
Bank of America	63	19.7	18.0	3.2
Morgan Guaranty	120	19.6	18.2	3.3
Standard and Poors Composite Index	92	23.0	18.2	3.0

earnings ratio of 13.5 based on 1964 earnings and an indicated growth rate of between 5 and 6%, the stock seemed to offer considerable attraction for accounts oriented toward long-term growth. However, to repeat, because of the low yield of 2.8%, it was not attractive for current income purposes.

In contrast, perhaps because of its recognized position as a leading New York bank, Morgan Guaranty seemed to be more fully valued than the others. Its rate of return and growth rate had been less favorable, yet it sold at a higher price in relation to earnings than the others. Bank of America seemed to represent a paradox. It had enjoyed the most favorable rate of growth in deposits and showed a rather high ratio of risk assets to capital, yet its payout ratio was well above National Bank of Detroit and its growth rate in earnings per share was lower. But its yield was above average and its price-earnings ratio did not appear excessive. Therefore, it might have been recommended for accounts interested in a combination of income and growth potential, although its earnings trend had been less favorable than might have been expected.

The comparison of earning asset values per dollar of market price of the stock also favored National Bank of Detroit. However, this measure of value is considered less significant than earnings levels and trends in relation to price because it does not reflect possible differences in operating efficiency but only the comparative potential for gross income from the loan and investment portfolio per dollar of market price. But the test confirmed the indications derived from the earnings analysis and, therefore, provided supplementary evidence to support the conclusion that National Bank of Detroit offered a superior comparative value at the prices prevailing in 1965.

~~~~~~

CHAPTER 21

Fire and Casualty
Insurance Companies

Insurance Operations

Types of Policies Written.   Fire and casualty insurance companies write very wide lines of insurance. Indeed, almost any kind of risk to property or persons can be covered by some type of insurance contract. Moreover, the line of demarcation between the traditional areas of fire insurance and casualty insurance has become quite vague. Traditionally, fire insurance provided indemnity against losses to all kinds of property due to fires, theft, or any natural disaster such as floods, windstorms, or earthquakes. Casualty insurance, in contrast, was concerned with personal liability and specialized in accident, health, auto liability, workmen's compensation, and surety lines. Both, however, have been engaged in such fields as automobile property damage and collision. The relative importance of the several types of insurance lines to the stock fire and casualty insurance companies is indicated by Table 21-1.

From the standpoint of total premiums written each year, these companies have enjoyed a remarkable growth because of both new types of policies and increases in the amount and values of insured properties. In 1955, to illustrate, total premiums written of the stock companies amounted to $7.6 billion, as compared to $12.3 billion in 1963. Moreover, the volume of business written has been reasonably stable, because for the most part it represents a highly essential service to business and

TABLE 21–1
CLASSIFICATION OF PREMIUMS WRITTEN FOR 1963
CAPITAL-STOCK FIRE COMPANIES

Type of Insurance:	Percentage of Total Premiums
Fire and home multiple peril	18.2
Motor vehicle	13.6
Casualty	3.07
Workmen's compensation	9.4
Inland marine	3.1
Other	25.0

Source: A. M. Best Company.

consumers. Stability in volume is indicated by the fact that in both 1958 and 1961, periods of modest recessions, premiums written increased over the preceding year. In brief, the past sales record and the economic characteristics of the demand suggest a happy combination of growth and stability.

Earnings Record on Insurance. Unfortunately, the net earnings from underwriting operations have not demonstrated these same desirable features. In fact, in the 1957–64 period most companies found it difficult to show any profits in their insurance business as such. The reasons for the unsatisfactory performance are rather complex, but a few might be briefly examined to show the unusual factors bearing on this phase of their activities.

First, the companies are subject to a considerable variation in the amounts paid out for claim losses. Actuarial tables have been much less reliable here than in life insurance. A series of disasters, like the severe tornados that struck the Middle West in the Spring of 1965, can have a serious impact on underwriting earnings. Although the companies attempt to diversify their risk exposure, these unforeseen events still cause troubles from time to time.

Second, inflation has had an adverse effect on underwriting results. Rates are subject to state regulation and are not quickly adjustable to new loss experience. Claims, however, adjust rather rapidly to new inflated cost levels. Auto property damage and public liability policies have been particularly affected by a continued escalation in costs of repair and claims awarded in court actions. Rate increases and attempts to screen applicants more closely have been only partially successful in reducing the underwriting losses in these areas.

TABLE 21-2
MEASUREMENT OF ACTUARIAL EXPERIENCE
(ratio of losses to premiums earned)

	Loss Ratio	
	1964	*Eight-Year Average (1957–64)*
Insurance Company of North America	67.7%	61.3%
Continental Insurance Company	64.0	62.4
Home Insurance Company	64.8	62.0

Source: Annual Reports.

The actuarial experience is measured by the ratio of claim losses to premiums earned. Recent trends and average experience should both be examined, and Table 21-2 shows results in this connection for three large firms in the industry. Over the years experience has indicated that a loss ratio of no more than 60% is necessary to show adequate earnings from the insurance side of the business. The fact that both the average and current loss ratios were above 60% for these companies provided clear evidence of continued problems on their underwriting activities. But despite the adverse actuarial results, the companies may still have attraction for investment purposes.

Accounting Distortion. Besides the poor loss experience, another factor contributed to the unsatisfactory reported underwriting results. Underwriting earnings, as reported, reflect a rather curious method of accounting which is required by state statutes. The law requires that the full amount of premiums collected be credited to the "unearned premium reserve," and then a pro-rata amount of the premium is allocated to earnings over the life of the policy. But included in the original premium collected from the insured is a sizable amount to pay sales agents' commissions and other expenses to get the business on the books. These expenses by law must be charged against earnings in the year incurred rather than, as might be logically expected, interpreted as a deferred charge and allocated to expense over the life of the policy.

The impact of these expenses can be estimated by relating the amount of underwriting expenses to premiums written in a series of years. Depending upon the efficiency of the company, they may amount to between 30 and 40% of premiums written, and might average about 35%. But in any case, assuming that losses run about 60% of premiums earned on the average (a very conservative estimate from the data in

Table 21-2), any new business giving insurance coverage for several years ahead will show a "loss" in the first year. And such policies constitute a large proportion of the total premiums written.

To illustrate, it may be assumed that a fire policy giving coverage for three years and calling for a premium of $300 is written on January 1 of a given year. Then the earnings experience on this policy as reported in the financial statements would be about as follows, assuming it must bear a loss ratio of 60% and original underwriting expenses on 35% of the total premium:

	Year 1	Year 2	Year 3
Premiums written—3-year period	300	0	0
Premiums earned—⅓ premium each year	100	100	100
Underwriting expenses—35% assumed	105	0	0
Claim losses—60% of premium earned	60	60	60
Net earnings	(65)	40	40

Over the life of the policy, under the given assumptions, the total net profit on the business was $15, or an average of $5 per year, although the first year showed a sizable deficit. Most analysts adjust for this unfortunate distortion by adding to reported underwriting earnings 35% of the excess of premiums written over premiums earned or subtracting 35% of any excess of premiums earned over premiums written. In the preceding example, the adjustment in Year 1 would be 35% of $200 (the $300 premiums written less $100 earned), or $70. In Years 2 and 3, 35% of $100 (premiums written zero compared with earned of $100) would be subtracted from reported results, and the net effect of all the adjustments would be to show earnings on the policy of $5 per year.

Adjusted Underwriting Results. There are several consequences of this accounting practice. First, during an inflationary or boom period, when the volume of new business increases rapidly, "statutory underwriting earnings" are likely to be unsatisfactory. These characteristics have marked the portwar period in general. In other words, growth can have adverse effects on reported earnings in the short run. Second, most analytical reports on these companies are likely to show figures for both "statutory earnings" and "adjusted earnings." Third, operating expenses other than claim losses are more realistically related to premiums written than to premiums earned. This ratio, known as the *expense ratio*, constitutes the second major test of efficiency in insurance operations. A measure of overall underwriting performance can be obtained by adding the loss ratio, based on premiums earned, to the expense

TABLE 21–3
APPRAISAL OF UNDERWRITING PERFORMANCE

	Expense Ratio		Operating Ratio*	
	1964	Average 1957–64	1964	Average 1957–64
Insurance Company of North America	33.6%	35.8%	101.4%	97.1%
Continental Insurance Company	39.6	41.4	103.6	103.8
Home Insurance Company	36.1	38.1	100.9	100.1

* Computed by adding loss ratios shown in Table 21–2 to expense ratio.

ratio, based on premiums written, and the result may be defined as an "adjusted" operating ratio.

Table 21-3 shows the operating ratios for three companies. A gradual improvement in the expense ratio has been the one redeeming feature of the underwriting activities in recent years. As the companies report continuing possibilities for reducing expenses, the insurance operations may show some improvement in future years. But as of 1965, the past eight-year average underwriting experience represented a negative factor in the status of these companies for investment purposes. But there is some merit in the view that fire and casualty insurance companies can be attractive investments without any underwriting earnings. Although a good underwriting record is desirable, the main source of returns to investors has been, and probably will continue to be, derived from their investment portfolios.

Appraisal of Investment Operations

Sources of Investment Funds. The fire and casualty companies have two major sources of funds for investment purposes. First, there are the premiums collected from policyholders that are shown on the balance sheet as the *unearned premium reserve* liability. Second, there are the funds represented by the common-stock equity in the company. To a considerable extent the proportions of these sources control the aggressiveness of the investment policy. When capital and surplus exceed the insurance liabilities, then common stocks may dominate the portfolio; on the other hand, high-quality bonds and preferreds are likely to dominate if insurance liabilities are more than about 150% of the stock equity. Because the earnings of these companies have been largely derived from the management of a discretionary investment portfolio, it is desirable to have management uninhibited by a weak capital position.

TABLE 21-4
INSURANCE LIABILITIES RELATED TO CAPITAL FUNDS: DECEMBER 31, 1964
(in millions of dollars)

	Capital and Surplus	Liabilities Unearned Premiums	Other	Total Liabilities as Percent of Capital and Surplus
Insurance Company of North America	$ 834.9	$402.3	$408.8	97%
Continental Insurance Company	1,180.8	317.0	373.5	57
Home Insurance Company	379.6	313.6	170.1	127

Source: Annual Reports.

When this situation exists, the so-called insurance exposure may control investment policy, and flexibility in investment operations may have to be sacrificed as a consequence.

Table 21-4 shows the relationship of capital funds to unearned premium reserves and other liabilities for the three companies whose underwriting operations were appraised.[1] The other liability classification represents for the most part current claims which are pending against the company and, therefore, are usually matched with highly liquid assets. The data indicated that Continental Insurance had an exceptionally strong equity; in fact its insurance exposure was so moderate that it almost appeared to be properly classified as an investment company. Only Home Insurance had an equity moderately on the low side, and to some extent its investment policies may have been constrained as a result.

Portfolio Composition. Unlike investment companies, the fire and casualty companies do not set forth the specific policies which guide their portfolio composition. However, there seems to be a general tradition that high-quality fixed-income securities and cash should be about equal to the total of the unearned premium reserve and other liabilities.[2]

[1] These companies report on both a parent company and a consolidated basis. As the operations are integrated in more or less homogeneous activities, the consolidated data were used in the statistical material when available. Some data, such as portfolio breakdowns, may be reported only on a parent-company basis, and to this extent the analysis of these companies is made more difficult.

[2] A specific statement to this effect was made by Samuel B. Jones, Vice President of the Fire Association of Philadelphia, in an article discussing investment policies of the fire companies. Jones, "The Point of View of a Fire Insurance Company Investment Buyer," *The Analysts' Journal*, May, 1952, p. 9.

TABLE 21–5
PORTFOLIO COMPOSITIONS RELATED TO STOCK EQUITIES
(as of 12/31/64)

	Total Stock Equity	Investment Portfolios (in millions)			Total Portfolio as Percent of Stock Equity
		Bonds and Preferreds	Common Stocks	Total	
Insurance Company of North America	$ 834.9	$602.3	$ 772.7	$1,387.3	167%
Continental Insurance Company	1,180.8	431.3	1,268.5	1,699.8	142
Home Insurance Company	379.6	318.6	376.2	694.8	182

To some extent, therefore, the insurance exposure controls investment policy, but on the whole the stockholder should welcome this degree of prudence. Presumably it would mean the companies can avoid severe financial difficulties even if the loss ratio approached 100%.

From the standpoint of the stock equity, the assets contributed by the insurance liabilities are in essence a form of leverage capital. But because the companies do not pay interest on these liabilities, any investment return on these assets increases total investment returns on the stock equity to an equal extent. In brief, the investment of the advance premiums collected from policyholders should be profitable leverage even though invested in moderate-yielding high-quality bonds and preferred stocks.

To illustrate, Table 21-5 shows the composition of the investment portfolios for the three companies and, for purposes of comparison, the size of the stock equities repeated from Table 21-4. The leverage factor was indicated by the fact that the investment portfolios significantly exceeded the amount of the stock equities. The excess for the most part represented the amount of premiums collected from policyholders which had been invested in earning assets in the form of fixed-income securities. However, it was also clear that the common-stock portfolios were roughly commensurate with the size of the stock equities. These portfolios suggest, therefore, that an investment in the common stock of many fire and casualty companies may constitute for the most part an indirect interest in a diversified common-stock portfolio similar to an investment company.

Liquidating Value Concept. When the assets of a financial institution are largely composed of securities valued at market values, the book

value per share based on such assets becomes an important indication
of the investment value of the common stock. In the case of fire insurance companies, however, it is arguable that the "true" book values
of their stocks significantly exceed the reported balance-sheet amounts
because of the highly conservative accounting policies forced on these
companies by state statutes. In the section devoted to a brief analysis
of underwriting operations, it was noted that the full amount of all
premiums collected from policyholders must be credited to the un-
earned-premium-reserve account even though immediate cash expenses
(taken into account, of course, when premium rates are set) amount
to about 35% of the total premiums. On the assumptions that the premium rates have no profit component, this would mean that the actuarial liability incorporated in the unearned premium reserve for future
claim losses would be about 65% of its stated balance-sheet amount.

As a consequence, it has become conventional procedure to add
about 35% of the unearned premium reserve to the common-stock
equity when estimating the "true" book value of the common stock at
any given balance-sheet date. The computed result is labeled *liquidating value.* It is based on the proposition that a fire insurance company
could realize in liquidation its stated capital and surplus plus 35% of
the unearned premium reserve. This computation for the three companies is shown in Table 21-6.

TABLE 21-6
LIQUIDATING-VALUE COMPUTATION: 12/31/64

	Capital and Surplus (millions)	35% of Premium Reserve (millions)	Total (millions)	Common Shares (millions)	Liqui- dating Value Per Share
Insurance Company of North America	$ 834.9	$140.8	$ 975.7	11.0	$ 88.70
Continental Insurance Company	1,180.8	110.9	1,291.7	12.6	102.40
Home Insurance Company	379.6	109.8	489.4	4.5	108.70

Total-Portfolio-per-Share Concept. Investment analysts have invariably given considerable attention to *liquidating value per share* as
representing a major element of value, on the theory that this "value"
is representative of the equity of each share in the portfolio assets. However, it does not express the total security portfolio per share on which
investment earnings are obtained, nor does it indicate the common-
stock portfolio per share, which may be of primary interest to the investor in these companies.

TABLE 21-7
PORTFOLIO BREAKDOWN PER SHARE: 12/31/64
(in millions of dollars)

	Bonds and Pre- ferreds	Common Stocks Insurance Companies	Other	Portfolio Total	Price 3/15/65	Price ÷ Port- folio Total
I.C.N.A.						
Per share	$55	$ 2	$69	$126	94	74%
Home Insurance						
Per share	71	14	69	154	72	47
Continental						
Per share	34	3	97	134	63	47

As there is a constant "float" of noninterest-bearing insurance liabilities, which in an investment sense contribute funds for security commitments without cost, there is no reason to deduct any of these liabilities in ascertaining the security investments working for the common stock. It is merely necessary to divide the total portfolio investments in fixed-income securities and common stocks by the common shares outstanding; the result shows the approximate market value per share of each type of security which is contributing investment earnings to the common stock. The portfolio values per share can then be compared with the market prices of the stocks to indicate the relative amount of portfolio values obtained per dollar of market price.

Table 21-7 shows the nature of this computation for the three fire insurance companies. Conclusions bearing on the desirability of these stocks as investments can be derived in two respects from this presentation. First and perhaps of primary importance, the relationship between the market prices and the indicated total portfolio values per share gave an indication of the comparative discounts at which the portfolios could have been obtained. Home and Continental, for example, were available at 47% of the total per share portfolio values, whereas Insurance Company of North America sold for 74% of such value. Assuming an equal investment performance, the result would indicate favoring the former companies. In a sense, the technique is analogous to computing the prevailing discounts from asset values on the prices of closed-end investment company shares.

Second, the analysis showed the characteristics of the security portfolio in which an indirect interest would have been acquired through the purchase of the insurance company's common stock. In these instances, the fact that Continental offered a common-stock portfolio per share well in excess of the market price suggested relative preference for its stock. As the objective in acquiring a fire company stock is to obtain qualified investment management, a substantial portfolio of common stocks is usually preferable, because it is here that professional investment management is most necessary.

In summary, the breakdown of the total portfolio on a per share basis related to the price of the company stock in the market may be recommended as an important analytical technique for the following reasons: (1) it reveals the percentage discount at which a given portfolio can be acquired, (2) it shows the composition of the portfolio per share of stock and per dollar of stock price. Moreover, it has the advantage of being easy to compute.

However, the results of the analysis must be considered in connection with the past investment management performance. Also, an apparent bargain in this respect can be partially negated by serious questions about the underwriting operations. The capacity of management to conduct investment operations is a particularly crucial factor.

Appraisal of Investment Performance. There are some unfortunate complexities involved in measuring the long-term investment results as a purely separate factor because changes in the stock equity and earnings are influenced by the underwriting operations as well as by the investment activities. However, the following procedure, shown for Insurance Company of North America, can be used to compute a performance *relative* for the investment operations:

	Per Share
Liquidating value, year-end 1964	$88.70
Add	
Dividends paid on stock, 1959–64	10.75
	$99.45
Subtract	
Underwriting earnings, 1959–64	1.93
Adjusted Liquidating Value, 12/31/64	$97.52
Liquidating Value, 12/31/58	$60.00
Performance relative, 1959–64	

$$\frac{\text{Adjusted Liquidating Value}-12/31/64}{\text{Liquidating Value}-12/31/58} = \frac{\$97.52}{\$60.00} = 162$$

Some comments on the logic of the computation might be useful to show why these adjustments were necessary to make several companies comparable and also overcome the shortcomings of the published financial reports. First, liquidating value was used as the beginning and ending estimate of the stockholders' equity per share in order to remove the unfavorable impact of the growth in insurance underwritings on the conventional book value of the stock. The nature of this effect has already been explained; suffice it to observe at this point that the liquidating-value concept merely makes the reasonable presumption that the immediate expenses incurred on new policies were set up as an asset deferred charge instead of being written off immediately against surplus as required by law. Unless this adjustment was made, those companies that had written the most new business during the period might have suffered in the investment-performance comparison.

Second, all dividends paid out to stockholders were added back to make the several companies comparable. If this was not done, then those companies which had paid out the smallest proportion of earnings would tend to show up best in the performance comparison. Finally, all reported underwriting earnings were deducted (or losses were added back in the cases of Home and Continental for 1959–64) because the intention was to isolate the investment results. Although a profitable underwriting record is certainly desirable, it should not enter into an appraisal of the results of investment management as such.

TABLE 21–8
INVESTMENT PERFORMANCE RELATIVES (1959–64)

	Performance Relative
Insurance Company of North America	162
Home Insurance Company	158
Continental Insurance Company	171

Table 21-8 shows the investment performance "relatives" for the 1959–64 period. As in the case of investment companies, the results must be interpreted in the light of the investment policy of the several companies. Home Insurance had a moderately higher proportion of fixed-income securities in its portfolio. As the 1959–64 period was exceptionally favorable to common stocks, part of the less favorable investment performance of Home may be ascribed to a more defensive investment policy. However, the performance "relatives" suggested that Continental had the most successful investment management and, as already indicated, offered the largest portfolio value of common stocks in relation to its market price. Based on the analysis of the investment operations, therefore, Continental appeared to be the most favorably situated of the three companies as of 1965.

Role of Past Earnings. When a common-stock portfolio constitutes a large proportion of a company's assets, reported earnings per share are of less significance in determining the investment value of its common stock. The reason is that a common-stock portfolio is expected over a period of years to give returns in two forms—current income and appreciation—and only the current-income component is included in reported earnings. All appreciation, whether realized or unrealized, is excluded from net investment income and shows up only as an increase in the book value of the stock equity on the balance sheet.[3]

Because insurance stocks have in the long run tended to reflect the book value of the stock equity, appreciation on the stock portfolio has ultimately been recognized in the market prices of the company common stocks. As a consequence, the portfolio values per share in relation to market prices and the record of management performance are considered of more importance in selecting an insurance stock than are reported earnings.

But reported earnings should not be ignored completely. In the first place, these earnings are the source of dividend payments, and many investors are interested in receiving a reasonable current-income return. In the second place, such earnings that are not paid out as dividends increase the stock equity and thereby the total portfolio per share working for the common stock. In this connection there seems to be a curious tradition among the fire companies that dividends should be limited to a major fraction of the net investment income and that all underwriting earnings (if any) should be plowed back to increase the capital cushion afforded the policyholders.[4]

It is, therefore, of some advantage to acquire these stocks at a reasonable price in relation to the earnings derived from the current income

[3] Between 1959 and 1964 inclusive, the liquidating value per share of Continental Insurance increased from $74.50 per share to $102.40 although because of recurrent deficits on adjusted underwriting earnings, dividends paid to shareholders exceeded total earnings per share. The appreciation on the stock portfolio, which was not reflected in earnings, was of course responsible for the increase in the stock equity.

[4] Underwriting results appear to affect dividends only if they are negative. In the 1957–64 period, such results have been generally unfavorable and the average payout of investment earnings declined from about 75% in the 1948–56 period to about 47% for twenty leading companies. Standard & Poor's *Industry Surveys: Insurance, Basic Analysis*, Sept. 17, 1964, p. 13.

TABLE 21-9
PER SHARE DATA: EARNINGS AND DIVIDENDS

| | Underwriting Earnings (1957-64 Average) | Net Investment Income | | Dividend Rate 1965 | Stock Data | | |
		1961-64 Average	1964		Price*	Price-Earnings Ratios†	Dividend Yield
I.C.N.A.	$ .28	$3.51	$3.98	$2.00	94	26.8 23.4	2.1%
Continental	(2.47)	3.84	4.13	2.40	63	16.4 15.2	3.8
Home	(1.22)	4.70	5.33	2.60	72	15.3 13.6	3.6

* As of March 15, 1965.
† Based on average and 1964 net investment income.

on the portfolio. In brief, some appraisal of the price-earnings ratios and dividend yields is justified for these companies, although their importance is considerably less than for industrial common stocks.

Analysis of Earnings Record. The published financial reports of the fire and casualty companies show two categories of earnings: (1) statutory underwriting profit and (2) net investment income. As mentioned above, it is also conventional practice to add about 35% of any increase in the unearned premium reserve during a given year to that year's underwriting earnings. If the reserve happens to decrease, about 35% of the decrease is subtracted from underwriting earnings.[5] The reasons for the adjustment have been explained and require no further comment at this point.

Selected earnings and dividend data for the three companies are given in Table 21-9. On the favorable side, it can be noted that the trend in net investment income was steadily upward and 1964 results were well above the four-year average. However, underwriting results were a negative factor in two of the companies and not important in the other. Because it appeared that there was a good probability that the underwriting deficits could be eliminated, the price-earnings ratios were based on net investment income only. However, it was ironic to note that if both Continental and Home had dispensed with the insurance business, their total earnings (as purely investment companies) would have been improved for these years, although the investment returns on the unearned premium reserve would have been lost.

As a qualitative risk element, the unsatisfactory insurance performance of these two companies could not be ignored. But assuming some measure of success in correcting the problem, the stocks appeared to be quite reasonably priced in relation to net investment earnings and the prevailing dividend rates, particularly in view of the favorable trend in net investment income generated largely by increased dividends on their large holdings of common stocks. In addition, the complete investment portfolios were then available at only 47% of the market values. Between Continental and Home, the former offered a larger common-stock portfolio per dollar of stock-market price, although the latter's underwriting results were moderately more favorable and its price-earnings ratios were slightly lower. On balance, more aggressive investors might have favored Continental because of the heavier emphasis

---

[5] It might be noted that both Moody's and Standard & Poor's follow this practice in their statistical presentations of these companies.

on common-stock investments which suggested a greater long-term appreciation potential for the common-stock equity of the company. A decision in favor of Continental would have implied, however, a willingness to discount the qualitative risk associated with its poor underwriting performance.

Insurance Company of North America appeared comparatively less attractive despite its favorable management record on both underwriting and investments. At the prevailing price, the price-earnings ratios were quite high and the dividend yield well below that offered by the other companies. Therefore, although analysis indicated it to be of superior quality, the price of the stock seemed excessive in relation to the other companies.

Summary. The fire and casualty insurance companies may obtain earnings from both underwriting activities and investment operations, but in the majority of instances the investment earnings have greatly dominated. Some companies have limited insurance exposure, and as a consequence, have been able to acquire large diversified common-stock portfolios which have been well managed and often have been available at wide discounts from their market values. Such companies would seem particularly attractive for investment purposes. Unfortunately they are complex and difficult to analyze. In summary, however, the following techniques appear pertinent to their appraisal:

1. The underwriting efficiency of a company is measured by combining the loss ratio and expense ratio over a period of at least eight years. The average experience, relative performance, and current trends of these ratios are indicative of the underwriting results of a given company.
2. Underwriting earnings have been highly unstable and actually were negative for a number of companies during the 1957–64 period. Reported earnings on this score also require adjustment for any increase or decrease in the unearned premium reserve.
3. The portfolio values per share compared to market price are good indications of relative values of these stocks. A large capital-stock equity in relation to insurance liabilities is desirable, because it makes possible greater flexibility of investment operations.
4. Investment performance "relatives" can be computed and are of some use in indicating potential managerial capacity in managing the portfolio.

5. Investment earnings have been more stable and have shown a favorable growth trend. However, because portfolio appreciation is not included in earnings, price-earnings ratios are of secondary importance, but may be used to indicate the potential current-income yield and possible evidence of a bargain price for net investment income.

PART VI

MUNICIPAL AND
GOVERNMENT OBLIGATIONS

CHAPTER 22

Municipal Bonds:
General Obligations

Introduction

The appraisal of municipal obligations is one of the most highly specialized areas of investment analysis. In fact, the techniques for establishing their quality are entirely different from those used in corporate-bond analysis. The major reason for the singular nature of municipal bonds rests in their status as obligations of governmental units. These units are not established to derive earnings from economic activities; their purpose is to supply governmental services to the general public. The taxation power is the typical means of financing these services, and under ordinary circumstances tax levies are designed to cover only the operating costs of municipal services plus any requirements for debt service, including interest charges and annual maturities.

As a consequence, a substantial "coverage" of interest payments is not expected on municipal obligations. And there is no residual equity to backstop the bondholders' claim. Indeed, in most cases there are no assets to which the bondholder can look in case of default. There is, of course, the estimated value of the properties subject to tax levies within the area concerned. But these are not available for foreclosure in case of default; moreover, estimates of taxable property values are not subject to conventional rules of determination as are corporate asset values. Therefore, security analysis enters an entirely new dimension when municipal obligations are under consideration, and to a considerable degree the analytical problems are more difficult and less subject to logical solution than is true for corporate securities.

For two reasons municipal securities are attractive only to a limited group of investors. First, they are available only in the bond form. Second, the income from them is tax exempt. As a consequence, municipals are usually attractive only to individuals and institutions primarily interested in fixed-income securities who would benefit by the tax-exempt feature.[1] The prices and resultant yields of municipal bonds naturally reflect the tax-exempt feature. For example, it is not uncommon for high-grade municipals to carry an effective yield of 2.5 to 3.0% when government bonds of equivalent maturities yield about 4%. Such a yield spread means that only investors in marginal tax brackets of roughly 30 to 40% or greater would obtain a higher after-tax yield on municipals than on governments.

Classification of Municipals

Obligations of States.   Strictly speaking, the bonds of the state governments are not properly included in the municipal group. Such obligations are more nearly comparable in legal theory with United States Government issues, because in both cases they are issued by sovereign jurisdictions against which no legal action can be taken without their consent. However, the several states lack important powers possessed by the federal government: that of printing legal tender, for one, and "last-recourse" financing of large bond issues through Federal Reserve cooperation, for another.[2]

---

[1] The special technique sometimes used of issuing long-term bonds with a very small coupon rate at a "deep" discount can make these bonds attractive to tax-exempt institutions. Here only a small proportion of the true yield is in tax-exempt income and the balance is a discount accrual to maturity. For example, if a city puts a coupon of .5% on a twenty-year bond, it will be priced at about 63 if the effective yield required by the market is 2.95%. One of the reasons for a city's doing this may be that it delays the payment of a large proportion of the effective interest until maturity of the bond. Sometimes sinking funds built up to anticipate the maturity can be invested in taxable government bonds (that are tax-exempt to the municipality) at rates higher than the real interest cost on the outstanding bonds.

[2] The placing of large bond issues in the banks during World War II with the Federal Reserve supplying the necessary bank reserves through open-market operations is illustrative of this point. In effect, the Federal Reserve seems to have assumed the implied duty of ultimately assuring placement of new or refunding issues of the federal government. Therefore, the money creation power of the Federal Reserve is an implied guarantee against default of U.S. bonds.

Therefore, the credit standing of a given state's bonds in essence depends on the financial prudence of its government in relation to the general wealth and income of its people. There is no recourse to "manufactured money" in case of severe financial difficulties. For this reason, state obligations closely resemble nonsovereign municipal governments and are, therefore, typically included in the municipal area. The only major difference between state bonds and municipal bonds is in the remedies available in case of default. And, because default remedies are a minor element in the appraisal of any fixed-income security, the difference is not regarded as highly significant.

General Obligations. These may be described as bonds issued by municipal corporations chartered by the states under which the full local taxing powers are pledged for payment. They are sometimes known as *full-faith-and-credit* bonds because they are dependent upon the willingness and ability of municipal corporations to levy any amount and type of taxes legally possible to discharge their debt. The "legally possible" qualification has led some analysts to distinguish between "limited tax" bonds and "unlimited tax" bonds. In fact, some have argued that where municipalities have strictly limited tax rates, including taxes required to service debt, the bonds are not truly general obligations. In general, this viewpoint seems tenable, but it should be noted that this is a controversial and unsettled point.

Most general obligations arise from the financing of capital improvements undertaken by cities, counties, and special districts. The latter are merely municipal corporations chartered for a particular governmental function, the most important and widespread example being school districts. These bonds are generally regarded as the basic type of municipals, and unless otherwise qualified in the bond description, it is usually presumed that a bond of a municipal corporation is a general obligation.

Revenue Bonds. When the interest and principal of an obligation issued by a governmental unit are payable solely from the sale of certain goods and services, it is called a *revenue bond*. These obligations are more closely allied to corporate issues than any of the other types, because, like corporates, revenues from the sale of some service or product are the source of the interest and principal payments. One of the most common types today is water-revenue bonds issued to finance municipally owned water plants, debt service being met from the sale of water to consumers. The close similarity between these and the bonds of electric-utility companies should be obvious.

A fairly recent development in revenue bonds has been the creation of governmental "authorities" with the power to issue revenue bonds. These are established by a special act of one or more state legislatures to carry out a particular function or provide services which are intended to be revenue-producing. The management of an authority is usually delegated to a small group of appointed individuals, and this group generally has autonomous powers to carry out its duties. These include the power of eminent domain, the power to issue bonds, construct necessary facilities, and set service rates.

One of the oldest and largest authorities from the standpoint of dollar value of bonds outstanding is the Port of New York Authority. Created in 1921 by the legislatures of New York and New Jersey with the consent of Congress, it consists of twelve commissioners, and is intended to provide terminal and transportation facilities within the port district. Pursuant to these objectives, it has constructed and operates tunnels, bridges, piers, truck terminals, and airports within the area. In 1965 this authority had about $240 million in bonds outstanding.

The widespread construction of turnpike expressways and bridges during the 1955–65 period has given rise to a large quantity of revenue obligations under authority-type arrangements. In some instances the authorities are empowered to issue bonds to finance the construction of roads, bridges, and related items which are payable either directly or indirectly from certain limited kinds of taxes or license fees. Here the obligations are not, strictly speaking, revenue bonds, but are more properly described as limited-tax bonds or even general obligations if the general taxing power is pledged directly or indirectly to meet interest and principal. The State Highway and Bridge Authority of Pennsylvania is a good example of the latter type of arrangement. Here, although the bonds are not general obligations of Pennsylvania, the bonds are secured by lease agreements with the state wherein lease rentals cover the bond interest and serial maturities.

As the legal arrangements may be complex, it is often necessary to investigate the sources of payment for authority obligations before they can be classified as revenue situations. When bonds are supported by certain tax powers, even if interest and principal payments are nominally to be met from service revenues, it is usually more appropriate to classify them as general or limited tax obligations.

Special-Assessment Bonds. These are usually issued by city or county municipal corporations with the proviso that they are payable only from certain special assessments against the specific property benefited by the improvements being financed. The theory is that certain municipal improvements may be highly desirable, but because the benefits flow to only a portion of the citizens or property, they should not be paid from general taxes on all properties within the municipal jurisdiction.

This type of obligation has declined in relative importance in the past twenty years or so. Perhaps the major reason is that in past years many such issues came out to develop unimproved subdivisions and the subsequent poor record of defaults created a prejudice against special-assessment bonds. Also, it is often relatively difficult for the outside buyer to obtain reliable data on the nature and value of the properties to be assessed. The assessed areas are not an entire municipal entity which maintains a more or less set status, but represent special areas which are of transitory significance only.

As a consequence, some of the so-called special-assessment bond issues are really general obligations, as the cities concerned pledge full faith and credit on the obligations with the intention of being reimbursed by assessment on certain properties within the city limits. For example, Midland, Michigan, has some outstanding bonds entitled "Water Main Improvement Special Assessment Bonds," but according to the terms, the title means only that the city sold the bonds in anticipation of the collection of a special tax assessment, although the full faith and credit of the city was pledged to the bondholders. In effect, therefore, they are general obligations of Midland in spite of their title. In short, municipal bonds cannot be classified solely on the basis of their nominal description, but an investigation of the specific contractual relationship is required before the bond can be "typed."

Tax-Anticipation Notes. These are typically used to obtain municipal operating funds in advance of tax-collection dates. As a consequence, they are almost always due within six months to a year and presumably are to be repaid from a known levy of taxes to be collected in the future. Usually they have the contractual status of general obligations in the sense that if the designated taxes are not collected in an amount sufficient to retire the notes, a general claim remains against the municipal funds.

However, in a few isolated instances—in Chicago, for example—the tax notes are a claim against the levy of a given year only and may be defaulted if collections are insufficient in that year. Such terms would seem inherently undesirable from the viewpoint of the noteholders. A very large margin of protection measured by the size of the tax levy relative to the size of the note issue might, however, extenuate the basically unfavorable contractual terms.

Technical Aspects of Municipal Bonds

Legality. In most states municipal borrowings are subject to restrictions under statutory law, and in some jurisdictions the power to borrow funds is not assumed to result from the general powers of municipal corporations. Moreover, certain definite procedural forms are usually required by law, and unless they are strictly followed in the bond-offering process, the resultant bond issue may be declared invalid and the municipality may be unable to pay interest and principal even though it may desire to do so.

Because of the legal complexities, which most investors are not competent or willing to evaluate in each case, it is customary for municipal bond offerings to be accompanied by a legal opinion of specially qualified attorneys. The opinion states that the borrowing power does in fact exist, that it does not exceed any statutory restrictions, and that all technical procedures have been followed as prescribed by law. Although not absolutely conclusive, of course, an unqualified opinion by one of the specialist law firms in this area is generally accepted as proof of the legality question.

In some states, other techniques to establish legality have been instituted. One is to have a state official bring a suit in court to have the municipality show cause why the bonds should not be validated, and a court decree is then issued conclusively validating the bonds. In New York the municipality need only affirm in the resolution authorizing the debt that the bonds are issued according to law; this has been accepted by the courts as conclusive evidence of legality. But, whatever the technique used, reasonable proof of legality should be established before any municipal bond is accepted by a prudent investor.

Maturities. Except for certain types of revenue bonds, it is customary for municipal bonds to carry serial maturities.[3] Such maturities are often required by law, and their purpose is to encourage prudent debt management by automatically retiring debt out of taxes or other sources of revenue. This feature has attracted certain types of taxable institutional investors, especially commercial banks, to municipal obli-

[3] This means that a portion of the total bond issue matures in each year, usually in roughly equal amounts.

gations. The investor usually has a wide choice of maturities available in a given municipal issue, and when spaced maturities are desired to provide liquidity and to limit market risk, the options provided by serial maturities are an attractive feature.

When term bonds are used, the indenture typically provides for regular sinking-fund payments as the means of preventing pyramiding of debt through continuous refundings on top of new issues. But unlike the usual terms of corporate bonds, it is not customary to find a special sinking-fund call price. The sinking fund must usually be invested in government or state obligations or else in the subject bonds purchased at market prices. Therefore, the terms are superior to the corporate sinking-fund arrangement, because the bondholder need not worry about his particular bond being drawn by lot for sinking-fund purposes at prices below his amortized cost.

Redemption Provisions. Most general obligations issued in serial form are not subject to a call price. The absence of a call price, of course, is a distinct advantage of municipal-bond contracts compared to corporate-bond contracts. In the few situations where serials are reedemable they are typically callable in inverse maturity order; the longest maturity must be called first and thence forward into the earlier maturity dates.

Revenue bonds, whether serial or otherwise, and general-obligation term bonds are more likely to be subject to redemption prior to maturity. The redemption provision is similar to that on corporates; they may be callable as a whole or in part at certain specific dates, and the premium above par at which the bonds are callable may decrease as they approach maturity. In view of the absence of a regular contractual practice and also because the statistical services do not furnish complete descriptions in all cases, a prudent investor should investigate carefully the possible redemption terms in the contract. Essentially the objective is to avoid the purchase of any bond at prices materially above any call price which may be operative in the near future.

Contractual Position and Remedies. In the case of corporate bonds, the willingness to pay the required interest and principal is always assumed strong, because the very life of the corporation is in jeopardy if there is a default. The situation is not quite so clear-cut in the case of municipal obligations. A municipality cannot be liquidated to satisfy the bondholder's claim.

The usual remedy under default conditions is to bring suit in an

appropriate court for a writ of mandamus ordering the municipal officials
to levy and collect sufficient taxes to meet the claim. But such a writ may
be difficult to enforce in practice if tax levies are seriously in arrears and
tax sales of delinquent properties are in prospect. Moreover, many municipal officials in a controlling capacity, such as mayors and aldermen,
are elected and act on a part-time basis. If they are unwilling or unable
to enforce the writ, they can resign from office and not be vitally in-
jured. In brief, if tax levy and collection practices are not effectively
administered or if there is a conscious desire on the part of a municipality to avoid debt claims, the legal remedies are difficult to apply
effectively in practice.

The purpose of this brief discussion of the contractual relationship
between municipalities and their bondholders is to suggest the need for
an inquiry which is usually assumed in corporate-bond work. This inquiry relates to the *willingness to pay*, or the indicated desire to treat
creditors equitably.

Tax Exemption. As previously mentioned, the feature which tends
to restrict municipal obligations to certain groups of investors is their
exemption from all federal income taxes. The exemption is judicial, arising from court decisions that the federal government does not have the
power to tax instrumentalities of the several states. There has been agitation from time to time for Congressional or Constitutional action to
remove the prerogative from municipal obligations, but to date at least
there have been no serious attempts to eliminate the tax-exemption
feature.

Table 22-1 shows the relationship between the after-tax yields on
taxable securities and municipal bonds for selected marginal tax rates.
The words "marginal tax" should be emphasized. In making a decision
as to whether an addition to an existing portfolio would give a higher
income yield in the form of a taxable corporate security (either bond or
stock) or in the form of a municipal, the highest tax rate on any additional income should be used to determine equivalent yields. But in the
allocation of an entire portfolio, each bracket of income should be considered separately for the purpose of determining the advantage of
the tax-exempt feature.[4] And in the case of many institutions, such as

---

[4] For example, the first $10,000 or so of income from a portfolio may be subject
to modest tax rates and nonexempt securities may be appropriate to produce income
up to this amount. Any principal still remaining may then be diverted to tax-exempt
securities if the tax rate on additional income is high. This point is discussed more
fully in chapter 28 on taxation and investment decisions.

TABLE 22-1
TAXABLE EQUIVALENT YIELDS
CORPORATE SECURITIES VS. MUNICIPALS

Tax-Exempt Yield	Equivalent Corporate Yield at Marginal Tax Rates Of			
	30%	50%	72%	90%
1.00%	1.43%	2.00%	3.57%	10.0%
1.50	2.14	3.00	5.36	15.0
2.00	2.86	4.00	7.14	20.0
2.50	3.57	5.00	8.93	25.0
3.00	4.29	6.00	10.71	30.0
4.00	5.71	8.00	14.29	40.0

commercial banks, the first increments of income on loans and investments are undoubtedly matched by operating expenses. Therefore, the advantages of tax exemption are not appropriately measured by comparing yields on the assumption of the marginal tax rate on all units of gross or even net income.

As a result of tax exemption, good-quality municipal bonds typically yield materially less than corporate and government obligations on a before-tax basis. For example, during 1964 the yield on the Moody's long-term Aa municipal bond index averaged about 3.2%, whereas similar maturity high-grade corporates could be purchased on about a 4.5% yield basis. The 1.3% difference in yields was about 30% of the total before-tax return on corporates. Therefore, municipals were then attractive only to accounts subject to marginal tax rates of 30% or more.

Marketability and Prices. Municipal obligations are bought and sold exclusively in the over-the-counter market. Investment banking and brokerage houses throughout the country maintain inventories and establish bid and ask prices for particular bonds in which they "make a market." The great number and diversity of municipals sometimes makes it difficult to buy or sell large blocks of these securities easily at indicated prices. However, the degree of marketability tends to vary with the size of the city and its general credit reputation. The larger the municipal unit, the greater the probability that a number of dealers will handle its obligations. Consequently it becomes easier to buy or sell in reasonably large quantities in short periods of time. Every day a "Blue List" several pages long is published by the National Association of Securities Dealers which shows the asked prices on various municipal bonds and the dealer making the offer.

Unlike corporate and government bonds, it is customary to quote municipal-bond prices on a yield basis rather than at a dollar price. For example, the "Blue List" might show a bond with a coupon rate of 2.5% maturing in five years, and the "price" would be shown as "2.25% basis." In order to compute the actual dollar price of the bond, it would be necessary to consult a bond-yield table, where we would find that a bond with a 2.5% coupon, five-year maturity, sells at 101.18 when it yields 2.25% to maturity. The price, therefore, of one bond ($1,000 denomination) is $1,011.80 plus accrued interest to date of purchase.[5]

Municipal-Bond Analysis: Willingness to Pay

Aside from a generally commendable desire on the part of most American citizens to meet their just debts, both as individuals and as groups, perhaps the basic incentive of municipal corporations to fulfill their existing debt obligations is the need to maintain an effective borrowing power in the future. The prudent municipality fully recognizes that any default on their bonded debt for whatever reasons (with the possible exception of an unintended legal technicality which makes it impossible to pay) will jeopardize their ability to market any future bond issues.

Debt Record. Occasionally, however, in periods of stress this long-run view may fade into the background, and the immediate operating needs of the municipality may seem more pressing than diverting shrunken tax receipts to bondholders who have no direct connection with or political influence in the community. To test this rather remote possibility, the debt record of the community in the past, especially during very adverse years, is closely inspected. If there have been any defaults or moratoriums on debt principal or interest which were not entirely beyond the capacity of the municipal unit to control, then the basic "willingness" may be called into question.

For example, the state of Arkansas decided in 1933 to take advantage of its sovereign status and undertook to force holders of maturing issues to

---

[5] Revenue bonds, especially toll-roads and authority issues, are often now quoted at a dollar price rather than on a yield basis. On the whole, "dollar pricing" should be encouraged, as it is more in accord with customary practices in other bond markets. Alexander Pinney puts the matter as follows: "what investor is edified to be told his sewer bond has gone up or down 20 basis points. Not having a yield book in his hip pocket and not knowing how to use one in any case, he will ask, like the American traveler abroad, 'How much is that in real money?'" Pinney, "A New Look for Municipals," *The Analysts' Journal,* May 1956, p. 83.

exchange them for lower-yielding obligations. Although admitting that the business and agricultural situation at that time was critical, this evidence of lack of "willingness" has led some municipal analysts to avoid Arkansas bonds ever since. On the other hand, some cities in extreme difficulties during the Great Depression did default, but because every effort was made to refund and subsequently retire the bonds in full, the "willingness" factor has not been regarded as unfavorable. Toledo, Ohio, for example, defaulted in 1933–34 on debt principal but exchanged the defaulted bonds for refunding obligations in 1935. Since then, both debt interest and principal have been promptly paid when due. As a consequence, Toledo's bonds are now rated top-quality by most municipal analysts.

In brief, the cause of any default in the debt record is evaluated. If because of circumstances largely beyond the ability of the city to control, the conclusion on willingness need not be unfavorable if every effort was made to meet the debt in full at a later date when conditions improved. But evidence of a default to avoid payment that could reasonably have been made is a tremendous black mark against a municipal bond credit.

Political Stability. A purely qualitative factor in estimating the willingness to pay of a municipality is the general nature and reliability of the political administrations and the electorate. These, of course, are very difficult to assess, and generally speaking, the analyst must rely on vague impressions. For example, the political administrations of the city of Chicago and Cook County have often been subject to unfavorable comment in the press; scandals of graft and corruption have been alleged and even proved in a few instances. The large slum population has also been cited as evidence of political unreliability. However, Chicago has a completely clear debt record, except for some bond issues in the 1920's, which were partially invalidated for legal reasons, and it is to the city's credit that ever since then it has endeavored to find a way of legally meeting these obligations. Therefore, in spite of a questionable political environment, Chicago has usually been rated good from a willingness standpoint.

It is, however, desirable to obtain rough impressions that (1) the municipal government has been marked by integrity and prudence, (2) the population has a dominant proportion of native-born citizens with above-average educational attainments and incomes, and (3) the political views of the electorate have been reasonably intelligent and lacking in radical tendencies. Certain statistical data on the community can be used as more tangible evidence of these factors, and these are shown for two Ohio cities, Toledo and Cincinnati, in Table 22-2.

Municipal-Bond Analysis: Ability to Pay

Social and Economic Factors. Data on population trends, educational achievements, family incomes, and property values within a community relate both to willingness to pay and ability to pay, because by and large there is a direct relationship between these elements and political reliability. Such data are collected at irregular intervals by the Bureau of the Census and published in a volume called *County and City Data Book* for all counties and cities having populations more than 25,000.[6] Much of the data are also reproduced in most of the Dun and Bradstreet municipal reports. In addition to providing evidence on the character of the people, they enable the analyst to determine if a city has been enjoying a relatively favorable growth trend and the relative degree of tax-paying ability of the inhabitants. Unfortunately, the figures are usually several years old, and as a consequence, current developments in these matters cannot be appraised in most cases. However, as the trends of population and income usually change slowly, the data still have considerable value.

Table 22-2 shows some selected social and economic statistics for Cincinnati and Toledo, Ohio, for their related counties, and for comparative purposes, the United States averages. The population figures show that Toledo and Cincinnati have been growing more slowly than has the population generally. However, a slower rate of population growth does not necessarily reflect a less rapid rate of growth for industry and commerce. It may be because of different policies in expanding the land area of the cities, combined with the growing trend toward locating residences in the suburbs. That this is true in these cases is suggested by the growth of the counties of which these cities are the metropolitan centers. Both Lucas County (Toledo) and Hamilton County (Cincinnati) show population trends about in line with the national average. It is reasonable to conclude, therefore, that these cities are not declining in economic stature, although the growth of resident population within the city limits proper may increase at a relatively slow rate, or even decline. Some evidence of maturity thus exists in both cases.

[6] Superintendent of Documents, U.S. Government Printing Office, Washington 25, D.C.

TABLE 22-2
Toledo and Cincinnati, Ohio
Selected Population and Economic Data: 1960 Census

	Lucas County	Toledo	Hamilton County	Cincinnati	U.S. Average
Percent of population increase					
1950 to 1960	15.5%	4.7%	19.4%	−0.3%	18.5%
1940 to 1950	14.9	7.5	16.4	10.6	14.5
1930 to 1940	−	−2.9	−	1.0	7.2
1959 Median family income	$6,533	$6,299	$6,451	$5,701	$5,660
Percent of foreign-born population, 1960	4.2%	4.8%	2.8%	3.3%	5.4%
Persons twenty-five years old and over					
Percent completed high school or more	40.9%	38.2%	39.2%	33.6%	41.1%
Percent less than five grades completed	5.4%	6.2%	6.2%	8.2%	8.4%

Source: Bureau of the Census, *City and County Data Book*, 1962.

The wealth and income data are favorable in both cities. Toledo showed a higher median family income in 1959 than Cincinnati, although both were above the national average. The incomes of the suburban county residents were even higher, to lend further support to the above-average income status of these areas.

The education and foreign-born data represent important social factors. The theory is that native-born and educated people are more likely to resist propositions which may result in unsound municipal finance and, consequently, unfavorably affect the bondholders. Moreover, it is generally accepted that illiterate adults are more likely to become public charges. The members of this group tend not only to earn less income to pay tax levies but to divert tax revenues to their own upkeep. Although Lucas County and Toledo show educational attainments about equal to the national average, Cincinnati and surrounding Hamilton County are below average. But both Toledo and Cincinnati have below-average percentages of foreign-born population.

Therefore, in general it appears that the population trends and characteristics of Toledo are superior to Cincinnati, with the latter below average in certain respects. However, both seem favorable so far as income characteristics are concerned.

Economic Factors: Industry Characteristics. The debt service on municipal bonds must be met largely from tax levies on the corporations and the people residing therein. These levies in turn can only be paid from a flow of income to business firms and individuals. Therefore, a general evaluation of the major sources of wealth and incomes is useful in appraising the potential of the community. In this connection the elements of growth, stability, and diversification are particularly significant.

Certain impressions about the economic strength of a community can be obtained from a general qualitative report on the major economic activities located within its boundaries or nearby.[7] To illustrate, the two cities in Ohio, Toledo and Cincinnati, might be compared in these respects. Toledo is an industrial city with numerous factories serving the automotive, machinery, and metal-products industries. Most of the products are classified as producer or consumer durables, although glass and oil refining are also important industries. The city is also an important shipping center with good rail connections and an excellent port on Lake Erie. Coal, oil, cement, and iron ore are among the bulk products handled in large quantities in the port area.

This condensed description of Toledo's economy suggests fair diversification and growth but a high degree of cyclical vulnerability. No one industry or company dominates, and most of the industries represented have good long-term growth trends. But the emphasis on durable goods indicates that employment and incomes in Toledo could fall drastically in the event of a sharp recession in general business activity. Therefore, Toledo's tax revenues could possibly be subject to wide variations. The high degree of cyclical vulnerability suggests a less favorable credit than would otherwise be the case.

Cincinnati, on the other hand, is less dependent upon the heavy-goods industries. There is a wider diversification of industrial activity, which includes soaps and detergents, chemicals, machinery, and paper and publishing. No one type of industry dominates. Moreover, the city is an important commercial center for nearby parts of Ohio and Kentucky. It is also an important banking and university area. Transportation facilities via rail and the Ohio River are good. The economic pattern of Cincinnati suggests considerably greater stability than for Toledo, although perhaps less secular growth. Diversification of industry and

---

[7] It is assumed that adequate information is available on all these matters. This would, at best, presume the availability of the excellent Dun and Bradstreet reports on municipal credits and, at the least, the more limited information contained in Moody's *Municipal and Government Manual.*

commerce is favorable. Therefore, Cincinnati gives an excellent impression from a general economic standpoint.

Ability to Pay: Debt Burden. But even a municipality with above-average economic characteristics may assume a quantity of debt which may prove embarrassing during any general setback in business conditions. In assessing the degree of debt burden, analysts are accustomed to look at two debt ratios. One is the relationship of total debt payable from taxes to the total estimated value of the taxable real property. The other is the ratio of the debt to the population of the community; this is referred to as *per capita debt.*

The first ratio is constructed on the theory that the principal source of tax revenues for municipalities is an *ad valorem* tax levied on the real property located within its jurisdiction. As a consequence, the value of such property implicitly indicates its tax potential, and when related to the debt, the resultant ratio purports to show whether a large proportion of the potential must be used to meet debt service or not. Moreover, to the extent that total property values represent an index of the total wealth and income of the community, the ratio also measures the debt burden in relation to the flow of income. It would, of course, be desirable to compare directly the debt burden with the total flow of personal and corporate income generated within the municipal unit, but such data are not available. As a consequence, even if the tax sources are not principally *ad valorem* taxes on real property, the ratio of debt to property values within the tax jurisdiction remains a significant statistical measure of the debt burden.

The per capita debt ratio is based on the theory that the people are ultimately responsible for the debt and that governmental units should borrow in relationship to the size of the community that is being served. However, the usefulness of the ratio is reduced somewhat by the common-sense observation that people alone without wealth and income do not add to the taxation and debt service capacity of the community. Conversely, where each family has a relatively high income, the debt capacity is correspondingly high on a per capita basis. Nevertheless, the trend of the per capita debt should indicate whether the city is expanding its services, provided by borrowed money, at a rate greater than the expansion of the population of the city.

Table 22-3 shows the ten-year trends of the debt and debt ratios for Cincinnati and Toledo. Before commenting on the debt burden in these two cities, one technical point should be explained, the inclusion of the "overlapping" debt. The "overlapping" debt represents obligations of

TABLE 22-3
DEBT-BURDEN RATIOS
CINCINNATI AND TOLEDO, OHIO

	Year	Net Direct Debt* (000 omitted)	Overlapping Debt (000 omitted)	Total Debt to Estimated† True Value	Total Per Capita Debt
Cincinnati					
	1955	$ 98,144	$48,444	6.6%	$298
	1957	107,511	56,382	6.9	327
	1959	129,378	58,502	7.2	376
	1961	139,709	58,825	7.3	398
	1963	143,633	55,864	7.3	398
	1964	160,882	62,597	8.4	446
Toledo					
	1957	$ 2,743	$10,493	1.0%	$ 41
	1959	2,629	12,330	1.1	49
	1961	1,901	33,369	2.3	117
	1963	4,777	37,649	2.5	141
	1964	10,134	38,292	2.7	161

* "Self-supporting" revenue debt such as water facility bonds are excluded from net direct debt to be borne by tax revenues.

† True value computed on basis of estimate that indicated assessed values represented 60% of true values.

Source: Dun and Bradstreet Inc., Municipal Credit Reports.

other governmental jurisdictions which levy taxes on the same property as does the city itself.[8] As these other units typically include taxable properties outside the city, the overlap burden is computed by taking the total assessed valuation within the overlapping unit and dividing it into the assessed values of the city. The resulting percentage is multiplied by the total debt of the overlapping unit, and the result is assumed to be the overlapping debt burden on the property within the city.

The most common types of overlapping debt in the case of cities are bonds issued by the related school districts and countries. As noted for Toledo, the overlapping debt can be much larger than the direct city debt, especially in recent years, when the school districts have greatly increased their debt to finance new school buildings.

As of 1965 the overlapping debt of Toledo consisted of 100% of the Toledo School District's debt and 69% of the Lucas County debt. Cin-

[8] If the boundaries of the other units are almost exactly the same, the debt might be called *coterminous* rather than *overlapping*; if the geographical boundaries of the other units are considerably smaller, the debt of such units may be called *underlying* in some instances. It is becoming increasingly common, however, to refer to all such obligations as the *overlapping* debt.

cinnati's overlap was 91 and 51% of the School District and County debt, respectively. It should be emphasized that the taxes to pay debt service and operating expenses of these other municipal units have equal claim with the taxes levied by the respective cities. Therefore, it may be assumed that any tax delinquencies resulting from a heavy tax burden to pay debt service on any of these units will prove equally serious to all of them. Therefore, the effective debt is the total of net direct debt plus the appropriate share of the overlapping debt as indicated in Table 22-3.

Although there are no scientific bench marks for these ratios, some specialists in municipals have suggested rough maximums for these ratios of $200 to $350 for per capita overall debt and 8 to 12% for debt to true values.[9] These standards apply to larger cities and are often scaled down for smaller cities on the ground that their tax revenues are likely to be more variable due to less economic diversification. Table 22-4 shows some suggested rough standards for these ratios by size of city which have been advanced by municipal analysts. It is, of course, possible for a municipality to have somewhat heavier debt burdens but still be considered a good-quality credit because of other factors of strength in the situation.

TABLE 22–4
SUGGESTED RANGES: DEBT-BURDEN RATIOS

Population	Per Capita Debt	Debt/True Value of Property
Over 500,000	$200–350	7–10%
100,000–500,000	100–250	5–8
50,000–100,000	75–150	5–8
under 50,000	50–150	3–6

A comparison of Toledo's debt-burden ratios with the suggested bench marks shows its debt to be well within the limits for cities in its population range (100,000 to 500,000). Particularly in relationship to estimated true value of taxable real property, the combined debt of the city and overlapping units was quite modest. Although the debt had in-

---

[9] True value is used instead of assessed value, because the rates of assessment may vary widely between different cities. However, it must be admitted that estimates of true value are difficult to compute and may be subject to serious error. Dun and Bradstreet municipal reports usually give estimates of true values based on the stated assessment policies, but these may be based on data which are a decade or more old as reassessments are infrequently made.

creased significantly since 1957, the growth in property values kept the burden well under the suggested range. However, a continuation of the debt trend might ultimately have adverse effects on the credit quality of Toledo's obligations.

Cincinnati's debt-burden situation was not quite so clear-cut. In the first place, it may be noted that the total debt increased substantially during the 1955–64 period. Specifically, the increase was from about $136 million to $223 million. As population has not increased, the consequence was that the per capita debt was well in excess of the suggested range. It is true that the trend of the debt-to-property-value ratio had not been especially alarming. But in view of the debt trend and its high level on a per capita basis, it could be argued that, despite the very favorable credit factors in other respects, Cincinnati should no longer be rated as a prime-quality municipal credit.

Ability to Pay: Tax Rates, Limits, and Collections. The most de-desirable combination of circumstances from the standpoint of credit quality would be to find low tax rates relative to true values, a complete absence of tax limits, and collection records showing few delinquencies. By and large these attributes logically go together. If tax rates are low as a percentage of property values, there should be considerable incentive for taxpayers not to become delinquent and not have their properties foreclosed by tax-sale proceedings. However, under very adverse economic conditions, when incomes of a significant number of taxpayers may be greatly reduced, delinquencies may increase, even though nominal long-term values of properties may appear unimpaired.

For this reason, the prevailing tax rates, their level in relation to tax limits (if any), and the tax-collection pattern should be examined. The tax-rate level may indicate two credit aspects. First, the degree to which new industry and residents will locate within a given city or beyond its limits may depend to a considerable extent on the tax rates. High tax rates can be a very real growth-retarding force. Second, low tax rates give a municipality considerably more flexibility in case of budget difficulties. Resistance to tax increases on the part of citizen groups may depend largely on whether rates are already relatively high or not. Therefore a municipal unit that shows a balanced budget at low tax rates is to be preferred. It is, of course, also desirable that flexibility not be reduced because of statutory tax limits. Such limits are most undesirable, especially when applicable to debt service as well as for general purposes. When tax limits apply to debt service, the bonds are generally accorded a lower-quality ranking even if existing tax rates are not near the statutory limits.

TABLE 22-5
TAX RATES AND COLLECTION RECORD
TOLEDO AND CINCINNATI, OHIO
(selected years)

	1933	1956	1962	1963	1964
Cincinnati					
Tax rates on assessed					
(per $1,000)	$21.96	$29.34	$34.90	$38.02	$38.22
Ratio—assessed to true value	100%	60%	60%	60%	60%
Tax rate—estimated true					
value	$21.96	$17.60	$20.94	$22.80	$22.93
Tax delinquency—this city	10.3%	1.6%	1.5%	2.2%	N.A.
Tax delinquency, 150 city					
median	26.3%	2.8%	3.3%	3.1%	N.A.
Toledo					
Tax rates on assessed					
(per $1,000)	$26.60	$22.74	$30.00	$30.10	$33.60
Ratio—assessed to true value	100%	60%	60%	60%	60%
Tax rate—estimated true					
value	$26.60	$13.64	$18.00	$18.06	$20.16
Tax delinquency—this city	32.3%	2.1%	2.6%	2.6%	N.A.
Tax delinquency, 150 city					
median	26.3%	2.8%	3.3%	3.1%	N.A.

Sources: Dun & Bradstreet Municipal Reports: Detroit Bank and Trust Co.

The tax-collection pattern not only provides a check on whether tax rates are onerous, but also represents a good index of the income variability of the residents and business. Above-average delinquencies during prosperous times would probably indicate an excessive tax-rate burden. But if delinquencies only become serious during adverse economic conditions, then the cause is probably a high volatility of business and personal incomes. As a consequence, both the average collection pattern and the results during depressions are given consideration.

Table 22-5 shows the tax-rate levels and collection records of the illustrative cities compared with the delinquency median for a number of large cities. Except for the trend of tax rates, Cincinnati through the years has shown a very favorable record along these lines. Tax rates on assessed values have substantially increased, but because assessed values have not kept pace with rising estimated true values, the real burden of taxes in 1962–64 was estimated to be about equal to that of 1933. As a rough bench mark, some municipal analysts have argued that if tax rates approach $30 per $1,000 of estimated true value, the municipality is vulnerable both to delinquencies and to industry "shift-outs" to avoid punitive tax rates. Cincinnati has never approached such a tax level, and therefore, the tax burden could be characterized as moderate. The good delinquency record confirmed this appraisal. Moreover, the markedly lower level of tax delinquencies in Cincinnati during 1933 suggests considerably greater stability of personal and business incomes than is true for the average city.

Toledo provides an interesting case of a city which was notably weak on the tax-burden and delinquency factors in the 1930's but as of 1962–64 appeared strong on both counts. In 1933 the tax-rate level was not too far away from the maximum bench mark of $30 per $1,000 and the delinquency record was atrocious—about one-third of the taxes levied in that year were not collected on time. However, as of 1962–64 both the level of tax rates and the delinquency record appeared to be more favorable than average. The pattern confirmed the qualitative appraisal that Toledo's economy is subject to considerable volatility. But at the level of tax rates prevailing in 1964, it was doubtful if delinquencies would be a serious problem in the future.

Both cities were nominally subject to a legal tax limit of $10 per $1,000 of assessed valuation. The limit was added to the Constitution of Ohio in 1934 during the Great Depression and applied to all property taxes, including overlapping units. Toledo's share of the maximum was only $4.45 per $1,000, whereas Cincinnati's share, fixed by charter, was $6.65 per $1,000. Fortunately, however, the inhibiting effects of the tax limits have been largely removed in two ways. First, the cities have been allowed to vote special taxes outside the limit to cover specific bond issues, and most of the bonds were of this character. Second, the cities have adopted an income tax as a major source of revenue (perhaps because of the tax limit), which has greatly increased their fiscal flexibility. However, it should be noted that income-tax revenues are probably more volatile than those derived from property taxes, which do not fluctuate directly with income.

The conclusion seems justified that Cincinnati definitely deserves a high ranking with respect to these credit factors, and to some extent the unfavorable implications of the high debt burden are offset thereby. Toledo had a favorable tax-burden appraisal, but its delinquency record was not impressive.

Ability to Pay: Debt Management. As already mentioned, most municipal obligations are issued in serial form. Moreover, in the less typical instance when term bonds are used, the indenture usually requires a sinking fund set aside to anticipate the maturity requirements. However, although any one issue may mature regularly, there may be a number of outstanding issues brought out from time to time that may add up to large maturities bunched in certain years in the future. There-fore, it is desirable to scan the maturity schedule of the combined issues with a view to estimating if any difficulty might be experienced in meet-ing principal requirements at any time in the future.

It is true, of course, that most municipal units could probably refund some maturing obligations under normal conditions in the economy and money market, but such action is typically considered evidence of negli-gent financial planning and lack of prudent debt-management policies. Moreover, if refundings are necessitated by a combination of heavy maturities and a degeneration in tax collections because of a decline in economic activity, there may be some real difficulty. Under such con-ditions, the market may be unwilling to buy the refunding issue and then a *de facto* default could conceivably result.

Most high-grade municipal credits show reasonable distributions of future maturities or alternatively regular sinking-fund accumulations to meet any single maturities of unusually large amounts. The existence of any large debt not anticipated in one of these two ways is evidence of inadequate financial management at best. It may lead, at worst, to a conclusion that should a significant economic downturn coincide with any extraordinarily large maturities, default could result.

TABLE 22–6
MATURITY DISTRIBUTIONS: CINCINNATI AND TOLEDO°

	Cincinnati	Toledo
1966	$7,638,000	$690,000
1967	7,316,000	621,000
1968	7,155,000	606,000
1969	6,972,000	589,000
Maximum year after 1969	6,798,000	520,000

° Excludes maturities on self-supporting debt; water revenue bonds principally.

Table 22-6 shows the maturity schedules of Cincinnati and Toledo as of the latter part of 1964. Both cities also operated "redemption funds" or "sinking funds" to which tax receipts sufficient to pay principal and in-terest plus a reserve were transferred. The maturity schedules of both cities seemed to be reasonably balanced, with no exceptionally heavy maturities indicated for any future year. Therefore, there was good evi-dence that these cities had a systematic and adequate means of retiring debt principal when it matured. However, Toledo, with its nominal debt maturities, seemed to be relatively stronger in this respect.

Ability to Pay: Financial Record.   The financial reports of municipal units are notorious for their sketchy and confusing nature. By and large the reports are in the form of a statement of receipts and disbursements wherein capital outlays may be mixed with recurrent operating expenses. Then, again, municipalities have a propensity for establishing different "funds," and transfers back and forth between the funds can be quite confusing. Finally, it is relatively rare to find a municipal unit giving any meaningful breakdown of operating expenses for analysis purposes.

As a consequence, the financial record is usually appraised with perhaps three objectives in mind. First, there is the question of the reliability of revenues to meet operating and debt requirements. Second, if possible it is desirable to ascertain if over a period of several years the unit has been able to maintain a balanced operating budget. Third, there may be the question of whether the unit is burdened by large expenditures for unprofitable services, such as transit systems.

With respect to revenue reliability, any onerous tax limits and the level of tax rates are pertinent factors, but these are not shown as such in the report of receipts and expenditures. The operating report, however, does usually show the major receipts by revenue sources. To illustrate, the operating statistics for the general funds of Cincinnati and Toledo are shown for 1958 and 1961–63 in Table 22-7. Both cities showed a definite trend toward replacing property taxes with an income tax as the major revenue source. The major reason for the adoption of city income taxes has been the tendency of the higher income groups to move outside the city limits but still derive their incomes from work within the city. The tax has the virtue of being collected by direct deduction from wages and salaries, and thus the delinquency problem is eliminated. On the other hand, as already mentioned, incomes tend to fluctuate more than property values, especially hourly incomes in the heavy industries which dominate Toledo. Therefore, greater volatility of this revenue source might be anticipated.

The reliability of state aid used to be subject to serious question, but with the passage of time a tradition for its continuance has gradually been built up. Ohio allows local units grants out of sales, inheritances, liquor, and intangible taxes. These grants are subject to yearly determinations by the state legislature and theoretically could be discontinued at any time. However, the practice is now well established to refund an established portion of these taxes to local units, and it seems inconceivable that they will be cut off on short notice. As the state taxes involved are mostly reliable sources of revenue, the state fiscal aid portion of each city's total receipts deserves a high ranking on a reliability basis.

TABLE 22-7
GENERAL FUND OPERATIONS
CINCINNATI AND TOLEDO: 1958 AND 1961–63
(000 omitted)

	1958	1961	1962	1963
Toledo				
Receipts				
Ad valorem taxes	$ 3,218	$ 3,413	$ 3,638	N.A.
State aid	1,785	1,986	2,181	N.A.
Income taxes	4,150	5,330	5,330	N.A.
Other	2,345	2,478	2,419	N.A.
Total	$11,498	$13,207	$13,568	$13,917
Expenses				
Operating expenses	$11,507	$13,164	$13,396	$13,070
Transfers	30	95	59	263
Total	$11,537	$13,259	$13,455	$13,334
Cash position				
General fund cash	$ 43	$ 106	$236	$754
Liabilities	366	213	124	678
Surplus or (deficit)	$(323)	$(107)	$112	$ 76
Cincinnati				
Receipts				
Ad valorem taxes	$10,483	$11,231	$11,194	$12,825
State aid	5,562	5,827	6,333	6,333
Income taxes	12,318	15,200	15,642	15,537
Other	8,323	9,699	8,983	9,572
Total	$37,046	$41,957	$42,152	$44,267
Expenses				
City hospital	$ 5,771	$ 6,408	$ 5,724	$ 5,778
City university	3,072	3,147	3,072	3,663
Department public works	4,351	4,601	4,688	4,823
Department safety	12,416	11,107	14,438	14,822
All other	12,410	14,933	15,543	14,859
Total	$38,019	$43,196	$42,465	$43,945
Cash position				
General fund cash	$2,865	$2,161	$1,847	$2,192
Liabilities	1,201	1,459	1,461	1,510
Surplus or (deficit)	$1,665	$ 702	$ 386	$ 682

To summarize, because of a heavy reliance in both cities on a more volatile income tax, the quality of the tax revenues appeared to be only fair. But although small deficits appeared in some years, both cities have maintained their budgets in reasonable balance. Toledo had a

minor deficit on balance in the operating fund in 1958, but the amount
was not serious. The fact that in the recession year of 1958 Toledo's income-tax revenues declined and the city experienced a mild deficit on
current account again confirms the above-average volatility of this city.
But expenditures in any one year may run beyond expectations because
of unforeseen needs; it is more important to pay attention to the average
record over four or five years. In this respect the records of both appeared reasonably adequate. In addition there was no evidence of
either city's operating fund being burdened by unprofitable services of
any significance. Therefore, it can be concluded that the fiscal operations were under satisfactory control, which adds to the stature of both
credits.

Summary of General Obligation Analysis. The following outline
summarizes the major analytical factors pertinent to an investigation of
a municipal credit. Each point has been fully discussed above with illustrative reference to two important cities in the state of Ohio, Cincinnati and Toledo.

A. Evidence of willingness to pay.
 1. A clean debt record especially in adverse years, is desirable.
    Defaults, if any, outside the control of the city should have been
    remedied at the earliest possible opportunity.
 2. Refundings of serial maturities should be at a minimum.
 3. The character of the population and the actions of the city
    administration should give evidence of political and fiscal reli-
    ability.
B. Evidence of ability to pay.
 1. The general economic and social factors should be favorable,
    such as growth, industry diversification, cyclical characteristics,
    wealth, and educational attainments.
 2. The debt burden in relation to true value of real property and
    on a per capita basis should be reasonable.
 3. Tax rates should be reasonable in order not to discourage
    growth. As a rule of thumb, a maximum rate of $30 per $1,000
    of true value is suggested.
 4. No onerous tax limits, however, should be evidenced. Bonds
    payable only out of limited tax rates should be evaluated sepa-
    rately because of their special vulnerability. In this case, it is
    desirable to find the tax rate well below tax limits. Other sources

of income, such as an income tax may eliminate some of the problems of tax limits.

5. The tax-collection record should be favorable. Better than 95% of the tax levy should be collected in the year of levy, and delinquencies in adverse years should be less than average.

6. Prudent financial planning should be evidenced by an even schedule of maturity distributions or adequate sinking funds.

7. The financial record should be satisfactory. This means approximately balanced budgets on the average over a three- to five-year period, reliable sources of revenue, and no significant drains because of unprofitable municipal services.

Comparing Toledo and Cincinnati with respect to these factors, it appeared that Toledo's debt record and economic stability were significantly less favorable than Cincinnati. However, the modest level of debt and the favorable record in all other respects in recent years suggested that Toledo bonds deserved a very high-quality rating. Cincinnati had a relatively high debt burden but because of an excellent economic position, above average performance under depression conditions, and an impeccable debt record, it also deserved a high-quality ranking, although perhaps as of 1965 not the very highest rating.[10]

[10] It is interesting to note that Moody's *Municipal Manual* of 1965 rated Cincinnati's general obligation bonds Aaa and Toledo's Aa. While admittedly a matter of judgment, on the basis of the above analysis it would be possible to reverse the ratings shown in Moody's largely on the basis of the relative size of the debt burdens.

CHAPTER 23

Municipal Revenue Bonds

Scope and Approach. The true municipal revenue bond can only be paid from the sale of some service to the public.[1] Therefore, the type of analysis appropriate for revenue bonds tends to be roughly similar to that of corporate fixed-income securities in general. In brief, the analysis requires a decision about whether the net income from the sale of a product or service will be sufficient to meet debt requirements in the future. Again, however, it must be noted that the purpose of municipal revenue units is not to maximize earnings. As there is no residual equity, the objective is to establish rates for the services which will adequately cover interest and principal amortization on the debt, with perhaps a modest excess for future contingencies.

The importance of revenue obligations in the total municipal market has been increasing. Thirty years ago they were relatively rare, but for several cogent reasons they now represent a significant share of total municipals outstanding. These reasons include the growth of quasi-gov-

[1] Bonds issued to finance properties leased to governmental units whose revenues come from taxes are difficult to classify. However, because the sources of payment are ultimately general taxes, which (in part) are then diverted to pay the necessary rentals, it is felt that such bonds really depend on the general credit of the municipal unit concerned and should not, therefore, be classified as revenue obligations. Other obligations, sometimes classified as revenues, are nominally to be paid from certain service revenues but are also guaranteed by a governmental unit, and as a consequence, would properly be classified as general obligations.

ernmental services, such as toll roads, airports, and parking facilities, wherein equitable considerations dictate that the user instead of the general public should bear the cost of the service. Also, revenue obligations can usually be issued without referral to the electorate, and various limits on debt assumption applied to general obligations do not apply to revenues. Their comparative importance may be suggested by the new issue statistics for the second and third quarters of 1964. During this period new revenue obligations (exclusive of rental revenues) were brought out in the approximate amount of $1.8 billion, which compared with new general obligation issues of about $2.9 billion during the same period.[2] These figures suggest that about one-third of new municipal bonds have been in the form of revenues, and the proportion may increase from time to time when large new issues, such as toll-road bonds, are brought to market.

Qualitative Credit Factors. The qualitative analysis of a municipal revenue situation covers essentially the same points covered in corporate appraisals. In both instances the nature of the demand for the product or service is of paramount importance. It is in this respect that there are wide differences in the quality of revenue obligations. At one extreme the demand for the product or service may be so stable and predictable, because of its absolute necessity to consumers, that the bonds financing the service may be ranked higher than the general obligations of the related municipality. Water-revenue bonds are an example. It can be argued that residents of a community may be inclined to meet water bills ahead of taxes should a choice be necessary.[3] Water consumption, except perhaps for industrial use, is likely to be highly stable and consumers must pay the bills or face a shut-off in service, and without water service, living conditions would be very difficult to say the least.

At the other extreme some revenue bonds actually defaulted during the 1955–64 decade because of a lack of demand of sufficient size to service the debt adequately. The bonds of the West Virginia Turnpike Commission may be offered as a case in point. These bonds, entitled State of West Virginia (West Virginia Turnpike Commission) Turnpike Revenue 3¾s and 4⅛s of 1989, were originally issued in 1952 and 1954 to finance the construction of an eighty-eight-mile toll road. The first issue of 3¾s amounted to $96 million, and when this amount proved inadequate to finance the construction, $37 million of 4⅛s

---

[2] Computed from the *IBA Statistical Bulletin,* November, 1964, pp. 2 and 7.

[3] Certain underlying water revenue bonds of Toledo are rated Aaa in Moody's 1965 *Municipal and Government Manual,* whereas the generals are rated Aa.

were sold. Construction was completed in 1955, but traffic has not been sufficient to provide adequate revenues to meet the annual interest charges of $5.126 million. Net revenues in fact were between $3 and $3.7 million during the 1957–64 period, and the bonds went into partial default in 1957 and intermittent interest payments have been made since then. As of 1965, interest payments were about three years in arrears. Although revenues have been increasing slowly, it is doubtful if the default can be corrected for a number of years.

Because of wide differences in the ability of various governmental projects to produce revenues sufficient to meet operating expenses and debt service, revenue bonds tend to vary more in intrinsic quality than municipals based on the general tax powers. In fact, the unsatisfactory performance of several revenue obligations has led some institutional investors, such as commercial banks, to eliminate such bonds from their portfolios. On the whole, the categorical rejection of revenues would seem to be an ill-advised policy. Two basic and relatively simple inquiries on the nature of demand can be applied which will ordinarily quickly separate the "good" from the "bad" in this respect. First, consider whether the service rendered is an essential consumer service whose use is highly stable. Second, if this is answered affirmatively, consider whether the total number of consumers using the service is likely to produce sufficient revenues to meet operating expenses and debt service at reasonable rates.

The second inquiry suggests a qualitative factor in most revenue-bond situations identical with the analysis of general obligations. This is the social and economic character of the area served. Because the service area of most revenue situations, like the tax area of general obligations, is restricted geographically, it is highly desirable to find the revenue generated in a locality where the population is growing, or at least stable. Even though the demand is highly stable (such as for water) if the total number of consumers is subject to erosion through the years, then the total volume of service sold may prove inadequate. In brief, a water plant in a ghost town is not a desirable basis to provide revenues to meet bond obligations.

Some revenue bond issues are accorded a high-quality rating almost entirely on the basis of these two qualitative factors alone. To take a case close at hand, the Dormitory Revenue bonds of the University of Michigan are well regarded by many investors, including conservative institutions. The quality of these bonds depends essentially on: (1) the stability and growth of demand for college educations in general and (2) the strategic position of the University of Michigan in relation to other colleges and universities. Because the proportion of high school graduates seeking college educations has been increasing and because the total number of students in high school is also increasing rapidly, the growth picture is good. And although college enrollments tend to vary cyclically to some extent, the lower-cost state universities tend to hold up better under depression conditions than higher-cost private colleges. Finally, the University of Michigan has been able to maintain through the years a favorable demand for its educational services. Therefore, because the University pledges that room and board rates will be sufficient to cover debt service, the Dormitory Revenue Bonds are normally given a high-quality rating.

Quantitative Credit Factors. However, the typical revenue bond is not of this type; more likely these bonds result from financing publicly owned utility operations of one kind or another. And in connection with these operations, the prospective investors should expect to have some specific financial data available to evaluate the quality of the credit. Such data would unquestionably be required for electric-power or water operations, and it usually should be required when quasi-utilities, such as toll roads are under consideration.

The relevant quantitative techniques are much the same as for private utility companies, although certain minor differences can be noted. These can be briefly summarized as follows:

1. The trend and stability of the revenues over a considerable number of years.
2. The trend and level of the operating ratio to indicate if expenses are under control.
3. The trend and level of the net revenue coverage of total debt service on a cash-flow basis. (This means the relationship between earnings before depreciation, on the one hand, and interest payments plus yearly serial maturities or sinking funds, on the other.)

Because the financial information released by municipal revenue units is often highly condensed or is not based on standard accounting practices, some techniques used in the analysis of utility companies are not feasible. For example, earnings are often only given before depreciation, and the amount of annual depreciation is not revealed in the financial statements; therefore, it is only possible to compute coverage on a cash-flow basis. This technique, however, should be sufficient in most cases.

Water-revenue bonds are perhaps the most common type (in terms

TABLE 23-1

FINANCIAL DATA: WATER DEPARTMENT
FLINT, MICHIGAN
(000 omitted)

Years ended June 30:	1956	1958	1960	1961	1962	1963	1964
Operating revenues	$2,818	$2,478	$3,193	$3,267	$3,348	$3,265	$3,420
Operating expenses	1,576	1,588	1,440	1,457	1,528	1,502	1,528
Net income before depreciation	$1,242	$ 890	$1,753	$1,810	$1,820	$1,763	$1,892
Bond interest and maturities	458	544	567	579	582	579	574
Operating ratio	56%	63%	45%	44%	46%	46%	45%
Cash flow to debt service	2.7	1.6	3.1	3.1	3.0	3.0	3.3

of number of issues) of municipal revenue obligations. To illustrate the use of the techniques previously suggested, it is appropriate to select a water-revenue situation of moderate size. Therefore, the water-revenue department of Flint, Michigan, has been selected for a brief analysis.

As the intention is to illustrate the use of quantitative analytical techniques, a detailed consideration of the qualitative factors bearing on the Flint credit will be omitted. Perhaps it will suffice to point out that although the growth characteristics of Flint have been good, it is almost entirely dependent on the automobile industry, and therefore, it may be drastically hurt by a serious downturn in business activity. The volatility feature suggests that the operating performance should be quite favorable in order to qualify the bonds for investment purposes.

Table 23-1 shows some selected data on the Flint Water Department for the years 1956–64. The ratios shown are illustrative of the quantitative techniques useful to appraise the quality of the credit. A review of these ratios suggests on the whole that the Flint Water Revenue bonds are a strong credit, despite some qualitative reservations on the economic characteristics of the city.

As is true of all financial analyses, the trends over a period of eight years or so are especially significant. And here they are reasonably reassuring. The revenue trend since 1956 shows unmistakable evidence of a good growth pattern, although the effects of the recession of 1957–58 were evident. Moreover, the operating ratio shows adequate control of operating expenses. Only in 1958, when adverse economic circumstances heavily affected Flint, did the operating ratio get to levels considered even moderately high. In addition, the cash flow from earnings and depreciation has been quite adequate; it has averaged 2.8 times combined interest charges and maturities on the debt. Debt-service requirements have held at a stable level and no large maturities in any one future year were indicated. On the basis of the total evidence, these bonds certainly deserved the A rating accorded them in Moody's *Municipal and Governmental Manual*. The rating meant they were classified as high medium-grade obligations with favorable investment attributes but with some long-term risks.[4]

Summary of Quantitative Standards. Although it is difficult to establish categorical bench marks of quantitative performance for all revenue bonds which finance a great variety of services, Table 23-2 indicates some conventional standards for high-quality revenue situations. It may

[4] Moody's *Municipal and Government Manual*, 1965, p. vi.

TABLE 23–2
QUANTITATIVE STANDARDS: MUNICIPAL REVENUE BONDS

Test	Stable Demand	Potentially Variable Demand
Revenue trend—ten years	neutral trend	increasing trend
Operating ratio—five years	40 to 70%	40 to 70%
Cash-flow coverage*		
Average, five years	1.5	2.5
Minimum, five years	1.25	1.5
Trend, ten years	neutral	neutral

* Using maturities and bond interest to net income before depreciation.

also be noted that a highly favorable indication in one respect may offset a moderate inadequacy in some other area. Finally, it should be remembered that most municipal revenue activities are not intended to produce large profits, and rates are set so that they only provide sufficient revenues to cover operating expenses and debt service with a modest margin to spare. Therefore, coverage standards can be considerably lower than for corporate obligations.

Contractual Terms

As in corporate bond appraisals, the specific legal covenants are regarded as less significant in the selection process than a strong qualitative and quantitative showing. In brief, the reasoning is that no amount of legal verbiage can assure payment of a bond issue which finances the production of a service or product that cannot be sold in an adequate and continuous volume. The basic economic and financial factors are, therefore, of prime significance, and the contractual terms have really negative importance only; they prevent the issuing entity from undertaking certain specific actions in the future which would prejudice the ability to meet future debt service requirements. In one sense, the covenants are aimed at preventing unethical or even fraudulent practices; in another they are designed to forestall imprudent management in certain crucial respects. In effect the contractual terms are supplementary to, but can never substitute for, the other phases of bond analysis. Therefore, it might be useful to examine and interpret the significance of a few of the major covenants typically found in revenue-bond contracts.

Rate Covenant. This provision consists of a promise to establish and collect rates for the particular service sufficient to pay all operating expenses plus interest and principal on the debt as required. Although the specific promise might be reassuring, its practical significance is doubtful. The original action of legally authorizing the sale of bonds to be paid from certain revenues would seem to imply the duty of charging rates sufficient to produce the required revenues. Moreover, the covenant does not and cannot guarantee adequate revenues to meet debt service. If consumer demand for the service is insufficient to provide the needed amount of revenues, then increasing rates may merely further reduce demand and possibly result in lower total revenues. The experience of certain toll roads may again be cited as cases in point. Therefore, the economic need for the service is a much more crucial factor than the rate covenant, although, of course, it does no harm.

Application of Revenues. A related provision requiring that rates be sufficient to allow for adequate maintenance and depreciation in addition to routine operating expenses would seem to be more significant. If the properties are allowed to deteriorate, then the long-term position of the bondholders may suffer, as the physical plant may finally be unable to produce the service effectively. This process would, of course, take time, and in the meantime full payments on debt service would preclude any action by the bondholders until it was too late. Where serial bond maturities are used, depreciation can be indirectly recognized by the regular retirement of debt out of net revenues. Sinking funds sufficient to retire term debt at maturity can serve the same purpose.

The experience of the Jacksonville, Florida, electric system may be cited as a case indicating the desirability of requiring adequate provisions for maintenance. This system, up until 1943, made no provision for depreciation. All revenues, after direct operating expenses and debt service (including clearly inadequate sinking funds) were transferred to the general operating fund of the city and greatly contributed to the general city operations. The lack of proper maintenance showed up in the early war years by an inability to expand service at that time, and a provision was incorporated into the Charter requiring the payment of 10% of net revenues into a replacement and renewal fund.

The new policy, plus more bond issues, made it possible to restore the electric plant to a very effective operating property as of 1965. The natural temptation of city officials to use all possible "excess" revenues from utility operations for ordinary city expenses (and thus possibly avoid unpopular tax increases) can be allayed by a contractual provision requiring adequate allocations for depreciation, maintenance, and bond sinking funds from available revenues.

Limitations on Additional Securities. Like corporate indentures, revenue-bond contracts usually have some provision restricting the issuance of additional bonds. The purpose is evident: to prevent the issuer from detracting from the credit quality of outstanding bonds by an excessive issue of new bonds with equal claim on the net revenues. In practice, however, it is doubtful if additional revenue bonds could be sold unless the pro-forma protection of all issues was satisfactory. Therefore, although a covenant prohibiting the issuance of prior-claim bonds is highly desirable, detailed restrictions on additional issues are not imperative, although they may discourage some degree of financial imprudence.

From the standpoint of the bondholders, restrictions on additional debt have most merit when they require a certain demonstrated earnings performance as a condition of new issues. For example, in the Flint water-revenue situation, a contractual provision requires that new bonds cannot be issued unless net income before depreciation for the past three years had been at least one and one quarter times the largest annual requirement for both interest and principal on both the new and outstanding bonds combined. As it allowed for no additional revenues on new properties financed by new debt, it seemed adequate to protect the outstanding bonds. In the case of water service a pro-forma coverage of one and one quarter times interest and principal would seem adequate; in other instances when the demand for the service is more variable a somewhat greater pro-forma coverage might be desirable.

Audits and Financial Reports. Municipal units are specifically excluded from any jurisdiction of the Securities and Exchange Commission. Therefore, they are not obliged to furnish detailed financial reports on the results of revenue operations. As it may be assumed that investors in revenue bonds would like to have, at the very least, annual financial reports in order to review the status of the credit, it is desirable to find a formal contractual provision requiring the routine submission of such information to bondholders.

However, where the revenue unit has a well-established practice of supplying the necessary financial data despite silence of the contract on this point, its absence is not regarded as a critical drawback. For example, the bond description in Moody's *Municipal Manual* for 1964 on the Flint Water Revenue bonds made no mention of a provision to furnish financial reports. Although not conclusive evidence of its absence (the descriptions must be condensed in a volume of this size), it is notable that reasonably adequate financial data have been promptly available for many years. So even assuming no contractual requirement in this regard, it is unlikely that Flint will suddenly reverse the precedents established in its reporting practices over the years. Although perhaps not crucial, it would be desirable, however, to have the reliability of the reports increased by outside audits, if they are not now required.

Revenue Bonds: Summary

Despite their sponsorship by governmental units, revenue bonds are only claims against business operations, and their credit quality depends entirely on the size and quality of the net revenues relative to the yearly requirements for debt service on interest and principal. Therefore, the appraisal techniques somewhat resemble corporate-bond analysis. But because most revenue operations are conducted under monopoly conditions, the size factor (indicating strong competitive position in the case of corporates) is less significant.

Because the nature of the services rendered by revenue operations vary widely, there are consequently wide differences in quality. The best revenue situations are typically found in city-operated utility departments, most often represented by water and sewer service but also including a number of electric-power and gas operations as well. In municipal departments providing essential services to residents of the community, the revenues are likely to be as reliable as taxes, and in some instances more so. Where there is no demonstrated economic demand of measurable size, such as for some toll roads and bridges, revenue bonds may be highly speculative. Therefore, a critical qualitative appraisal of the basic economic status of the service rendered is of prime importance in selecting revenue obligations.

The primary statistical techniques used to evaluate these bonds are: (1) the cash flow of earnings plus depreciation related to combined annual interest charges and serial maturities or sinking funds on debt principal, (2) the trend of revenues, and (3) the trend of the operating ratio. The application of these techniques was illustrated by an analysis of the Flint, Michigan, Water Revenue bonds.

Finally, the specific covenants incorporated in the bond contract, although less important than basic credit quality, should provide assurance of an intention to maintain adequate service rates, adequate maintenance, adequate provision for debt retirement from revenues, some recognition of the necessity to exercise prudence on future debt issues, and recognition of the rights of the bondholders to regular financial reports on the operations.

CHAPTER 24

Federal Government Securities
and Yield Curves

Scope of Analysis

The analysis of corporate fixed-income securities is two-dimensional. The first dimension is the determination of the investment quality of the subject corporation to establish the degree of credit risk. The second is the investigation of the contractual terms and yields offered on a given issue to decide whether the terms and yields are attractive. In the special case of United States Government Bonds the first dimension can be entirely eliminated.

Reasons for Assuming Credit Quality. The impeccable credit quality of government securities has sometimes been ascribed to the unlimited taxation power of a sovereign government. In brief, it is held that the government, by means of taxation, can exercise a first lien on all assets and income within its domain. Therefore, it is further argued that its obligations by definition take precedence over any corporate security. In practice, however, obligations of sovereign governments, particularly those payable in foreign currencies, have defaulted when private corporations still had resources which, if confiscated through taxes, might have avoided the defaults. Experience indicates there are practical if not theoretical limits on the ability of a government to exercise this so-called first lien of the taxing power.

However, although the taxation power appears to have practical limits, there is another power of the federal government which can be exercised more readily to avoid any default on its obligations payable in dollars. It is the unlimited power to create new dollars, assuming that under extreme conditions the gold reserve requirements of the Federal Reserve would be waived.

Assume for the moment that the federal government is running a deficit, Congress is unwilling or feels practically unable to increase taxes, and new issues and refundings of government obligations are experiencing real difficulty in finding a market. If these conditions confronted a private borrower, default would appear inevitable. Not so the United States Government. Under these circumstances the Federal Reserve would be in practice induced to underwrite the necessary financing by supplying reserves to the banks through buying substantial quantities of government obligations or perhaps reducing reserve requirements. These additional "free" reserves would then enable the banks to buy the required amounts of government debt. But this process, as elementary courses in money and banking bring out, would result in an increase in bank deposits to the extent of the debt so purchased. And it is pertinent to note that bank deposits are the major form of money in our economy.

In brief, the Treasury can always meet its debt requirements and thereby avoid defaults by manufacturing additional money of one sort or another. In modern states this fact is the essential reason why there is no credit risk as such on government obligations payable in domestic currency, and the so-called unlimited tax power is of lesser practical significance. It can be assumed that the government will fulfill its contract by creating additional money if other means prove inadequate. Although the assumed situation might create or intensify the risk of inflation bearing on portfolio management, there would still be no credit risk attached to government securities.

Significance of Terms. The major reason for directing special attention to the study of government obligations is because the contractual terms vary extensively among the various types of issues. Moreover, these terms often establish a significantly different relationship between investors and the government than is conventionally established between investors and corporations. By and large, the contractual terms are more favorable than those offered by corporations. Therefore, although the technical terms vary in detail from one issue to another, it can be generalized that government bond contracts are preferable to any other type.[1] The only reason to consider corporate or municipal obligations is that the yields may be greater than on governments. The purpose of this chapter, therefore, will be to set forth the major contractual terms of the various government securities and explain their investment significance.

In addition, because government securities are devoid entirely of credit risk, their yields represent the "pure" interest rate or price of money as such. Any differences in yields between various government-bond issues necessarily arise out of the differences in contractual terms and the interpretation of their relative attractiveness at a given time. One of the major terms which is interpreted differently from time to time is "maturity." By studying the yield relationships that prevail between government bonds of various maturities, it is possible to obtain some insight into both the current status of the bond market and expectations for its near-term future. The analysis involves the construction of "yield curves" and explaining the significance of the typical shapes of this curve as they have appeared from time to time. Therefore, the nature and interpretation of yield curves will also be considered.

Government Obligations: Technical Features

Types and Quantities. As of the end of 1964, the total interest-bearing debt of the federal government amounted to about $318 billion, and the debt was available to investors in a wide variety of forms. Table 24-1 shows the major debt classifications according to the types of issues. There are three classifications which are of only academic interest. First, the special and miscellaneous nonmarketable issues are sold only to government trust and pension funds (such as Social Security), and they are not available in the market. Second, the convertible bonds cannot be sold or purchased in the market. Existing holders of these securities must either retain them or convert them into fully marketable five-year 1½ % notes twice a year. All the other issues shown in Table 24-1 may be acquired by individual investors. However, institutional investors, such as banks, may not for the most part purchase savings bonds.

Treasury Bills. Treasury bills may be defined as obligations due within one year whose entire yield come from a discount on the purchase price from par rather than a coupon payment. Also, Treasury bills are

[1] This observation does not apply to convertible or participating senior securities which are considered special types because of their common-stock characteristics.

TABLE 24–1
UNITED STATES GOVERNMENT DEBT: NOVEMBER, 1964
CLASSIFIED BY TYPE OF SECURITY
(in billions of dollars)

Treasury Bills	$56.5
Treasury Notes	58.9
Bonds	
Marketable Treasury bonds	97.0
Convertible bonds	3.1
Savings bonds	49.7
Special Issues	46.7
Miscellaneous nonmarketable issues	2.2
Total outstanding issues	$314.1

Source: Federal Reserve Bulletin, December, 1964, p. 1570.

originally sold to investors through competitive bidding and then are quoted by dealers on a yield-to-maturity basis. For a number of years the Treasury has followed the regular practice of issuing a thirteen-week and a twenty-six-week bill every week[2] In addition, special bill issues with maturities up to one year have also been issued about once a month. As a consequence, bills can usually be obtained to mature in any week for the subsequent six months and monthly thereafter up to about a year.

These obligations are extremely useful to any investor, corporate or otherwise, with the problem of investing seasonal funds. For example, a bank or a manufacturing corporation may have funds flowing in at one time during the year for which there is no immediate business use, but it is expected that the funds will be required in the business in, say, five months. Under these assumed conditions, a Treasury bill maturing at the time of expected need would be a natural investment. During the intervening period the short maturity combined with excellent marketability characteristics makes it possible to sell them at any time at very stable prices. Their primary use, therefore, is to provide an outlet for short-term funds on which a high degree of liquidity is required.

Treasury Certificates and Notes. At the time of original offering, Treasury certificates mature within one year and notes from about one

---

[2] For example, in the week ended January 15, 1965, applications for thirteen-week bills amounted to $2.1 billion of which $1.2 billion were accepted at prices of $99.031 to 99.038 to yield 3.833% to 3.806%. In the secondary market, bills can be acquired through banks or brokers but the yields are usually moderately lower than on the new issues typically by about ten basis points.

up to five years. Both pay interest, usually semi-annually, and the coupon rate is established by the Treasury in the light of prevailing market conditions. Generally they are sold by the Treasury at par or at small discounts, but in the secondary market the price may be either above or below par, depending upon the movements of interest rates. Denominations are in multiples of $1,000 on both.

With the practice established of offering bills of longer maturities than the traditional thirteen-week obligations, it is questionable whether certificates will continue to be used in the future. In fact, in the last half of 1964 there were no outstanding certificates, although the Treasury may find it expedient to use them in the future. It is notable that government-bond dealers have recommended the complete elimination of certificates on the grounds that they "clutter up" the maturity schedules and are not really adaptable to the needs of the short-term money market.[3] Their investment functions are almost identical with bills except that the maturities are not regularly spaced.

Notes, on the other hand, provide an intermediate maturity to investors, although the outstanding issues, as they approach maturity, have roughly the same liquidity characteristics as bills and certificates. But obviously those issues with current maturities of three to five years hence may be subject to considerably wider price fluctuations in response to changing levels of interest rates. For example, the 3⅝% notes of February 15, 1967, fluctuated from about 100-6 to 98-20 during the years 1963–64.[4] The moderate price fluctuations suggest that Treasury notes do not offer the necessary degree of price stability for the investment of seasonal funds, but at the same time their prices tend to be more stable than those of long-term bonds. Some investors, particularly banks, often establish a policy of having a staggered maturity schedule running from perhaps one year to fifteen years. Treasury notes may provide the majority of maturities available within one to five years.

Notes are not redeemable by the government prior to maturity. Therefore, there is no redemption risk on these issues. Moreover, in recent years the Treasury has regularly conducted "advance refunding" operations wherein a year or so before maturity the holder may exchange a note for another intermediate or long-term obligation on which the yield is slightly above prevailing market yields. With this option, the investor can easily "roll over" his holdings into new issues as portfolio objectives suggest might be desirable at the time.

[3] Aubrey G. Lanston & Co., "Treasury Debt Management and Debt Lengthening," Part 2 of letter dated July 28, 1958, p. 6.

[4] Prices of government obligations change in units of 1/32 rather than of ⅛ as is true of stocks. Thus 98-20 represents $98 plus twenty thirty-seconds of $1.

Treasury Bonds. These are issued for an original term of more than five years, and the outstanding regular series are available in a wide variety of coupon rates and maturity dates. As of 1965, for example, the coupon rates varied between 2½ % and 4%. It was possible to find maturities for most of the years between 1968 and 1974; after the latter date about three to five year gaps existed between maturities. Most of these bonds are available in denominations as low as $500, and a few have $50 or $100 units.

For the most part, Treasury bonds are similar to municipal or corporate obligations, but a few features deserve special comment. First, most of them are not callable although some have an optional call date. This means that the Treasury can redeem such bonds at par about three to five years prior to final maturity on any interest payment date (semi-annually). About four months advance notice, however, must be given on the redemption. On these bonds, the first call date is always expressed in the bond description. For example, one outstanding bond was described as the 2½ of 9/15/67–72, which means the obligation was first callable by the Treasury in 1967 and on any interest payment date thereafter with final maturity September 15, 1972.

Between about 1935 and 1952 the Treasury always redeemed bonds on the first call date, but since 1952 redemptions have only been made if the issues could be refunded at lower interest costs than the coupon rate. The existence of optional call dates creates some confusion in computing yields to maturity, as it is not known whether an issue will actually run only to first call date or to final maturity. Customary practice is to consider that bonds will run only to first call date if they are selling above par and to final maturity if they are below par. Therefore, if a bond is purchased or sells in the market at a premium above par, the effective maturity is regarded as first call date for yield determination, whereas final maturity is used if the bond is purchased or sells at a discount.

The reasoning is that a price above par suggests that the bond can be refunded at a lesser interest cost than the coupon rate, whereas a price below par indicates refunding would not be expedient. But as interest rates can and do change, a bond which is now at a premium can be selling at a discount at the first call date and vice versa, so that the above procedure of computing yields on bonds with optional call dates is subject to some uncertainties.[5] It does result, however, in the most conserva-

---

[5] If the yield on a bond purchased at a premium is computed to first call date and then it is not called at that time, the annual yield for the preceding years was understated, as the premium has been in effect written off more rapidly than necessary.

tive determination of the yield. Premiums are fully amortized by the first call date, so that if in fact redemption does take place at that time, a capital loss is not incurred. If the bond is not redeemed, then the coupon rate becomes the recognized subsequent yield until final maturity. Similarly, the accrual of the discount on a bond purchased below par means the bond is written up to par value only over its entire remaining life. If final maturity is used as the term, then the investor's "book value" will increase at a less rapid rate and recognized annual income will be less.

Another special feature of Treasury bonds worthy of brief mention is their tax status. First, the income from all government obligations is exempt from all state and municipal taxes. Second, most Treasury bond issues, but not other types of federal obligations, are acceptable at par in the payment of the Federal Estate Tax. When interest rates are high and these bonds sell at large discounts, they may have special investment attractiveness for accounts which may be subject to the Estate Tax in the reasonably near future. The bonds, however, must be owned by the decedent at date of death in order to be used in this manner. But all interest payments on Treasury obligations issued since 1941 are subject to the federal income tax.

Federal Agency Obligations.   Through the years Congress has created a number of government agencies and corporations to implement desired objectives of national economic policy. When pertinent to their purposes, such government instrumentalities are given the power to issue notes and bonds in limited amounts as set forth in the enabling statutes. These become the direct obligation of the agency concerned, and legally the United States Government is not obliged to pay interest or principal in case the agency's resources prove to be inadequate. However, as they are sponsored by and operate under the direct control of the federal government, the consensus of opinion is that Congress would, without doubt, appropriate sufficient funds to meet the obligations of any agency which experienced operating difficulties for one reason or another.

A complete review in detail of the various agencies would be highly tedious. Therefore, The Federal National Mortgage Association, better known as "Fannie Mae," can be cited as a typical example. This association is a federal corporation, headed by an appointee of the President, and has the purpose of promoting a secondary market in government insured residential mortgages. To carry out its purpose, it is authorized to buy, sell, and maintain inventories of mortgages, and it is further authorized to issue bonds up to specified limits in order to finance

TABLE 24–2
YIELD COMPARISONS: F.N.M.A. BONDS AND GOVERNMENT BONDS
(prices as of January, 1965)

Federal National Mortgage Association

Issue	Price	Yield to Maturity
3⅝%, due 3/11/68	98–20	4.10%
4⅜%, due 4/10/69	101	4.11
4½%, due 9/10/71	101–24	4.20

U.S. Government Bonds

Issue	Price	Yield to Maturity
3⅞%, due 5/15/68	99–21	3.99%
4%, due 2/15/69	100–2	3.98
4%, due 8/15/71	99–16	4.09

its mortgage acquisitions. About $2 billion of such obligations have typically been outstanding. Table 24-2 shows the prices and yields of several "Fannie Mae" issues as of January, 1965, and for purposes of comparison the prices and yields of similar maturity government obligations are also shown. It can be noted that the "Fannie Mae" bonds offered slightly higher yields than comparable governments probably because it is assumed that there is some slight credit risk. As such yield differentials are typical and as the risk appears minimal, federal agency obligations may be considered attractive substitutes for treasury issues. It may be mentioned that, like governments, they are not callable, which is a decided advantage in comparison with most corporate issues.

Savings Bonds: General Features. These obligations are primarily designed for the modest-sized individual investor rather than for large accounts. As of 1965, only two types, Series E and H, were available for purchase, and in both cases acquisitions were limited to $10,000 maturity value per year. But where several individuals, such as members of a family, have a joint-investment operation, these bonds could be purchased up to $10,000 times the number of individuals concerned. The primary difference between the two types is that returns on Series E take the form of an increase in redemption value, whereas Series H pays interest semi-annually by check to the holder.

As pointed out elsewhere, the great contractual advantage of savings bonds is the call feature in reverse—they are redeemable at the option of the investor rather than at the option of the issuer. In this sense they closely resemble a bank savings account, although of course their form is a security rather than a book account. As a consequence,

TABLE 24-3
SERIES E SAVINGS BONDS
REDEMPTION AND YIELD SCHEDULE*

Time of Holding	Redemption Value	Effective Yield To Date of Redemption	Effective Yield On Redemption Value to Maturity
Issue Price	$75	—	—
1st ½ year	75	0	3.75%
½ to 1 year	75.64	1.71	3.89
1 to 1½ years	76.76	2.33	3.96
1½ to 2 years	78.04	2.67	4.01
2 to 2½ years	79.60	3.00	4.01
2½ to 3 years	81.12	3.16	4.03
3 to 3½ years	82.64	3.26	4.05
3½ to 4 years	84.28	3.36	4.06
4 to 4½ years	86.00	3.45	4.06
4½ to 5 years	87.80	3.53	4.04
5 to 5½ years	89.60	3.59	4.03
5½ to 6 years	91.44	3.64	4.02
6 to 6½ years	93.28	3.67	4.01
6½ to 7 years	95.16	3.70	4.01
7 to 7½ years	97.08	3.72	3.99
7½ years to 7 years, 9 mos.	99.00	3.74	4.06
7 years, 9 mos.	100.00	3.75	—

* Schedule changed in 1966 to offer 4.15% to maturity.

they offer perfect liquidity to the holder and are, therefore, quite useful for the investment of "contingency funds" which may have to be used for other purposes at indeterminate times in the future.

Yield and Redemption Terms: Series E. Series E bonds have been by far the most popular type with investors. Typically there have been $35–40 billion of E bonds outstanding, as compared to $6–8 billion of Series H.[6] Series E bonds were first offered in 1941. As interest rates have generally increased since then, the government has been obliged to increase the yields available on these bonds several times; the most recent change was effected in September of 1959. Table 24-3 shows the yield terms of Series E bonds in effect since that date. These terms are confusing to some investors because although they offer a compounded yield to maturity of 3.75%, to obtain the full yield the bonds must be held for the full period of seven years and nine months. For example, reference to Table 24-3 shows that if the investor redeemed after holding for two years, the yield would only be 2.67% for the pe-

[6] Moody's *Municipal and Government Manual*, 1964 edition, pp. 5–6.

TABLE 24-4
SERIES H SAVINGS BONDS
SUMMARY OF YIELD TERMS: AS OF 1965

Term of Holding	Interest Paid*	Effective Yield To Date	Effective Yield From Date to Maturity
½ year	$ 8.00	1.60%	3.88
1 year	14.50	2.25	3.95
1 and ½ year	16.00	2.56	4.00
2 thru 10 years	40.00†	2.91 to 3.75	4.00

* Per $1,000 bond during each period.
† Semiannual payments of $20.00 made per $1,000 bond.

riod. But after holding a Series E bond two years the investor would have to obtain about 4.01% on the reinvestment of the redemption proceeds in order to equal the return offered for the five years and nine months of its remaining life. Therefore, in deciding whether it would be advisable to redeem existing holdings and reinvest, the pertinent reference in Table 24-3 is the yield on the redemption value to maturity.

On Series E bonds the government has allowed investors to retain the bonds beyond maturity and obtain a return at the rate of about 3½% compounded semiannually. However, under the conditions prevailing in 1965, the advisability of the purchase or retention of these bonds beyond maturity may be questioned. Commercial bank savings accounts and certificates of deposit offered 4 to 4¼% yields with the same option of immediate redemption. Unless the rates offered by banks decline in future years, or unless the yields on savings bonds are scaled upward to 4% or more, they would appear to be unattractive in comparison with alternatives for contingency funds on which a high degree of liquidity is desirable. (In 1966 yields were increased.)

Yield and Redemption Terms: Series H. These bonds are sold at par and are redeemable at par six months after the issue date.[7] The interest on these obligations is paid by check semiannually, and they offer a 3.75% yield if held for the entire term of ten years. Like the Series E bonds, however, the terms are arranged to offer a lower yield in the earlier years and a greater return in the final years. Table 24-4 shows a summary of the terms in this respect; to illustrate, after one

[7] Series H bonds can only be redeemed on the first day of a calendar month after 30-days notice. Effective notice may be given by presenting the bond for redemption at any bank. Series E bonds, on the other hand, are redeemed immediately on presentation for payment.

year the bonds offer a return of 3.95% for the remaining nine years but only 2.25% if the bonds are redeemed one year after purchase. However, the entire structure of yields on these obligations seemed unattractive as of 1965.

One further technical point which might be noted in connection with savings bonds is that they are not transferable, and they are payable only to the registered owner or the legal heirs thereof. This means they cannot be used as collateral on loans or to secure the performance of any obligation. Regular Treasury bonds, on the other hand, may be hypothecated under a loan agreement which may be of some advantage to certain investors.

Government Securities: Rights Value. In view of the large size of the debt and the chronic inability of the federal government to establish a budgetary surplus, most marketable government securities are refunded at maturity by offering exchange rights to the holders of the maturing obligations. Such rights mean the maturing securities can be exchanged at par for the new issues, and often the new issues are not originally available to other investors. To encourage investors to exchange rather than demand cash payment as is their option, the Treasury usually offers a higher yield on the new obligations than prevails in the market on securities of a similar maturity. Under these conditions it is probable that the new issue will sell at an immediate premium above par. As a consequence there is a *rights value* attached to the maturing security in the amount of the expected premium. Because of this value some issues approaching maturity have in the past sold on negative yield basis in the market, although the yield becomes positive if proper allowance is made for the value of the rights.

To illustrate, suppose that a 3% bond is near maturity and the Treasury announces that it can be exchanged for a 4% bond with a ten-year maturity. Assume that ten-year obligations are currently selling on a 3.90% basis. The yield conditions suggest that the new issue should sell for about $100.82 in the market.[8] The maturing bonds, therefore, a few days before maturity should sell for almost $100.82 (about $100^{26}\!/_{32}$), or literally show a negative yield to maturity. The expected premium on the new issue for which it can be exchanged is of course responsible for this condition.

The rights value exists only when holders of maturing securities have

[8] Because the new bonds result in a greater availability of obligations of that maturity, the new market yield may be slightly higher than that prevailing on outstanding bonds. The premium in case of such an expectation would be somewhat less than shown above.

the sole rights to obtain to new obligation. If cash subscriptions are also accepted, then there should be little if any value to the exchange rights. Also, it should be mentioned that the value of such rights can change rather dramatically if new conditions confront the bond market and change the level of interest rates. By and large, therefore, transactions in securities with anticipated rights values should be confined to highly sophisticated investors.

Government Securities: Yield Curves

Mechanics of Yield Curves. A yield curve may be defined as the relation that exists at a given time between the yields on obligations similar in all respects except as to maturity. In other words, it expresses graphically in a continuous way the prevailing yields on similar bonds of different maturities. Although in theory a yield curve can be constructed for corporate obligations, differences in credit quality and contractual terms tend to obscure the single factor of maturity as an influence on the relative yields. As the purpose of the yield curve is to isolate and interpret the effect of this factor, the homogeneity of government obligations makes them particularly suitable for this purpose.

It should be mentioned, however, that the rules for computing income taxes distort the implications of a yield curve based on before-tax yields when some of the issues are selling at sizable discounts. Then bonds of identical pretax yield to maturity may offer different after-tax yields to various investors. The principal factor causing the discrepancy is the differential tax treatment of that portion of the yield which takes the form of accrued discount. Under existing tax laws, the discount portion of the yield is taxed at maturity at the capital-gains tax rate, whereas coupon income is subject to the ordinary income-tax rates. For example, one bond with a 3% coupon might sell at 90 and show the same yield to maturity as another issue with a 4% coupon selling at par. However, for investors in a high tax bracket, the first bond will give the greatest after-tax yield because the discount portion of the yield (90 to 100 over its life) is taxed at a lower rate. Therefore, each investor in effect must construct his own after-tax yield curve.

But as it is impossible to assume any given tax rate for investors, Figure 24-1 shows the construction of two pretax yield curves derived from the market yields on government obligations at given times about three years apart. Table 24-5 shows the prices and yields of some of the issues included in the graphic presentation.

In January of 1961 there was considerable unemployment and a

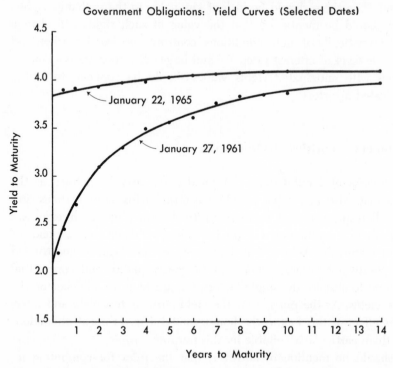

FIGURE 24-1

Government Obligations: Yield Curves (Selected Dates)

general concern with the failure of the economy to show an adequate rate of growth. Under these conditions, the Federal Reserve was following a policy of "easy" money, as evidenced by about $700 million of net "free" reserves in the banking system.

In the first part of 1965, however, the economy was enjoying highly prosperous conditions. But in the absence of strong inflationary pressures and because of a desire to maintain the level of economic activity, the Federal Reserve was permitting a nominal amount of "free" reserves to exist in the banking system despite strong demands for borrowed funds in most markets. But there was also official concern with international balance-of-payment problems, with the result that yields, particularly in the short-term area, were at above-average levels, but not at extremely high levels.

Yield Curves: Interpretation. The interpretation of the different shapes of the yield curves can be suggested in the light of the above information on the state of the economy at each point in time. The upward-sloping curve of early 1961 indicated a strong preference for short-term maturities. As these provide much greater price stability and are,

TABLE 24–5
Yield-Curve Data: Selected Issues

	Appropriate Term	Price	Yield
January 27, 1961			
Bills of 4/27/61	3 mos.	–	2.23%
3⅛s of 8/1/61	6 mos.	100–11	2.43
3s of 2/15/64	3 years	99–1	3.34
3⅛s of 5/15/68	7 years	100–21	3.77
4¼s of 5/15/75–85	14 years*	103–10	3.95
January 22, 1965			
Bills of 4/22/65	3 mos.	–	3.80%
Bills of 7/22/65	6 mos.	–	3.91
3⅛ of 5/15/68	3 years	99–21	3.99
4s of 2/15/72	7 years	99–8	4.12
4s of 2/15/80	15 years	98–10	4.16

* About fourteen years to first call date in 1975 as of 1961; yield and term computed to that date because of price above par.

Source: Aubrey G. Lanston & Co.

therefore, more suitable for investors requiring liquidity (such as banks), it is arguable that these obligations normally should carry lower rates.

But for two reasons the yields on short maturities are likely to be particularly low in relation to long maturities when an active easy money policy is in effect. First, a large supply of free reserves enables the banks to be aggressive buyers in the market. As these institutions generally prefer to hold the bulk of their investment portfolios in five-year maturities or less, their demand tends to hold rates down in this area. Second, when rates are at low levels, the probabilities of a future increase logically become greater than of further significant declines. And whenever expectations lean toward higher interest rates in the future, long-term bonds are at a disadvantage in the market, because their prices fall much more drastically when and if interest rates do in fact move upward.

In 1965, however, the flat shape of the yield curve suggested that expectations favored a possible decline in rates within a year or so. Long maturities are more attractive under these conditions because they enable investors to obtain the indicated yields for a longer future period. Holding short maturities of course would require reinvestment of the maturing obligations within a year or so. In addition, if rates did subsequently decline, the prices of long-term bonds would advance much more than short-term issues, which also results in a preference for long maturities when expectations favor a later decline in rates.[9]

There have been instances when a down-sloping yield curve has prevailed in the market. This condition suggests that there are strong expectations of a future decline in interest rates, because it evidences a heavy preference for long-term securities. These are desirable under conditions of an anticipated decline in interest rates for the reasons indicated. However, other explanations might be advanced for a market condition marked by higher yields on short maturities than on long maturities. First, a very high demand for loans coupled with a restrictive monetary policy may force significant liquidation of bank holdings of short-term obligations, which will act as a depressant on their prices. Second, certain institutional investors, such as pension funds and insurance companies, naturally gravitate toward long-term securities. If there is a large supply of such funds seeking investment and the supply of bonds in this area is moderate, then long-term bonds may sell for lower yields than the more liquid short-term obligations.[10]

Yield-Curve Analysis: Investment Significance. By and large only large investors, particularly institutional investors, are directly concerned with yield curves in reaching investment decisions. However, even moderate-sized individual investors might find an understanding of yield curves of some help in conducting their investment operations. In summary, the shape of the curve at a given time, and its changing pattern through time might influence investment decisions in the following ways.

First, the graphic picture enables the investor to obtain the maximum yield commensurate with liquidity requirements. For example, the curve on January 27, 1961 (Figure 24-1) showed that yields could have been increased substantially by investing in one- or two-year maturities rather

[9] A special factor also appeared to be operating in 1965 to produce somewhat higher yields in the short-term sector than might otherwise have prevailed. It was the conscious attempt of the Treasury and Federal Reserve to keep short-term rates attractive in relation to yields abroad. Then foreign holders of funds required for liquidity purposes would keep them invested here rather than transferring the dollars into foreign currencies and thereby aggravating the existing balance of payments problems facing the United States at that time. To implement the policy both the Treasury and the Federal Reserve took action to increase the supply of bills available to investors; the Treasury by increasing the size of new issues, the Fed by reducing its portfolio of bills.

[10] The fact that some large institutional investors (banks) are oriented toward short-term obligations and others toward long-term bonds because of the inherent nature of their investment requirements is sometimes described as the "compartmentation" of the market. The implication is that different types of investors operate largely in independent sectors of the market.

than in three-month obligations. Therefore, if liquidity requirements permitted and significant immediate increases in rates were not considered probable, funds might have been diverted in larger than usual amounts to these maturities. Second, the shape and position of the yield curve in relation to the pattern of the past may suggest the degree of market risk inherent in current commitments. In 1961, the shape of the curve suggested the probability of increased future rates which might have restrained aggressive operations in the long-term sector of the market.

Finally, the pattern of yield curves through time clearly shows a greater fluctuation in yields on short-term securities than on long-term securities. Therefore, investors concentrating in short-term bonds can expect large variations in the rate of income from their portfolios, as they must reinvest constantly at widely different levels of interest rates. This fact suggests an interesting paradox. A continuous portfolio of short-term securities offers the probability of more stable market prices but less stable income through time than is true of long-term obligations.[11] As a consequence, investors whose basic needs are stability of income rather than stability in market value of the principal may find long-term securities more appropriate despite their greater fluctuations in price.

[11] For an excellent discussion of this point and a more detailed treatment of the interpretation of yield curves and their different shapes through time, see Sauvain, "Changing Interest Rates and the Investment Portfolio," *Journal of Finance*, May, 1959, pp. 230–244.

PART VII

PORTFOLIO MANAGEMENT FOR THE INDIVIDUAL INVESTOR

CHAPTER 25

Portfolio Objectives and Investment Risks

Introduction

In a sense an individual might consider that his "investments" consist of all personal assets which are not destined for immediate consumption. Thus purchase of a house or an automobile would be a form of investment, and plans in these regards would be incorporated into an investment program. This view, however, results in a concept of the investment management problem which is exceedingly broad—the determination of a logical pattern of expenditures for all financial resources not devoted to immediate consumption needs. It would lead into many areas not even remotely related to securities and consequently would increase the scope of investment management well beyond its accepted role in the framework of finance.

Therefore, a distinction might be made between a *financial plan* and the more restricted concept of the *investment program*. The financial plan would take account of all the family's economic needs and objectives as a going concern. Of course, few family units are highly scientific in the matter of financial planning. They do not establish formal projections of income and expenditures; instead, they are inclined to decide individual financial needs as they arise, and out of a succession of somewhat haphazard decisions a financial plan emerges. In this way most people decide upon the amount of funds to be kept in a checking account, the amount of liquid contingency reserves needed in the form of savings accounts, the needs for insurance protection, and the desirability of owning a home rather than renting. All these matters are highly important and deserve careful attention; in fact, they generally have precedence over the construction of a security portfolio, but they are regarded as outside the scope of the investment program per se.

An *investment*, in the restricted sense of the word, is a financial commitment with the objective of obtaining a monetary return. Although it is true that some of the previously mentioned considerations in the financial plan have income elements, they tend to be ancillary to other needs. The investment program, therefore, can be defined as the management of that portion of an individual's resources on which the primary objective is to obtain some monetary yield either in the form of current income or appreciation, or both. Although financial investments can conceivably take a variety of forms, for most individuals they are likely to be in securities of one kind or another. Therefore, it will be assumed that the investment program will largely be concerned with the development of a consistent plan to guide the construction of a security portfolio.

The general objective of any investment program is to obtain the maximum benefits from the available funds and yet provide adequate protection against the various types of risk that are inherent in our economic and political system. But a general statement of the investment-management objective is not very helpful in working out a particular program, because what is "adequate" protection against risk will depend largely upon the unique economic and family circumstances of the individual. Therefore, it is often said that a realistic program must be "tailor-made" to fit the person. However, because it is impossible to consider in detail all the possible individual variations, the principal concern will be to develop the general principles and techniques which are relevant to the determination of an investment program, and then, to make the discussion more specific, these principles and techniques will be applied to several illustrative cases.

The following steps would appear requisite to the formulation of a specific investment program. First, it is necessary to evaluate the personal needs and obligations which determine the specific investment objectives. Second, it is then desirable to appraise the relative importance of the several types of risk, or put another way, the problems and obstacles that confront the investor in achieving the positive objectives. Third, it might be useful to define and classify the various broad groups of securities according to the risks they assume and the opportunities they afford. This is their "functional classification." Fourth, it then should be possible to plan the specific portfolio strategy in a rational manner. As a corollary of the last step, it is important to understand the significance of diversification to the achievement of objectives and to the control of risk.

Step 1—Analysis of Specific Portfolio Objectives

In the course of a casual conversation investment analysts are sometimes asked to recommend a "good stock" for "investment purposes."[1] The request is analogous to asking a doctor to recommend a "good medicine" without any further qualification. Just as the choice of medicine should depend upon a thorough diagnosis of the physical symptoms, the choice of securities should be preceded by a careful diagnosis of the personal circumstances of the individual. Only when this step has been completed can individual securities be suggested that would be appropriate in the given instance.

For purposes of convenience in analysis, it is useful to distinguish between what might be called the "family" factors and the "economic" factors. The former are concerned with the status of the family group in a physical way, while the latter are concerned with the financial assets and liabilities of the group. The more important considerations under each of these headings may be listed as follows:

1. Personal family situation.
   a. Ages of individuals that are to be primary beneficiaries of the portfolio.
   b. Health of these individuals.
   c. Number of dependents and their ages and health.
   d. Possibilities of additional dependents.
2. Personal financial situation.
   a. Approximate size of funds available for portfolio.
   b. Nature of occupation (if any).
   c. Amount of income expected from occupation—tax bracket.
   d. Income from other sources—both present and prospective.
   e. Amount of debt and its maturity schedule.

[1] It usually turns out that what the person has in mind is a stock that "will double in price or so in the next few months." Why this "pot of gold" idea is so often associated with commitments to securities is difficult to explain, except that everyone has heard of a stock that has performed in this manner.

f. Potential benefits under estates, trusts, or retirement plans.
g. Extent of training and experience in financial and investment matters.

The analysis of personal data provides the basis for establishing the specific objectives of the portfolio. Some have suggested that investors should have one primary objective, such as growth or assured income. While this may be true in certain cases, most individuals are likely to have a mix of such objectives, although perhaps of different priority. It is, therefore, usually desirable to plan the portfolio in appropriate segments classified according to the various objectives that have emerged from an analysis of the personal information.

Because the several possible objectives are necessarily related to the several types of risks which are an integral part of economic society, it will be necessary to anticipate partially the subsequent specific discussion of these risk factors. However, the risk factors are essentially obstacles to be taken into account after the main purposes have been resolved. The following objectives, although perhaps not inclusive of all possibilities, are likely to be present in some degree or other in the majority of instances.

Recoverability of Principal. When considerable volatility of occupation income is indicated and when there are several dependents, one of the primary functions of the investment portfolio may be to provide a reservoir of readily available funds. During periods of reduced income a major portion of the funds might well be needed to help meet ordinary family living expenses. The need might be intensified by the existence of contractual debt of a substantial amount. In these cases it is hoped that the unfavorable exigencies will never arise but ordinary prudence would dictate considering them when constructing the portfolio.

Recoverability also becomes an important factor when certain large and unusual expenditures are in sight for the future. For example, outlays for college educations might be on the horizon, or for a house. Another potential expenditure might be the need to meet large estate and inheritance taxes.

Finally, when the size of the investment fund is limited and the persons concerned are elderly or in ill health, partial recoverability is often a necessary feature. As a general rule, it is more prudent to supplement limited income from a small account with partial consumption of principal rather than reach for income by assuming considerable risk.

Under these circumstances it may not be necessary to keep the entire fund in a highly recoverable form, but only that portion which over a reasonable period of years might be needed to supplement the income from the portfolio or other sources.

Growth of Principal. The growth objective is pertinent when the income needs from a portfolio will be significantly greater a decade or more hence than at the present time. Perhaps the most typical example would be a well-established person in a reasonably secure occupation between the ages of 40 and 60. Although such a person is often covered by a pension plan, his income from noninvestment sources usually decreases considerably at the time of retirement. Moreover, the rate of taxation of current income can be assumed to be high. Therefore, it would be most desirable for the portfolio to produce capital gains rather than generate dividend or interest income. Near or at retirement the primary function of the portfolio might change, and then there might be a major shift in its composition.

For younger individuals the situation may not be so clear-cut. If these persons are fortunate enough to have any funds available for investment purposes, perhaps from estates or gifts, then it would seem entirely logical to desire some current income from their investments to supplement a salary which can be expected to increase as they become better established in their occupation. The dependency status might also influence the emphasis in these cases. If there are no dependents, of perhaps only a wife, then a decision to subordinate current income to growth possibilities might appear desirable. On the other hand, if there are young children, then an adequate living standard from a modest salary may be difficult and additional current income could be quite desirable. At a later time when and if increased income from the occupation materializes, there could well be a gradual shift to growth as the major purposes of the portfolio.

Current Income. The ultimate purpose of most investment portfolios is to derive a reasonable income return from the fund. For retired individuals dependent upon the portfolio for part or all of the living expenses, it is clearly the major objective. The widow, confronted with the problem of investing insurance proceeds and other resources from an estate, is a typical case wherein current income is paramount. The personal circumstances in most instances indicate modest income from other sources and usually advanced age. But in any family situation wherein immediate consumption expenditures are pressing relative to the income generated from other sources, current income is one of the logical objectives of the investment account.

Stability is ordinarily considered a desirable adjunct of an income objective. However, "stability of income" is in itself an ambiguous concept. It can mean stability in terms of dollars or in terms of purchasing power. Most investors probably should be interested in a reasonably stable real income, because their usual purpose is to obtain a constant flow of goods and services required in ordinary living. But, although theoretically desirable, it is difficult to attain in practice, and some have chosen to interpret stability entirely in terms of dollars which is easily attainable. This position seems basically unsound, because it assumes away the inflation risk. Unfortunately, it appears more conservative in that it does not involve fluctuations in market values and dollar income as is likely to prevail under the real-income approach. In recent years, however, there has been some progress in this connection. Thirty years ago an investor desirous of current income probably would have been advised to emphasize fixed-income securities and dollar returns almost entirely. Today most experienced investors recognize the need for including in such a portfolio some securities which promise larger returns under inflationary conditions even though they are likely to yield decreased income and suffer market losses under deflationary circumstances.

When approaching a portfolio aimed at producing current income, considerable care must be exercised. One pitfall in the planning is to estimate first the amount of income considered desirable and then attempt to obtain securities on which the yield is sufficient to provide the predetermined requirement. Such an approach could lead to the assumption of a very high degree of risk which may be entirely unwarranted. For example, assume that it was decided $5,000 annual income was required and then, because the amount of available principal was only $50,000, securities were selected which would provide an average yield of 10% on cost. Unless both the bond and stock markets were at unusually depressed levels, the net result would necessarily be a portfolio filled with low-quality securities whose immediate yield was high because their prospects were unfavorable for the future. Ultimately, of course, both the amount of income and the value of principal could significantly deteriorate under these conditions. It would be considerably more prudent to recognize the need for limiting risk exposure and the inherent limitations on the amount of income that can be safely obtained from a given investment fund.

On the other side, it is certainly desirable to maximize the returns from a portfolio within the limits of tolerable risk. For example, just because an investor may "need" only $4,500 income from a $150,000 portfolio is no excuse to settle for a 3% return in U.S. Governments, if substantially larger returns can be achieved at only moderate increases in the risk exposure.

Preservation of Purchasing Power. The Social Security Law, passed by Congress in 1936, set in motion a trend toward universal participation in retirement plans throughout industry. To illustrate, it is only necessary to point to the growth in pension funds during the past fifteen years or so. For the most part the benefits derived by participants are in terms of a fixed number of dollars. Therefore, a growing number of individuals have as part of their financial resources a sort of built-in fixed-income security portfolio. Although the income is not generally available until retirement, it means that the emphasis of many investment portfolios can and should be changed to meet the new conditions.

Primarily these conditions suggest that any funds available for discretionary investment in securities might be increasingly designed to protect against the possibility of inflation. In some instances where the retirement benefits are likely to be a considerable amount—say, $5,000 per annum or more—the investment program of a person near retirement age might emphasize this objective almost entirely. It should be made clear that there are no easy means of attaining protection against potential inflation. As shown later, those securities which might be most suitable for the purpose are extremely volatile and most difficult to evaluate intelligently. Nevertheless, assuming a reasonable degree of skill on the part of the investor or his advisers, it is legitimate to establish the maintenance of purchasing power as a major objective, even though an attempt to achieve it in practice may well require assumption of other risks which it would be desirable to avoid.

A combination of certain other personal circumstances might also lead to emphasis on the purchasing-power objective in an investment account. Income from the occupation could be highly secure in the sense that it would continue under adverse business conditions. However, in many secure occupations salary increases often lag well behind any advance in the price level. School teachers and career governmental employees are perhaps good examples. To these individuals prospects of volatile market prices and income on their securities should not be serious problems, except perhaps from an emotional standpoint. On the other hand, they might find it increasingly difficult to maintain an adequate standard of living from their relatively stable occupation incomes under inflationary conditions. Therefore, it would seem quite reasonable for these individuals to emphasize purchasing-power protection in their investment portfolio.

It should be emphasized again that the several objectives are not mutually exclusive. All of them conceivably could be considered appropriate to some extent in a given account. In short, the analysis of the personal factors really determines the relative emphasis that might be placed on recoverability, growth, current income, or purchasing power. It then follows that specific securities should be selected for the portfolio only with the full recognition of the purpose that each is supposed to accomplish.

Step 2—Survey of Investment Opportunities and Risks

In the several chapters on the analysis and selection of fixed-income securities and common stocks, emphasis was on the appraisal of the potential opportunities and risks associated with a given company—its growth potential, management, financial position, competitive situation, and so forth. But the security-analysis process could not completely ignore an evaluation of the broader economic factors which are pertinent to a company's desirability for investment purposes. For example, the dynamic behavioral characteristics of the economy as a whole as to long-term growth features, cyclical fluctuations, and inflation trends were considered in relation to their impact on alternative investment strategies and on particular companies. However, these factors were not considered in relation to the formulation and implementation of an investment program. Therefore, it would seem desirable to review the sources of the major long-term investment opportunities and risks with reference to specific portfolio objectives and to various types of securities.

Long-Term Industry Trends. One of the inherent elements of economic progress is the development of new products and new means of producing established goods and services. Dynamic economies are marked by rapid growth in sales and profits of some industries and concurrent declines in others. When products are rendered obsolete by technological developments, a company must adjust to the situation or perish, and in some cases adjustment is difficult if not impossible. The misfortunes of the street railway and transit companies provide an extreme example; the anthracite coal-mining industry may be cited as another instance in which investors have suffered material erosion in the value of their commitments.

The first implication of the dynamic growth process is that no corporate security of any type can be regarded as a "strong-box" security, one that can be put away for decades with the assurance that its value will always remain inviolate. Reappraisal of industry developments must be made periodically, and the decisions consequent to such reappraisals are often not an easy matter. They are often based largely on qualitative information and the conclusions involve a considerable amount of conjecture. Ability to adapt productive facilities, relative costs, and potential changes in consumer preferences are all important elements.

Fortunately, there is another side of the coin associated with a dynamic economy. It also signifies that certain industries and companies may have prospects for remarkable increases in sales and profits over a decade or so. Although in some cases the prospects may be fully reflected in the price of a common stock, and therefore the long-term appreciation in market price may not match the growth in profits, the fact that there are such companies is essentially an opportunity for investors. Where growth is the primary portfolio objective, common stocks in companies promising above-average long-term increases in per share earnings remain the traditional means of implementing the objective.

Moreover, economic history is reasonably reassuring to the investor owning common stocks in a cross-section of American industries. The secular growth of the economy as a whole and its implications to investment strategies in common stocks were considered in Chapter 5. Although there is no absolute assurance that the future rate of growth will equal that of the past, there is at least a strong presumption in favor of continued progress. However, economic growth may not be at a steady rate as exemplified by the flat earnings trend of the 1955–61 period.

The nature of the dynamic long-term changes in the economy has several implications for investment management. The caution against strong-box securities has already been mentioned. Second, it means that many investors should seek to diversify among several industries. Paradoxically, however, it also means that enterprising investors seeking growth might be advised to concentrate in a few dynamic industries. Third, it means there is a legitimate argument for the inclusion of some growth stocks even in portfolios where growth is not a major objective. The purpose is to offset possible secular declines in the other sections of the account. Finally, the average investor should probably avoid declining industries, regardless of apparent bargains.

Cyclical Fluctuations in Business Activity. The study of business cycles has been one of the principal preoccupations of economists and financial analysts. Innumerable volumes have been written on business fluctuations, and entire careers have been spent studying their various characteristics and developing theories of their causation. It is manifestly impossible to summarize in a brief space the many important aspects of cyclical variations. But, at risk of some oversimplification, a few generalities on the implications of cyclical fluctuations to investment-management decisions might be suggested.

First, the prices, earnings, and dividends of many common stocks have varied widely as business conditions have moved up or down. But it is also true that significant downward movements in common-stock prices, such as in 1962, have occurred without any major change in the level of business activity. Second, business fluctuations have had a few common characteristics, such as wider movements in the heavy-goods industries, but have been remarkably dissimilar in duration and intensity. Moreover, there has been no regularity of their timing as might be implied from the word *cycle*. Third, there is a wide variety of opinion as to the major causes of business fluctuations. Fourth, the economic data at any given time are likely to be contradictory, and forecasts of changes in the direction of business activity have been notoriously unreliable. Finally, there has been an increasing tendency in the past few decades for the government to take increasing responsibility for the control of economic fluctuations. Monetary and fiscal policies have been the primary means of attacking the problem, and the general economic record since World War II suggests that drastic declines in business activity are not probable, but that modest recessions and interruptions in the growth trend of the economy may well take place from time to time.

The investment opportunities and risks related to cyclical movements in the economy, however, remain highly controversial. Some still argue that the primary task of investment management is to buy and sell securities in accordance with the business outlook, and thereby attempt to secure capital gains from the associated price movements. Others have been impressed with the highly unpredictable features of security-price movements and have concluded that buying and selling on this basis is likely to be a highly unprofitable endeavor. On the whole, cyclical timing operations have not appeared to be particularly opportune since World War II because the growth trend has been strong as compared to the fluctuations around the trend. Therefore, the possibilities for modest economic downturns and interruptions in the growth trend of corporate earnings are viewed more as a hazard to portfolio management rather than as an opportunity for gains.

One subtle investment-management problem arises out of the relation of business fluctuations to the selection of common stocks. In Chapter 14 it is shown that the values of most stocks are essentially a function of their current and projected earnings and dividends per share. But in many cases, these involve implicit or explicit forecasts of both the rate of general economic growth and the average level of business activity. Should growth rates and business activity fail to measure up to the assumed projections, there may be constructive losses as a result. Reasonably cautions projections are the basic means recommended to meet the problem. Also, the principles of "time" diversification can be used to moderate its impact.

In addition, there are some problems created by the very fact that stock prices have in the past been subject to sharp fluctuations. Some of the price movements have been touched off by economic developments and others by political events. The causation, however, is really unimportant; what is important is that investors must recognize the fact in portfolio planning. The most significant consequence, perhaps, is that price volatility makes common stocks generally unsatisfactory for that section of the portfolio where recoverability is the paramount objective. There is never any guarantee that funds committed to common stocks can be drawn out intact at any particular time in the future, no matter how carefully they are chosen.

The business cycle also presents problems to the income objective in an investment portfolio. Cyclically vulnerable common stocks typically offer greater than average dividend yields during prosperous periods, and it may appear that the average yield potential is quite favorable, but lack of stability represents a drawback to an emphasis on such stocks in income oriented accounts. The result may be a very practical dilemma —the desire to maximize income yield versus the desire to obtain reasonable stability under all possible economic conditions. There is no easy answer to this problem, but it does require the investor to weigh the possible consequences of reaching for income by purchasing common stocks with above-average dividend yields but with considerable vulnerability to cyclical disturbances.

Monetary Inflation. From the standpoint of investment management, inflation may be defined as a major and sustained rise in the general price level of goods and services. Historically, inflation in the United States has accompanied or followed every major war. It can be noted, for example, that during the Civil War wholesale prices rose about 120%; during and following World Wars I and II the increase was about 170% and 115%, respectively. Moreover, there is increasing evidence that there has been an inflationary bias even in the peacetime economy. Under the Full Employment Act of 1946, the prevention of unemployment and deflation is clearly given priority to the maintenance of a stable price level as a goal of national economic policy. The empirical evidence of the decade 1955–64 lends support to the view that the economy has a definite inflationary bias. During this period, the consumer price index of the Bureau of Labor Statistics increased from about 93 to 109, or by almost 17%. And although cold-war tensions existed during these years, they must be classified as peacetime in character. In view of these trends, it would seem absolutely imperative that portfolio planning should take specific cognizance of the probability of at least a slow inflationary trend. The assumption of a stable monetary unit, not an uncommon one in earlier years, seems entirely unrealistic in an era of international tensions and widespread governmental policies with inflationary implications.

The origins of a rapid or "burst" inflation are typically in a substantial increase in the money supply. In earlier periods the process was quite obvious; the government merely turned out fiat currency on the printing press. However, this crude method is no longer necessary with our modern institutional arrangements. Most of our present-day money is in the form of demand deposits in banks. The banking system is able to increase these deposits by extending loans or purchasing government bonds by several times their available reserves. And the Federal Reserve System is able to keep the banks well supplied with reserves by purchasing government obligations in the market. For example, between 1961 and 1964 currency and adjusted demand deposits increased from $139 billion to $159 billion, or by 14%, whereas the total loans and investments of commercial banks increased from $239 billion to $276 billion.[2] The easy money policy of the Federal Reserve during most of these years was the obvious factor responsible for these increases.

To bring about any substantial inflation, however, the increase in the money supply must be large relative to any change in the quantities of available goods and services. In brief, the usual conditions of inflation are an increasing amount of money competing for a restricted supply of goods. As a consequence, pressures are likely to be especially severe under wartime conditions. Then productive facilities are diverted to military products, so that there might be an actual decline in goods available for consumer use; at the same time, the fiscal needs of the

[2] Federal Reserve Bulletins: September, 1962, pp. 1185–86 and February, 1965, pp. 275–76.

government require a large increase in bank-held debt with the consequent effects on the money supply.

However, in the 1955–64 decade the economy was confronted by inflationary influences of a somewhat different sort. Although there was a moderate expansion in the money supply, the rate of production of goods and services increased at least as fast as the money supply during this decade.[3] Yet price levels continued to creep upward at a relatively slow but persistent rate.

Economists are by no means in agreement concerning the causes of the phenomenon, but several plausible reasons have been suggested. First, there is the "cost-push" explanation. Here it is noted that strong labor unions have been able to obtain wage increases in excess of increases in productivity. The result has been higher unit costs which have been passed on to consumers because, it is alleged, many prices are now established by administrative determination rather than by open-market competition. Second, many have held that the concepts of the "welfare state" inevitably lead to a creeping inflation. Farm subsidies, high minimum wages, and subsidies to the housing industry are illustrative of policies which have the effect of sustaining or increasing prices. Third, there has been superimposed upon welfare-state subsidies and cost-price pressures a national economic policy directed toward full employment at all costs. This policy has complemented and reinforced inflationary pressures because effective consumer resistance to the upward drift in the price level would probably have resulted in lesser sales of goods and services to consumers. But this countervailing pressure would have reduced output and employment, and the government has been unwilling to allow such adjustments to take place.

The purpose of the brief review of accepted national economic policy is to show that the importance of the inflation problem has greatly increased since World War II. Moreover, there seems to be little evidence that the problem will disappear from the scene in succeeding years. In addition, these trends also suggest that the relative importance of cyclical fluctuations have diminished, although certain highly vulnerable industries and companies may still experience wide fluctuations in earnings

[3] Between 1955 and 1964 inclusive the money supply, consisting of adjusted demand deposits and currency outside banks, increased from about \$129.7 billion to about \$158.6 billion, or by about 22%. During the same period the Federal Reserve index of industrial production, a measure of physical output, increased from an average of 97 in 1955 to about 131 in 1964, or by about 34%. Although this is a rough comparison as services are not included in the production index, it strongly suggests that physical output increased at least as fast as the money supply throughout the decade.

during modest recessionary periods. But on the whole, there seems to be a strong probability that inflation will prove to be a more serious problem to the long-term investor than wide and protracted cyclical movements in the economy.

Portfolio management becomes a much more difficult matter when inflation is specifically recognized as a major problem. Securities which are the most conservative from the standpoint of price stability and assurance of income are exposed to constructive losses under inflationary conditions. Reference here is to high-grade fixed-income securities. It can be argued, therefore, that a portfolio consisting solely of such securities is not really conservative at all but amounts to a speculation that there will be no inflation in the future. On the other hand, there is no assurance that any particular kind of securities will vary proportionately in income and value with changes in the price level. There is merely the probability that some common stocks with particular economic characteristics are likely to perform in this manner. Nevertheless, even where the personal factors dictate the need for maintaining integrity of principal and regularity of income, some of these stocks should be included in the portfolio.[4]

The Interest-Rate Risk. The fact that the price of money, represented by the yields on high-quality fixed-income securities, can fluctuate up or down must be recognized as a special problem in portfolio management. Typically, fluctuations in bond yields are related to business fluctuations, as for the most part interest rates tend to move in accord with changes in the demand for and supply of investable funds. Although demand from borrowers, as might be expected, is usually high under good business conditions and low under recession conditions, the supply factor is more erratic because to a considerable extent it is controllable by the Federal Reserve authorities. But although other considerations may intervene, such as balance-of-payments problems, Federal Reserve policy can be expected to allow interest rates to increase during booms and to decline during recessionary conditions.

The investment consequences of fluctuations in interest rates are related to the stability of both security prices and the income derived from fixed-income securities. One of the inevitable consequences of a rise in interest rates is generally lower prices for fixed-income securities.

[4] It has even been suggested that regulations requiring trustees to invest primarily in fixed-income securities should be reversed and that such trustees should be prohibited from acquiring fixed-income securities. Bach, *Inflation*, Providence, R.I.: Brown University Press, 1958, p. 82.

And long-term bonds and preferred stocks are subject to the greatest price decline. Vice versa, of course, long-term obligations show the greatest price advances should interest rates decline, although as brought out earlier, the redemption price on many corporate bonds can limit a price increase in response to a decline in interest rates. Therefore, these securities are not stable in price even though they may be of the highest quality from a credit standpoint.

However, although short-term bonds do not fluctuate as much as long-term bonds, the amount of income obtained from a portfolio constantly invested in short-term obligations will probably fluctuate to a greater extent. As brought out in the discussion of yield curves, the apparent paradox arises from the fact that interest rates have varied over a wider range in the short-term markets. As a consequence, a short-term portfolio must be recurrently reinvested at different levels of interest rates. Long-term rates are more stable (but not prices), and the reinvestment of a long-term portfolio is a gradual process. For example, $100,000 invested in one-year obligations may produce a yield of 2%, or $2,000 income, in a given year and then 4%, or $4,000 income, when reinvested at maturity in another year. In contrast, if a $100,000 investment is made in twenty-year bonds at (say) 4.5% to produce $4,500 of income, this income would be forthcoming in the specified amount for twenty years regardless of interest-rate fluctuations in the interim years, assuming adequate call protection. Therefore, so far as bond investors are concerned, the interest-rate risk has two dimensions. One is the risk associated with variations in market prices, and the other is the risk of variable income. A long-term bond portfolio is more exposed to the first, whereas a short-term portfolio is more exposed to the second.

It can be argued that an increase in interest rates should have depressing effects on the prices of other types of securities. Because when taken as a completely separate factor, higher interest rates mean that fixed-income securities offer greater yields relative to other securities than before. Therefore, it might be reasoned that prices of other securities, including common stocks, would decline to maintain the same relative yield relationship. But this effect is often obscured by other factors bearing on the prices of lower-grade bonds, preferreds, and common stocks. For example, rising interest rate levels are typically associated with boom conditions in the economy, and the improved earnings outlook associated with such conditions may well produce higher prices and lower yields for common stocks despite the increase in interest rates. Therefore, the interest-rate risk can be considered directly relevant only to high-quality fixed-income securities.

To conclude, it should be apparent that portfolio management in essence involves a compromise between maximizing return opportunities and minimizing risk exposure. If the portfolio structure gives recognition to all the potential risks, then returns substantially above average should not be expected. Such returns can only be achieved by sacrificing risk protection in some way, but for some individuals a conscious assumption of considerable risk may be entirely legitimate.

CHAPTER 26

Classification of Securities:
Objectives and Risks

The next logical step in the portfolio planning process is to classify various types of securities according to the objectives they are designed to meet and the risks they assume or protect against. The investor may then select from each functional group as the specific objectives seem to justify. A note of caution, however, is necessary. There is never any guarantee that the securities within a particular functional group will achieve the desired results, but only that within a given group there is a greater probability of being able to accomplish a specific objective.

High-Grade Fixed-Income Securities. High-grade bonds and preferred stocks are those wherein the investment contract seems certain to be fulfilled in the future. Their primary function in a portfolio is to produce a given income under any conceivable economic conditions. In investment accounts requiring a high degree of stability of dollar income, these securities would occupy a significant role.[1] Historically their yields have usually been less than on other types of securities, but in the 1959–65 period, their immediate yields have been higher than on common stocks.

A portion of the group also provides for dollar recoverability. Savings accounts, certificates of deposit, and Savings Bonds are examples. In

[1] As indicated in Chapter 22 on municipal obligations, tax-exempt returns are also obtained through such securities issued by state governments and municipal units.

435

corporate obligations, however, only the short-maturity issues would promise a high degree of price stability. As previously indicated, long-term bonds and all preferred stocks are exposed to considerable price fluctuations as the level of interest rates moves up or down.

The primary risk is inflation. Returns are solely in terms of dollars, and consequently, they do not solve the income problem in real terms. To a lesser extent high-quality long-term corporate bonds and preferred stocks are exposed to adverse long-term changes in the position of industries and companies. The problem arises out of the inherent limitations of security analysis. A thorough investigation and the insistence on rigorous standards can clearly promise satisfactory performance for perhaps five or ten years, but security analysis cannot promise that a company will maintain its economic position for thirty or forty years. The difficulties of certain high-grade railroad bonds of thirty or forty years ago may be cited as a case in point.

Government bonds, however, represent an exception, as the government always has the power to pay dollars, because it has the means of creating them. As a consequence, individual investors are well advised to use government obligations for dollar safety of income and principal if the income sacrifice is nominal. To a lesser extent, certificates of deposit and savings accounts in banks have the same features because they are insured for $10,000 by a government agency.

Medium-Grade Fixed-Income Securities.   Medium-grade bonds and preferred stocks by definition do not measure up to the standards of performance required of top-quality bonds and preferreds. Therefore, there is some risk that internal company problems or a general economic decline will result in an interruption of income payments. Their nominal function is to provide an intermediate position between high-grade obligations and common stocks. Yields may be significantly greater than on top-quality bonds and preferreds, yet it is felt the returns will be somewhat more stable than on common stocks.

However, these securities are usually an undesirable investment medium for individual investors, although large institutional investors, such as life insurance companies, have obtained adequate results from them. In summary, the view is that higher current-income yield alone is not adequate compensation for exposing a major part of principal to a significant risk of loss unless a very extensive diversification of commitments is possible. Therefore, the assumption of substantial risk seems unwise unless there is some possibility of realizing a substantial appreciation on a security. The fact that the appreciation potential of this group is usually quite limited, because of the nature of the investment contract, is a serious drawback to investment attractiveness.[2]

The real purpose of fixed-income securities in the individual investor's portfolio is to assure continuity of income or to provide recoverability. On both counts medium-grade obligations are likely to prove unsatisfactory. Wide price movements may take place as the degree of credit risk appears to be increasing or decreasing. And under unfavorable economic conditions, when the investor might be most in need of income to balance reduced returns from common stocks, some of these securities may shut off their income payments altogether. A combination of high-grade bonds and preferreds and common stocks would seem to be a much superior distribution of a portfolio where current income is the primary objective.

Common Stocks. The characteristics of common stocks in relation to specific investment objectives vary widely in accord with the economic nature of particular situations. As a result, for portfolio management purposes, they are a much more complicated medium than fixed-income securities. A bond or preferred serves the same function in a portfolio, regardless of the nature of the company. For example, the investment returns on a bond will be the same whether the company involved has tremendous growth possibilities or is likely to be highly stable without any growth potential. But in the case of common stocks the objectives served by growth companies are entirely different from those served by such stable companies. For this reason it seems desirable to classify common stocks into certain subgroups for the purpose of establishing their relationship to the risks and objectives of the investment program.

Income common stocks. The primary features of most income common stocks would be (1) a high dividend-payout percentage and (2) a neutral secular trend. These two features, which are not entirely unrelated, have historically resulted in a somewhat greater dividend yield relative to alternative commitments. Yield differentials exist within the group; yields may also vary over a period of time for the general class as a whole. First, within the group, the yields on different stocks depend on the economic stature of the companies and their vulnerability to

---

[2] For example, in Chapter 11 on the analysis of financial policies, it was found that the growth potential of Georgia-Pacific Corporation might have made the common stock a suitable long-term investment, but that the top-heavy debt structure made the nonconvertible senior securities unattractive from the standpoint of the individual investor.

cyclical variations. Second, the general popularity of common stocks as a whole is the primary factor controlling the fluctuations in average market yields on these stocks. In fact, during periods when the stock market is at a high level, the availability of quality common stocks primarily for income purposes may be quite limited because advances in prices may bring the indicated yields to an unfavorable level in relation to alternative commitments in fixed-income securities.

Income stocks typically offer either stability of current income at moderate yields or a higher average income that may, however, fluctuate to a considerable extent. Any common stock, of course, is subject to dividend variations at the discretion of the board of directors. But when a company is relatively insulated from cyclical disturbances, dividend rates may in fact be maintained at constant levels for a long period of time. Certain companies in the food products, tobacco, and electric-power industries illustrate the stable type of income stocks. When the personal circumstances show that only modest variations in current income can be tolerated, then these stocks would have obvious appeal if available at adequate yields in relation to alternatives. If subclassifications are considered desirable, the stable situations could be placed in a special group and perhaps labeled "defensive income stocks." In some instances, such stocks may also offer the probability of some protection against the creeping type of inflation, so in moderate amounts they might be included even if comparative yields are not favorable.

"Aggressive income stocks" may be defined as those more vulnerable to cyclical variations. They might be appropriate when the income from an occupation, a retirement annuity, or high-grade fixed-income securities provides an adequate amount of defensive income and the main objective in the stock account is to maximize average income and obtain some degree of protection against inflation. And nongrowth cyclical stocks, because they are more volatile, usually tend to sell on a higher yield basis even though they may represent well-established companies. For example, in the chapter on common-stock selection, it was found that Borg-Warner offered a dividend yield of 4.4% in 1965, when stocks in general offered only about 3.0%.

Many income-type stocks, however, are probably more vulnerable to adverse secular developments than other securities, because these companies almost by definition are relatively mature. The high dividend payouts usually suggest limited growth potential, and although some may continue to show moderate growth, others could well show a significant decline in their economic position over the years. For this reason, a portfolio consisting almost entirely of common stocks with above-average dividend yields might show a gradual erosion in principal throughout a long-term period unless considerable care is exercised.

Growth stocks. A growth stock has been defined as a common equity on which per share earnings will probably increase more rapidly than average. As a consequence it is anticipated that they will show greater than average long-term appreciation in market price.

The typical characteristics of growth stocks might be described as follows. First, the dividend payout is usually low, because earnings are needed to finance expansion in facilities. Second, market prices relative to existing earnings levels tend to be high. It follows, of course, that immediate dividend yields may be almost negligible. Third, a number of large and seasoned companies are in the growth category, International Business Machines and Minnesota Mining, for example. But they might also be new arrivals on the industrial scene, such as Xerox, which until about 1961 was a relatively small and unlisted company with about $40 million of sales and about $45 million of assets. In both instances, how- ever, the average and marginal rates of return on the equity are well above average and promise to continue at these levels.

The major difficulty with these stocks, as indicated in the section on common-stock selection, is to determine whether the probabilities favor a continuance of the growth rate for a sufficient number of years to justify the premium prices. If the growth rates do in fact continue, then quite favorable appreciation results are often obtained; if they do not, then below-average returns may be obtained, such as was the case with Alcoa and Dow Chemical between 1956 and 1965.

Undervalued Issues. A second type of stock sometimes recom- mended for the possibility of above-average appreciation is the under- valued issue. The theory behind the purchase of these stocks is that the stock market will ultimately reflect elements of value that were not recognized by the market at the time of purchase. The companies need not be growth companies in the usual sense; indeed, it is most probable that they will not be. To obtain growth in this fashion is not, however, an easy matter. In the first place, the investor must possess considerable analytical skill and must be willing and able to devote a great deal of time and effort to appraising many companies. In the second place, the operation requires great courage and patience. The investor must be willing to act contrary to general opinion and usually in the face of a discouraging current performance. And subsequent market experience might be unfavorable for a considerable period. Several years might

TABLE 26-1

STANDARD AND POOR'S STOCK PRICE INDEXES

(prices, earnings, and dividends: selected years)

Year	Industrial Index			Public Utility Index			Railroad Index			Cost-of-Living Index†
	Price*	Earnings	Dividends	Price*	Earnings	Dividends	Price*	Earnings	Dividends	
1940	$10.37	$1.01	$ .63	$13.08	$1.28	$ .99	$ 9.47	$1.42	$ .68	48.8
1946	14.75	1.06	.66	19.58	1.63	.91	15.61	1.89	1.89	68.0
1947	15.18	1.70	.82	16.28	1.64	.98	14.46	2.22	.97	77.8
1948	15.12	2.34	.91	16.04	1.60	1.00	13.92	3.06	1.10	83.8
1949	16.49	2.40	1.14	19.93	1.67	1.08	13.86	2.35	1.11	83.0
Percent increase 1940–49	58	138	81	52	32	9	46	64	63	70
1955	$48.44	$3.78	$1.68	$31.70	$2.09	$1.42	$34.17	$4.08	$1.75	93.3
1956	50.08	3.53	1.70	31.76	2.22	1.54	31.36	4.00	1.87	94.7
1957	42.86	3.50	1.84	32.14	2.25	1.63	20.95	3.33	1.67	98.0
1958	58.97	2.95	1.79	43.28	2.37	1.67	34.39	2.89	1.60	100.7
1959	64.50	3.53	1.90	44.74	2.48	1.77	33.82	3.04	1.66	101.5
1960	61.49	3.41	2.00	51.76	2.69	1.86	29.55	2.45	1.70	103.1
1961	75.72	3.38	2.08	64.83	2.81	1.96	33.25	2.15	1.62	104.2
1962	66.00	3.87	2.20	61.09	3.06	2.05	32.73	2.90	1.64	105.4
1963	79.25	4.22	2.38	66.42	3.23	2.16	40.65	3.18	1.72	106.7
1964	89.12	4.85	2.61	74.18	3.50	2.30	45.64	3.55	1.95	108.1
Percent increase 1955–64	85	28	54	103	66	64	32	−13	12	16

* At year end for each index.
† Average for each year; 1957–59 = 100
Source: Standard and Poor's Security Price Index Record, 1965.

elapse before a correct judgment on such a stock is vindicated by an appreciation to reflect true value.[3]

Whether there are more opportunities to achieve growth through the undervalued-issue approach than in the traditional approach is highly controversial. The advantages are that it is based on careful analysis of known performance and does not neglect the price factor. The theory also implies that stocks become more attractive for ultimate growth as they decline in price, whereas the growth-stock theory sometimes results in a greater enthusiasm for a stock the more it has appreciated in the past. The main disadvantage is that it requires a high level of training and experience. A corollary drawback is that it tends to concentrate commitments in problem companies, which typically reduces the general quality of the portfolio and often increases the exposure of the account to long-term or cyclical risks.

Inflation stocks. There is a familiar line of argument which suggests that all common stocks should tend to protect the investor to some extent against inflation. In summary, the theory is as follows: common stocks represent the residual ownership of the physical facilities of production, and under inflationary conditions the dollar values of such real properties should increase and lead to a commensurate appreciation of stock values and prices. If the theory could be accepted at face value, the solution of the inflation problem would be relatively easy: merely acquire a diversified list of common stocks.

Unfortunately, there is a basic error in the simplified version of the supposed relationship between common stocks and inflation. The theory assumes that economic values of properties and the related common stocks are largely a function of replacement costs, which of course tend to advance during inflation. But in the real world replacement costs may not be very significant in the determination of the economic value of corporate properties. It is the prospective earnings from the productive use of the facilities that fundamentally determines the real value of corporate assets. Therefore, a true inflation company is more properly defined as one where the level of earnings and dividend payments is likely to increase under inflationary conditions.

To show more specifically the possible divergencies, the performance of three broad groups of stocks for selected years since 1940 is shown in Table 26-1. Although it would have been highly desirable to show a

[3] See Chapter 5 for specific examples of the problems and possible opportunities in the undervalued issue strategy of common stock operations.

breakdown of the industrial average into major industry classifications, unfortunately the data were not available. However, it is clear that during the major price inflation of 1940–49 the earnings and dividends on industrial common stocks increased by more than the rise in the cost-of-living index, whereas the same was not true for the public-utility and railroad groups. Therefore, it seems reasonable to conclude that it is within the industrial classification that investors should seek protection against rapid inflation of the classic monetary type. However, not all industrial stocks are satisfactory for this purpose. Differences in performance are very wide, so a more selective approach to the problem is advisable.

Moreover, the statistical data must be interpreted in the light of general economic conditions that prevailed in those years. In 1940 complete recovery from the Great Depression had not yet been achieved, whereas postwar boom conditions had only slightly moderated in 1949. As a consequence, there is no assurance that equally favorable trends in earnings and dividends would be enjoyed if a rapid inflationary surge was superimposed upon a period of favorable business activity. For example, the surprisingly favorable performance of the railroads was probably largely due to a cyclical recovery. In 1940 a number of the railroads were still in receivership, and the subsequent financial re-organizations greatly improved the postwar results by a drastic scaling down of capital structures. The fact that earnings of the rails actually declined between 1955 and 1964 suggests that they are a dubious means of obtaining protection against the inflation risk.

During the strong inflationary surge of 1946–48, the performance of the public utilities was unfavorable, as earnings actually declined and dividends advanced only moderately. The lag in rate adjustments behind cost increases seems to be the most plausible explanation of their performance. Therefore, the quantitative results of utility common stocks were not highly reassuring under rapidly developing inflation.

However, under the "creeping" inflation witnessed in the 1955–64 decade, the performance of the utilities was the most favorable. Under these conditions, the growth features and also technological improvements, which largely offset the slow increases in costs, were able to produce a consistent growth in earnings and dividends at a rate above the increase in the consumer price level. In brief, stable growth characteristics have provided the best protection against a slow inflation. The record of the industrials was less favorable during this decade. Their more erratic performance was especially notable in 1955–61, when earnings actually declined in the face of a 10% rise in the price level. The reduced rate of activity in the durable goods sector of the economy was probably responsible, but it suggested that returns on the common stocks of cyclical companies may not in the short run offset slow increases in living costs. However, such stocks provided the best protection against a rapid inflation in commodity prices such as occurred between 1946 and 1948. In summary, the record of the 1946–64 period was rather paradoxical. It suggested that the companies providing the best protection against monetary inflation were less reliable as protection against a slow upward drift in the price level, whereas utilities, which showed good results under the latter conditions, were undesirable hedges against a rapid monetary inflation.

Because the latter type of inflation has the more damaging impact, portfolio policies may desire specific representation of common stocks whose characteristics offer the maximum probability of increasing earnings under these conditions. In theory, their economic characteristics should be as follows: costs should be relatively fixed and selling prices relatively sensitive. Integrated companies producing essential raw materials or products fabricated from these materials may be cited as examples approaching these characteristics. Being integrated, they usually have large investments in natural resources, and fixed costs, such as depletion and depreciation, are quite important. It is also desirable of course that there be at least moderate growth in total demand for the products.

The integrated petroleum and copper companies may be used to illustrate these characteristics. These all have large "sunk" costs in the form of natural-resource reserves and low levels of labor cost per unit of output with large investments in plant and equipment. Depreciation and depletion are thus important items of cost, and the prices of the products tend to be sensitive, as indicated by Table 26-2, although to varying degrees.

The increase in profit levels for the two largest companies in the industries from 1939–40 to 1947–50 lends empirical support for their classification as inflation stocks. Table 26-3 shows the earnings and dividends per share for these years for Standard Oil of New Jersey and Kennecott Copper, and it is notable that shareholders in each of these companies enjoyed average earnings and dividends in 1947–50 more than double those of 1939–40.[4] Then through the Korean War and the

---

[4] This relatively favorable showing was no doubt due in part to the cyclical recovery which took place between 1939 and 1947–50. Therefore, to repeat, proportionate increases in earnings and dividends might not occur when a price inflation was superimposed on a boom level of general business activity, although if the reasoning is correct, earnings of these companies would tend to advance considerably under a monetary inflation producing a general rise in commodity prices of a substantial magnitude.

TABLE 26-2
PRODUCT PRICES FOR SELECTED YEARS: YEARLY AVERAGES

Years	Copper (Per Lb.)	Crude Oil (Per Barrel)
Preinflation		
1939	$.1022	$1.04
1940	.1084	1.02
Postinflation		
1948	.2233	2.59
1950	.2158	2.54
1952	.2450	2.56
1954	.2994	2.82
1956	.4200	2.83
1958	.2631	3.06
1960	.3234	2.97
1962	.3100	2.97
1964	.3200	2.93

Source: Standard & Poor's Industry Surveys.

capital-goods boom which followed, the earnings and dividends on these stocks continued to advance. But subsequently the erratic price and demand conditions in the copper industry resulted in declining earnings for Kennecott Copper. Standard Oil of New Jersey was also subject to earnings variations of a considerable magnitude as inflationary pressures lessened and competitive conditions became more intense. Fortunately the growth in sales and cost reduction programs enabled Jersey Standard to record new highs in earnings in 1963–64, despite lower crude-oil and refined-product prices.

As suggested by these examples, the primary risk on these stocks is their instability. The same features that make for protection against inflationary developments also expose them to fluctuations in earnings. A relatively large incidence of fixed costs combined with product price sensitivity tends to magnify any decline in demand resulting from a general economic setback or because of special conditions within the industry. For example, both Kennecott and Standard Oil suffered substantial declines in earnings during the mild recessions of 1949 and 1958. Thus although investors should realize greater returns during inflationary periods, they should also anticipate and be reconciled to substantial reductions in returns at other times.

Summary. In summary, common stocks differ widely in their investment characteristics, and therefore it is appropriate to classify them into

TABLE 26-3
EARNINGS AND DIVIDENDS RECORD PER SHARE

Year	Standard Oil of N.J. Earnings*	Dividends*	Kennecott Copper Earnings	Dividends
1939	$ .54	$ .30	$ 3.14	$2.00
1940	.76	.20	4.05	2.75
1939–40 average	$ .65	$ .25	$ 3.59	$2.37
1947	$1.64	$ .66	$ 8.49	$4.00
1948	2.17	.33	8.67	5.00
1949	1.48	.66	4.45	4.00
1950	2.25	.83	8.15	5.50
1947–50 average	$1.86	$ .62	$ 7.44	$4.62
1956	$4.11	$2.10	$13.23	$9.25
1957	3.96	2.25	7.32	6.00
1958	2.62	2.25	5.44	5.00
1956–58 average	$3.58	$2.20	$ 9.00	$6.75
1962	$3.88	$2.50	$ 5.94	$5.00
1963	4.73	2.75	5.15	4.00
1964	4.87	3.00	5.98	4.00
1962–64 average	$4.49	$2.75	$ 5.69	$4.33

* Adjusted for all stock dividends and splits.

functional groups according to the purposes they satisfy in the portfolio. Some appear suitable for income purposes, some for long-term growth, and some especially desirable to protect against various types of inflationary developments. Although it is doubtful if a given common stock can be desirable both for income and growth, it is possible that certain stocks might be attractive both for inflationary protection and for either income or growth. Finally, it may be noted that, in general, common stocks cannot be used to satisfy the recoverability objective because their prices are subject to considerable variations. Emotional as well as economic developments produce these price swings. However, on a comparative basis, the stable, slow-growth stocks (such as those of many of the major public utilities) have been subject to a much narrower range of price fluctuations than other types of common stocks.

CHAPTER 27

Principles of Diversification

The Theory of Diversification

One of the hard facts of investment management is that those securities which offer the greatest probability of meeting a given objective are entirely inappropriate for other purposes. It would be absurd to look for the Utopian security to provide adequate and stable income, growth potential, price recoverability, and protection against inflation. The natural consequence is that an investment portfolio is usually made up of a group of securities. This aspect of investments is called diversification. But it should be emphasized that it is essential to limit portfolio diversification to reasonable proportions; otherwise the burdens of appraisal and periodic reviews might become an intolerable task. A portfolio should never include more securities than can be diligently reviewed at periodic intervals.

One of the most common undesirable features of portfolios which have been constructed without systematic planning is an excessive number of securities. The most probable reason is that from time to time securities are added because they appear promising for one reason or another, but the individual selections are not related to the status of the portfolio as a whole. The ultimate result is that a number of securities may be acquired more or less independently of each other. Finally the investor is confronted with an intolerable situation: the inability to review the status of the specific holdings without an undue amount of time and effort. To guard against this contingency, a simple rule can be recommended. It is that a limit should be placed on the total number of securities to be included in a portfolio and once the limit is reached any new acquisition should be matched with the disposition of an existing holding.

Moreover, it should be strongly emphasized that adequate diversification is not achieved through the mere acquisition of a number of different issues; it is possible to acquire a great many securities with the same general investment characteristics. For example, an investor conceivably could have fifty common stocks all in the heavy industries. Broadly viewed, portfolio diversification is designed to accomplish two objectives: (1) to obtain the maximum achievement of the positive portfolio objectives, and (2) to obtain adequate protection against the several risks. However, the problem is that these two objectives are not always compatible; in other words, obtaining substantial risk protection may be at the expense of maximizing the positive aims of the portfolio. As a result, compromises are often required.

Perhaps the most common instance of a conflict is found where the major positive objective is to obtain better than average long-term appreciation. The nature of the conflict can be indicated by noting the natural results of diversification. First, it reduces the impact on the total portfolio of mistakes in the selection of individual issues. Second, it is often designed to limit the adverse effects of changing conditions in the economy, such as a general downturn in business activity. But a third result inevitably follows from the first; diversification also dilutes the effects of an outstanding performance of a given company. The result is inevitable because diversification means that the proportion that one security bears to the total is necessarily limited. In fact, in a common-stock portfolio, it would be logical to expect that as diversification increases, the probability increases that portfolio returns will resemble those achieved on the stock-market averages, neither better nor worse. On the other hand, the less the diversification, the greater the probability that results will be different than the averages; superior selection should lead to superior returns on the one hand, but the impact of selection mistakes will be accentuated on the other.

For this reason, enterprising investors often consider extensive diversification a drawback rather than an advantage. In these cases, the compromise might be to sacrifice risk protection and concentrate on a relatively few issues.

Diversification might also be of a special nature. For example, it might appear that one or two industries offer a potential for superior growth, but the uncertainties are great concerning the fortunes of the specific companies constituting the industry. This situation, it may be mentioned, is often typical of highly dynamic new industries. Assuming risk protection can appropriately be sacrificed, then the entire portfolio may consist of a package of several companies in these industries. But allowing for wide differences in objectives, it might be suggested that most individual investors might have from five to about fifteen securities in their portfolios at a given time.

Principles of Risk Diversification

Diversification against Long-Term Risks. The forces which generate long-term growth or decline are usually industry-wide. In a typical case a series of technological developments will make the products of some industry obsolete and promote the growth of another. Therefore, the natural means of protection is to diversify the portfolio by industries. The dispersion of industries should insure that they are independent of each other in their economic operations. For example, the auto-parts industry would not be regarded as sufficiently separate from automobile manufacturing for this purpose. Unfortunately, the fortunes of many industries are to some degree intertwined, and it is often difficult to decide whether a secular decline in one would result in permanent deterioration of another. For example, it is an open question if the steel industry is sufficiently independent of the automobile in this respect. In general, all that can be said is that when a major objective is risk protection, the portfolio should include a group of industries with independent demand features.

Obtaining representative industries is perhaps most important in common stocks, because the direct and immediate impact of a secular decline is on the stock.[1] However, if part of the portfolio is devoted to high-grade corporate bonds and preferred stocks, it is also prudent to allow for the secular risk by appropriate industry diversification. It would be especially pertinent when maturities are long or in the case of pre-

[1] The wave of mergers in recent years has resulted in a number of companies with products in a number of industries. The Olin Mathieson complex of products might be cited as an example. However, these companies do not usually report a breakdown of sales and earnings by industry or product areas, so that, while the effect of these mergers may be a reduction in risk, it is almost impossible to determine the degree to which risk has been lessened.

ferreds where there is no maturity. The reason is that risk increases as the period of time for which the investment is made lengthens. The unhappy experience of holders of railroad bonds in the 1920–40 period can be cited as a practical example of the impact of the secular risk on fixed-income securities.

Cyclical Risk Diversification. Although the general acceptance of aggressive national economic policies to prevent or offset recessions have probably reduced the portfolio risks incident to business fluctuations, prudence would still dictate some attention to the possibility of moderate cyclical swings. The following consequences are perhaps of most importance to investment management: (1) the possibility of substantial variations in security prices, (2) fluctuations in income payments on many common stocks, and (3) possible valuation errors in situations where earning power is essentially a function of the future average level of business activity.

The first of these specific possibilities may suggest the desirability of diversifying commitments in terms of time of purchase. In the case of common stocks several investment-management concepts have been advanced to preclude all acquisitions at stock-market peaks, and these are considered in more detail later. For bonds, other than savings bonds, systematic purchases at regular intervals can be accomplished by maturity diversification. A staggered maturity schedule once set up results in the run-off of some bonds every year or so; it is then possible to maintain the schedule by reinvesting the proceeds in bonds which mature a year or so beyond the longest then held. Thus there is a constant reinvestment at various interest rates, and in this way the bond section of the portfolio would obtain a yield approximating the average level of interest rates.

The potential variability of dividend income is not a risk of general applicability to all portfolios. But where regularity of income is a primary objective, it suggests that diversification by type of security is desirable. High-grade bonds and preferred stocks serve to offset any fluctuations in income on the common stocks by providing a "storm cellar" income level. Another means of meeting the dividend-instability problem is to emphasize reasonably stable companies in the common-stock portion of the portfolio. However, there may be "costs" related to this procedure, as stable companies are often valued more generously and thus offer lower yields and possibly less appreciation potentials. Also, as previously mentioned, highly stable stocks generally offer less protection against certain types of inflationary developments in the economy.

Valuation Risk Diversification. In considering the problems of common-stock valuations it was found that their long-term investment values are largely dependent upon estimates of potential earning power. Because forecasts of earnings are inherently subject to errors, the related portfolio problems are sufficiently important to warrant special attention.

First, even though a particular industry as a whole prospers, the earnings of certain companies may turn out to be less than anticipated. Perhaps the primary cause of such a deterioration in earnings is the fact that the capacities of management may change. Atrophy of management has occurred in apparently strong companies to the serious distress of outside investors. Concentration on the leading companies is one means of reducing the probabilities of serious earnings declines because of internal corporate problems. Therefore, defensive investors are likely to concentrate on the large "blue chip" companies. The investment "costs" of achieving such protection are typically lower dividend yields and perhaps less appreciation prospects than on the common stocks of less dominant companies.

Second, errors in valuation can result even though specific adverse developments do not occur within the company. The company may merely fail to live up to the growth-rate expectations which were incorporated into the valuation estimate. Above-average returns are quite often realized if the company maintains the projected rate of growth; if it does not, then losses may be experienced even though the company had moderate success in its operations. But as mentioned earlier, the degree of diversification used in a growth-stock portfolio may well be limited because of a decision to sacrifice risk protection for the possibility of better than average returns. If the latter is emphasized, then only a few such issues would be acquired in order to obtain the maximum impact from their anticipated superior performances.

Third, on the majority of common stocks the valuation risk also tends to change as the general level of the market moves up or down. If common stocks are available at reasonable prices relative to existing earnings and dividends, then optimistic growth-rate projections are not required in order to justify the acquisition prices. Because under these conditions the risk of valuation errors is reduced, less diversification of the common-stock portfolio may be needed even for defensive investors.

Functional Diversification. The point of introducing functional diversification as a separate concept is to make sure that the portfolio is in fact constructed according to the various positive needs of the investor. The most typical specific objectives, which can be found in some combination or other, are recoverability, growth, a reasonable level of current income, and preservation of purchasing power. Although it is possible that any one of these might be the sole function of an account, this situation is probably not typical. The family and financial factors are more likely to suggest that an investment account is multiple-purpose.

It is desirable, therefore, to plan the portfolio to make sure the functional characteristics of the securities selected are in accord with the several purposes of the fund. The following list of objectives and types of securities relevant to each suggests the nature of investment management applied to the functional construction of a portfolio.

Recoverability. For this need Government Savings Bonds, shares in savings and loan associations, savings accounts with commercial banks, or short-term marketable securities are appropriate. The dollars committed are obtainable from either redemption or from sale in the market at any time without any appreciable loss.

Growth. Certain types of common stocks are the means of meeting the growth objective. Investing in a few companies with favorable growth prospects is the normal means of implementation, although experienced investors might also consider the possibility of seeking out undervalued common stocks.

Current Income. For certainty of dollar income, long-term U.S. Government bonds, high-quality municipals, and corporate obligations may be recommended, depending upon the relative prevailing yields. For investors in high tax brackets, tax-exempt municipals are of course appropriate. Savings accounts in banks or savings and loan associations may also be used, but the drawback is that the rate of income is not guaranteed and it may be reduced if interest rates in general decline substantially.

In principle, these accounts would also find it advantageous to include a substantial proportion of "income stocks." These usually provide a higher rate of return on the average, and if emphasis is placed on stable companies, a reasonable degree of consistency might also be expected. Such common stocks, however, can occasionally become unattractive because of very high market prices and consequent low yields. Some improvement in average returns might be enjoyed by including some cyclical stocks. This may be justified if greater fluctuations in income can be tolerated in the common-stock portion of the portfolio.

Maintenance of Real Income. It is suggested that most portfolios should include some representative "inflation stocks" in at least moderate amounts. To make absolutely sure that they are included, it is desirable to establish them as a distinct component in the account. Only when the nature of the occupation income is such that it is likely to vary with changes in the price level can this function be largely ignored. It must be remembered, however, that these stocks are typically vulnerable to considerable swings in prices and dividends; in brief, the valuation and cyclical risks are likely to be relatively heavy.

Principles of Time Diversification

Nature of Problem. In the discussion of alternative investment strategies in common stocks, it was argued that the propensity of the stock market to fluctuate might result in two natural reactions to the phenomenon, both of which are wrong for a long-term investor. One is to become excessively timid with respect to the acquisition of common stocks. In extreme cases, stocks may be practically excluded from consideration because of an almost morbid fear of a price decline subsequent to their purchase.[2] This aversion may exist even though stocks may be acquired at attractive prices and there is not the remotest need to sell in the foreseeable future. The result is that potential returns on the account may be artificially restricted. Moreover, certain types of commons are the only means most investors have of coping with the risks of inflation; therefore, an undue fear of price declines may unwittingly expose the portfolio to the risk of inflation.

The second reaction, almost diametrically opposite, is to become increasingly engrossed with the notion that market fluctuations can be a source of tremendous gains. By hindsight these profits look deceptively easy. Merely by reviewing past market movements the investor can mentally chalk up the theoretical results which would have accrued from buying at a previous low, then selling at a subsequent high, and later repeating the process. He then becomes fair game for the services of "market outlook letters"; securities are purchased more with their anticipated short-term market performance in mind than with their desirability as investments for the long pull. In brief, he becomes a trader instead of an investor, although personal circumstances may make it highly desirable to refrain from the considerable risks of market speculation.

---

[2] A modification of this attitude is holding back purchases of stocks on the ground that the stock market is likely to decline sometime in the future and acquisitions can then be made at more favorable prices. To many investors prices are always likely to be more favorable later on, so the effect is that stocks are never purchased.

But assuming these pitfalls can be avoided, it is still desirable to acquire more stocks when the market is low than when it is high even though they are to be held for the long pull. A number of alternatives have been suggested to meet the problem. The following discussion will analyze some alternatives and indicate their possible merits and drawbacks, based on the assumption that the objectives are to consider both risk exposure and potential returns.

Dollar-Cost Averaging. The solution to the timing problem which has been increasingly advocated in recent years is to recommend diversification with respect to time of purchases. The postulates underlying the recommendation are as follows: (1) the magnitude of fluctuations around the long-term trend is likely to be considerable and thus justifies some attempt to acquire stocks at low points in the general market, (2) recurrent highs and lows will take place in the market, but it is not possible to forecast the timing and extent of such fluctuations, and (3) investors using discretion are more likely to be optimistic when the market is high and be pessimistic when the market is low. Therefore, they are well advised to adopt a technique which will result in purchasing common stocks at the average market levels prevailing through the acquisition period.

The mechanics of dollar-cost averaging are simple. It requires the commitment of a constant amount of money at prescribed intervals. Common stocks are thereby acquired at the average prices prevailing on the dates of purchase. However, the principal advantage attributed to dollar-cost averaging is that a larger number of shares will be acquired at lower prices. As a result, the average cost per share will be less than the unweighted average of the several purchase prices. These results are illustrated in Table 27-1. In this hypothetical example, the average price of the stock prevailing over the assumed five periods was $20 per share, but a $2,000 dollar-averaging program would have produced an average cost per share of $17.84.

During the 1955–65 period, however, the first major postulate of dollar averaging has been open to question, that is that the magnitude of fluctuations around the trend will be large in relation to the upward slope of the trend. Because if the market moves in a strong upward pattern for a number of years, with only minor setbacks of relatively short duration, then most of the hypothetical results may not be enjoyed. This comment would especially apply to the specific problem of investing a single sum, such as cash proceeds from an inheritance, rather than to the case where regular amounts become available for investment over a period of time. In the lump-sum case, time diversification produces

TABLE 27-1
DOLLAR-COST AVERAGING: ILLUSTRATION

Period	Amount	Price per Share	No. of Shares Purchased
1	$ 2,000	$ 10	200
2	2,000	20	100
3	2,000	25	80
4	2,000	20	100
5	2,000	25	80
Total	$10,000	$100	560
Average of prices, unweighted		$ 20	
Average cost per share			$17.84

lower acquisition costs (relative to a single outright commitment) only if the stock market does in fact decline for some subsequent period to lower levels than those prevailing at the time the funds became available for investment.

To illustrate, reference is made to Figure 27-1 which shows the monthly average of the Standard and Poor's industrial stock index for 1960 through the first half of 1965. It is apparent that during this period common-stock prices have shown only one decline of any significance—May through December, 1962. Suppose then that a lump sum had become available during 1960. An immediate outright commitment would have been less costly than averaging purchases on a monthly basis for the following four years, because even at the high for 1960, the index was materially lower than it averaged in the subsequent several years. As a matter of fact, dollar-cost averaging would probably have resulted in favorable acquisition prices only if it had been instituted in late 1961 and had been completed by the latter part of 1963. However, the record of these years should not be regarded as necessarily indicative of future probabilities, but only that dollar-cost averaging does not guarantee acquisition costs below those obtained by outright purchases.

Finally, although the dollar averaging process may remove the temptation to procrastinate or engage in market timing operations, conceivably it could lead to a tendency to ignore the price factor entirely in common-stock purchases. On the hypothesis that the *average* price of a stock will not be excessive, there may be a complacent attitude toward buying a stock at any price once the inherent quality of the company has been found to be satisfactory. Therefore, if the market stubbornly proceeds to excessively high levels for several years, then there might be continued purchases at an increasing level of overvaluation. Although admittedly conjectural, the growing use of a purely mechanical dollar-cost averaging

FIGURE 27-1

Standard & Poor's Index of 425 Industrial Stocks
Monthly Average of Index

technique by institutional investors, especially pension and retirement funds, may be responsible for some leading stocks remaining indefinitely at prices which seem unreasonably high. In brief, it is at least arguable that even the average price may be an unsound basis for the acquisition of some common stocks.

A rather curious paradox is suggested by these comments. A device aimed at removing the temptation to speculate on price movements may result in another form of risk. Perhaps a reasonable compromise is to suggest that maximum potential values be established for specific stocks on the basis of admittedly generous standards and that further commitments cease when prices exceed these values. It is unlikely that all stocks held in, or considered for, a portfolio will be in this position at the same time, so this policy would not ordinarily mean holding back purchases of common stocks. It does mean maintaining a critical and analytical attitude as equities show marked advances in price and consequently become less desirable as long-term holdings. Switches from overvalued situations to more reasonably priced stocks may also be a part of the program.

Formula Plans. Formula plans are more complex techniques designed to prevent acquisitions of common stocks at market peaks. However, they typically go one step farther. Most plans not only are oriented to establishing reasonable buying levels but also require the sale of stocks when the market, on the basis of some preconceived standards, is considered to be approaching a cyclical high. As conventionally set forth, therefore, they do not entirely accept the buy-and-hold theory, but are aimed at obtaining appreciation greater than long-term growth by cyclical switching of stocks to bonds and vice versa. They can, however, be modified to include only the "buy side" and, as a consequence, conform to a theory of holding common stocks on a long-term basis.

The postulates of formula plans can be summarized as follows: (1) it is not possible to forecast the future direction of the market at any given time, (2) the probable range of fluctuations over a long period of time can be predicted with some degree of assurance, (3) common stocks should be purchased when a selected stock average is below its normal in the estimated range and sold when it is above normal, and (4) the dollar quantities of purchases and sales should be established in accordance with predetermined rules of action and should not involve discretionary judgment, except as to the specific securities selected to carry out the prescribed action. The notion that it is possible to develop a mechanical means whereby stocks are automatically purchased at low levels and sold at high levels is certainly attractive in theory. Furthermore, the formula plan concept eliminates the need for agonizing decisions on what course of action is desirable at any given juncture.

Formula Plans: The Range Forecast.   The critical problem, however, is in connection with postulate (2) above; the market must fluctuate within the preconceived range or the plan will fail to accomplish its objectives. If, for example, stock prices move above the limits of the established range and persistently remain there, the formula plan technique may result in a portfolio almost devoid of stocks for an indefinite period. That serious consequences can ensue from an error in forecasting the range of stock prices is indicated by noting that the market range used by a number of plans completely missed the range of the market in the 1957–65 period.[3] Although the details differed, several plans were based on arithmetic trend projections of the historical pattern of the market. Such projections based on the long-term market trend up to about 1956 suggested eliminating most common stocks at about 500 on the Dow-Jones industrial average. As the average had moved to well above the 900 level by 1965 and had not at any time fallen below 500, it was clear that these plans had failed to indicate the range of fluctuations in the 1959–65 period.

[3] Feyler, *Income Growth with Security: The Formula Plan Solution,* New York: Macmillan, 1958, pp. 70–92.

Various other means to project the "norm" of the market and the expected range of price fluctuations have been used.[4] One such method is an "intrinsic value" approach. For example, the normal "intrinsic value" in one approach is obtained by multiplying the estimated earnings of the Dow-Jones Industrial Average by the historical average price-earnings ratios prevailing on this average.[5] In a sense the method merely adapts a particular valuation approach to a stock index instead of limiting it to individual stocks. But unfortunately it did not produce the desired results. In the 1963–65 period a "normal" value of about 600 was estimated for the Dow-Jones Industrial Average and it consistently sold well above that level.

In short, it appears almost as difficult to forecast the future range of stock price fluctuations as it is to forecast the direction of the market at a given time. As a result, formula plans have not been successful during most of the postwar years. The problem is that structural changes in the economy can make past experiences an unreliable guide to the future. Greater stability in the economy accompanied by an inflationary bias could logically have greatly improved the quality of corporate earnings and thus have made past price-earnings ratios quite unrealistic for a determination of the future range of prices.

Rules of Action. The "rules of action" under formula plans can either be based on a constant ratio of stocks to bonds in the portfolio or on a variable ratio. In addition, there may be various other rules adopted to guide action which, although useful at times, greatly increase the administrative complexity of execution.[6] Under the constant ratio plan the portfolio is divided into a set proportion of bonds and stocks. Typically this ratio is fifty-fifty, although other proportions may be considered desirable in the light of the personal needs of the investor. For example, if the primary objectives are those typically associated with common stocks, say inflation protection or growth, then the ratio might be set at 80% stocks and 20% bonds. When and if the market values of the stocks increase, stocks are sold and bonds acquired to restore the preconceived ratio. On market declines bonds must be sold and stocks bought to effect the correction. This type of plan is designed to produce only modest "timing" gains, but it has the advantage of maintaining a constant proportion of market value participation in common stocks at

---

[4] See *ibid.*, pp. 52–65, for a complete discussion of these methods.

[5] Graham, Dodd, and Cottle, *Security Analysis*, New York: McGraw-Hill, 1962, p. 422.

[6] See Cottle and Whitman, *Investment Timing—The Formula Plan Approach*, New York: McGraw-Hill, 1953, pp. 169–175, for a thorough discussion of these rules.

all times which may be desirable for the general portfolio needs of the investor. Moreover, it should be noted that failure to forecast the range of fluctuations is less serious under a constant-ratio plan.

The variable-ratio rules are designed for more aggressive action and results. Here as the reference stock index moves upward by prede-termined stages, the ratio of stocks to bonds in the entire portfolio is reduced. For example, assume that the plan at a given time calls for a fifty-fifty ratio at the 800 level of the Dow-Jones average. Then at 850 it might be established that stocks should be sold to reduce stocks to 40% and increase bonds to 60%, then at 900 the ratio may be reduced further to twenty-eighty. If the index moves below 800, then stocks would be bought and bonds sold to increase the ratio in the opposite direction. In these plans it is quite essential to predict the range of fluctuations reasonably accurately or else the account may be indefinitely weighted heavily with one type of security or the other.

Despite its apparent plausibility, the prospects of obtaining good results by formula-plan "timing" are by no means assured and in fact may produce inferior long-term returns. Only if the market fluctuates around the prognosticated "norm" will the desired results ensue. To re-peat, if a major structural change in stock-market conditions takes place, then because formula plans are established on the basis of inflexible rules, they may fail to yield as much in the way of gains as other approaches to portfolio management.[7] The consequences of errors in fore-casting the range are particularly serious in variable ratio plans; here it is possible for the portfolio to be seriously distorted for a number of years. As a result, the objectives provided by one type of security or the other may in effect be foregone. For example, if the range is established un-realistically low, then the account will be consistently devoid of com-mons and thus exposed to the inflation risk and lack growth potential entirely.

However, in accounts where there is a steady accretion of new money for investment, such as in pension funds, it may be possible to adapt certain aspects of formula plans to the acquisition of *new* securities in the portfolio. The idea is to avoid the complete inflexibility of dollar-cost averaging by committing new money according to whether the ratio of stocks to bonds in the *existing* portfolio has increased or decreased on a market value basis. If stocks have declined in price, thus decreasing

[7] The inability of formula plans to adjust to dynamic changes in the economy was one of the principal criticisms of the formula plan technique advanced by J. Fred Weston in "Some Theoretical Aspects of Formula Timing," *Journal of Business*, University of Chicago, October, 1949, pp. 249–270.

their percentage in the existing portfolio, then a larger proportion or perhaps all new money would be directed to stocks. Vice versa, if the market moves up, stocks would *not* be sold, and therefore the equity percentage of the total portfolio in terms of the market values of common stocks would increase. This would then be balanced by a lesser investment of new funds in stocks.

Serious distortion of the portfolio should not result from such a procedure as may occur under the conventional types of formula plans. In addition, the process of buying stocks automatically on an uncritical basis (true of dollar averaging) might then be avoided. One main advantage of formula plans would still be obtained; forcing investors to buy when the market declines instead of being "scared off" by the general pessimism usually predominant in bear markets. The technique of adjusting new money commitments may be quite useful when a portfolio is subject to policy direction by people who lack experience in the investments area. Such individuals may be inclined to "panic" during market declines and not only recommend no purchases of stocks but advise substantial sales. A preconceived plan about the commitment of new money to stocks as the market value ratio of stocks to bonds varies in the existing portfolio should prevent erratic changes in policy as general psychology moves back and forth from optimism to pessimism concerning the market outlook.

CHAPTER 28

Taxation and

Investment Decisions

Introduction

The primary purpose of this chapter is to examine the more important tax rules imposed on long-term investment returns and transactions with a view to appraising their influence on the objectives and execution of investment policy. Secondarily, some consideration will be given to methods for minimizing the tax burden through specific transactions executed solely for their tax effects. Most investors, of course, are subject to some taxation on their security portfolios. But not all investors should modify their policies because of taxation problems. For example, the retired person, supplementing modest pension and Social Security income with income from a moderate-sized security portfolio, would probably not find the rate of taxation sufficiently great to justify substantive changes in his portfolio composition.[1]

At the other extreme, however, the composition of some portfolios may be almost entirely dominated by tax considerations. The obvious and prime example is the very large account of several million dollars on which the income automatically is large and subject to high rates of

[1] This does not necessarily apply to certain legal mechanics of policy such as holding the securities in joint name or via gift of a part of the corpus reducing potential estate taxes. These mechanics should always be investigated for minimization of tax liabilities.

taxation. Here the portfolio may largely consist of tax-exempt municipal securities, solely because of the taxation factor. As a general proposition, the objective of all investors is to maximize returns on an after-tax basis and at the same time to safeguard the principal against the hazards inherent in a dynamic economy. If a large part of the gross returns is likely to be absorbed by taxation, then policy naturally becomes more concerned with tax minimization.

The great majority of investors are probably in an intermediate position with respect to the taxation factor. Specific investment decisions may be influenced to a moderate degree by tax considerations, but they do not (or should not) control the construction and management of the account. The positive objectives and a recognition of the inescapable investment risks should control basic policy decisions. In this framework the tax factor enters the picture as a supplementary element which may suggest certain modifications in the practical execution of investment management.

The Income Tax

The federal government and a number of the states impose taxes on income derived from most securities. The principal exception is the complete exemption from federal income taxation of the income derived from municipal securities. As state income taxes vary widely in nature but are usually quite moderate in rate, attention will be concentrated on the incidence of the federal tax. Moreover, there are many intricate and detailed provisions in the income-tax statutes to cover all kinds of unusual specific transactions and types of income. In order to avoid confusion resulting from a morass of detail, only the major provisions of the tax statutes as related to long-term investments will be considered.[2]

Basic Principles. The framework of the income tax may be described as follows. First, a relatively small amount of income is exempt; each individual and dependent thereof receives a $600 exemption per year (doubled for individuals 65 years and older) under the statute in effect as of 1965. Second, certain deductions are allowed against income which may be either itemized in full or taken at a flat 10% of gross income, but the percentage deduction is limited to a maximum of $1,000. Third,

[2] For example, the rules on short-term gains and losses on securities held less than six months will not be considered in detail, because by definition long-term investors would not have much if anything in this category.

TABLE 28–1
TAX RATES ON INCREMENTS OF INCOME TO $100,000
(1965 statute: joint return)*

Income Increments	Tax Rate
$ 000–1,000	14%
1,001–2,000	15
2,001–3,000	16
3,001–4,000	17
4,001–8,000	19
8,001–12,000	22
12,001–16,000	25
16,001–20,000	28
20,001–24,000	32
24,001–28,000	36
28,001–32,000	39
32,001–36,000	42
36,001–40,000	45
40,001–44,000	48
44,001–52,000	50
52,001–64,000	53
64,001–76,000	55
76,001–88,000	58
88,001–100,000	60

* For single taxpayers or if separate returns are filed, the incremental rates apply to one-half the above amounts. For example, the 60% rate applies to taxable income between $44,000 and $50,000 for single taxpayers.

income beyond the exemptions and deductions is subject to a minimum tax of 14% with increments of income taxed at the rates shown in Table 28-1. The sharp progressivity of the income tax is evident from the rate schedule, and of course it means that investors with large incomes have a materially different problem from those with modest incomes.

Taxation of Investment Returns. The tax rules on investment returns modify this basic outline to some extent. First, dividends from most stocks are exempt from income taxes up to $100 ($200 if held jointly by spouses). Second, if investment returns take the form of appreciation, there is no tax imposed until it is actually realized by a sale and then only half the gain (assuming the securities have been held more than six months) is included in taxable income.[3] Moreover, the

[3] If the appreciation is never realized prior to the death of the individual holding the securities, it is then not subject to a capital-gains tax as such. After payment of estate and inheritance taxes, if any, the new cost basis to the heirs for capital gains becomes the market value of the securities either at date of death or one year thereafter depending upon which is used for determination of the estate tax.

maximum rate of tax on the taxable portion of long-term capital gains (one half) is restricted to 50%. Put another way, the maximum rate of tax on *total* long-term capital gains is limited to 25%, but if the investor's marginal tax rate is less than 50%, the lesser rate is applied to one half the gain.

Treatment of Capital Losses. Third, all long-term realized capital losses (a negative investment return) can be deducted from ordinary taxable income up to $1,000 in any one year. If, unhappily, the loss exceeds $1,000, the excess can be subtracted from regular income for the subsequent years in a maximum amount of $1,000 per year. Thus there is no limit on the amount of a long-term capital loss that can ultimately be used to offset ordinary income from other sources, but this would preclude obtaining any *current* deductions from additional realized capital losses. However, capital losses in all cases must first be deducted from realized gains before the net gain or loss is established, and, of course, an unlimited amount of realized losses can be so deducted from such gains.

Treatment of Bond Premiums and Discount. Finally, although of minor consequence to all except large investors, the rules on the tax treatment of bonds bought at a discount or premium from par might be mentioned. The discount portion of the interest yield on a bond purchased in the secondary market is taxable as a long-term capital gain at maturity, whereas the premium on a bond purchased above par must be amortized against the regular coupon return and is thus deducted from interest income. For example, if a bond is purchased at $90 to mature in ten years, then the $10 gain realized at maturity is considered a long-term capital gain and is taxed as such.[4] If sold or redeemed by the company at the call price before maturity, any realized gain is also taxed at the capital gains rate assuming the bond has been held more than six months.

It might be noted that capital gains on municipal bonds are taxable, although the regular coupon income is fully tax exempt. Thus the after-tax returns on taxable bonds are increased by having part of the gross yield to maturity take the form of accrued discount, but in the case of municipals the after-tax yield is decreased when part of it takes this

[4] However, if a bond is first offered to the public at a discount below par, this so-called original discount is taxable as ordinary income. This rule is to prevent corporations from in effect lowering the tax rate on the effective interest return paid to their bondholders.

form. For tax reasons, therefore, it is preferable, when before-tax yields on several taxable bonds are about equal, to buy the one offering the maximum portion of its yield in the form of accrued discount. But, for the same reasons, it would be desirable to choose the municipal bond offering the maximum portion of its total return through regular coupon income.

On the other hand, if either a corporate or municipal bond is purchased at a premium above par, the premium must be regularly amortized in appropriate installments against the coupon income and cannot be treated as a capital loss at maturity. Of course, if any bond is sold before maturity at a price below its amortized cost value at that time, the difference is allowed as a capital loss and is deductible pursuant to the rules set forth above.

Income Tax Effects on Current-Income Portfolios. Having established the major rules pertinent to the taxation of returns on securities, it is now possible to suggest their impact on investment policy decisions. First, there are those cases where current income is the primary portfolio objective. In this case the appropriate analytical procedure would be to consider the tax burden on incremental units of investment income with a view to establishing when municipal bonds give a higher net yield than alternative securities. Although the general principle sounds rather obvious, some intensive analysis may be required to execute it in practice. For example, assume that a married man in semiretirement has a discretionary portfolio of $500,000 and that other taxable income from professional or business interests after all exemptions and deductions amounts to $10,000. Referring to Table 28-1, it can be established that additional income from investments beyond the $10,000 from other sources will be subject to tax as follows:

Investment Income Unit	Tax Rate
1st $2,000	22%
$ 2,001– 6,000	25
6,001–10,000	28
10,001–14,000	32
14,001–18,000	36

But in order to prevent the taxation factor from causing unwise decisions, it should be noted that although tax-exempt municipal bonds can be selected to produce highly safe dollar income, they are entirely exposed to the inflation risk. It would seem highly desirable that all investment accounts protect against possible inflationary developments even though it can only be done imperfectly at best. Therefore, for essentially defensive reasons (protection against a specific risk) a significant proportion of the discretionary portfolio—say, $150,000—might be diverted to common stocks. This step would be advisable even if after-tax returns on good-quality stocks were significantly lower than on municipal bonds. In the first part of 1965, for example, yields on such stocks (Standard Oil of New Jersey, for example) were only about 3.3% before taxes, or on a $150,000 portfolio the gross income would be $4,950, on which the tax would be 22% on the first $2,000 and 25% on the balance, or a total of about $960. Net income after taxes would be about $3,990, or 2.66% on the $150,000. As our hypothetical investor could have obtained about 3.2% on municipals, a significant sacrifice in income was required to obtain adequate inflation protection.

Yields on high-grade taxable bonds as of 1965 were about 4.7%, or after taxes as follows: 3.52% at a 25% rate, 3.39% at a 28% rate, and 3.19% at a 32% rate. Therefore, at the indicated yield spread between municipals and taxable corporate bonds, it would have been advisable for income purposes to have bought taxable bonds until total income from the portfolio exceeded $10,000 and then tax-exempt bonds to obtain additional increments of income. Assuming the stock income of $4,950, this would mean $5,150 of taxable bond income could be purchased before tax-exempts would be indicated, or about $110,000 at a 4.7% yield.

To generalize, the following steps would seem pertinent in the management of a portfolio emphasizing current income to take account of the income-tax problem: (1) establish the effective rate of tax on successive units of investment income, (2) determine the net after-tax yields obtainable on municipal securities, corporate fixed-income securities, and common stocks, (3) invest in common stocks as required to achieve the necessary inflation protection, (4) invest in additional taxable common stocks or bonds up to the point where the net yield after deducting the incremental tax rate equals the yield from municipals, and (5) allocate the remainder of the account to municipal obligations. The application of these principles to the hypothetical $500,000 account would mean at least $150,000 in common stocks, $110,000 or so in taxable bonds, and the balance of about $240,000 in municipals.[5] Finally, it should be noted that if municipal bonds become part of the portfolio, they provide the same portfolio functions as any long-term bond both as to positive objectives and risk protection.

[5] These allocations were based on the comparative yields and tax rates prevailing in 1965. They might of course be modified under different yield relationships and tax rates or because of the introduction of other portfolio objectives.

Income Tax: Appreciation vs. Current Income. The preferential tax treatment of long-term capital gains means, of course, that the net returns per dollar of long-term appreciation are greater than current income. Therefore, the obvious suggestion is usually made that when current income is not a pressing need, the portfolio should logically emphasize common stocks wherein long-term growth in value is likely to pre-dominate rather than dividend income. In theory this is certainly a sound principle, but, like many policy generalities, it is easier to state than to implement it in practice. By and large it means seeking common stocks that are: (1) retaining a large portion of the earnings and (2) showing clear prospects for profitable use of these retained earnings by virtue of a consistently high average and marginal rate of return on the book value of the stock equity, and (3) selling at prices that are reasonable in relation to projected earnings and the payout period.

If stocks meeting these requirements are available, then the tax structure would dictate their use to an increasing degree as the marginal tax rate on current income increases. However, it is necessary to recognize that investment selections directed specifically toward obtaining apprecia-tion require a greater degree of sophistication than when directed toward producing current income. It is also true that the appreciation return may be more irregular because of the propensity of the stock market to vary over a reasonably wide range. On the other hand, the taxation factor reinforces the principle that where growth in the account is the prime objective, a large part of the portfolio might logically consist of common stocks selected primarily for their possible long-term appreciation char-acteristics.

Income Tax: Sales from Portfolio. So far the discussion has been oriented to the influence of the income tax on the construction of the basic portfolio. For long-term investors this is by far the most important question, as presumably decisions to sell one security and buy another would be dictated only by (1) a change in portfolio objectives due to new financial or personal circumstances, (2) clear evidence of the un-desirability of a security now held either because of a price advance to a distinct level of overvaluation or a change for the worse in the appraisal of a company's long-term future. By and large these conditions under the buy-and-hold theory of investment operations should arise rather infrequently; indeed, some investors need to be warned recurrently against an undue amount of switching for transitory or even capricious reasons.

Tax considerations may, however, suggest some specific changes in

TABLE 28-2
COMPUTATION OF EFFECTIVE PRICE AFTER TAXES

Cost*	Net Proceeds*	Result	Tax Effect†	After-Tax Proceeds
$4,040	$2,970	$1,070 (loss)	40% of $1,070 saved	$2,970 + $428
2,020	2,970	950 (gain)	40% of $475 taxed	2,970 − 190

* Includes assumed acquisition costs on original purchases of $40 and $20 respectively and estimated selling costs of $30.

† Assumes no other gains or losses and also carry forward of loss in excess of $1,000.

portfolio composition now and then even though not dictated by fundamental policy or security-analysis factors. However, a definite and substantial tax saving should be indicated; minor tax advantages should not tempt the investor to engage in an excessive turnover of the securities embodied in the account. It might be mentioned that the mechanical costs of purchases and sales (commissions, transfer taxes, and odd-lot premiums) may amount to more than the tax savings on such transactions. But assuming that for one reason or another portfolio sales are contemplated, tax factors may affect the decision in two primary ways. First, they change the effective price data on which the decision to sell is predicated. Second, they may suggest a certain desirable "timing" pattern of the sales.

The after-tax price on an issue which is a candidate for sale should be the criterion for final decision. This price may be greater or less than the indicated market quotation. It is greater if there is a tax loss involved; here the amount of the tax saving should be added to the total proceeds, because the sale will produce a retention of funds which otherwise would be paid to the government. On the other hand, if there is a capital gain, the proceeds are reduced by the indicated tax liability. To illustrate briefly, assume that an investor is contemplating the sale of 100 shares of a common stock priced at 30 in the market. Further assume that the marginal tax rate is 40%. In Table 28-2 a computation of the effective proceeds from the sale is shown first when a cost basis of $40 per share produces a loss and second when a cost basis of $20 per share produces a gain. In the first instance the investor really obtains $3,398, or about $34 per share after the tax saving, whereas in the second the net price per share becomes $27.80.[6] These respective prices are

[6] The amount of the tax saving or deduction will vary, of course, with the marginal tax rate of the investor, and in the case of tax savings the amount of such savings will depend on whether the loss is offset by gains or exceeds the total allowable deduction.

really the logical data for deciding whether the contemplated sale should be consummated.

The desired "timing" pattern of sales for optimum tax effects is not the same for all investors; in fact, it is possible to suggest diametrically opposite courses of action depending on the circumstances. However, some general concepts can be established. First, relatively small investors would usually be well advised to take long-term gains and losses in different years. Here it is presumed that the total amount of losses on securities considered for disposition will not exceed $1,000 or so per year. As losses up to $1,000 can be deducted from ordinary income in a given year, whereas only half a long-term gain is subject to tax, it is desirable on small accounts not to offset realized gains with losses in a given year.

For example, suppose two securities are to be sold, one of which shows a long-term loss of $800 and the other a similar gain of $1,200. It would then be desirable to "time" the sales in different years. The consequences would be that the entire $800 can be deducted from ordinary income in one year and only $600 of the gain is added to taxable income in the second year. The net effect would be a $200 reduction in taxable income over the two-year period, whereas if they were both sold in the same year, there would be a net gain of $400, of which $200 would be added to taxable income. There is not even any need to take the risk that the market price of one of the stocks will move down if sale is delayed. The risk can be obviated by making a short sale of one while holding the original stock to cover the short sale next year. The real gain or loss will be determined when the short sale is made, but it will be recognized for tax purposes only when the original stock is used to cover the short sale.

Second, large investors usually take capital gains and losses in the same year in order to obtain the full deduction for tax purposes of the losses. However, because of the carry-forward rule on losses, it is somewhat difficult to be categorical on the desired policy. But large losses in any one year should usually be "timed" to coincide with realized capital gains, because only $1,000 per year can be carried forward to the succeeding years. Therefore, if potential realized losses exceed an average of $1,000 per year over a period of time, then capital-gain offsets must be taken to obtain a tax deduction for the excess.

The Washed-Sale Rule. A "washed sale" may be defined as the sale and immediate repurchase of the same security for the purpose of registering a realized capital gain or loss for tax purposes while recording the reacquisition at a new cost basis. The action is permissible when the result of the transaction is a capital gain; therefore, capital gains to offset losses can be registered without any substantive change in the portfolio at the cost of broker's commissions and other charges of a minor nature.

However, if a security is sold to establish a loss for tax purposes, the same security cannot be purchased thirty days before or after the sale. Although the indicated tax saving may sometimes justify assuming the risk that the subsequent repurchase may have to be at a significantly higher level, the waiting interval suggests that purely mechanical tax switching on the loss side must be conducted with care. If the tax saving is considerable, it might be possible to find a similar security of equal quality for immediate substitution which would avoid the market risk and at the same time maintain the desired portfolio structure. It is probable, however, that only relatively large investors in the higher tax brackets would find it desirable to incur the costs and conduct the investigations necessary to justify switching purely for tax reasons.

Determination of Cost Basis. The cost of a security for tax purposes includes all acquisition expenses. The total sum shown on the broker's invoice is thus the cost for tax purposes of that unit of securities. If the entire unit is sold intact at a later date, there are, of course, no problems in determining the amount of the realized profit or loss in connection therewith. But some special problems may arise to complicate the cost-basis determination.

First, the investor may sell a part of his holdings of a given security acquired at different times and prices. In this case it is possible to designate which blocks are to be sold, and, of course, the designations should obtain the maximum tax advantage possible in the circumstances. If no specific designation is made, then the "first-in, first-out" rule is applied which means the first unit acquired is assumed to be the first unit sold. Second, if there have been stock dividends or splits and only a part of the holdings are sold, it is necessary to compute the cost basis per share.[7] This can be done simply by dividing the total cost on each invoice by the new number of shares held after the declaration of the stock dividend or splits.

Third, for stock acquired through the exercise of stock rights, the

[7] The receipt of stock dividends in the same class of stock as that held creates no taxable income under existing law unless the shareholder has the option of receiving cash or other property in lieu of the stock dividend. This latter situation is relatively rare.

cost basis is the subscription price unless the market value of the stock rights is more than 15% of the value of the outstanding stock.[8] Except for small or new companies, such a market value on rights would be highly unlikely. If the rights are sold, their cost basis is considered to be zero and a capital gain equal to the net proceeds results. The gain is considered long-term if the related stock has been held more than six months.

Fourth, the cost basis for determination of capital gains taxes becomes the value shown on the estate tax return for securities received from an estate.[9] For example, an investor may have purchased a security at $10 per share and then held it for some considerable period until at his death its market value was $50 per share. To the heirs the cost basis for capital gains taxes becomes the latter amount. The rule means that many elderly investors desiring to preserve the maximum corpus for their heirs may find it undesirable to sell securities on which very substantial unrealized gains exist. If held until death, these securities are subject to the estate tax discussed below, but the proceeds from any prior sale would be subject to the capital-gains tax and the remainder to the estate tax as well.

Death and Gift Taxes

Nature of Death and Gift Taxes. Death taxes are imposed both by the federal government and the several states, whereas the gift tax is exclusively federal. Taxes on the transfer of property from a decedent to the heirs can either be levied on the estate as such or on the heir. In either case, however, the burden usually falls on the estate or properties resulting therefrom. As it has worked out in practice, the estate tax is used by the federal government whereas inheritance taxes on the heirs are mostly used by states. However, a few of the latter have recently converted to the principle of the estate tax. The federal gift tax is related in that its basic purpose is to prevent tax-free disposal of property to heirs before death and thereby in effect eliminate the incidence of death duties.

---

[8] If the market value of the stock rights exceeds 15% of the value of the outstanding stock, then the cost basis of the new stock is increased and that of the old stock decreased via an allocation formula.

[9] The value shown on the estate tax return is ordinarily computed as of date of death. However, in recognition of the time necessary to probate an estate, the values may be alternatively taken one year following date of death. This prevents the inequity which might result if the stock market declines drastically.

The specific details and computation of these taxes are quite complicated and involve many legal, accounting, and statistical principles. The essential concepts, however, can be briefly outlined as a frame of reference for investment decisions. Those of the estate tax are as follows: (1) all assets owned in any way by a decedent on date of death are included in the estate; (2) deductions for charitable bequests, expenses of administration, and debts of decedent are then made; (3) then assets passing to a surviving spouse can be deducted up to one half the remaining estate; (4) a specific exemption of $60,000 is allowed before any tax is imposed on the "net estate." In brief, when the major heir is a spouse, the net estate after payment of all debts and expenses must amount to more than $120,000 before any tax is imposed and $60,000 when the heirs do not include a surviving spouse. The estate tax rate, however, is quite progressive on additional assets. For example, it starts at 3% on the first $10,000 of taxable assets, it is 22% between $50,000 and $60,000, and it increases to 28% between $100,000 and $200,000.

The inheritance taxes imposed by the states vary widely, and, therefore, specific generalizations are difficult. However, these usually provide for a smaller exemption than the federal estate tax, but the rates are ordinarily considerably lower. In addition, state inheritance tax rates may vary with the relationship of the heir to the decedent. Property passing to spouses and children is usually taxed at a lesser rate than when the relationship is more distant. Moreover, property held jointly with the right of survivorship, although not subject to inheritance taxes on the death of one of the joint owners, is included in the purchaser's estate for federal estate tax purposes. Unless evidence to the contrary is supplied, it is assumed that the male spouse supplied the funds for the acquisition of property held jointly by husband and wife; such joint properties, therefore, are included in their entirety in the estate of the husband for tax purposes. Therefore, holding property in the joint name of husband and wife is usually undesirable when the total value is much in excess of $120,000. Gifts to the wife or children of at least the exempt amounts might then be recommended.

The federal gift tax is imposed on the donor. It was designed to remove part of the tax saving which can result by transferring income-producing assets from high-income-tax-bracket members of a family to low-bracket members while at the same time eliminating the assets from the prospective estate. The general rules of the gift tax as of 1965 were as follows: (1) a donor has a specific lifetime exemption of $30,000; (2) gifts up to $3,000 per year may be made to any number of individuals without tax; (3) a husband and wife may treat gifts to third parties (children usually) as though they were made one half by each, although the property given can be owned by one spouse only; (4) gifts to a spouse are exempt to twice the indicated amounts (the "marital deduction" principle); (5) rates are progressive and are about three-quarters of the estate tax schedules; (6) to determine the rate bracket in any year all prior years' gifts are added to those of the current year.

This last rule means that a wealthy individual cannot distribute his assets through time to his prospective heirs at relatively low tax rates. To illustrate, if a gift of $10,000 in excess of exemptions is made to a child in one year and then repeated in a later year, the gift tax rate on the second distribution would be that of a $20,000 gift applied to the $10,000 actually given in that year.

Death and Gift Taxes: Relation to Investment Decisions. Estate and inheritance taxes have only a limited impact on investment decisions, and some of the appropriate adjustments are more mechanical and legal than substantive. To a large extent these taxes influence the method of holding investment assets rather than their composition. Decisions to establish trusts as the legal nominee or to give a certain proportion of the portfolio to one's spouse or children in order to reduce the prospective estate tax levy are typical of the type of considerations involved.

These are really in the area of estate planning, and when it appears that the total assets may be considerably above the prescribed exemptions, assistance from a trust department of a bank or a qualified lawyer should be obtained. It might be noted that it is not as difficult for a prospective estate to amount to more than $120,000 as first might be presumed. All assets are included in the gross estate including housing, insurance proceeds, business interests, and personal property besides assets of an investment nature. Competent estate planning can often greatly reduce the possible incidence of death taxes without any major disadvantage to the person concerned. But as the details of estate planning are essentially legal, they are outside the scope of investment management as such. For example, the use of trusts is a major element in estate planning for large investors, and a thorough knowledge of the law applicable to trusts is required so that legal advice rather than investment advice is pertinent to their use. However, where trusts are not considered desirable and where the total assets of a family are between $120,000 and $250,000, holding half the assets in the name of one spouse and half in the name of the other will tend to minimize estate taxes to the surviving spouse. As noted previously, this arrangement can be accomplished through regular lifetime gifts within the limits of the gift-tax exemptions.

In planning the portfolio composition, the principal effect of estate taxes is to create a possible need for liquidity that would otherwise not be required. The estate and inheritance taxes become cash claims against the indicated values of the assets and forced liquidation of assets to meet these claims may lead to severe injury on the heirs. Some U.S. Government bond issues can be used to pay the federal estate tax at their par value, and if these are available in the market at a discount, they are natural acquisitions for a portfolio where estate taxes may arise within several years. This liquidity can also be provided through insurance payable to the estate; alternatively, savings accounts or savings bonds can provide the necessary amount of liquidity.

CHAPTER 29

Portfolio Management:
Case Studies

The preceding chapters on the concepts pertinent to the composition and management of a security portfolio have necessarily been general. Moreover, in order to avoid undue complexity, the analyses of the several major policy issues confronting investors have been somewhat isolated from one another. Therefore, a discussion of a few hypothetical investment situations might be useful as a means of integrating the issues of investment management. However, as has been emphasized earlier, each individual investor is in some ways unique, and relative conditions in the securities markets tend to change through time. Therefore, although the cases have been designed to depict typical situations, they are not intended to provide specific portfolio recommendations for various classes of investors at all sequences in time.

Furthermore, it should be remembered that investment management decisions cannot be clearly defined as either right or wrong. Considerable modification of portfolio distributions can always be justified because of different conclusions about personal objectives and the opportunities and risks that seem to be evident in the securities markets. The purpose of these case discussions, therefore, it not to establish specific solutions for different types of portfolios. Rather, the purpose is twofold. First, it is to give a summary review of the major issues and approaches to investment management. Second, it is to illustrate the nature of the decisions required in various types of situations.

Case 1. As of 1965, Robert Maxwell is 40 years of age and is married with three children, ages 16, 13, and 10. All the family are in good health, and his life insurance program is adequate. He also has adequate hospitalization and disability insurance for himself and his family. He is a vice president of a medium-sized bank, with a current salary of $19,000 per year. There are no other sources of income at the present time, but under a retirement plan and Social Security he will receive an estimated $600 per month upon retirement at age 65. At the present time his assets consist of a $25,000 house with a $10,000, 5% mortgage; $1,500 in a checking account, $12,000 in a 4% (current rate) savings account at the bank; and 100 shares of bank's common stock, with a market price of 40, on which the yield is 3.6% By considerable effort he is able to save in cash about $2,000 per year after taxes. His potential benefits from estates of older relatives may be estimated at $40,000.

The following conclusions from this information seem pertinent to the determination of the investment objectives of this individual. First, he seems to be well established in his job, and, in view of the nature of the banking industry it is unlikely that any downturn in general business activity will result in a cessation of salary. Second, the need for contingency funds is moderate in view of the stable occupation and adequate insurance program. Third, there may be some presumption that he will obtain gradual advances in occupation income in the future. Fourth, there may be a considerable exposure to the inflation risk in the sense that the salary increases may lag behind any substantial increase in the cost of living over a period of a few years. Fifth, the fact that he has four dependents of an age that could enjoy vacation trips, clubs, and other higher-level discretionary expenditures, plus the likelihood of a higher salary later on, provides evidence of the importance to the Maxwell family of current disposable income. Assuming $3,000 in itemized deductions and five exemptions of $600 each, his taxable income may be estimated at $13,000, on which the marginal tax rate is 25%. Sixth, assuming that college educations are desired for the children, there might be some provision for additional resources at that time, although use of current savings and expected normal salary increases should largely take care of this need. Seventh, although retirement income presently provided is moderate, potential benefits from estates should assist in this connection and also should add to the ultimate estate available to his wife and children.

The objectives suggested by the review of the personal and financial factors would seem to be to (1) obtain some protection against any significant increase in the cost of living, (2) maintain a modest amount of liquidity to take care of contingencies or larger than ordinary family expenditures, such as travel or a new car, (3) supplement salary income with current income if possible, and (4) obtain a moderate growth in the size of the portfolio through time. The relative priority of the objectives would seem to be roughly in the order listed, although some might prefer to reverse (3) and (4).

To implement the program pursuant to these objectives, one major step might be instituted immediately: a program of dollar averaging in "inflation stocks." Four purchases a year in a total amount of $6,000, ($4,000 from the savings account and $2,000 from current savings), and rotated among perhaps six companies in three industries might be considered appropriate. The total objective in such stocks might be final commitment of $15,000 to $20,000, to be achieved over a three- to four-year period. It is not necessary, of course, to select all six companies in advance, as prevailing prices in relation to indicated earnings projections and dividends can change over a period of time. Moderate diversification builds up gradually, which is all that can be expected in the formulative stages.

Dividends derived from the common stocks will be small in total amount for several years and might also be irregular, because inflation stocks are typically exposed to cyclical fluctuations. However, moderate growth characteristics on these stocks would seem preferable to high current income. But any dividends can be used to increase the amount of income available for ordinary living expenses or added to the stock-purchase fund if more rapid growth of the investment account is desired. Any increase in available funds due to salary advances could be advantageously used to step up the rate of acquisition of these stocks. After achieving the appropriate inflation protection, additional commitments might emphasize growth or current income, as personal preferences dictate.

Retention of the bank stock already owned would probably be advisable for personal reasons. Some degree of prejudice toward one's own company is natural, especially in the executive ranks, but ordinarily it is poor practice to tie the fortunes of an investment account to the same source from which a salary is received. In this case it may be less serious, because the degree of business risk in a bank is ordinarily moderate in both a cyclical and secular sense. Also, although as a general principle the investor should avoid a large concentration of commitments in his own company, the ability to make a more penetrating analysis than outsiders might be the source of an unusual investment opportunity. The obtaining of favorable stock options may also be a cause for exception to this general rule. Maintenance of between $2,000 and $4,000 in the savings account would also appear desirable, the current return is good and it provides absolute assurance of recoverability at any time.

Specific programming of portfolio requirements beyond a decade or so in advance except for well-defined needs, such as education, is probably not worthwhile. Personal and financial circumstances tend to change extensively, and considerable flexibility must be maintained. In short, it would be advisable for Mr. Maxwell to review his complete investment program periodically and adjust the account to any new conditions.

Case 2. To indicate the evolutionary nature of an investment program, let us take the same family situation as in the preceding case but assume that ten years have passed. Now Mr. Maxwell is 50 years of age and is Executive Vice President of his bank at a salary of $28,000 a year. one child is still in college, but with his higher salary the educational expenses are not a significant strain on his financial resources. From the implementation of the original program, he has accumulated a portfolio of inflation stocks worth $26,000 at current market prices with a cost of $20,000; annual income on these stocks as of 1965 was expected to amount to $800 per year. In addition, an inheritance of $25,000 in cash has recently been received.

His home is owned free of debt, and other assets consist of a $2,000 checking account, a $5,000 savings account, and 200 shares of the bank's common stock with a market value of 50. Income on this stock from dividends amounts to $400 annually, and for business reasons retention of this stock is considered desirable. The insurance program remains adequate and estimated retirement income at age 65 remains $600 monthly.

The personal circumstances now suggest that the major positive objective of the investment program is long-term growth of principal. Several aspects of the situation seem to lead to this conclusion. First, the marginal tax rate should be about 36% assuming normal exemptions and deductions of about $6,000 from the gross income of about $30,000. As a result, there is a significant tax benefit achieved if returns on the investment account take the form of capital gains. Second, the current amount of income derived from his occupation and existing investments appears quite adequate for regular consumption needs, although Mr. Maxwell might well desire to use some of the returns from the investment portfolio (either from current income or realized capital gains) to finance a major expenditure from time to time, such as a trip to Europe. In short, there is no reason why a growth objective should dictate a Spartan existence for a man in this fortunate position. But, aside from these special uses, there are no pressing needs for large cash returns from the portfolio. Third, it is probable that Mr. Maxwell will find it difficult to maintain his accustomed standard of living on $600 a month on retirement some fifteen years hence, and the existing $66,000 in available cash and stocks invested at 4% would only produce another $220 per month. Therefore, increasing the size of the fund would seem to be a logical objective. Finally, it may be presumed that there is some desire to provide an inheritance to his family to the greatest extent possible, and this fact would also indicate a growth objective.

The primary negative risk factor of concern to Mr. Maxwell is still the possibility of continued inflation. His insurance, retirement income, and to a lesser extent his salary are all exposed to inflationary developments. But as there are now $26,000 of inflation stocks in the portfolio, only moderate additional attention to this risk would seem desirable. Moreover, growth stocks by definition should protect against "creeping inflation" of the type characteristic of the peacetime American economy. Therefore, the $25,000 in cash and such net savings as may materialize in the next fifteen years may well be committed entirely to growth stocks.

In making this recommendation, however, it is assumed that the investor by temperament, training, and experience is qualified to be an "enterprising" investor, because these stocks are likely to be both volatile and difficult to appraise on a long-term basis. Furthermore, because of the price factor, dollar-cost averaging at the rate of $2,000 per quarter ($8,000 per year) of the $25,000 cash inheritance might be suggested. Temporary commitments to bank certificates of deposits at 4.25 to 4.5%, maturing in ninety days to one year, might be justified for the funds held back on the dollar-averaging program. However, should the stock market decline significantly or should particular stocks be discovered which are attractively priced, an "enterprising" investor might well decide to depart from a rigid dollar-averaging program. In a growth investment program a reasonable degree of flexibility would seem appropriate.

Finally, as a technical point, Mr. Maxwell might be advised to consider making a gift of the $50,000 in negotiable assets to his wife by transferring the existing cash and stocks to her name. Subsequent acquisitions to the investment account up to $6,000 a year, the amount exempt from the gift tax annually in the case of a wife, might also be in her name until total assets so held reach about $120,000. This action is advisable because all other assets of the family would presumably be included in his estate for tax purposes, including the home and all insurance proceeds. It is quite probable that such assets already exceed $120,000 and thus the present values in the investment account would be fully subject to the estate tax in the case of his untimely death. As noted in Chapter 28, property passing from one spouse to another is exempt from the estate tax up to $120,000 in value, so that it is usually desirable to divide between a husband and wife the legal ownership of family assets up to about $240,000 in total values.

Case 3. Mr. Fred Johnson is 52 years of age and is self-employed as a manufacturers' agent for a group of small companies selling components to the automobile companies. His commissions have averaged $20,000 annually for the years 1960–64. In 1961, however, his income declined to $14,000 and in 1962 it recovered only to $16,000. However, he expected that in 1965 his occupation income would advance to about $25,000, in view of the favorable outlook for automobile production. He has a wife and three children, one of whom is working after graduating from college and another who graduates from college in June of 1966. The third, a girl, is a junior in high school and intends to enter college in September of 1966. All are in good health. He has life insurance of $75,000 with a cash value of $20,000, owns a $30,000 home outright, and after age sixty-five on retirement will obtain $110 monthly from Social Security with death benefits to his widow of about $75 monthly. From his own savings and an inheritance he has accumulated the following: eight good-quality steel, automotive, and oil stocks currently worth $60,000, with a capital-gains tax base of $30,000; ten miscellaneous common stocks of cyclical secondary companies worth $30,000, with a tax base of $26,000, although on three of these issues there are unrealized losses of $4,000 at their current market of $14,000; a $2,000 checking account; and a savings account of $7,000 in the same bank. He has no significant amount of outstanding debts.

These data suggest a personal situation almost the opposite from that of Mr. Maxwell. The income from the occupation is exposed to considerable risk both in terms of a general decline in business activity and in terms of the competitive uncertainties that the companies he represents will be able to maintain their contracts. Inflation, however, is not to be greatly feared, because commissions should tend to increase with any rise in the price level over a period of years. Considerable outlays on education for the children are now required and presumably will continue for about six years. If earnings continue at the expected 1965 level, the education expenses could probably be met without assistance from the investment account. Reasonable prudence, however, would indicate the desirability of stand-by resources to insure the completion of this responsibility. Moreover, it is conceivable that some of the investment account will be needed for various contingencies, including living expenses in case of a serious loss of earning power. Fortunately, the debt situation is favorable, which reduces fixed family expenses somewhat, but regardless of this fact, it can be argued that a significant portion of the portfolio should protect against the risks associated with a decline in business activity.

As Mr. Johnson may contemplate complete or partial retirement within fifteen years or so and existing provisions for retirement income are very modest, the investment program must also take on the responsibility of providing Mr. Johnson with a reasonable standard of living upon retirement. After the children are educated, however, ordinary family expenses should decline and a larger proportion of his income can be diverted to investments. At the same time the needs for stand-by funds will be reduced. Under existing tax laws his effective tax rate is probably between 25 and 32%, depending on the level of the occupation income. Although not an extremely high tax rate, it suggests the desirability of emphasizing growth rather than current income on any common stocks that might be included in the portfolio.

From these facts, it might be concluded that the investment objectives of Mr. Johnson are: (1) dollar recoverability of a significant amount, especially for the next five years and (2) long-term growth of principal for the next fifteen years or so, until retirement. These two objectives indicate that the portfolio should really be divided into two major components for investment-management purposes. One would be invested in highly "defensive" securities wherein stability of dollar income and principal values would be emphasized. The other would seek growth through relatively enterprising investments in common stocks, assuming competence in investment selection techniques on the part of Mr. Johnson or his advisers.

The existing portfolio of Mr. Johnson clearly requires considerable revision in the light of these objectives. First, the existing common-stock portfolio is largely concentrated in cyclical issues, although some may have demonstrated reasonable growth characteristics. Second, the dollar assets of about $9,000 appear inadequate in view of the potential variations in his business income and the considerable family obligations.

However, an investment adviser to Mr. Johnson might be well advised to work out a flexible program for portfolio adjustments over a period of time rather than institute immediate radical surgery for two reasons. First, clients tend to be disturbed by wholesale disposition of holdings that have given good results over the years. Secondly, the

TABLE 29-1
COMPARATIVE YIELDS: BONDS AND EQUIVALENTS
(as of January 1965)

	Yield
U.S. Governments	
182-day bills	3.94%
Three-year maturities	4.15
Five-year maturities	4.17
Ten-year maturities	4.20
Corporate (average yields)	
Aa long-term	4.49%
A long-term	4.57
Municipal (average yields)	
Aa long-term	3.06%
A long-term	3.24
Five-year, A	2.70*
Ten-year, A	2.95*
Fifteen-year, A	3.10*
Commercial Banks	
Passbook accounts	4.0%†
One-year certificates of deposit	4.25†
Savings and loan share accounts	4 to 4.25†

* Estimated from new issue yields in week of January 11 to 15, 1965.
† Current rate offered in metropolitan areas of midwest.
Source: *Moody's Bond Survey*, January 18, 1965.

favorable outlook for his business income suggests that realized capital losses rather than gains are appropriate, although tax considerations probably should not inhibit sales of some lower-quality stocks which were then selling at favorable prices.

With these considerations in mind, the first step might have been to review the common stocks, and particularly the cyclical secondary companies to obtain perhaps $15,000 to $20,000 of funds for conversion into defensive securities or their equivalent. Those with unrealized losses might be prime candidates. The question then emerged as to what items were appropriate for the investment of these funds. Table 29-1 indicates the available yields on various alternatives as of January, 1965. For historical perspective it might be noted that these yields were neither extremely high nor low in terms of the spectrum of yield curves for the past decade. Therefore, the opportunities in the bond market appeared reasonably attractive, although there is never complete assurance that higher interest rates may not prevail in the future and lead to declines in the prices of long-term obligations.

At a marginal tax rate of 32%, three- to five-year governments would have produced after-tax yields of about 2.8%, or above that on municipals of similar maturity. One-year certificates of deposits at commercial banks or savings and loan share accounts offered slightly higher after-tax returns of about 2.9%. On the other hand, the after-tax yields on long-term corporates of about 3.05%, assuming purchases on about a 4.5% yield basis, compared unfavorably with those obtainable on long-term municipals.

On the basis of the comparative yield data, the first inclination might have been to concentrate on a combination of certificates of deposits (or savings and loan shares) and long-term municipals. But short-term securities, which certificates of deposit represent, were subject to the risk that a decline in general interest rates may lead to lower yields when they are "rolled over" the following year. However, they did promise recoverability at any time, although at lower rates if redeemed before maturity. Therefore, some additional "tying down" of the returns then available in the market might well have been considered prudent. The purchase of some intermediate term governments of about three- to five-year maturities offered a compromise between obtaining assurance of continued returns at existing levels and reasonable stability of price, especially as they would become short-term obligations in a year or so.

On balance, a staggered maturity portfolio of bonds along the following lines might seem appropriate in the light of the level and structure of interest rates shown in Table 29-1.

Item	Yield	Source
$ 7,000 savings account	4%	existing
4,000 certificates of deposit	4.25%	stock sales
4,000 three- to five-year governments	4.15%	" "
12,000 ten- to twenty-five-year municipals	3.2%	" "
$27,000		

The account, as constructed, provided assured recoverability through the $11,000 in savings accounts and certificates of deposit. These funds would be available at any time for personal needs, or for allocation to long-term obligations should interest rates increase substantially at some future time. At higher rates, such a shift might be made because the liquidity features of long-term bonds improve as they are acquired at higher yields. The reasoning is that the probabilities of additional increases in yields (lower prices) gradually diminishes as the yield curve as a whole moves upward toward a historical high. Secondly, the $16,000 in intermediate and long-term obligations stabilized the income potential on the account and provided modest opportunities for capital gains in the event of a decline in interest rates. If such a decline in rates was associated with an easy money policy due to a recession in the economy, then these long-term securities could be sold at higher prices and the proceeds used to offset the probable decline in business income which the record indicated was exposed to cyclical variations.

A maximum of perhaps $30,000 to $35,000 might be considered sufficient in the bond account to meet the defensive objective and the additional funds might come largely from current savings from the high levels of business income expected for the next year or so. A gradual orientation of the balance of the account, about $70,000 in total, to the growth objective would subsequently have seemed desirable. Tax considerations, the level of the individual stock prices in relation to the estimated earnings and growth rates, and the need to improve quality to a modest degree were among the important factors which might guide the gradual evolution of the common stock portfolio to its revised status.

Case 4. Mrs. John Fletcher, whose husband passed away in 1962, is 66 years of age and in reasonably good heath. She has no direct dependents, but there are two adult daughters; one is married and the other is employed as a secretary in a large corporation. Their ages were 37 and 33, respectively. Mrs. Fletcher receives about $90 per month from Social Security and another $50 per month from insurance contracts which will continue for twenty years. The sale of her home, insurance paid to her in cash, and bank accounts of her husband resulted in $40,000 cash assets, of which all but $2,000 was in a savings account earning 4% currently. She had also the following common stocks.

Number of Shares	Company	January, 1965 Price	Total Value	(1964 Rate) Total Dividends	Dividend Yield
50	Dow Chemical	76	$ 3,800	$ 98	2.4%
50	Corning Glass	205	10,250	125	1.2
100	Scott Paper	34	3,400	90	2.6
20	Du Pont Chemical	250	5,000	155	3.1
200	Detroit Edison	36	7,200	260	3.6
40	Amerada Petroleum	84	3,360	96	2.8
	Totals		$33,010	$816	2.5*

* Average yield on portfolio at market prices.

Mrs. Fletcher rented an apartment near her married daughter for $100 a month. She had no life insurance but continued a hospitalization policy which she had maintained with her husband.

These personal data show the widow problem, long a favorite subject of investment management. Actually, the specific investment objectives of this individual were relatively simple. First, there was a definite need to supplement the assured dollar income provided by Social Security and the insurance contracts. Second, a modest amount of recoverable funds might be useful to provide for any emergency or unusual expenditure needs. Third, the major positive objective would appear to be maximum current income in real terms consistent with a high degree of continuity. Fourth, it might be presumed that Mrs. Fletcher would desire to preserve the major part of the estate for her children if possible and therefore avoid consumption of the principal unless absolutely necessary.

It is a somewhat more difficult task to translate these objectives into a concrete portfolio. In this case returns from the investment portfolio have to provide for the major amount of living expenses. As a result, it seems imperative to obtain adequate protection against the major investment risks and in addition achieve a reasonable income level. Second, it appears that Mrs. Fletcher should be classified as a "defensive" investor. In other words, it is essential to maintain quality and forego any attempt to secure greater returns from more enterprising investment operations. It would not be appropriate, for example, to seek undervalued stocks even if their current income returns appear attractive. The risks of such an investment strategy are too great to be assumed by a modest-sized portfolio on which regularity of income is required. Third, "time diversification" seems desirable on any common-stock commitments unless the desired stocks are available at yields above bond yields.

The problem in this case is essentially the creation of a substantially new portfolio with the approximately $73,000 in cash and market values then available.[1] The existing items in the form of savings accounts and growth stocks for the most part are not suitable for a current-income account. However, retention of perhaps $1,000 in the form of cash and $5,000 in savings accounts for operating and contingency purposes could be recommended. Also the Detroit Edison stock is a good-quality stock with demonstrated growth and considerable stability; thus retention seems justified.

Table 29-2 has been prepared to indicate a suggested distribution of the account in the light of conditions prevailing in early 1965. The reasoning on which the portfolio was constructed might be summarized as

---

[1] For purposes of the illustration, it was assumed that the market values of the stocks approximate their values on the estate tax return which means no capital gains taxes would be payable on their sale.

TABLE 29-2
SUGGESTED PORTFOLIO DISTRIBUTION: MRS. JOHN FLETCHER
(as of 1965)

Item	Amount	Approxi- mate Yield	Annual Income	Portfolio Function
Social Security plus insurance		—	$1,680	Stable dollar income
Savings account	$ 5,000	4.0%	200	Stable income, recoverability
Corporate bonds, high quality	32,000	4.5%	1,440	Stable income at maximum assured rate
Total fixed income	$37,000		$3,320	
Common stocks	$27,800	3.5%	973	Maintain purchasing power
Detroit Edison	7,200	3.6%	260	Income and purchasing power
Totals	$72,000		$4,553	

Suggested diversification
  Savings account
  Bonds

Corporate	6	in different industries
Inflation stocks	6	leading companies in different industries
Stable, slow growth	1	high-quality utility
Total	13	

follows. First, an adequate degree of recoverability for emergencies plus a favorable current income was most conveniently available in a savings account with a bank or savings and loan association. Second, Social Security, insurance, and the savings account provided an annual income of about $1,900. As such income was clearly inadequate, the primary objective was to obtain the maximum amount of reasonably safe income from the portfolio. As of 1965 such income could best be obtained from long-term corporate bonds. After the acquisition of $32,000 of such securities, the total basic income from top-flight fixed-income sources would be about $3,300 or an amount required for a basic standard of living under adverse economic conditions.

Under different comparative yield conditions in the securities markets, high-quality income common stocks might be substituted for perhaps $20,000 of the corporate bonds. For example, if as a result of a recession, interest rates fall and stock prices decline, so that income-type commons offer yields of between 4.5 and 5.5% and corporate bonds yield less than 4%, the sale of bonds up to about $20,000 might be justified and the proceeds used to buy common stocks. In brief, the objective would be to obtain the maximum amount of relatively safe income from whatever source offered the best opportunity at a given time.

Third, there is a definite need to seek additional real income. The fixed-income securities, of course, will not provide additional income under inflationary conditions. Therefore, the suggested portfolio included $27,800 of several leading industrial corporations, such as Standard Oil of New Jersey and General Motors. These should show increased dividends in the event of a general inflationary surge and probably a slow but perhaps erratic growth in dividends otherwise. Although there is the risk that the market will continue to advance rather consistently, the acquisition of these stocks by using a dollar-averaging process of perhaps $3,000 quarterly seems prudent in view of the market levels prevailing in early 1965, when both earnings and dividend yields were historically low. In the meantime, the funds held back would actually give higher returns in a savings account or certificates of deposit.

Finally, the high-quality utility stock in the portfolio should be retained. It appears to offer an above-average and stable yield with slow growth in the dividend payment probable. Therefore, it offers some additional protection against a possible "creeping" inflation because of these characteristics.

Conclusion. The purpose of these several hypothetical cases has been to show how specific investment programs may be adapted to the particular needs of the individual and to the prevailing conditions in the securities markets. Although there is always room for individual judgments on the methods of achieving various objectives, the important principles are that portfolio strategy and its implementation should be subject to careful advance planning and should also be flexible to adjust to new developments in the economy and securities markets. Moreover, periodic reviews of the entire structure of the portfolio are almost as essential as reappraisals of individual securities. A common mistake is to accumulate a random collection of miscellaneous securities that "looked good" at the time in and of themselves but that are not consistent with the basic objectives and adequate risk protection.

On the other hand, investors should guard against undue switching of the securities held in the account. If the specific portfolio items have been carefully selected with long-term objectives in mind, there should be clear and convincing reasons for any subsequent dispositions. Perhaps one of the greatest temptations is to sell a security which has been disappointing in its market performance for six months to a year and buy another which has enjoyed a favorable "action" in the market. Once transactions along these lines are allowed to develop, long-term investment management considerations are likely to be forgotten and "trading" for market profits becomes the principal objective. For most nonprofessional investors this change in approach usually leads to disaster.

APPENDIX TABLE 1
CONDENSED COMPOUND INTEREST TABLE: 3% TO 25% RATES

Years	3%	4%	5%	6%	7%	8%	9%	10%	12%	14%	16%	20%	25%
1	1.03000	1.04000	1.05000	1.06000	1.07000	1.08000	1.09000	1.10000	1.12000	1.14000	1.16000	1.20000	1.25000
2	1.06090	1.08160	1.10250	1.12360	1.14490	1.16640	1.18810	1.21000	1.25440	1.29960	1.34560	1.44000	1.56250
3	1.09273	1.12486	1.15762	1.19102	1.22504	1.25971	1.29503	1.33100	1.40493	1.48154	1.56090	1.72800	1.95313
4	1.12551	1.16986	1.21551	1.26248	1.31080	1.36049	1.41158	1.46410	1.57352	1.68896	1.81064	2.07360	2.44141
5	1.15927	1.21665	1.27628	1.33823	1.40255	1.46933	1.53862	1.61051	1.76234	1.92541	2.10034	2.48832	3.05176
6	1.19405	1.26532	1.34010	1.41852	1.50073	1.58687	1.67710	1.77156	1.97382	2.19497	2.43640	2.98598	3.81470
7	1.22987	1.31593	1.40710	1.50363	1.60578	1.71382	1.82804	1.94872	2.21068	2.50227	2.82622	3.58318	4.76837
8	1.26677	1.36857	1.47746	1.59385	1.71819	1.85093	1.99256	2.14359	2.47596	2.85259	3.27841	4.29982	5.96046
9	1.30477	1.42331	1.55133	1.68948	1.83846	1.99900	2.17189	2.35795	2.77308	3.25195	3.80296	5.15978	7.45058
10	1.34392	1.48024	1.62889	1.79085	1.96715	2.15892	2.36736	2.59374	3.10585	3.70722	4.41144	6.19174	9.31323
11	1.38423	1.53945	1.71034	1.89830	2.10485	2.33164	2.58043	2.85312	3.47855	4.22623	5.11726	7.43008	11.64153
12	1.42576	1.60103	1.79586	2.01220	2.25219	2.51817	2.81266	3.13843	3.89598	4.81790	5.93603	8.91610	14.55192
13	1.46853	1.66507	1.88565	2.13293	2.40984	2.71962	3.06580	3.45227	4.36349	5.49241	6.88579	10.69932	18.18989
14	1.51259	1.73168	1.97993	2.26090	2.57853	2.93719	3.34173	3.79750	4.88711	6.26135	7.98752	12.83918	22.73737
15	1.55797	1.80094	2.07893	2.39656	2.75903	3.17217	3.64248	4.17725	5.47357	7.13794	9.26552	15.40702	28.42171
16	1.60471	1.87298	2.18287	2.54035	2.95216	3.42594	3.97031	4.59497	6.13039	8.13725	10.74800	18.48843	35.52714
17	1.65285	1.94790	2.29202	2.69277	3.15882	3.70002	4.32763	5.05447	6.86604	9.27646	12.46768	22.18611	44.40892
18	1.70243	2.02582	2.40662	2.85434	3.37993	3.99602	4.71712	5.55992	7.68997	10.57517	14.46251	26.62333	55.51115
19	1.75351	2.10685	2.52695	3.02560	3.61653	4.31570	5.14166	6.11591	8.61276	12.05569	16.77652	31.94800	69.38894
20	1.80611	2.19112	2.65330	3.20714	3.86968	4.66096	5.60441	6.72750	9.64629	13.74349	19.46076	38.33760	86.73617

APPENDIX TABLE 2
PRICE-FUTURE EARNINGS RATIOS (PAYOUT PERIODS)

Price-Earnings Ratio (Current Earnings)	Estimated Annual Growth Rate of Earnings Per Share													
	1%	2%	3%	4%	5%	6%	7%	8%	9%	10%	12%	15%	20%	25%
12	11.4	10.9	10.4	10.0	9.6	9.3	9.0	8.7	8.5	8.3	7.9	7.4	6.7	6.2
13	12.3	11.7	11.1	10.7	10.3	9.9	9.6	9.3	9.0	8.7	8.3	7.7	7.0	6.5
14	13.2	12.5	11.9	11.3	10.9	10.5	10.1	9.8	9.5	9.2	8.7	8.1	7.3	6.7
15	14.0	13.2	12.6	12.0	11.5	11.0	10.6	10.2	9.9	9.6	9.1	8.4	7.6	7.0
16	14.9	14.0	13.3	12.6	12.0	11.5	11.1	10.7	10.4	10.0	9.5	8.8	7.9	7.2
17	15.8	14.8	13.9	13.2	12.6	12.1	11.6	11.2	10.8	10.4	9.8	9.1	8.1	7.4
18	16.6	15.5	14.6	13.8	13.2	12.6	12.1	11.6	11.2	10.8	10.2	9.4	8.4	7.6
19	17.5	16.3	15.3	14.4	13.7	13.1	12.5	12.0	11.6	11.2	10.5	9.6	8.6	7.8
20	18.3	17.0	15.9	15.0	14.2	13.5	12.9	12.4	11.9	11.5	10.8	9.9	8.8	8.0
21	19.2	17.7	16.5	15.5	14.7	14.0	13.4	12.8	12.3	11.9	11.1	10.2	9.0	8.2
22	20.0	18.4	17.1	16.1	15.2	14.4	13.8	13.2	12.7	12.2	11.4	10.4	9.2	8.4
23	20.8	19.1	17.8	16.6	15.7	14.9	14.2	13.6	13.0	12.5	11.7	10.7	9.4	8.6
24	21.6	19.8	18.3	17.2	16.2	15.3	14.6	13.9	13.4	12.8	12.0	10.9	9.6	8.7
25	22.4	20.5	18.9	17.7	16.6	15.7	15.0	14.3	13.7	13.1	12.2	11.1	9.8	8.9
26	23.2	21.1	19.5	18.2	17.1	16.1	15.3	14.6	14.0	13.4	12.5	11.4	10.0	9.0
27	24.0	21.8	20.1	18.7	17.5	16.5	15.7	15.0	14.3	13.7	12.7	11.6	10.2	9.2
28	24.8	22.5	20.6	19.2	17.9	16.9	16.0	15.3	14.6	14.0	13.0	11.8	10.4	9.3
29	25.6	23.1	21.2	19.6	18.4	17.3	16.4	15.6	14.9	14.3	13.2	12.0	10.5	9.5
30	26.4	23.7	21.7	20.1	18.8	17.7	16.7	15.9	15.1	14.5	13.5	12.2	10.7	9.6
32	27.9	25.0	22.8	21.0	19.6	18.4	17.4	16.5	15.7	15.1	13.9	12.6	11.0	9.8
34	29.4	26.2	23.8	21.9	20.4	19.1	18.0	17.1	16.3	15.5	14.3	12.9	11.3	10.1
36	30.9	27.4	24.8	22.7	21.1	19.7	18.6	17.6	16.8	16.0	14.7	13.3	11.5	10.3
38	32.4	28.5	25.7	23.6	21.8	20.4	19.2	18.1	17.2	16.5	15.1	13.6	11.8	10.5
40	33.8	29.7	26.7	24.4	22.5	21.0	19.7	18.6	17.7	16.9	15.5	13.9	12.1	10.7
45	37.3	32.4	28.9	26.3	24.2	22.5	21.0	19.8	18.8	17.9	16.4	14.7	12.6	11.2
50	40.7	35.0	31.0	28.0	25.7	23.8	22.2	20.9	19.8	18.8	17.2	15.3	13.2	11.7
60	47.2	39.8	34.8	31.2	28.4	26.2	24.4	22.8	21.5	20.4	18.6	16.5	14.1	12.4
70	53.3	44.2	38.3	34.0	30.8	28.3	26.2	24.5	23.1	21.8	19.8	17.5	14.9	13.1

Index